Rethinking
Productive Development

Rethinking Productive Development
Sound Policies and Institutions for Economic Transformation

Edited by
Gustavo Crespi, Eduardo Fernández-Arias, and Ernesto Stein

Inter-American Development Bank

palgrave
macmillan

RETHINKING PRODUCTIVE DEVELOPMENT
Copyright © Inter-American Development Bank, 2014.

All rights reserved.

The opinions expressed in this publication are those of the authors and do not necessarily reflect the views of the Inter-American Development Bank, its Board of Directors, or the countries they represent.

The unauthorized commercial use of Bank documents is prohibited and may be punishable under the Bank's policies and/or applicable laws.

First published in 2014 by
PALGRAVE MACMILLAN®
in the United States—a division of St. Martin's Press LLC,
175 Fifth Avenue, New York, NY 10010.

Where this book is distributed in the UK, Europe and the rest of the world, this is by Palgrave Macmillan, a division of Macmillan Publishers Limited, registered in England, company number 785998, of Houndmills, Basingstoke, Hampshire RG21 6XS.

Palgrave Macmillan is the global academic imprint of the above companies and has companies and representatives throughout the world.

Palgrave® and Macmillan® are registered trademarks in the United States, the United Kingdom, Europe and other countries.

ISBN: 978–1–137–40559–3 (hardback)
ISBN: 978–1–137–39716–4 (paperback)

Library of Congress Cataloging-in-Publication Data

    Rethinking productive development : sound policies and institutions for economic transformation / edited by Gustavo Crespi, Eduardo Fernández-Arias, and Ernesto Stein ; Inter-American Development Bank.
      pages cm
    Includes bibliographical references and index.
    ISBN 978–1–137–40559–3 (hardback)
    ISBN 978–1–137–39716–4 (paperback)
    1. New business enterprises. 2. Industrial policy. I. Crespi, Gustavo. editor of compilation. II. Fernandez-Arias, Eduardo, editor of compilation. III. Inter-American Development Bank.

HD62.5.R487 2014
338.9—dc23   2014018504

A catalogue record of the book is available from the British Library.

Design by Newgen Knowledge Works (P) Ltd., Chennai, India.

First edition: September 2014

10 9 8 7 6 5 4 3 2 1

Contents

List of Boxes	vii
List of Figures	ix
List of Tables	xv
Preface	xvii
Acknowledgments	xxiii
List of Contributors	xxvii

Part I The Role of Productive Development Policies

1	Rethinking Productive Development	3
2	A Conceptual Framework for Productive Development Policies	33

Part II Sound Policies in Key Areas of Application

3	Investing in Ideas: Policies to Foster Innovation	61
4	The Start-Up and Scale-Up of High-Productivity Firms	107
5	Beyond the Classroom: Preparing People to Produce	145
6	Giving Credit to Productivity	175
7	More Than the Sum of Its Parts: Cluster-Based Policies	203
8	A World of Possibilities: Internationalization for Productive Development	233
9	Selecting Priority Sectors for Productive Transformation: An Elephant in the Room?	279

Part III Institutions for Successful Policies

10	The Hard Part: Building Public-Sector Capabilities	321
11	Two to Tango: Public-Private Collaboration	359
Notes		391
References		423
Index		451

Boxes

1.1	EMBRAER and Brazil's Informatics Policy: A Contrast	16
1.2	PDPs and WTO Rules	20
2.1	Addressing the Self-Discovery Problem with Subsidies to Export Pioneers	39
2.2	A Tale of Two Interventions	48
2.3	The Caribbean-Brazil Air Bridge	52
3.1	Fostering Innovation through Government-Sponsored, Mission-Oriented Research and Public Procurement: The Case of the United States	74
3.2	Innovation Policy Building through Catch-Up: The Case of South Korea	76
3.3	FONTAR's Toolkit: Basic Rules for Allocating Subsidies vs. Credit	84
3.4	Competition and the Impacts of Innovation Grants: The Case of Chile	96
4.1	Impact of One-Stop Shops in Portugal and Latin America	124
5.1	How Much Does the Status Quo Cost? How Long Can the Reforms Take to Show Results?	151
5.2	Does Higher Education Respond to Market Demands? The Montevideo Software Cluster	156
6.1	Development Banks as Agents of Economic Intelligence: The Opinion of Bank Managers	200
6.2	The Cases of BNDES (Brazil) and KfW (Germany)	201
7.1	Zonamerica: An Island of Excellence	208
7.2	CIDETER: An Agricultural Machinery Cluster Engaged in Internationalization Policies	217
8.1	Incentives for FDI	248
8.2	Two Cases of Sectoral Targeting to Attract FDI	258
9.1	The Case of Auto Parts in Durango	289

9.2	Tax Waivers in Jamaica: The Winds Are Changing	291
9.3	Quality: The Missing Dimension	295
9.4	The Attraction of Sterilization Services in Costa Rica	302
9.5	The Cluster Program and Sector Selection in Chile	305
10.1	The Corporate Governance of Executing Agencies	331
10.2	The EFA Cycle at Work: The Experience with Produce Foundations in Mexico	355
11.1	The Smell of Success in Colombia's Flower Sector	369
11.2	Self-Organizing Investment Boards	383

Figures

1.1a	Relative GDP per Capita (Percentage): Typical Latin American Country vs. Typical Country from the Rest of the World	4
1.1b	Relative GDP per Capita (Percentage): Typical Latin American Country vs. the United States	4
1.2	GDP per Capita Decomposition: Typical Latin American Country Relative to the United States (1960=1)	5
1.3	Productivity Gap Relative to the United States	6
2.1	A Typology of PDP Interventions	34
B2.1	Rice Productivity in Argentina and Costa Rica, 1990–2012	49
2.2	Solving Coordination Failures in Tourism in Costa Rica	51
3.1a	Innovation in Latin America and the Caribbean at a Glance: R&D Expenditures as a Percentage of GDP and Source of Performance	63
3.1b	Innovation in Latin America and the Caribbean at a Glance: Innovation Investment in Firms	64
3.1c	Innovation in Latin America and the Caribbean at a Glance: Researchers per 1,000 in the Labor Force	64
3.1d	Innovation in Latin America and the Caribbean at a Glance: TFP Growth, 1960–2010	65
3.2	Social Returns to R&D, Latin America and the Caribbean vs. the OECD	71
3.3	Star Performers' R&D Investment	73
3.4	Direct Government Funding and Tax Incentives for Business Innovation (Percent of GDP)	87
3.5	Manufacturing Firms That Received Public Support for TEPs (Percent)	90

B3.1	Innovation Policy and Competition: Evidence from Chile	97
4.1	Net Job Creation by Age of Firms in Chile, 2006–09 (Percentage)	108
4.2	Number of New Formal Firms per 1,000 People of Working Age, 2004–11	110
4.3	How Access to Funds Affects the Entry of New Projects and Firms	113
4.4	Reducing Barriers to Entry and Rates of Return of Entrants	123
4.5	Venture Capital as a Share of GDP in Various Countries	133
4.6	Firm Age and Size in the United States, Mexico, and India	139
4.7	Average Cost Curve for a Firm with Multiple Local Minimum Costs	141
5.1a	Expansion of Years of Education of Adult Population and Labor Productivity, 1970–2012: Brazil	150
5.1b	Expansion of Years of Education of Adult Population and Labor Productivity, 1970–2012: China	150
B5.1	GDP per Capita under Different Reform Scenarios in Chile, 2010–50	153
5.2	Survey of Skill Demand in Argentina, Brazil, and Chile (Average Points Assigned)	155
5.3	Enrollment in Secondary Technical/Vocational Education by Specialty Sector, Chile, 2010	160
5.4	Human Capital Gaps in the Mining Sector in Chile, 2012–20	170
6.1	Credit to the Private Sector, 2005–10 Average	176
6.2	Interest Rates on Loans with Maturity Greater Than One Year, 2011–12 Average	176
6.3	Financial Depth and Productivity Growth	177
6.4a	Government Ownership of Banks: All Countries	192
6.4b	Government Ownership of Banks: Advanced Economies	192
6.4c	Government Ownership of Banks: Latin America and the Caribbean	192

6.4d	Government Ownership of Banks: Other Developing Countries	193
8.1a	Trade, Vertically Linked Subsidiaries and Level of Development, Latin American and Caribbean Countries, 2010: Exports and Level of Development	234
8.1b	Trade, Vertically Linked Subsidiaries and Level of Development, Latin American and Caribbean Countries, 2010: Export Diversification and Level of Development	235
8.1c	Trade, Vertically Linked Subsidiaries and Level of Development, Latin American and Caribbean Countries, 2010: FDI and Level of Development	235
8.1d	Trade, Vertically Linked Subsidiaries and Level of Development, Latin American and Caribbean Countries, 2010: Number of Subsidiaries and Level of Development	236
8.2	Local Export Spillovers in Peru (2000–11)	240
8.3a	Distribution of the Number of Followers and Share of New Exporters for New Products Introduced between 2003 and 2006: Chile	241
8.3b	Distribution of the Number of Followers and Share of New Exporters for New Products Introduced between 2003 and 2006: Colombia	241
8.3c	Distribution of the Number of Followers and Share of New Exporters for New Products Introduced between 2003 and 2006: Costa Rica	242
8.3d	Distribution of the Number of Followers and Share of New Exporters for New Products Introduced between 2003 and 2006: Peru	242
8.4a	Absolute and Relative Size of EIPOs, Latin America and the Caribbean vs. the Rest of the World, 2007–10: Absolute Size	251
8.4b	Absolute and Relative Size of EIPOs, Latin America, and the Caribbean vs. the Rest of the World, 2007–10: Relative Size	252
8.5	Presence Abroad of EIPOs, Latin America and the Caribbean vs. the Rest of the World, 2007–10	253

8.6	Impact of Foreign Missions on Countries' Intensive and Extensive Margins of Bilateral Exports, Latin America and the Caribbean, 2000–07	254
8.7a	PROCHILE's Export Promotion Instruments: Number of Instruments	256
8.7b	PROCHILE's Export Promotion Instruments: Persistence of Targeting	257
8.8a	Some Measures across Groups of Firms Participating in Different Export Promotion Programs in Colombia: Distribution of Total Exports	263
8.8b	Some Measures across Groups of Firms Participating in Different Export Promotion Programs in Colombia: Number of Export-Destination Countries	263
8.8c	Some Measures across Groups of Firms Participating in Different Export Promotion Programs in Colombia: Number of Products	263
8.9a	Average Effect of Export Assistance Programs in Colombia: Total Exports	264
8.9b	Average Effect of Export Assistance Programs in Colombia: Number of Products	264
8.9c	Average Effect of Export Assistance Programs in Colombia: Number of Countries	264
8.9d	Average Effect of Export Assistance Programs in Colombia: Average Exports per Product and Country	264
8.9e	Average Effect of Export Assistance Programs in Colombia: Average Exports per Product	264
8.9f	Average Effect of Export Assistance Programs in Colombia: Average Exports per Country	264
8.10a	Costa Rica Provee: Sales, Links, and Products Sold, 2002–12: Sales	267
8.10b	Costa Rica Provee: Sales, Links, and Products Sold, 2002–12: Links	267
8.10c	Costa Rica Provee: Sales, Links, and Products Sold, 2002–12: Products Sold	267
8.11	Estimated Impact of Costa Rica Provee on Exports	268
9.1a	Complexity of Export Baskets in Korea and Latin America and the Caribbean: Korea	285

9.1b	Complexity of Export Baskets in Korea and Latin America and the Caribbean: Latin America and the Caribbean	285
9.1c	Complexity of Export Baskets in Korea and Latin America and the Caribbean: Typical Latin American Country	286
B9.1	Productivity Index in Jamaica and Latin America and the Caribbean	292
B9.2	Sector Selection in the Chilean Cluster Program	306
9.2	Complexity and Distance for Product Communities in Colombia	311
9.3	Failure to Seize and Expand Opportunities	313
9.4	Strategic Value and Distance for Product Communities in Colombia	314

Tables

3.1	Explaining the Gaps in Business R&D: The OECD vs. Latin America and the Caribbean (Percent of the Total Gap)	70
3.2	Innovation Policies in Developed Countries: A Taxonomy	78
3.3	Fiscal Incentives: Subsidies vs. Tax Incentives	82
B3.1	Basic Rules to Allocate Funding to Innovation Projects: The Case of FONTAR	85
3.4	Effects on Innovation Investment (Input Additionally): Testing Crowding-in/Crowding-out Effects	92
3.5	Output Additionality: Testing for Productivity Impacts	95
3.6	The Search for Spillovers	99
4.1	Classification of Policies According to the Stage of a Firm's Development and Targeting of the Real vs. Financial Side of the Venture	121
B5.1	GDP per Capita in 2050 under Different Reform Scenarios	152
5.1	Share of Trained Workers to Employed Workers and Cost of Training	158
8.1	New Products Introduced in 2003–06: Pioneers and Followers	240
8.2	Characterization of Exporters Participating in the Different Programs: Median Export Indicators and Test of Differences in Medians	275
8.3	Complementarity between Export and Innovation Promotion	276
10.1	Key Features of Public Policies since the 1980s: Cluster Analysis	343

Preface

Latin America and the Caribbean represent around 8.5 percent of the world's GDP and a similar proportion of the planet's population. In the last three decades, the region has grown, has managed to reduce poverty, and has been able to lift the income of its citizens, adjusted for purchasing power parity, to US$ 13,000. However, it has been unable to close the gap in well-being that separates it from the most developed countries.

The Inter-American Development Bank (IDB) has dedicated a good part of its research agenda to delving into the factors that limit the region's convergence with the levels of income and well-being in the most prosperous countries. The analyses carried out, particularly our 2010 edition of the flagship series, Development in the Americas (DIA), titled *The Age of Productivity: Transforming Economies from the Bottom Up*, have identified the region's insufficient growth in productivity as the principle cause of this relative lag. During the past fifty years, the region's active population and capital stock have grown far more than those of the United States. The region's level of education and its access to technology have improved. But the sustained increase in the gap in relative productivity has meant that compared to citizens of the United States today, citizens of Latin America and the Caribbean today have per-capita incomes less than those of their fathers and grandfathers.

For that reason, the principal goal of the region's sustainable development strategy is to create conditions that will boost the rates of productivity growth.

There is no single recipe for achieving that goal. For example, productivity increases could be achieved simply by reassigning the factors employed in companies and sectors of lesser productivity to more productive activities. But the same goal could also be achieved by creating the conditions and incentives needed to accelerate the process of productive factor accumulation and improve the quality of human and physical stock.

Many analytical efforts have emphasized the importance of the first path. The validation of the close link between labor informality and the financing of contributory and noncontributory schemes of social insurance, fiscal and labor policies, and at the level of the company, the access to credit, and the limited capacity to incorporate new technologies, has led us to identify reducing informality in labor markets as a priority for improving long-term productivity and sustainable growth. On the other hand, last year's DIA, *More Than Revenue: Taxation as a Development Tool*, focuses on the second path, emphasizing the region's need to undertake tax reform that, in addition to improving collection, reestablishes fiscal neutrality, increases fairness, eliminates distortions, and promotes saving and investment.

Although progress has been significant, the persistence of the productivity gap testifies to how much must still be understood and achieved.

The motivation for this book lies in that concern, as expressed in its very title: *Rethinking Productive Development: Solid Policies and Institutions for Economic Transformation*. Our goal is to present a perspective that complements those used to date to address the productive transformation of Latin American and Caribbean economies. This book is a collective effort by professionals from eight departments and operational divisions of the IDB and was coordinated by Gustavo Crespi, Eduardo Fernández-Arias, and Ernesto Stein.

It is not an ideological book. Nor is it an instruction manual for productive reforms. The methodologies are still being developed and cannot provide flawless answers to all our doubts. It is not a compilation of possible good practices either. Rather, it is a work, supported by the best available data and a common methodology, that addresses how Latin America and the Caribbean can rethink its policies of productive development both in terms of content and with regard to the institutions necessary to execute them and measure their impact.

What we here denominate productive development policies might to some evoke memories of the "industrial policies" that took root in the continent during the last century.

They are not.

Their scope is the totality of the economy and not accelerated industrialization; their emphasis is competitiveness and integration with global value chains, not import substitution; and the instruments of intervention are not public companies or subsidies to declining sectors or SMEs of low competitive potential but rather policies of innovation, improvement in human capital, facilitating entrepreneurship and clusters, promoting internationalization, and, especially, an active public and private collaboration.

But they are not unprecedented either.

In the world and, of course, in Latin America and the Caribbean, policies of a very varied nature and effectiveness continue to be implemented to promote productive transformation.

Rethinking productive development in Latin America and the Caribbean allows us to review our immediate past and learn from its successes and failures, with a ready openness to new perspectives and approaches. The emphasis in this publication is on the cause and quantification of the direct and indirect effects of some of the policies of productive transformation recently developed within and beyond the region. These policies cover a spectrum ranging from subsidies to projects of innovation, the opening of agencies promoting exports and investment, the establishment of incubators for new companies, development clusters, programs to create and attract technology, and specialized companies in very specific sectors.

In order to draw clear conclusions from this diversity of experiences, we have subjected each policy to an examination, including three conceptually clear and concise questions:

- What failure of the market—static or dynamic—does it try to fix?
- What instrument could be used to resolve this failure of the market?
- What types of institutions, with what characteristics, are necessary to develop the policy with success?

We have differentiated productive development policies applied to specific sectors or companies—vertical policies—from horizontal policies, which potentially affect the entire economy. And we have differentiated policies whose direct effects are entirely on the firm's profitability from those that constitute public inputs to facilitate production.

Of the many lessons contained in the book's eleven chapters, five deserve emphasis.

The first is that the nonexistence of—or partial or insufficient access to—a good, service, or critical factor for development does not necessarily justify intervention or the creation of a productive policy. What makes productive development policies necessary is the existence of a market failure, static or dynamic.

The second lesson to highlight is that the solution to this market failure lies in choosing the most appropriate policy in terms of efficiency, cost, risk, and simplicity. Consider a simple example: low financial penetration does not necessarily justify the creation of a public bank. Rather, it urgently calls for examining the financial sector's degree of competence, the protection of the property rights of creditors, and access to reliable registries that provide the financial records of potential clients.

The third is potentially controversial but nonetheless indispensable. Even in the case of a market failure, and even when the productive development policy needed to address it is plainly identified and is the most efficient alternative, an adequate institution or institutions is needed to develop that policy. If those institutions do not exist, it is preferable to invest first in creating them rather than insisting on applying the correct policy without them.

The fourth lesson is that the policies that assume intervention in markets entail more risks than those limited to producing public goods. And the policies that assume vertical interventions pose more complex scenarios than the horizontal policies from which no sector or agent can be excluded.

Finally, given the specifics of each economy and the proven absence of exclusive solutions, is that instead of seeking out best practices, policymakers must choose the policies that effectively correspond with the economy's institutional capacities.

The goal of this book is to reorient the focus of productive development policies in Latin America and the Caribbean, in terms of both policy design and the institutional capacities needed to carry them out. It accepts that the methodologies used are not definitive and that it does not offer all the necessary answers, or even all the necessary questions.

Nonetheless, the book is a valuable contribution to the already pressing debate over what Latin America and the Caribbean should do to grow in a sustainable and inclusive manner.

Luis Alberto Moreno
President
Inter-American Development Bank

Acknowledgments

This book was prepared by the Research Department and the Institutions for Development Department of the Inter-American Development Bank.

The overall coordination of this project was undertaken by Gustavo Crespi, Eduardo Fernández-Arias, and Ernesto Stein. Ricardo Hausmann, Andrés Rodríguez-Clare, and Alberto Trejos provided support as external advisors. Gonzalo Rivas carefully read and commented on the entire manuscript. Santiago Levy and José Juan Ruiz provided guidance throughout the project.

The principal authors are:

Chapter 1: Manuel Agosin and Eduardo Fernández-Arias
Chapter 2: Ernesto Stein
Chapter 3: Gustavo Crespi, Alessandro Maffioli, and Alejandro Rasteletti
Chapter 4: Rodrigo Wagner and Ernesto Stein
Chapter 5: Marina Bassi, Graciana Rucci, and Sergio Urzúa
Chapter 6: Eduardo Fernández-Arias, Ugo Panizza, and Fernando de Olloqui
Chapter 7: Gabriel Casaburi, Alessandro Maffioli, and Carlo Pietrobelli
Chapter 8: Juan Blyde, Carlo Pietrobelli, and Christian Volpe Martincus
Chapter 9: Eduardo Fernández-Arias and Ernesto Stein
Chapter 10: Jorge Cornick, Ernesto Stein, and Eduardo Fernández-Arias
Chapter 11: Eduardo Fernández-Arias, Alberto Trejos, and Ernesto Stein

Lorena Caro and Sergio Rodríguez-Apolinar provided superb research assistance for the project as a whole. In addition, David Alfaro

Serrano, Daniel Alonso, Alonso Bucarey, Lorena Caro, Allison Cathles, Lucas Figal Garone, Alejandro Graziano, Fiorella Pizzolón, Sergio Rodríguez-Apolinar, and Fernando Vargas Cuevas provided excellent research assistance for individual chapters. Special thanks to Aglae E. Parra for overseeing the administration of the project.

Many other individuals participated in the preparation of the report, by writing background material, by writing specific boxes, or by leading workshops on relevant issues including Roberto Álvarez, Matt Andrews, Alejandro Artopoulos, Sebastian Auguste, José Miguel Benavente, Sebastián Bustos, Ernesto Dal Bó, Frederico Finan, Jeffrey Frieden, Gustavo García, Claudio Maggi, Valerie Mercer-Blackman, Juan Carlos Navarro, Juan José Price, Lant Pritchett, Gonzalo Rivas, Andrés Rodríguez-Pose, Charles Sabel, and Muhamed Yildrim.

This book benefited from background research projects based on country studies coordinated by bank economists including:

- Industrial Policies in Latin America and the Caribbean: http://www.iadb.org/en/research-and-data/project-details,3187.html?id=3776
  Public-Private Collaboration for Productive Development Policies: http://www.iadb.org/en/research-and-data/project-details,3187.html?id=4448
- The Next Step in Evaluating Productive Development Policies: Spillovers, Program Complementarities and Heterogeneous Impacts: http://www.iadb.org/en/research-and-data/project-details,3187.html?id=8709

Numerous officials from many public and private institutions graciously accepted to be interviewed during the preparation of this book. These institutions included National Agricultural Technology Institute (INTA), Banco Ciudad, Cideter Foundation, Ministry of Science, Technology and Productive Innovation (MINCYT) in Argentina; the Brazilian Development Bank (BNDES), the Funding Authority for Studies and Projects (FINEP), and the Federation of Industries of the State of São Paulo (FIESP) in Brazil; Private Council for Competitiveness in Colombia; Ministry of Finance (Unit of Economic Productivity) and Nacional Financiera (NAFIN) in Mexico; and Ministry of Industry, Energy and Mining (MIEM) and National Research and Innovation Agency (ANII) in Uruguay.

Many individuals made valuable comments and suggestions as this book was prepared and revised. The authors wish to particularly thank Verónica Alaimo, Carlos Álvarez, Gregorio Arévalo, Martin Chrisney, Seth Colby, Robert Devlin, Arturo Galindo, Susana García Robles, Jorge Katz, Juan Ketterer, David Kupfer, Bernardo Kosacoff, Pablo García, Jaime Granados, Fernando Jiménez-Ontiveros, Daniel Lederman, Ernesto López-Córdova, Ricardo Navarrete Gómez, Nobuyuki Otsuka, Manuel Pacheco, Carmen Pagés-Serra, Guillermo Perry, Luis Porto, Andrew Powell, Gerardo Reyes-Tagle, Ben Ross-Schneider, Pablo Sanguinetti, Teresa Ter-Minassian, and Emiliana Vegas.

Rita Funaro managed the editorial production of this book, with extensive assistance from Nancy Morrison. Cathleen Conkling-Shaker and John Dunn Smith also contributed to the editorial process. Gabriel Dobson and Alberto Magnet were responsible for translations, and Claudia Pasquetti edited the Spanish edition.

The authors and editors are responsible for any errors in information and/or its analysis. Likewise, the opinions and policy recommendations stated in this book are those of the authors and do not represent the official position of the IDB, its president, or board of directors.

Contributors

Manuel Agosin, a US/Chilean citizen, holds a PhD in Economics from Columbia University. He is currently dean and professor at the Faculty of Economics and Business, Universidad de Chile.

Marina Bassi, an Argentine citizen, holds a PhD in Economics from the University of California, Los Angeles. She is sector senior specialist in the Vice Presidency of Sectors and Knowledge of the Inter-American Development Bank.

Juan Blyde, a Venezuelan citizen, holds a PhD in Economics from the University of Colorado at Boulder. He is a senior economist in the Integration and Trade Sector of the Inter-American Development Bank.

Gabriel Casaburi, an Argentine citizen, holds a Masters in International Relations and a PhD in Political Economy from Yale University. He is a lead private sector specialist in the Competitiveness, Technology, and Innovation Division of the Inter-American Development Bank.

Jorge Cornick, a Costa Rican citizen, holds a PhD in Agricultural Economics from the University of Wisconsin-Madison. He has worked in the Costa Rican public sector on fiscal and regulatory issues, and works as an independent consultant on policy and development issues.

Gustavo Crespi, an Argentine/Italian citizen, holds a Masters in Economic Growth and International Trade from the University of Chile and a PhD in Science and Technology Policies from Sussex University, UK. He is a principal specialist in the Competitiveness and Innovation Division of the Institutions for Development Sector at the Inter-American Development Bank.

Eduardo Fernández-Arias, an Uruguayan citizen, holds a PhD in Economics and a Masters in Statistics from the University of California at Berkeley. He is principal economist at the Research Department of the Inter-American Development Bank.

Alessandro Maffioli, an Italian citizen, holds a PhD in Economics of Production and Development from the University of Insubria, Italy. He is a lead economist at the Office of Strategic Planning and Development Effectiveness of the Inter-American Development Bank and an adjunct assistant professor at the McCourt School of Public Policy of Georgetown University.

Fernando de Olloqui, a Mexican citizen, holds Masters degrees in Development Studies from the London School of Economics, United Kingdom, and in International Business Administration from the Mexico Autonomous Institute of Technology. He is a lead financial markets specialist at the Inter-American Development Bank.

Ugo Panizza, an Italian citizen, holds a PhD in Economics from Johns Hopkins University. He is a professor of International Economics and Pictet Chair in Finance and Development at the Graduate Institute of International and Development Studies in Geneva, where he is also the head of the Department of Economics.

Carlo Pietrobelli, an Italian citizen, holds a PhD in Economics from the University of Oxford, UK. He is a lead economist in the Competitiveness and Innovation Division of the Inter-American Development Bank and a professor of Economics (currently on leave) at the University of Roma Tre, Italy.

Alejandro Rasteletti, an Argentine/Italian citizen, holds a PhD in Economics from the University of Maryland. He is a specialist in the Fiscal and Municipal Management Division of the Institutions for Development Sector at the Inter-American Development Bank.

Graciana Rucci, an Argentine citizen, holds a PhD in Economics from the University of California, Los Angeles. She is lead specialist at the Labor Markets and Social Security Unit of the Inter-American Development Bank.

Ernesto Stein, an Argentine citizen, holds a PhD in Economics from the University of California at Berkeley. He is principal economist at the Research Department of the Inter-American Development Bank.

Alberto Trejos, a Costa Rican citizen, holds Masters and PhD degrees in Economics from the University of Pennsylvania. A former minister of foreign trade of Costa Rica, president of CINDE and professor of Economics at INCAE, he is currently president of the board of the Arias Foundation for Peace and Democracy and a senior partner at CEFSA.

Sergio Urzúa, a Chilean citizen, holds a PhD in economics from the University of Chicago. He is an assistant professor of Economics at the University of Maryland, NBER research faculty, IZA research fellow, and CLAPES-UC international fellow.

Christian Volpe Martincus, an Argentine and Italian citizen, holds a Masters in Economics from the University of La Plata and a PhD in Economics from the University of Bonn. He is a lead economist at the Integration and Trade Sector of the Inter-American Development Bank.

Rodrigo Wagner, a Chilean citizen and economist, holds a PhD from Harvard University. He is assistant professor of International Economics and Finance at University of Chile's Business School, assistant professor from Tufts University (currently on leave), and an associate member of the Center for International Development at Harvard.

Part I

The Role of Productive Development Policies

1

Rethinking Productive Development

Latin America and the Caribbean is a middle-income region. The typical country in the region has an income per capita about 25 percent above the typical country in the world, but 80 percent below the income per capita of an advanced country like the United States.[1] The region's relative position is declining: 50 years ago, it was much better off than it is today compared to the rest of the world (ROW), and despite recent strides, it has been unable to converge with respect to the United States (Figure 1.1). Why is the region so much poorer than the advanced countries in the world? Why is the region lagging behind while other parts of the world are catching up with the leaders? And most important, what can the region do about it?

Behind the region's disappointing performance in income per capita lie substantial shortfalls in its productive capabilities. Measured against the United States, workers are less productive because they have less capital and schooling with which to multiply the fruits of their labor. Important as these shortfalls in production factors are, however, they miss a key part of the problem. The main driver of the region's disappointing performance, and the one factor on which to lock the policy radar, is the low productivity with which factors of production are utilized. In economists' jargon, the key to understand the region's underperformance is total factor productivity (TFP) (for details, see Daude and Fernández-Arias, 2010).

In fact, economic performance over the last 50 years has been held back by declining TFP compared to both the most advanced economies and the successful developing economies. Figure 1.2 shows

Figure 1.1 Relative GDP per Capita (Percentage)

a. Typical Latin American Country vs. Typical Country from the Rest of the World

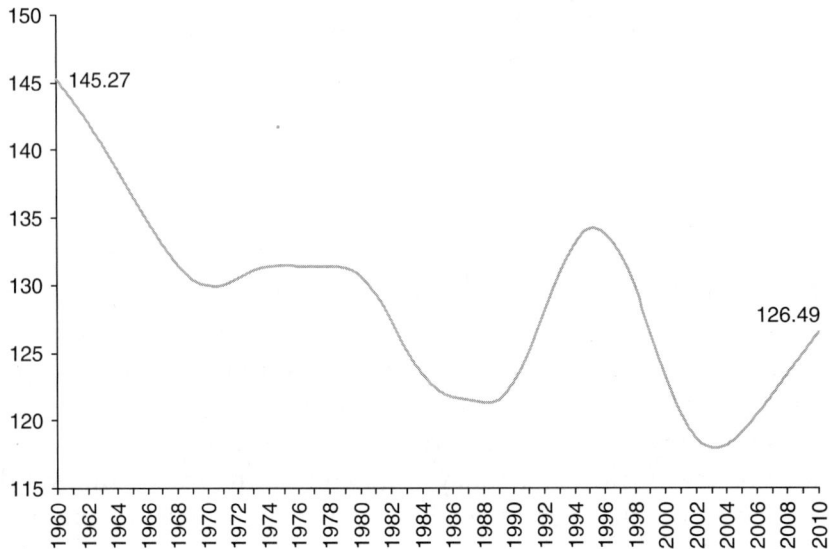

b. Typical Latin American Country vs. the United States

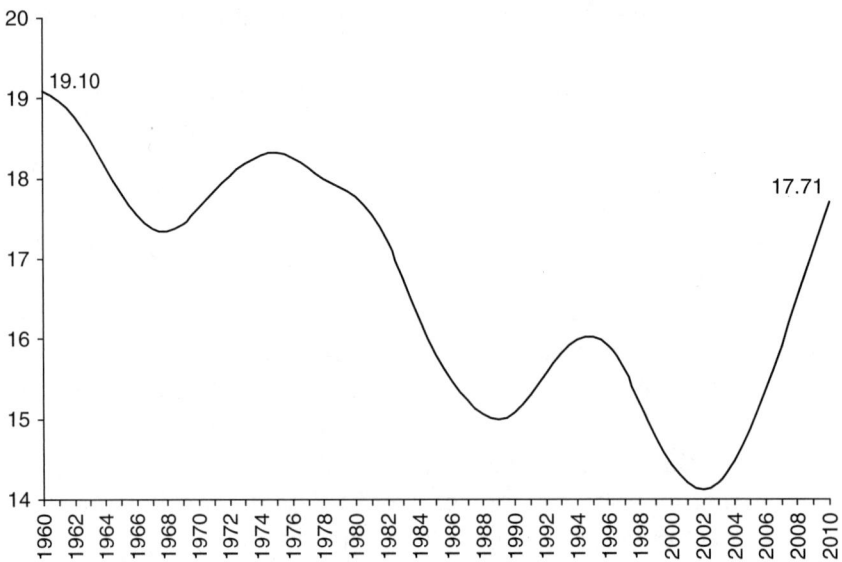

Source: Authors' calculations based on Feenstra, Inklaar, and Timmer (2013).

Figure 1.2 GDP per Capita Decomposition: Typical Latin American and Caribbean Country Relative to the United States (1960=1)

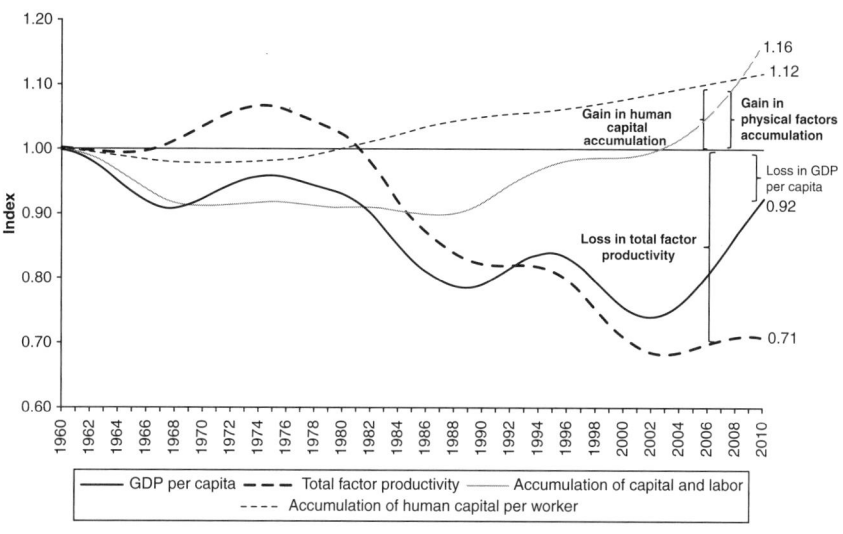

Source: Authors' calculations based on Fernandez-Arias (2014).

that, relative to the United States, the typical country in the region has had faster factor accumulation (the gaps in both physical factors, capital and labor headcount, as well as schooling of the labor force have been reduced), but its gap in TFP has increased. In fact, the productivity gap greatly widened, from 27 percent to 48 percent (Figure 1.3). At the same time, the typical East Asian tiger[2] narrowed its productivity gap significantly, from 51 percent to 33 percent.

The region's substantial productivity shortfall suggests an overarching policy objective: set the conditions to improve productivity to match the pace of other, better-performing countries. There are multiple ways to strive for this objective. Better productivity policies may aim at a better use of existing factors of production. This applies to resources not only within existing firms but also their reallocation from low- to high-productivity firms and sectors. Crucially, policies may also aim at better incentives for future factor accumulation to obtain sound productive transformation.

This report does not cover the entire public policy agenda that could be relevant for productivity improvement and faster growth along these fronts. For example, it does not discuss how to reduce

Figure 1.3 Productivity Gap Relative to the United States

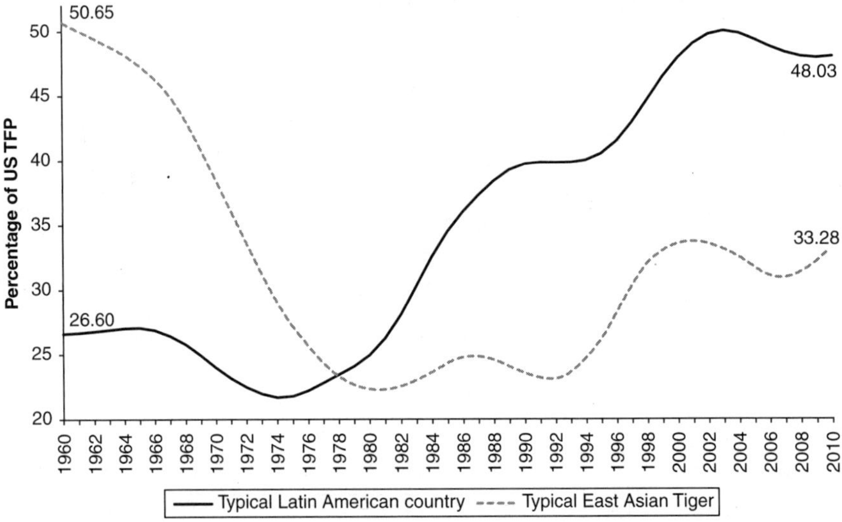

Y-axis: Percentage of US TFP

Values labeled: 50.65, 26.60, 48.03, 33.28

Legend: —— Typical Latin American country   ---- Typical East Asian Tiger

Source: Authors' calculations based on Fernandez-Arias (2014).

low productivity in the informal economy, reform labor or financial markets to facilitate the overall efficiency of allocating factor inputs across the economic structure, structure fiscal revenues with productivity in mind, or improve the overall quality of the education system. In contrast, this report focuses specifically on policies directed to the activities of the productive sectors of a national economy, or productive development policies (PDPs) (Melo and Rodríguez-Clare, 2006). This policy focus is highly relevant but restrictive: faster growth and strong economic development require a successful balance across all fronts of the policy agenda, not only sound PDPs. The importance of each policy front and the appropriate time path of the policy mix depend on the stage of development and other country circumstances. PDPs by themselves are no panacea; they are part of the toolkit of policymakers concerned with economic development to complement the rest of the policy agenda outside the scope of the report.

PDPs vary widely and encompass both broad-based and selective policies, discussed in chapter 2 under the headings of horizontal and vertical policies, respectively. They include diverse areas such as promoting technological upgrades at the level of the firm; encouraging the creation and growth of high-impact, high-productivity firms; stimulating efficient collaboration among firms to resolve coordination problems at the sector level; ensuring that public goods such as infrastructure are provided appropriately; and more generally, supporting a market-friendly business environment. In this report, these policies are not geared toward industrialization or the manufacturing sector, but encompass all sectors of the real economy, including the primary and service sectors.

PDPs are important for the economic development of all countries in the region. However, some countries may benefit from them more than others and some policy areas may be more important than others depending on country circumstances. Country heterogeneity in the region implies that uniform policy priorities are bound to be inadequate; in fact, policies that are appropriate in a given country may not work in another. The report emphasizes principles for policy and institutional design that can be useful under a wide range of country circumstances, more than explicit prescriptions for policies and agencies that may be maladapted to the specifics of particular countries. However, while the effort to collect detailed country data in this report made possible a thorough assessment of many policies and programs, relevant information for some countries remains a challenge to overcome in the future. In order to offset the lack of comprehensive and comparable data for all countries, in-depth information obtained from numerous country studies conducted in the region was also utilized whenever possible.

The report strongly emphasizes the need for sufficient institutional capabilities to conduct effective policies, particularly for policies that may involve risks. Some of the policies discussed will become progressively viable as countries reach more advanced stages of development and get farther along in building their institutional capabilities to successfully attempt high-impact policies soundly and safely. The report provides a road map for building capability to enable countries to advance in their path toward more effective PDPs.

The report is motivated by the region's development challenges but does not view the poor outcomes as a license for remedial policies. Crucially, a poor outcome—for example, the realization that firms invest too little in research and development (R&D) compared to those in other regions—is not in itself a valid justification for policy intervention. Effective policy needs to make sure that poor outcomes are actually caused by market failures; then policy must be designed to address the root failures, rather than superficial symptoms.[3] Governments have attempted and continue to attempt to deal with these serious productivity shortfalls through various policies, but not always with clarity, and sometimes in a wrongheaded fashion. Furthermore, even policies that may be justified because of market failures may turn out to be counterproductive in practice. As discussed later in the book, the market may fail to provide the right incentives to firms—for example, to innovate or to coordinate firms' actions to secure collective inputs if profits are dispersed to free riders—but at the same time the government may fail even more if it intervenes, owing to issues such as capture by the private sector or political manipulation. In this context, it is fundamental to be mindful of the government capabilities required to conduct PDP effectively.

Thus, the report places particular emphasis on the proper conceptual justification of PDPs, not simply the will to achieve results. It is intended to help readers think about them as a way to address specific market failures. At the same time, it places emphasis on the institutional capabilities needed to derive the potential benefits from these policies while mitigating the risk of government failures.

As analyzed below, the region has a rich and long history of industrial policy from which to learn. While its experience includes some successes that did advance economic development, it is also filled with failures that discredited the effort. Eventually, there was a push to dismantle the structures of industrial policy as a liberalizing paradigm emerged from the macroeconomic crisis of the 1980s. While this new paradigm contributed a good number of sound recommendations that paved the way for better macroeconomic policies throughout the region, so far it has not been sufficient to foster productivity and growth to satisfactory levels. While distorted industrial policy and public-sector overreach was a very serious problem, wholesale elimination of industrial policy was not the solution. Today's rethinking of productive development is not backtracking but rather moving forward, searching for different approaches to solve the growth problems that continue to dog the region. This requires sound policies and institutions based on new ideas and new evidence from policies within and outside the region. It also requires an understanding of what went wrong, not in order to reassess the past, but rather to make sure that new solutions avoid the same mistakes.

The rest of this chapter reviews in more detail some of the key components of the rethinking that this book proposes. The next section reviews the region's experience with industrial policy, the subsequent liberalizing backlash against it, and the unsatisfactory growth performance of both strategies. Against this background, this report proposes to rethink the challenges and policy responses with conceptual clarity and a pragmatic approach, learning from experience. The approach taken for this rethinking is outlined at the end of the chapter.

The analysis leads to a wide range of conclusions, both conceptual and practical, about desirable policy features and the institutional framework (agencies and processes) that support them. To help the reader interested in PDPs and institutions appreciate the breadth of topics analyzed in this report, the following questions provide a taste of the extensive menu of issues that inspired this research effort.

Policy Features

- Do policies to reduce the cost of starting a business attract the right type of firms?
- Should countries rely more on subsidies or tax incentives as a way to foster business innovation?
- How can pioneers be rewarded in order to maximize productivity gains at the national level?
- Does it make sense to subsidize new technological equipment?
- How should the private sector be involved in labor training policies?
- Do immigration policies have a role in PDPs?
- How can countries stimulate the emergence of new export activities?
- What to look for when attracting foreign direct investment (FDI) and connecting to global value chains?

- Does it pay to have special programs for small or young firms?
- Should credit promotion policies rely on guarantees, loans, or grants?
- Should the provision of public inputs for clusters be conditional on beneficiaries sharing the costs?
- How should the PDP mix change as countries develop?

Institutional Framework

- Why is the "best practices" approach to PDPs flawed?
- What role does experimentation play in PDPs?
- Does impact evaluation really measure policy effectiveness?
- How can development banks be propped up to be more effective and safe?
- How do countries accumulate technical, operational, and political (TOP) capabilities to carry out PDPs?
- How can the public sector organize in order to ensure needed interagency cooperation for PDPs of wide scope?
- What kind of public-private interaction is more effective to design and implement PDPs?
- What mechanisms can be set up to encourage more collaboration and less capture from the private sector?
- How can a country set up a process to identify sectors worth supporting?

Industrial Policy Past and Present: Black Sheep or Sacrificial Lamb?

The development challenges of the region are not new and have been actively confronted by industrial policy. The current state of PDPs in the region, to a large extent, has been shaped by its history.[4] The shock of the Great Depression was enormous. In the region as a whole, between 1929 and 1932, export volume shrank by over 25 percent, while the purchasing power of exports fell by 40 percent; meanwhile, since international financing was unavailable, import volumes contracted by over 60 percent (Bértola and Ocampo, 2012). Eventually, the shortage of manufactured goods, accompanied by a variety of measures to economize on imports and balance external accounts in the face of unprecedented declines in export values (quantitative restrictions, the abandonment of fixed exchange rates, and the ensuing real depreciations), resulted in a strong process of unintended, and largely welcomed, industrialization. During World War II, the unavailability of imports continued to give a boost to domestic manufacturing. It was only after the war that trade policy was used more deliberately with protectionist intent. The economic strategy that willy-nilly emerged during this period had a number of elements, of which import restrictions played a central role.

The import-substitution industrialization (ISI) that started in the early postwar period in the mid-1940s both within and outside the region was an attempt to solve the market failures that worked against productive transformation, against the backdrop of the historical conditions of that period. Policymakers had to address market failures in the context of weak and risk-averse domestic private sectors, rudimentary capital markets, international financial market disintegration, and shrunken levels of international trade. Developed economies emerged from World War II with average tariffs on imports of around 40 percent, which were reduced only gradually through subsequent internationally negotiated "rounds" of the General Agreement on Tariffs and Trade (GATT) ending 50 years later. The solution attempted under these conditions was to pursue ISI through trade restrictions and other state-directed measures, such as high-import tariffs, quantitative restrictions, import prohibitions, import licensing, and onerous interest-free prior import deposits. Some countries also restricted FDI in order to reserve protected sectors for domestic producers.[5]

Thus, policymakers in the region attempted to solve the lack of dynamism by stimulating a wide spectrum of manufacturing activity—to an important extent in a selective way. The coordination problems among producers were tackled through a variety of policies. Several of the favored sectors, such as steel, were capital intensive. In the face of weak private sectors and embryonic and risk-averse private capital markets, some of these new undertakings were carried out by state-owned enterprises (SOEs). The provision of finance was also problematic. Therefore, development banks sprang up in several countries, and state-directed credits to favored sectors were adopted widely. Development banks set up in the period (such as

Banco Nacional de Desenvolvimento Econômico e Social [BNDES] in Brazil, Corporación de Fomento de la Producçión [CORFO] in Chile, and Nacional Financiera [NAFIN] in Mexico) channeled domestic and international financial resources to favored sectors and to other private producers upstream or downstream (particularly to suppliers of non-tradables, such as electricity). The solution to coordination problems also involved the construction of roads and other forms of infrastructure, and efforts to increase the supply of human capital; engineering schools and schools of economics and business throughout the region date from this period. Governments invested heavily in these.

Import restrictions can encourage productive diversification in a number of ways. They raise the rate of investment in the protected sectors when enacted. Particularly in sectors with economies of scale, declining unit costs may eventually make these sectors internationally competitive.[6] In several countries, particularly those with large domestic markets, the strategy was initially successful, although it later ran into difficulties. By the second half of the 1960s, the Latin American development model began to exhibit diminishing returns, while growth began to decelerate. The state was increasingly embroiled in mounting implicit liabilities and impaired assets related to its financial support of weak private and public enterprises that failed to become competitive. At the same time, the consensus on ISI began to break down as some of the more irrational aspects of the policy came to the fore; eventually a "new consensus" emerged that favored free markets and specialization according to comparative advantage.

What went wrong? Part of the blame for the eventual stall in the effort to create internationally competitive industries was the failure to proceed with initially ambitious economic integration goals, in imitation of the European countries, which moved rapidly to establish a common market without exceptions. Most Latin American countries, perhaps with the exceptions of Brazil and Mexico, were too small to sustain industries with large economies of scale. Furthermore, integration efforts failed to improve infrastructure within the region. The problems with ISI and the manner in which it was implemented in the region became evident as time went on. To begin with, the narrowness of domestic markets was bound to result in declining rates of growth, even had the policy been pursued with technocratic rigor, unhampered by error or favoritism. As import substitution progressed from goods with relatively large markets (consumer nondurables) to those with much smaller markets (consumer durables, industrial inputs, and capital goods), the spurts of growth brought about by new bouts of protection could have been foreseen to be even shorter-lived.

ISI strategy in the region generally assumed that international competitiveness would be acquired spontaneously through a process of learning by doing. Yet this generally did not happen, and the strategy became a drag as protected sectors found the domestic market increasingly constraining. Protection of individual sectors was not transitory but tended to become permanent—even when it was not leading to any useful purpose. In a sense, this can be attributed to the political economy of protection: tariffs and other import restrictions created large rents for favored sectors that were later difficult to take away (see Little, Scitovsky, and Scott, 1970; Krueger, 1974). Business and labor banded together to prevent the reduction in protection that would have made economic sense had favored industries either moved down their learning curves or proved their lack of viability in the long term. At the same time, when a government is in the business of granting tariff protection to certain sectors, others soon appear claiming strong "developmental" benefits. In addition, protection was granted without any quid pro quo from the favored sectors (such as targets for sustained increases in international competitiveness). Rather than removing protection after a certain period of learning, when policymakers shifted their attention to new sectors, they piled new protective measures upon the existing ones. In the end, the intricate set of measures (including high tariffs, prohibitions, nontariff measures, and favored credits) became increasingly irrational, to the point where outcomes (in terms of sector growth rates) were more the result of happenstance than of explicit policy. In fact, a number of sectors ended up being granted negative effective protection in the net.

The ISI model as practiced in Latin America and the Caribbean had two other specific problems. First, by the early to mid-1960s, nominal tariff rates for manufactures in several countries had risen to levels that could hardly be justified by an argument in favor of shaping the productive structure. And, as soon became evident, wide dispersion of tariffs for final goods led to even wider and arbitrary dispersion in the protection of value added in different activities. The notion of "effective rates of protection" exemplifies this contention. The basic intuition behind this concept is that when a tariff (or tariff equivalent) on a final good is higher than the tariff rates on the inputs used in its production, the protection to value added in that particular activity can be much higher than the nominal tariff rate itself.[7] As should become clear, the stakes of this protection game were quite high, further fueling rent seeking, in turn made possible by policy discretion.

Second, the heavy reliance on import substitution caused the real exchange rate to appreciate relative to its free-trade level, and thus introduced an anti-export bias that intensified the concentration of exports in a few primary commodities. The anti-export bias of widespread protection had been noticed as far back as the 1970s (see Balassa, 1989). Perhaps as a result of the export successes of Asian countries, beginning in the late 1960s, policymakers made efforts to take this criticism on board. Policies adopted included crawling peg exchange rate regimes, in some countries multiple exchange rates favoring new exports, and various export subsidies. However, rather than rationalizing the incentive system, these new policies tended to be superimposed on the older ones. In any event, the pro-export policies proved too weak to counter the bias of the incentive system toward inward-oriented growth.

In a nutshell, export incentives were weak or absent in the region, and new exports did not receive the priority they might have deserved. This is in sharp contrast to industrial policy in high-growth Asian economies. Interestingly, the Asian countries that were later to be successful exporters of manufactures (Indonesia, the Republic of Korea, Singapore, Taiwan, and Thailand) followed the same path, initially. However, the Republic of Korea and Taiwan, the most successful among them, soon blended incentives to produce for the domestic market with support to close the competitiveness gap and export subsidies. Indeed, they made successful exporting a success indicator for initially protecting production for the domestic market.[8] There were export incentives (and punishments for not complying with export goals), which compensated for the anti-export bias of protection early on.

Perhaps a deeper question relates to the relationship between the state and the private sector. While in the countries of Asia that initially applied some of the same policies as in the region (especially the Republic of Korea and Taiwan) the state was able to establish temporary incentives and to tie them to performance, governments in Latin America and the Caribbean were unable to manage these policies effectively and granted incentives with no quid pro quo; they then tended to become permanent. In many cases this resulted in fiscal losses. In contrast, in Korea the authorities decided to promote the emergence of large conglomerates (*chaebols*) to act as an internal capital market to channel profits (assured by protection and export subsidies) into investments earmarked for development (Amsden, 1989). These contrasting experiences suggest that the institutional capabilities of productive development agencies in Latin America and the Caribbean were not up to the task of steering the private sector with resolve.

Nevertheless, industrial policy in the region was not all excess and failure. The evidence is mixed. First, the overreach of past industrial policy was partly dictated by the weak private productive capacity and underdeveloped financial system prevailing at the time. ISI, the region's version of industrial policy, was a very unreliable policy for achieving international competitiveness, but on occasion it did. The Brazilian experience provides examples of policies that turned out to be successful in creating new industries that eventually became internationally competitive, and policies that did not leave a trace on the production structure of the country. (Box 1.1 contrasts the EMBRAER success story with the failed information technology policy of the 1980s.) Even when failing, ISI sometimes created productive capabilities in the private sector and institutional capabilities in the public sector that were later useful as a platform for development. This evidence suggests that a reformulated industrial policy geared more toward achieving international competitiveness along the lines of the East Asian version could have brought economic development in Latin America and the Caribbean.

Box 1.1 EMBRAER and Brazil's Informatics Policy: A Contrast

Brazil's experience with industrial policies has been long and varied, ranging from great successes to not so successful endeavors. It is instructive to contrast two cases, one the successful effort to build up a global player in aeronautics (EMBRAER) and the other the failure of the 1984 policy to create an entire information technology industry from scratch, largely through protection.[9]

Empresa Brasileira de Aeronáutica (EMBRAER) was founded as a state enterprise in 1969 by the military government that had ruled Brazil since 1964. The company's mandate was to produce military as well as small commercial aircraft, well adapted to Brazil's domestic transportation needs, to fly to a multiplicity of low-traffic destinations. Since early on, EMBRAER's strategy was to concentrate on aircraft design, the production of the fuselage, and assembly, with components purchased from abroad for practically the entire aircraft. This allowed EMBRAER to produce technologically advanced planes competitively and avoid the need to develop technologically complex components—a very costly process—without having the comparative advantage to do so. In this way, foreign suppliers also had an interest in making sure that their home markets were open for the final product. EMBRAER's timing was perfect: just as the *Bandeirante* (a 15–21-passenger turboprop) was rolled out, the United States deregulated its air travel market, which led to the creation of hub-and-spoke networks, and, as a result, a very substantial spike in the demand for regional aircraft that could service these routes.

A key pillar of EMBRAER's success derives from institutional development. In the late 1940s, Brazil established the Aerospace Technological Center and the Aeronautical Technological Institute, where specialized human resources were trained. These institutions were crucial to ensure that Brazil had the productive capabilities needed for the success of the sector and the entire cluster that developed. The Aeronautics Ministry played an important role in providing financing and strategic planning, giving needed support to the process of learning by doing that was essential to its eventual success. In turn, this venture generated important spillovers for other segments of Brazilian industry, which materialized thanks to the alliances between multinational companies, domestic entrepreneurs, and industrial federations.

Brazil's various macroeconomic crises during the 1980s and early 1990s left their mark on the company. Skyrocketing oil prices and the difficult state of government financing in the early 1990s led to its privatization in 1994, with BNDES retaining a 6.8 percent in the ownership of the company. Both BNDES and the new private owners injected important capital resources into the company between 1994 and 1996, which improved its finances and allowed it to attempt a new and successful venture, with the launch of its regional ERJ-145 jet in international markets.

EMBRAER, together with over 430 multinationals (including some of its own suppliers), is located in the industrial complex of São José dos Campos. Its proximity to other sophisticated producers solves many coordination problems and facilitates joint production arrangements. A large and well-trained labor force is certainly one of the advantages. Today EMBRAER is the largest producer of regional jets in the world, having outpaced sales of rival Bombardier for the last eight years.

The story of EMBRAER is not without critics, however. Some question the reliance on subsidies, in the form of export financing through the PROEX program. These subsidies, and similar ones provided by the Canadian and Quebec governments to rival Bombardier in the form of export credit and loan guarantees, were the subject of trade disputes between Canada and Brazil within the WTO at the end of the 1990s and beginning of the new century. As a result, both governments adjusted their subsidies to make them WTO-compatible, but did not eliminate them. Both companies would be profitable if subsidies in both countries were eliminated. Their only justification is that the other country is extending them. Thus, both countries would be better off if, instead of engaging in trade wars, they would negotiate their joint elimination.[10]

In contrast to EMBRAER, the Brazilian informatics policy, launched in the 1970s and expanded in 1984, shows why pure protectionism in technologically dynamic industries where the importing country has no comparative advantage is usually ineffectual. The 1984 law defined a market reserve for computer hardware by stipulating that only firms with Brazilian majority ownership would be allowed to sell in the domestic market. The reserve applied to microcomputers, minicomputers in existence at the time, and some peripherals. These pieces of equipment had to be produced in the country and were granted heavy tariff protection. The regulations forced foreign companies in the computer business to enter into minority joint ventures with Brazilian partners and to manufacture in Brazil, if they wished to sell in the Brazilian market. Very few did so. Significant restrictions also applied to software production and sales. Foreign companies were not allowed to market their products freely in the country, especially if the government's Secretariat for Information could identify domestic producers of similar products.

> In contrast to EMBRAER's focus on selected production areas in which it could eventually compete, and agreements with foreign partners to make the transition, the strategy followed to develop informatics-promoted protection through isolation. Brazilian informatics did progress but, despite substantial resources devoted to its development, could never catch up in an extremely dynamic industry in which the technological frontier was constantly pushed by advanced economies. Nowadays, there are no Brazilian computers in the international market. Since information and communication technology (ICT) is a general-use technology, these policies may have slowed down economic growth in Brazil.

By the time of the debt crisis of the 1980s—dubbed "the lost decade"—ISI had run its course. The debt crisis was a macroeconomic phenomenon of excessive public and private spending (the latter mostly on consumption and not on investment) for a protracted period of time, leading to an accumulation of foreign debt that was eventually viewed as unsustainable by international creditors. When it erupted, it led to a drop in incomes, an abrupt decline in the rate of investment, and high rates of unemployment in the majority of countries in the region. Whereas the ISI policy of altering market signals to channel investment resources in new directions was increasingly doing more harm than good, it was not the main factor generating or prompting the debt crisis. However, it tended to be blamed for it by association.

Be that as it may, the debt crisis was the last straw after ISI's mounting failures. By the end of the 1980s an animus against any industrial policy had spread, along with almost universal support for leaving the allocation of investment to markets. The rejection of industrial policy became intertwined in the minds of observers and policymakers with what came to be known as "the Washington Consensus." The Washington Consensus, as originally formulated by John Williamson in 1990, had little to say about industrial policy per se and focused instead on macroeconomic management, so it cannot be made directly responsible for the backlash. However, the injunction to liberalize imports was a frontal blow to the ISI strategy, the backbone of industrial policy in the region, and, more generally, was taken as a call to return to a laissez-faire approach to development. Later formulations of the Washington Consensus, such as Williamson (2003), did come out firmly against industrial policy, on the grounds that business decisions should be left to the private sector, while the government should concentrate on the framework within which private decisions are made. This flat rejection of sectorial policies involving "picking winners" did in fact win the day, and became for the most part the accepted boundary for PDPs. By the early 1990s, most countries had liberalized their trade policies extensively, many SOEs had been privatized, development banks had been scaled back, financial repression had ended, and the economies in the region had been opened to international financial flows.

Reforms over the past 20 years furthered the goal to "get the prices right" by dismantling industrial policy and its institutions. A market-friendly business climate and macroeconomic stability rightly promoted by these reforms, however, proved insufficient for economic development in Latin America, as laissez-faire policies delivered disappointing growth outcomes. As a result, the backlash against industrial policies has softened in recent years and made room for forward-looking rethinking. While misguided protectionist policies and political abuse gave industrial policy a bad name, PDPs appear to be needed for growth.

Now the challenge is to put into practice a new generation of policies. Fortunately, the national and international environment has changed significantly and may now support active, modern PDPs. Domestically, private sectors have shown increasing muscle and capacity to undertake uncertain, long-term investments. Deeper domestic financial markets have emerged in a number of countries. In many of them, finance can be raised through stock and bond markets—something that was unthinkable in the 1940s. Internationally, the export pessimism that dominated development thinking in the early days of ISI has subsided, as international trade has boomed and barriers to trade have fallen. By the same token, countries have become increasingly integrated into international financial markets.

On the other side of the ledger, some of the export promotion policies that were used successfully by Korea and other developing countries that are catching up are currently barred by the World Trade

Organization (WTO). WTO agreements support the free-trade regime vital for productive transformation, but at the same time impede the application of some export-promoting PDPs. While the system provides for some flexibility and ways to implement policies that foster pro-growth transformation of export activities, clearly, navigating WTO rules designed to support free trade complicates PDPs (see Box 1.2 for details). Moreover, specific trade agreements signed by individual countries to facilitate trade and investment may also include additional provisions constraining PDPs. In fact, the free-trade agreements signed by several countries in the region and developed countries often impose rules on many of the WTO-related subjects that are stricter for developing countries in terms of their depth and scope than the disciplines set by the WTO itself.[11] The point is that trade agreements constrain PDPs and need to be designed, and evaluated, with this interaction in mind. By contrast, exchange rate policies are not restricted by the WTO, and trade agreements more generally, and could be used as PDPs to foster exports in lieu of prohibited subsidies. However, they would be blunt PDPs that run the risk of introducing inflation and distortions and whose ability to foster productive transformation is not well established.

Box 1.2 PDPs and WTO Rules

Several recently industrialized countries (Korea, Taiwan, and even Finland) used subsidies to diversify their production and export structures (Amsden, 1989; Jäntti, Saari, and Vartiainen, 2005; Wade, 1990). These subsidies were temporary and meant to compensate for the anti-export bias of protection. In addition, many of these sectors were favored with interest rates that were lower than those charged to other firms and sectors. Most of these policies were adopted in the 1960s and 1970s, well before countries had agreed to fairly stringent disciplines on subsidies in the context of the Uruguay Round of Trade Negotiations, which concluded in 1993 with the creation of the WTO and the adoption of a large number of codes (e.g., on subsidies and countervailing measures, on trade-related investment measures, on so-called trade-related matters of intellectual property rights, and on trade in services).

The main obstacles to using trade policies that affect prices introduced in the Uruguay Round are of two kinds. In the first place, WTO members have generally "bound" their tariff rates.[12] This means that members who have done so are committed to refrain from raising tariffs unless they provide an offsetting tariff reduction and have the approval of the WTO, a fairly cumbersome process that has been rarely used. However, several countries have sought to circumvent these restrictions. Developing countries binding their tariffs have done so at levels higher than those that they effectively apply, giving them some leeway to increase them in case of balance-of-payments problems or even to encourage individual sectors.

Second, and more importantly for modern PDPs, the Code on Subsidies and Countervailing Measures severely limits the kinds of subsidies that are allowed. Export subsidies and subsidies tied to the use of domestic inputs are banned. So are all other subsidies that, although not aimed directly at exports, could affect export prices and the competitiveness of domestic firms in foreign markets. The intent of the Code is to eliminate international trade distortions by means of assistance to individual firms or industries (which will be labeled vertical market interventions in this report). Supports that are general in nature and not firm- or industry-specific are still allowed.

The Subsidies Code has a de minimis clause for exports from developing countries. Their export subsidies are not considered actionable when they do not exceed 2 percent of the export value. They are also not actionable by an importing country when they do not exceed 4 percent of the total imports of similar goods by the importing country.[13] This is an interesting option for countries wishing to use transitory export subsidies that are withdrawn once the exports of a good exceed a certain threshold (as was the case with Chile's *reintegro simplificado*, analyzed in chapter 2, notified by the authorities as an export subsidy in 2003).

A particular cause for concern for developing countries was the inclusion of income tax exemptions contingent upon exportation in the definition of prohibited export subsidies. Several countries (most Central American and Caribbean countries) use income tax exemptions as part of their arsenal of measures to attract multinational firms to their Export Processing Zones. Moreover, these exemptions apply even to national subcontractors of multinationals. On several occasions, developing countries have succeeded in postponing the elimination of such income tax exemptions. However, given that 2015 is the final deadline to eliminate those export-related tax exemptions, several countries in the region have already started to reform their Export Processing Zones regimes. The 20 least-developed countries that are identified in Annex VII of the Code were initially exempted from these disciplines until the time their per capita GNPs exceeded US$ 1,000.[14]

The new disciplines on intellectual property ("Trade-Related Intellectual Property Rights") and on investment ("Trade-Related Investment Measures," TRIMs) also pose important challenges to PDPs. Intellectual property rights have been considerably tightened, and they have been brought under the purview of the WTO. This means that violators of the strengthened regimes for patents, copyrights, trademarks, denominations of origin, and other forms of intellectual property may face retaliation in the form of protectionist measures on their exports. As regards TRIMs, the most important issue is the banning of local content requirements for foreign investors, a measure greatly in use in the 1970s and 1980s, but much less so in recent times, although some countries have revived them recently without challenge.

Productive development in the region is now ripe for rethinking. Countries are increasingly attempting to find new ways to conduct active PDPs—what might be called a second-generation industrial policy, radically different from the original.

- Policymakers have become much more respectful of comparative advantage, both actual and potential. Protection of the domestic market has given way to a strategy of export transformation.[15] Development strategies are outward-oriented, and export agencies play an important role.
- The emphasis on manufacturing is largely gone. In countries that have large manufacturing sectors, such as Brazil and Mexico, policymakers have continued to think of diversification partly in terms of manufactures, but with the central objective of helping firms in new sectors become internationally competitive. Much of the new emphasis has gone into moving up the technological ladder in industries that have proven successful (agriculture, food products, and mining).
- Policies are largely guided by the perception of market failures. There is stronger willingness to tackle them in a horizontal fashion but also a growing recognition of the power of specific, vertical interventions to address bottlenecks. Encouraging

clusters of firms with backward, parallel, and forward linkages in their production network to sectors that have a demonstrated comparative advantage have been the hallmark in some countries.
- Interventions gradually tend to emphasize innovation. Following the lead of successful catch-up developing economies, an increasing number of countries in the region now have an agency dedicated to innovation and technology diffusion, and many support it through tax breaks and outright subsidies.
- There has been a switch from state-led and state-implemented development to giving the private sector a central role. The state is viewed as a facilitator of the production decisions that must be carried out by private agents, which puts a premium on public-private collaboration. In modern PDPs, the policy process tends to be bottom-up rather than top-down.
- The attraction of FDI has played a prominent role in the new PDPs. While policies toward FDI have become welcoming in general, some countries have made efforts to attract FDI into specific, technologically advanced sectors and to undertake the actions required to ensure success in this effort. In some cases, state agencies have played a coordinating role, sometimes unwittingly, as foreign companies have made known their requirements for investing in the country. The need to increase the supplies of human resources in industry-specific and generic skills has figured prominently in these efforts.

At the same time, the failed experience with industrial policy in the region concerning the overreach of a state with weak institutional capabilities and the risks of "picking winners" leading to "rent seeking" is a clear warning that the new PDPs need to be established on different institutional bases in order to avoid the risk of past failures. Sound policies for productive development will require new roles for public agencies, and more active involvement of the state in conjunction with the private sector. One key challenge is to design these institutions in a sound way to make sure that history is not repeated and to grow the capabilities required to advance and strengthen them.

Rethinking Productive Development

The question is then, how does a country go about fostering higher productivity and sustained growth? How does it improve the drivers of productive transformation? The region has searched for various policy answers over time but the good results achieved elsewhere have eluded it. Policies have usually run their course without becoming engines of sustained development. On the one hand, transformational processes demanding the accumulation of new productive capabilities have not typically occurred to satisfaction in the context of laissez-faire policies. When successful, they have involved a more active role of the state to enable countries to become competitive in the production of a wider, more advanced range of products. On the other hand, misguided policies have also led to distorted development or outright transformational dead ends. It is high time to rethink the role of public policies aimed at productive development in order to successfully navigate the hazardous waters of productive transformation.

The Policy Agenda Today

PDPs in the region as measured by direct public spending and indirect assistance in the form of tax expenditures, as well as risk exposure, are substantial and somewhat haphazard. An active PDP agenda is not necessarily about expending more fiscal resources, but rather about how to find savings by curtailing policies that are not justified or do not work in order to strengthen those that deliver and make way for new ones that are promising. Policymakers in most countries in the region are searching for policies and institutions that work over a wide range of areas, whether in the form of broad-based incentives (such as matching grants for R&D), focused attention to specific productive needs (such as cluster programs), or establishing institutions able to conduct modern policy processes (such as public-private collaboration). The challenge for each country is to find a good constellation of policies and institutions, slashing useless or distortionary policies while engaging in well-chosen active policies, carried out by effective productive development agencies with the capabilities to design and implement them.

As mentioned, effective policy needs to address market failures in a consistent way, from diagnosis to implementation. Unfortunately, all too often this is not the case. Furthermore, policies have been used too frequently to pursue social and other objectives with the pretense of enhancing productivity; adding objectives to PDPs creates confusion and degrades them. Moreover, the risk of political abuse and capture by the private sector prompted by past industrial policy looms large; effective PDPs require institutional capabilities to confront these perils. For all these reasons, a systematic review to weed out detrimental policies in place using this optic may be very useful as a starting point.

At the same time, there is now a growing consensus among policymakers and analysts alike that by putting all industrial policy out of bounds, the region may have thrown out the baby with the bathwater. More and more, the question is not put in terms of "whether" to do active PDPs but rather "how" to do them.

The Scope of This Book

This book on PDPs does not center on manufacturing; instead, it encompasses the region's traditional primary sectors and fledgling service sectors.

The theme of this book is production—specifically, productive development. The tools of PDPs may also be used to deal with social concerns, with the purpose of redistributing opportunities or outcomes. These objectives are very legitimate but are outside the scope of the book because they involve an entirely different set of issues. This analysis assesses policies and institutions only with respect to their effects on productive development. For example, the merit of policies concerning small or family enterprises is assessed strictly on the basis of their overall productive impact, disregarding the social impact that is sometimes argued to favor them. In this sense, the report puts a proper perspective on issues such as the supply of easy credit to small and medium enterprises (SMEs). While the discussion notes some of the implications of PDPs on social issues, an integral evaluation of these policies and whether they are well suited to deal with social objectives would require taking into account factors that are not addressed in this report. In the same way, the use of PDPs to soften the blow suffered by declining sectors or to protect sectors from cyclical downturns is relevant for this analysis only to the extent that they are part of a long-run strategy of productive development.

The informal economy is also outside the scope of the book. As is well known, the informal economy is a salient characteristic of the region's economies; without a doubt, it is an important part of the region's dismal productivity performance, and deserves in-depth treatment. However, the tools of PDPs and their institutions are generally not well suited for reaching the informal sector. The issues of informality, which were one of the main focuses of the 2010 report, *The Age of Productivity*, are best treated separately (Pagés, 2010). For this reason, this book touches upon the informal economy only inasmuch as PDPs designed for the formal economy may have an indirect impact on informality: for example, when discussing the reduction of steps required to start a (formal) business (chapter 4 on new firms) or programs to facilitate the access to (formal) financing that may provide incentives for formalization (chapter 6 on financing).

Macroeconomic policies are also outside the scope of this report. The development implications of the structure of fiscal revenues were the main focus of the 2013 edition of Development in the Americas entitled *More than Revenue* (Corbacho, Fretes Cibils, and Lora, 2013). Macroeconomic stability and the quality of macroeconomic policies may have a first-order impact on productive development, but are best dealt with separately because they follow a different logic. Exchange rate policy could be to some extent an exception in this regard because for some it is a key PDP tool (such as Rodrik, 2008). However, both the productive development rationale of currency undervaluation (the market and government failures it would address) and whether it is amenable to policy intervention on a persistent basis to have an effect on exports are open to debate in academia and among policymakers. Furthermore, an exchange rate policy of currency undervaluation would be a blunt instrument, substantially less precise than the PDPs analyzed in this report that are targeted to meritorious activities and sectors. For example, undervaluation may expand export volume but not necessarily improve its composition. For these reasons, this report leaves aside this potentially important issue for productive development and concentrates on more targeted PDPs. For the most part, macroeconomic developments are taken into account only as a critical context for PDPs.

Finally, basic public functions underpinning the so-called business climate, such as the enforcement of property rights, are underemphasized in order to focus more intensely on policies specifically related to productive development (as explained in the policy typology in chapter 2). The book recognizes the critical importance of these broad-based policies and institutions as a foundation for productive development but chooses to de-emphasize them because they are by now noncontroversial and generally well understood throughout most of the region.

This Book's Approach to Rethinking Productive Development

This book is not ideological; it is based on analysis and evidence. The checkered past of industrial policy in the region merits a pragmatic approach that builds on its experience, dealing with the nuances and trade-offs of the practice of PDPs. Rethinking productive development includes being mindful of the lessons from the past, both successes and failures. As a result, the analysis assumes that conclusions are dependent on context, and that there is no best practice to emulate. More than recommendations, the book offers information and a way of thinking about these issues.

The report has an analytic approach, which is used throughout to assess the justification of policies. At its core, before embarking on policy thinking, it asks the seemingly simple question of why it is that presumably desirable productive developments are not undertaken by the market. Policymakers in market economies can benefit enormously by understanding the apparently failed behavior of market agents that possess deep business information and a strong profit incentive to use it. The report systematically applies two tests to start the policy analysis.

- *What is the plausible market failure that has been diagnosed to justify the policy?*
- *Is the alleged policy remedy—whether it entails alleviating the failure or redressing its impact—a good match for the diagnosis?*

Beyond the sound guidance derived from these two tests, the report makes an effort to evaluate the impact of policies implemented by productive development agencies on the basis of solid evidence and rigorous evaluation. To this end, it applies the same analytical approach to identify the precise indicators of outcomes that would reveal whether the policy has in fact had a beneficial impact specifically in terms of addressing the market failures that justified the policy. For example, if policy is justified by the spillovers it is expected to generate beyond the direct beneficiary, as in the case of the diffusion of innovations, impact evaluation needs to measure spillovers. Policy impact evaluation based on evidence of proximate outcomes, in this case effects on direct beneficiaries, can yield useful information about the mechanism through which policy is expected to work, but is not a test of the effectiveness of policy in achieving its final objectives resulting from spillovers. When possible, statistically rigorous impact evaluation techniques are used to assess policy effectiveness, based on the relevant indicators for policy evaluation. This report showcases evaluations done or coordinated by the Inter-American Development Bank (IDB) that may be seen as models to build on in the future.

The book builds on a new policy paradigm that is emerging: namely, that PDP is a learning process.[16] The premise, supported by experience, is that policymakers cannot know what the right policy interventions are and need to set up a process to discover them. Therefore, the aforementioned two tests to validate policy are subject to substantial imprecision that would be reduced over time. A learning process also involves tentative, even experimental, policy design and implementation with a built-in capacity to iterate and adjust as a matter of refining policy. This implies a premium on exploration and a calibrated risk of failure, and represents a substantial shift from conservative policy paradigms based on perceived safety. Finally, a learning process implies that policies are designed to be evaluable and are discontinued unless validated by a pertinent evaluation, which require institutions well equipped for learning.

The book puts a very strong emphasis on the institutions behind the policies. The institutional capabilities required to explore, design, implement, monitor, and evaluate policies are key for the viability and success of policies. Without them, government failures may trump market failures and the medicine may be worse than the disease. One of the main insights of this report is that institutional development holds the key for better PDPs, minimizing the risk of repeating some of the mistakes and overreach of past industrial policy. The focus ought to be not on policy "best practices" but on policy "best matches" with institutional capabilities. This is the third test to validate policy.

- *Are institutional capabilities sufficiently strong to design and carry out policy as intended?*

The approach taken in this report emphasizes that sound institutions require solid capabilities and collaboration with the private sector.

- Sound institutions require efforts to develop and effectively deploy public sector capabilities for the task at hand. Besides the technical capabilities needed to deal with complex policy matters—a well-known issue in public administration—the required set of capabilities includes steps to coordinate actions across public sector agencies and effectively engage in collaboration with private sector actors, whose demands may straddle various public agencies, as well as the capacity to protect agencies from undue political pressure. The book discusses how technical, operational, and political capabilities limit the range of policies that can be carried out in the short term without overreach, and suggests how to grow capacities over time and ratchet them up.
- Sound institutions for productive transformation cannot just operate from the top down: they require public-private collaboration. On the one hand, the private sector has privileged

knowledge of some aspects of market failures and government failures, as well as direct knowledge concerning policy design, implementation, and evaluation. The pieces of knowledge available to the public and private sectors are complementary and require collaboration to harness them. On the other hand, the private sector has a profit motivation that deviates from the collective welfare perspective of the public sector; this mismatch may lead to the manipulation of information and rent seeking. The book discusses the types of policy operations that are more subject to a conflict of interest, and thus may be prudent to avoid. It suggests a number of principles to set up cooperation mechanisms that keep tabs on private incentives to help prevent them from degenerating into demands for favorable treatment and other types of rent-seeking behavior as well as, in the extreme, corruption.

This report emphasizes economic transformation consistent with international competitiveness. This is not the only route to growth. Producing more of the same through factor accumulation and producing the same products at lower costs—a productivity gain—are certainly important for growth and incomes. So is the reallocation of factors of production from less productive to more productive existing firms and sectors. However, transformation is a key factor that lies behind the virtuous dynamic of sustained economic growth. This book emphasizes these transformational aspects of PDPs, such as those helping product innovation; the creation and growth of firms with high productivity potential; the provision of public inputs needed for the development of emerging sectors; and well-functioning factor markets to facilitate reallocation to new and dynamic activities.

International competitiveness is key in the analytical framework of this report. As mentioned, international competitiveness is a test of efficiency (sustaining tradable products that do not reach competitiveness after policies run their course is welfare-reducing). Competitive export products can be scaled up, thus magnifying the aggregate policy impact. Furthermore, domestic producers facing ample world demand share common interests, rather than competing for limited domestic demand; this facilitates collaboration, and, consequently, the conduct of public policy. Consistent with this outward orientation, the report purposely frames PDPs in a globalized world. It emphasizes the opportunities afforded by a globalized world in terms of exports, as mentioned, as well as the attraction of FDI and insertion in global value chains.

Finally, the report frames the question of PDPs in the context of countries on the road to development, which is the most fruitful for analyzing the region. On the one hand, the region is not at the productivity frontier. On the other hand, most countries in the region have the resources required to be able to learn from those economies at the frontier and adopt or adapt. Therefore, the report emphasizes policies in the context of a catching-up process. More generally, it stresses the dimensions that are most relevant for the circumstances of the countries of the region.

With an aim at conceptual clarity, detailed evidence grounded in the realities of the region, and a view toward pragmatism, this book explores a way forward to build sound policies and institutions for productive development. It is about principles rather than prescriptions.

2

A Conceptual Framework for Productive Development Policies

Chapter 1 made the case that the relevant question is not whether productive development policies (PDPs) should be pursued; rather, the question is how. What types of policies can help address the many market failures that beset the process of productive development—without repeating the errors of the past—and pave the way for a better future? In this regard, the oft-cited image of a pendulum, by which past industrial policies have swung out of vogue and are now back in fashion, is simply not appropriate. It would be more accurate to say that certain well-designed policy interventions may be worthwhile; they have stood the test of time, or can be crafted to meet new challenges. Other types, however, may lack proper conceptual justification or may be too risky to implement effectively. What types of policies should be favored? Which ones should be set aside? There is a need to rethink PDPs, to screen them in order to separate the wheat from the chaff. Rethinking these policies starts with a proper conceptual framework.

What Types of Policies Are Needed?

PDPs differ in a variety of dimensions. This framework emphasizes two. The first dimension pertains to their scope. They can focus on specific sectors (vertical policies). Or they can be broad-based and not attempt to benefit any industry in particular (horizontal policies).[1]

The second dimension relates to the type of intervention. Support can take the form of *public inputs* or *public goods* that the state can provide in order to enhance the competitiveness of the private sector, such as general improvements in infrastructure or protection of property rights. Or support can take the form of *market interventions*—such as subsidies, tax breaks, or tariffs—that affect the incentives faced by private actors, and thus influence their behavior. These two dimensions can be combined in a 2×2 matrix, which divides the universe of PDPs into four quadrants (Figure 2.1).

On the horizontal dimension, an example of a horizontal public input would be an intervention that reduces the transaction costs of starting a business. It is a public good provided by the state, and it is not specifically intended to benefit any particular sector. An example of a horizontal market intervention would be a matching grant scheme for R&D. On the vertical dimension, an example of vertical public input would be the provision of phytosanitary controls that prevent plagues from contaminating food products. An example of vertical market intervention would be giving tax breaks to a specific sector, such as tourism.

Why focus on these dimensions? For a simple but powerful reason: Because the public policy considerations to take into account when analyzing the merits of PDPs differ in each of these quadrants.

This is particularly true when it comes to the problems of rent seeking and capture precisely the type of problems that gave industrial policies a bad reputation in the past. Interventions in these quadrants differ importantly in the degree to which they are subject

Figure 2.1 A Typology of PDP Interventions

	Horizontal policies	Vertical policies
Public inputs		
Market interventions		

to these problems. Generally, these problems tend to be more pervasive in market interventions such as subsidies, tariff protection, or tax breaks than in the provision of public inputs. Even when the policy rationale calls for temporary measures, market interventions tend to produce ongoing benefits with open-ended time frames, and thus create strong constituencies that lobby for continued support. By contrast, public inputs supplement productive efforts by the private sector and usually have no reason to be discontinued, and thus do not face the same problems.

Rent-seeking problems are also likely to be more prevalent in the case of vertical interventions. As these policies generate concentrated benefits, and the stakes for beneficiaries tend to be higher, vertical interventions tend to create incentives for the sectors to lobby for support, and facilitate the necessary collective action at the sector level to sustain such lobbying.[2] Taking both the ongoing nature and the high stakes profile into account, interventions in the vertical/market intervention quadrant seem riskier from a political economy point of view, and thus require particularly careful safeguards (see Dal Bó and Finan, 2014).

The discussion that follows presents a bird's-eye view of the type of considerations that should be taken into account when thinking about the merits of policy interventions in each of these four quadrants.

Horizontal Public Inputs

This quadrant includes interventions that ensure respect for property rights, efforts to improve the quality of education or the general quality of the infrastructure, and measures to streamline the steps and costs of starting a business.

Of all the quadrants, this is the least controversial. Even the most ardent defenders of the free market would agree that the state has a central role to play in this type of policy. Many of the interventions in this quadrant are associated with the cost of doing business in a country, and many of them are captured by indexes such as the Doing Business Index of the World Bank, and the Global Competitiveness Index of the World Economic Forum. Governments around the world have often made these indexes the focus of their competitiveness policies. Rather than analyzing the merits of state intervention, which are not under discussion, the key in this quadrant is to consider whether the particular policies pass three key tests: whether the design of the interventions is appropriate for achieving the desired objectives, whether these interventions have the desired impact, and whether they are cost-effective.

These policies are obviously very important, and they involve substantial challenges. But because they are less controversial, they are in less need of rethinking. For these reasons, the discussion of policies corresponding to this quadrant—mainly in this chapter, and to some extent, later in this book—will be left aside, in order to focus on interventions in the other quadrants.

Horizontal Market Interventions

These interventions are not aimed at favoring specific *sectors*, but rather at stimulating certain *activities*. Examples include tax breaks to attract foreign investment, subsidies for job training, for investment in machinery, or subsidized credit to small and medium enterprises (SMEs). Are such interventions justified by a sound rationale? This is the critical question in this quadrant. And the answer is... It depends.

The key is to identify the market failure that these interventions seek to address. A *market failure* implies that the net social benefit of productive activities differs from the net private benefit perceived by market agents that control these activities: that is, these productive activities generate spillover effects that may benefit or impose costs on other agents. In some cases, these market failures are clear. Consider a firm's decision to invest in training its workers. The firm faces the following problem: some of the trained workers may go on to work for other firms—perhaps even competing firms. Thus the firm cannot appropriate all the benefits associated with the training. In this case, there is a spillover: when deciding how much to invest, the firm will take into account only its own private benefits associated with the training, not the total benefits to society, part of which will be appropriated by others. As a result, the firm's investment in training will be less than what would be desirable from the point of view of society as a whole (that is, the market fails to achieve a socially appropriate solution). In such cases, a subsidy to promote training can be justified, so that the firm has incentives to provide the socially optimal level of job training.[3] A similar case can be made for subsidizing R&D that has spillovers beyond the firm.

Compare this with the case of investment in machinery. Assume that the machine will increase the productivity of a firm. Is this a good enough reason for the state to intervene with a subsidy? The answer is no. To the extent that the firm can appropriate all the benefits associated with this increased productivity, the firm itself would have all the right incentives to invest without the need for a subsidy. Unless there are special circumstances that determine the existence of a market failure, state intervention would not be justified in this case.[4]

Once a market failure has been identified, a second important question is whether the intervention proposed or adopted is designed so as to address as precisely as possible the market failure that has been identified. For example, although an investment in research and development can clearly create positive spillovers, certain R&D activities are more likely to generate them than others. Collaborative R&D activities between groups of firms, or between firms and research institutions, tend to reduce duplication costs and create more spillovers than R&D activities within individual firms, which could have an interest in limiting dissemination of the knowledge acquired. Therefore, interventions designed to encourage collaboration in R&D projects have more chance of successfully addressing market failures than interventions that stimulate R&D regardless of how it is done. These and other aspects of the design of R&D incentives are discussed in detail in chapter 3 on innovation and technology diffusion.

A similar case can be made with respect to tax breaks to attract FDI. The justification for these exemptions is that there are positive spillovers associated with the installation of foreign companies in the host country. The literature, however, is inconclusive in this respect. Studies such as Aitken and Harrison (1999) suggest that spillovers could be negative, particularly within the sector, since new companies compete with existing ones for productive resources, resulting in higher factor costs. In contrast, other studies suggest that there could be positive spillovers through linkages to local suppliers (provided that they have the human capital required to absorb the foreign company's technology), the development of specialized inputs, or the mobility of labor (if employees trained in the foreign firm then go on to work in other companies or start their own businesses).[5] Interventions aimed at fostering these spillovers (for example, tax breaks linked to certain labor training commitments, or a foreign firm's support for programs to develop local suppliers) can be preferable to interventions aimed at promoting foreign investment across the board.

A third important question has to do with the size of subsidies or exemptions. In general, the size of the subsidy should be related to the size of the spillover. In the job training example, unless turnover is very large, a substantial part of the training benefits is captured by the firm that is making the investment in training, in the form of the increased productivity of its workforce. In this case, a subsidy amounting to a small fraction of training costs might be warranted, but not a grant that covers the full cost of training.[6] In the case of exemptions or subsidies to attract foreign investment, the ideal would be to offer the minimum necessary for the investment to occur, as long as this minimum is less than the size of the spillover.[7] In this way, the host country—and not the foreign firm—can capture a larger share of the benefits associated with the new investment.

Another aspect that can be important in certain cases has to do with the timing of the benefits associated with certain market interventions. Consider the case of attracting FDI. While the installation of the firm in the host country is a one-time event, the instruments used to attract it may differ in terms of their timing. They could take the form of a one-time benefit, such as an installation grant, or a benefit that is extended over time, such as an exemption from certain taxes for a certain number of years. In addition to the potential issue that recurring benefits may be difficult to discontinue, another political economy issue may come into play. In the case of the tax exemption, most of the sacrifice in terms of fiscal resources may fall on future administrations, particularly if the investments do not bear fruit for a few years. Current governments may accrue the immediate political benefits associated with extending tax breaks, without internalizing the costs. Thus incentives may be overly generous, with the corresponding cost to future taxpayers.[8]

In addition, interventions in this quadrant can also be used to stimulate the development of competitive new export activities. What Hausmann and Rodrik (2003) have called the process of "self-discovery" is of particular policy interest. According to these authors, the activity of exploring new sectors with potential comparative advantages occurs less often than it should because of the presence of spillovers. Developing a competitive new export activity—and in the process "discovering" that the country has comparative advantages in its production—requires costly experimentation. While the pioneer must cover these costs—and therefore will suffer the corresponding losses if the experiment does not pan out—success can give rise to imitation. Thus the successful pioneer cannot appropriate all the benefits associated with the "discovery" because some of the benefits will be enjoyed by the followers. This may call for a subsidy to stimulate discovery activities by compensating pioneers for this spillover. Box 2.1 presents a scheme to do precisely this, which also serves as an illustration of how policy instruments in this quadrant can be designed so as to address market failures in a precise way.

Box 2.1 Addressing the Self-Discovery Problem with Subsidies to Export Pioneers

The case of blueberries in Argentina is an excellent example of the type of externalities involved in self-discovery (see Sánchez et al., 2012). At the beginning of the 1990s, the pioneer Francisco Caffarena was searching for investment alternatives with export potential in the agricultural sector. Blueberries had the potential to get to market during the Northern Hemisphere off-season, when prices, and thus profits, were expected to be high.

Since blueberries were not produced in Argentina at the time, he faced uncertainty. Would the climate and soil conditions be favorable? What would be the ideal location within the country? What varieties of blueberry would be more appropriate for the local conditions? When would he be able to harvest, and at what price would he be able to sell? To launch his business, Caffarena had to invest in experimentation. He hired US experts to advise him in matters of production and sanitation; he imported several different varieties of blueberry plants and learned to reproduce them; he planted different varieties in different locations. Altogether, the initial investment was approximately US$ 200,000.

He discovered that local conditions were appropriate for blueberry production. But in the process, he also discovered something of great value: he could harvest one month before anyone else in the world, thus avoiding competition and fetching very high prices. Not surprisingly, soon he had many followers. Furthermore, since Argentina as a source country did not have competition at the time of the early harvest, the presence of followers led to lower prices and eroded his profitability.

In response to these developments, the pioneer moved upstream (a nursery to supply plants to other producers) and downstream (export services to the followers). Predictably, in time, competition in these activities emerged as well. By 2005, his share of exports was less than 5 percent. Clearly, the pioneer was not able to appropriate all the benefits associated with his discovery. Diffusion generated a positive externality, benefiting followers and contributing to the country's export diversification.

In this case Caffarena, somehow, decided to invest. Whether or not he underestimated the extent to which he would be followed, he obviously thought that his expected private benefits would exceed the costs, which they did. Many other would-be pioneers, however, may be discouraged from experimenting. As a result, some potentially competitive products may be left undiscovered. What is the best way to address this market failure? Three potential interventions will be discussed:

i. Ex ante Subsidies for Self-Discovery

The idea, proposed by Rodrik (2004), is to identify potential pioneers and subsidize their investment in experimentation. But how can pioneers be identified ex ante? How can the process be protected from rent seeking and favoritism? Rodrik proposes a contest in which entrepreneurs present pre-investment proposals to compete for public funds. Eligible projects would relate to substantially new activities and demonstrate potential to generate spillovers. Selected projects would be subject to audits and oversight. Given that experimentation in self-discovery is risky, many projects would not pan out, and not generate spillovers. As Rodrik would put it, however, each success would compensate for many failures. But the question remains, is it possible to do better?

ii. The Simplified Drawback in Chile

In 1985, Chile implemented a simplified drawback, or *reintegro simplificado*. In lieu of reimbursements for tariffs paid on imported inputs (drawbacks), exporters received a subsidy of up to 10 percent of their export value, as long as total exports of the sector did not exceed $7.5 million.[9] Once this threshold was breached, export subsidies in the sector were automatically eliminated. One strength of this intervention is that it did not require picking winners. Subsidies were assigned automatically to every exporting firm in a new sector, thus making the development of new or incipient sectors more attractive to pioneers and early followers. Unlike Rodrik's proposal, those that experimented but failed would not receive support. There were, however, a few downsides. First, the subsidy would not just go to the pioneer who invested in experimentation, but to early followers as well. While experimentation was encouraged, the early imitation that exacerbates the appropriation problem was encouraged as well. Second, the successful pioneer was subsidized whether or not he generated spillovers, that is, whether or not he was followed. Third, given that the subsidy was eliminated as soon as the threshold was breached, the pioneer had incentives to discourage diffusion and thus minimize spillovers, since faster diffusion led to earlier phaseout. The *reintegro simplificado* was dismantled in 2003.

iii. Addressing the Self-Discovery Problem More Precisely: A New Policy Proposal

The idea, proposed by Stein (2012), is to simply subsidize export pioneers in proportion to the exports of their followers (thus not including their own exports). As in the case of the *reintegro simplificado*, picking winners is not required. Subsidies go automatically to those that generate a successful discovery as long as they are followed. The proposed scheme addresses the three weaknesses of the *reintegro simplificado*: (i) it benefits only the pioneer, not the followers; (ii) it benefits him only to the extent that he generates spillovers; and (iii) it generates the right incentives for the pioneer to encourage diffusion.[10] The subsidy would not need to be large. In the case of blueberries discussed above, for example, Stein (2012) estimates using Argentina's customs export data that a subsidy of 2 percent of exports of followers would have paid the pioneer about $1.2 million between 1998 and 2005, more than enough to compensate for the cost of experimentation.[11]

This program would be fully compatible with WTO rules for the case of agricultural products, such as the blueberry case discussed above, provided the parameters of the subsidy fall within the limits agreed upon

> by the country in the Uruguay Round (see Box 1.2 in chapter 1). More generally, to the extent that this scheme is understood as an incentive for research and development, it would be compatible with the spirit of WTO restrictions. Furthermore, while WTO rules prohibit subsidies conditioned on export performance (with the exception of agriculture), under the proposed policy the subsidy would not be conditioned on own exports, only on those of others. Even if the subsidy were classified by the WTO within the "prohibited" or "actionable" categories, making it sufficiently small (below 2 percent) would ensure that it is not challenged, provided the export share of the country in the destination market is sufficiently low, owing to WTO special de minimis provisions for developing countries.[12] Larger subsidies may simply require this proposal to be adjusted so that it does not discriminate whether pioneers and followers export or produce for the domestic market.

In some cases, interventions in this quadrant involve the participation of agents that help connect the demand for public support with the corresponding supply, intermediating between the state and the beneficiary firms. Examples include first-tier commercial banks, which intermediate between second-tier state development banks and the private firms that receive their credit; incubators, which intermediate between a state agency dealing with entrepreneurship and the aspiring entrepreneurs that receive subsidized services from the incubator; and providers of different types of technological or managerial services, which intermediate between a development agency that promotes SMEs and the target beneficiaries. These intermediary agents may play a crucial role because they are closer to the clients and know their needs. They bring an element of flexibility and a private sector perspective into the selection of beneficiaries, and may act as screening devices, identifying opportunities that would otherwise go unnoticed given the more rigid structures of the public sector.[13]

At the same time, interventions provided through intermediary agents are subject to well-known principal-agent problems. The objectives of the intermediary agents are not necessarily aligned with those of the principal. Thus mechanisms may need to be put in place to align their incentives so that the development objectives can be achieved.¹⁴ In the case of incubators, for example, it is important that these intermediaries receive compensation on the basis of the success of incubated firms, rather than simply the number of firms subject to incubation. This provides them with the right incentives to select the right projects, and to add value during the incubation process. These issues are discussed further in chapter 4 on entrepreneurship, with a particular focus on a change in incubator policy in Chile.¹⁵

To summarize, when analyzing the merits of policy interventions in this quadrant—whether grants, tax breaks, subsidized credit, or other types—the key is to identify the market failure (if any) that justifies the intervention, and adjust the policy instruments to address the identified market failure as precisely as possible.

Vertical Public Inputs

This quadrant encompasses public inputs provided or arranged by the state that generate benefits for specific sectors. Examples in Latin America and the Caribbean include phytosanitary controls; the promotion of tourism from abroad; the creation of specific university degrees to attract a certain type of investment; research by public agencies to create new, more productive crop varieties; or coordination of critical aspects of logistics to facilitate export of specific products, such as cold chain logistics to allow the export of certain fruits and vegetables.

Policies in this quadrant are selective, and thus favor some sectors and not others. These policies are more controversial, since they involve the highly contentious issue of "picking winners," which became a lightning rod for criticism, particularly during the period of the backlash against industrial policy, and remains controversial today.

Should certain sectors be chosen to receive support? If so, how should these sectors be picked? How can a public-private dialogue be structured to identify the public inputs that are needed? How should the state organize itself in order to be able to deliver the required public inputs or help the private sector produce the collective inputs they need? How can problems of capture be avoided? As can be appreciated, the important questions in this quadrant are very different from those of the last one.

It is worthwhile asking first if the state should provide public inputs that benefit specific sectors, or if instead it should focus solely on providing the type of public inputs that are horizontal in nature. The answer is an emphatic yes: the state should get involved in this quadrant. As Hausmann and Rodrik (2006) convincingly argue, most public inputs, by their very nature, tend to benefit specific sectors. Implementation of cold chain logistics can be a key input for the fruit and vegetable sector, but not for the textile sector; a good intellectual property law can be a key input for the biotechnology sector, but not for footwear; development of a university degree in mechanical engineering in the public university (as Costa Rica did to attract Intel) can be a key input for the electronics industry, but not for agriculture. To reserve state action only for those public inputs that have neutral effects on different sectors would mean leaving out a number of interventions that clearly contribute to the productivity of the economy or to the sound functioning of certain markets, which in most cases would not be provided spontaneously by the private sector.

While there is a clear case for the state to provide vertical public inputs, the public sector does not necessarily need to pay for them. In fact, many of these interventions are actually collective or club goods that benefit a specific set of firms, which ought to be willing to foot the bill. While in some cases sectors may be able to organize and provide the collective goods themselves, in others the state may have to help solve a coordination problem that may preclude atomized firms from providing their own solution. A case in point is discussed in Box 2.2, which describes efforts to promote rice production in the province of Entre Ríos in Argentina. More generally, policies in this quadrant should normally include provisions for the private sector to share at least some of the costs of financing the solutions to their problems. In fact, their willingness to pay for a public input is a key test of whether the intervention in question is money well spent. These issues will be discussed in more detail in chapter 11.[16]

If the state has a role in securing these public inputs, how should it choose which inputs to provide? Whose needs should be dealt with first? Hausmann and Rodrik argue that the specific nature of the benefits generated by public inputs, combined with budgetary constraints and the limited attention span of policymakers, mean that policymakers are "doomed to choose." But that does not necessarily mean that the sectors need to be selected a priori. While some countries have preselected sectors—such as Chile, with its cluster program, and Colombia, with its Productive Transformation Program (PTP)—another possible strategy is to initiate a dialogue with any sector that organizes itself to ask for public input support, and then choose which of the problems are worth solving without defining in advance the sectors to be supported. The relative merits of these different strategies may depend on the characteristics of the country in question, a matter that will be discussed in more detail in chapter 9, which addresses the issue of sector selection in vertical policies in detail.

If governments do choose sectors a priori, what criteria should they use? An obvious criterion is to target export sectors in which world demand is growing and in which the country has demonstrated, or at least can be presumed to have, latent comparative advantage. Chapter 1 suggested that countries may also want to focus on sectors that are relatively sophisticated or complex, or that have strategic value in that they open avenues for later redeployment of productive capabilities to other worthwhile sectors. As with the discussion of the previous quadrant, however, choosing sectors with these criteria makes sense only to the extent that there are market failures that prevent the private sector from developing these promising sectors or allowing them to reach their potential. These issues will also be tackled in detail in chapter 9.

Regardless of the criteria used to select sectors, though, it is important to ensure that the selection mechanism is based on an in-depth analysis of the sector's challenges and opportunities and is largely free from political interference and from the vested interests of the sectors involved. For example, Chile heavily involved an international consulting firm, the Boston Consulting Group, in the selection of the sectors in its cluster program. It is also crucial that support be quickly abandoned if it becomes clear that the sectors do not have competitive potential.[17]

For the state to be able to help solve the problems holding back the development of a certain sector, it must be able to identify what those problems are. To carry out this diagnosis, the dialogue between the public and private sectors is absolutely essential. This dialogue often takes place within the context of cluster development programs (CDPs), studied in chapter 7. How the state structures this dialogue, and the nature of the conversations that take place within it, are key for the success of interventions in this quadrant. It is important that the sector-level dialogue focuses on the public inputs, the solutions to coordination problems, or the removal of obstacles required by the private sector to become more productive—and not on subsidies, tax breaks, or other market interventions that may improve profitability without making a dent in productivity. The public sector's role in shaping this dialogue is to allow the necessary exchange of information and support public-private collaboration, while limiting the likelihood of rent seeking. Chapter 11 addresses these issues of how best to structure public-private interaction for PDPs.

Once the priority actions have been identified, it is important to understand how to organize the public sector's response to the private sector's needs. A good response capacity requires good coordination within the public sector because the public agencies that identify needs in dialogue with the private sector are not necessarily the ones that will be responsible for providing the public inputs required to meet these needs. For example, the minister of tourism may identify the need to improve a road required to develop a tourist destination, but the agency that has the resources and the responsibility to deal with road construction and maintenance may be the Ministry of Public Works. Without a system in place that allows authority, information, and resources to flow within the public sector to deliver the necessary public inputs, identified inputs will not be delivered appropriately, and the private sector may be discouraged from participating in the sector-level dialogue.

The Productive Transformation Program in Colombia illustrates some of these points. In this program, a number of sectors—some of them emerging, some more traditional—have been selected with the aim of taking them to world-class status. In each of them, public-private collaboration has been structured to identify obstacles, public inputs that are needed, and coordination problems, and come up with an action plan to address them, with the help of an international consulting firm. The rules of the program clearly delimit the nature of the conversations that can take place in the sector-level dialogue: there is no scope to discuss subsidies, protection, or other market interventions. While there has been some partial success in some sectors (for example, cosmetics), critics charge that the program's Achilles heel relates to failures of public-public coordination. More specifically, the public leaders of the clusters, who are supposed to articulate the needs of the sector within the public sector, typically have lacked the authority or the backing needed to elicit collaboration from the public sector agencies responsible for delivering what is needed.

Vertical Market Interventions

This quadrant is without a doubt the most controversial. Subsidies or protection for specific sectors can lead to rent-seeking behavior by the private sector actors that benefit from these interventions, and can lead to arbitrariness or favoritism by the political and economic authorities. It is mostly interventions in this quadrant—heavy-handed subsidies, protection, state production, or directed credit to specific sectors—that have given industrial policy a bad reputation. For these reasons, policies in this quadrant should be pursued with great care.

Interventions in this quadrant may pursue very different goals. Some interventions are aimed at protecting sectors in decline or that lack current or potential comparative advantages, but have a strong lobbying presence. Rice protection in Costa Rica (see Box 2.2) is a case in point. This type of intervention, which responds to rent seeking and not to the pursuit of efficiency, should clearly be discouraged. This does not mean that governments should never become involved with declining sectors. But when policies are necessary to protect workers or installed productive capacity, this should be done in ways that facilitate the reallocation of the factors of production into more productive sectors, and not by resorting to interventions that preserve these factors in unproductive sectors with limited potential.

Box 2.2 A Tale of Two Interventions

Dysfunctional Market Interventions in Costa Rica

Rice is one of the most protected commodities in Costa Rica. Tariffs are high (35 percent) and prices are controlled at each stage of the production process. Overall, rice subsidies in Costa Rica amount to 45 percent of the domestic price, higher than those in the United States (31 percent) and the European Union (32 percent) (Monge-González, Rivera, and Rosales-Tijerino, 2010). A central player in the rice policy has been the Corporación Arrocera Nacional (CONARROZ), created in 2002 to protect producers from international price shocks and improve local production conditions. But the efforts of CONARROZ, which has strong lobbying capabilities, have focused entirely on the first objective (protection) and not the second (productivity).

When local rice production falls below local demand (as is typically the case), import quotas are allocated to private sector actors, who can import rice without paying the corresponding tariffs. CONARROZ manages the quotas, which are assigned to rice processors in proportion to their processing capacity. Thus, processors can purchase rice at international market prices and sell the processed rice in Costa Rica at prices that reflect the high level of protection and subsidies. This generates extraordinary rents for rice processors, particularly the large ones. Altogether, rice policy in Costa Rica implies important transfers from consumers (in particular, the poor, for whom rice represents a large share of their consumption basket) to medium and large rice producers and processors.

Effective Public Inputs and Resolution of Coordination Problems in Entre Ríos, Argentina

The experience of Costa Rica contrasts with that of Entre Ríos, Argentina, where problems in the rice sector were addressed using public inputs. In this case, the key players have been the National Agricultural Technology Institute (INTA) and Pro-Arroz, a foundation of local rice producers. Until 1998, this province produced one low-quality, low-productivity variety, mainly for export to the Brazilian market. With the devaluation of the Brazilian currency in 1999, the sector lost competitiveness. Since the early 1990s, INTA had been developing a new variety of rice (Camba) of better quality and higher productivity.

Rather than lobbying for protection or subsidies, Pro-Arroz organized the producers to complement the financing of the local chapter of INTA, INTA-Concepción, by coordinating its members' contributions. Later, and at the request of Pro-Arroz, the provincial government introduced a tax on producers that went directly into financing the research activities of INTA-Concepción. This is a clear mechanism to prevent free riding, where the state helps to solve coordination problems of the private sector. Rice producers collaborated by lending their fields for the necessary experimentation with the new variety. Thanks to the successful introduction of the new variety, the sector's productivity rose rapidly, boosting its competitiveness. INTA went on to become a global leader in rice technology, and has since developed a more sophisticated variety (Puita), which has been successfully introduced in many countries, in association with BASF, the German chemical company. The results in each country in terms of productivity are very clear, as seen in Figure B2.1.

Figure B2.1   Rice Productivity in Argentina and Costa Rica, 1990–2012

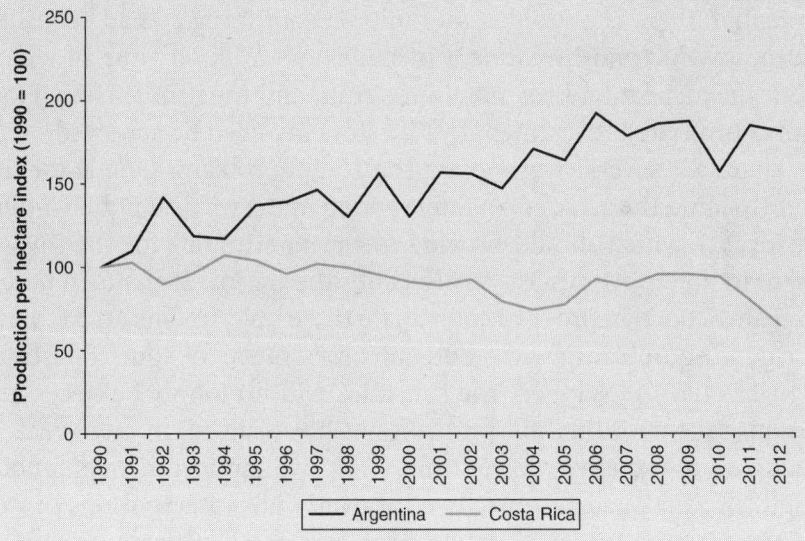

Source: Authors' calculations based on FAO (2013).

Sources: For the case of Costa Rica, see Monge-González, Rivera, and Rosales-Tijerino (2010) and Cornick (2012). For the case of Entre Ríos, Argentina, see Sánchez, Butler, and Rozemberg (2011).

On the other hand, this quadrant also includes interventions designed to develop sectors with competitive potential that would not develop without them. Does it make sense to offer market interventions in these cases? While mainstream economists have long been skeptical of this type of intervention, there are theoretical arguments—and some successful experiences—for supporting industries with latent comparative advantages, even if there are short-run social costs to doing so. Naturally, in order for interventions to be warranted, the overall benefits to society must be demonstrably greater than the costs.

One particular case in which interventions in this quadrant may be justified is when they help solve coordination problems in sectors with latent comparative advantage. A typical example would be the development of a new tourism destination. Such a development might face the following problem: without an airport, it makes no sense to invest in hotels, but if there are no hotels, it makes no sense to invest in the airport. Assuming that the destination has real potential, there is a problem of multiple equilibria: a "bad" equilibrium, in which no investment is made, and a "good" one in which both the airport and the hotels are built, and tourism thrives. How can coordinated investment by all actors involved be achieved?

There are several ways to approach this problem. One is for the state to build the airport (an intervention in the vertical public inputs quadrant), which should provide sufficient stimulus for the investment in hotels. Another is to offer subsidies to investments in hotels and an airport, in order to coordinate these investments and achieve the good equilibrium with good outcomes. Once the tourist destination has been developed, the subsidies will no longer be necessary because the coordination problem has been solved; in any event, if required, the activity can continue to receive support through public inputs (in the quadrant discussed above). Thus interventions in this quadrant to solve coordination problems are justifiable only on a temporary basis.

A good example is Costa Rica's tourism strategy. In 1985, the country introduced a series of incentives for the sector, mostly in the form of tax breaks, covering hotel investments, air and water transport, travel agencies, and car rentals, among others. As a result of this policy, investment in the sector took off, and the rate of arrivals and spending on tourism grew significantly. In 1992, most of these exemptions were eliminated without slowing the growth of the sector (see Figure 2.2). Later, the state assisted the sector by providing sector-specific public inputs geared toward the emergence of the sustainable tourism that the state wanted to develop. These included the creation, in collaboration with the private sector, of the national brand, "no artificial ingredients," the conservation of natural areas, and the creation of a program of sustainable tourism certification. Thus the intervention in the vertical market quadrant was temporary, and later replaced with interventions in the public inputs quadrant.

In these cases, the size and the duration of the subsidy should be the minimum necessary to resolve the coordination failure without imposing undue fiscal costs. In principle, it should be possible to coordinate the investments at little or no cost to the treasury by guaranteeing a certain return to each investor. If the project is in fact profitable provided everyone invests, everyone could reap the

Figure 2.2 Solving Coordination Failures in Tourism in Costa Rica

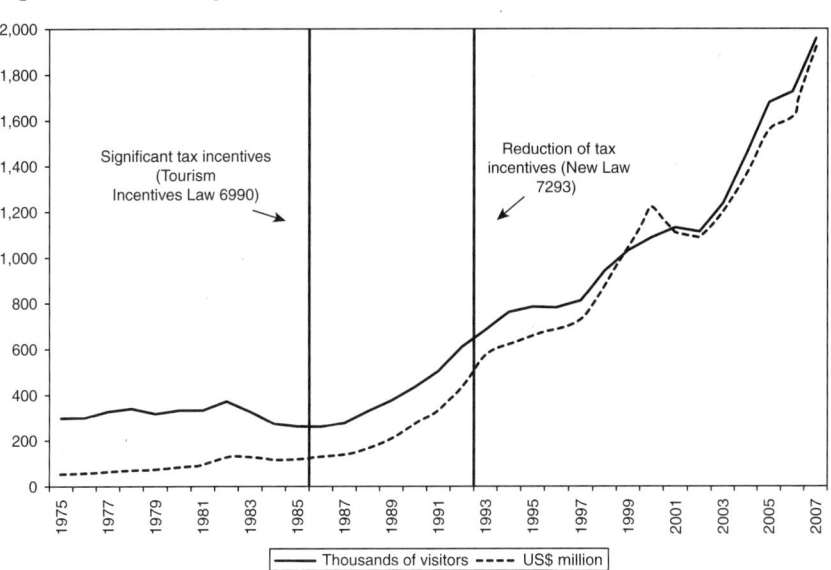

Source: Monge-González, Rivera, and Rosales-Tijerino (2010).

returns needed so that no actual outlays are required. The government of the province of Salta, Argentina, situated nearly 1,000 miles northwest of Buenos Aires, followed a hybrid strategy to develop its tourism sector. It offered subsidies to investment in hotels, and a minimum occupancy guarantee to a start-up airline, Andes Líneas Aéreas. At the time (2005), Salta was served by only two flights a day from Buenos Aires, and the lack of flights was considered a key obstacle for the development of the sector.[18] The government guaranteed the occupancy of 65 percent of seats in the airline, and had to transfer resources only during the first few months. A similar idea has been proposed to attract Brazilian tourists to the English-speaking Caribbean (see Box 2.3).

> **Box 2.3 The Caribbean-Brazil Air Bridge**
>
> Tourism flows depend on the strength of the links between the tourism destination and originating countries. The tourism sectors in the region of the CARICOM countries depend on two main markets: the large English-speaking countries in the neighborhood (the United States and Canada), and the European countries where there are strong colonial-era ties (the United Kingdom and the Netherlands for the six IDB-member countries). The United States and the United Kingdom alone concentrate nearly 60 percent of the market. The high season is from November to April when visitors come to the islands to enjoy the sand, sea, and sun.
>
> The financial crisis of the end of the decade led to a significant drop in tourism revenue from these countries. The Caribbean countries first responded by offering hefty discounts—such as loyalty discounts or 2-for-1 deals—aimed at preserving tourists from these traditional markets. Nonetheless, the recovery has been slow and is unlikely to sustain much growth in the long term. Even traditional British and European visitors, who tend to stay for longer periods and spend more than visitors from the Western Hemisphere, are dwindling following the economic events in Europe. Therefore, the Caribbean countries have begun searching for new markets, preferably the more dynamic countries in the neighborhood.
>
> Competition is strong and attracting tourists from new markets requires establishing a brand and airline connections. For this reason, tourism countries focus on specific markets from which they try to attract their

visitors. Having a direct connection is an obvious advantage for potential visitors, but airlines are reluctant to start a new connection without guarantees that seats will be filled. In addition, attracting tourists requires specific and substantial marketing expenses. These are two costly, up-front investments that the private sector might not be willing to make on its own.

First, attracting tourists to one Caribbean country may have significant spillovers on others, especially if visitors become interested in visiting more than one destination in a single trip, or if knowledge of one destination in the area prompts further interest in other destinations for subsequent trips. For this reason, promotion activities may be subject to a free-rider problem, if left to the private sector in each country alone. Thus, they need to be undertaken in a coordinated fashion. Second, there are important synergies between these two types of interventions. Marketing will not make a difference if connecting flights are inconvenient. And a minimum occupancy guarantee on a flight will be very expensive if the promotional efforts do not bear fruit.

Recently, the IDB conducted a pilot marketing study of outbound tourism from Brazil to analyze the merits of creating a "Caribbean-Brazil air bridge." The study, conducted in São Paulo airport (a metropolitan area of more than 20 million people), suggested that Brazilians are interested in international travel, and in many of the features that the English-speaking Caribbean has to offer. However, they are mostly unfamiliar with this region. Nonetheless, if the Caribbean region could successfully arrange frequent and direct flights from Brazil and attract just 1 percent of this potential market, tourist arrivals would increase by more than 80,000 visitors per year, a very significant number. Marketing efforts are thus essential to drive awareness and subsequently obtain greater tourism value added for the Caribbean.

While promotional activities such as marketing and advertising are not cheap, a cost-benefit analysis suggests that investing in the combined scheme would be worthwhile. The idea is that joint investment in promotional activities will address an information externality. The air bridge, in turn, would greatly enhance the returns of the promotional activities. Together, these interventions would help create a market to a destination that Brazilians did not previously know about. If so, repeat visits could eventually lead to a self-sustaining destination, at which point the minimum occupation guarantee would no longer be costly, or necessary. All this, in turn, would become a source of renewed growth for the Caribbean countries.

Aside from the resolution of coordination problems, there are other sound theoretical justifications for policies in this quadrant to help sectors achieve latent competitiveness that the market alone is unable to realize.[19] Most of them involve the "infant industry" argument. The most obvious case is that of so-called Marshallian spillovers, by which the productivity of the sector increases with its size. Since increase in size takes time, true or "latent" productivity of a certain sector may be revealed only by a fully mature industry. "Learning by doing" has often been invoked as a rationale for industrial policy: while an industry may be uncompetitive early in its life cycle, it may become competitive over time as management and workers learn to do their jobs more productively. However, individual firms have the incentive to wait until the industry is mature and profitable rather than investing in starting a process from which later entrants will benefit. Subsidies or protection may help spur the early entrants.

The benefit of industry maturation may disseminate through backward and forward linkages to other sectors of the economy. If so, the case can be made that the growth of a "strategic" sector that sets in motion this positive chain of events is worth fostering with industrial policy. Chapter 9 examines the strategic value of certain directions of productive transformation in detail. It presents a methodology to identify good candidates for a thorough analysis of whether their strategic value may merit some of the policies in this quadrant.

Melo and Rodríguez-Clare (2006) have labeled interventions like these "strategy-driven" policies—as opposed to "demand-driven" or "bottom-up" policies that respond to a sector's needs—and pose the greatest risk in terms of capture. These interventions involve governments making bets on developing a specific set of industries, many times from scratch, through a combination of aggressive market intervention policies to jump-start the sectors. Accordingly, they require a tested institutional setup that ensures competence and transparency in decision making.

Defensive PDPs

The PDPs considered so far and analyzed in depth in the following chapters are "constructive": they seek to repair the failure of the market to deploy its capabilities in an effective way. However, building up is not all in productive development: the gains achieved must also be defended from threats. Adverse shocks that put development gains at risk include episodes of macroeconomic instability, financial crises, and patches of currency overvaluation due to extraordinary capital inflows or commodity price booms, as well as more permanent shocks such as the loss of competitiveness of a specific sector for irreversible technological reasons. The region has ample experience with the costly effects of these shocks on productive development, which at least in the case of large macroeconomic crises have caused permanent productivity losses (Blyde, Daude, and Fernández-Arias, 2010). "Defensive" PDPs to safeguard productive development from backsliding are an important complement to "constructive" PDPs in the overall policy portfolio.

While constructive PDPs aim at helping the market achieve what was latent in its capabilities (as in establishing a new competitive export activity), defensive PDPs aim at avoiding the loss of capabilities (as in closing down a competitive export activity or dismantling specialized equipment). To the extent that the cost of defensive PDPs is less than reconstructing capabilities once circumstances normalize, these PDPs are part and parcel of the formula to foster productive development. This cost/benefit test is critical: defensive PDPs only make sense when valuable productive capabilities are at risk of being destroyed. Temporary shocks fit this description only if they would destroy productivity, not simply because they cause financial pain to firms. Permanent shocks may also fit this description but only when policy is needed to soundly reallocate resources to other sectors of the economy, not to keep alive nonviable sectors.

A defensive PDP should be disciplined by the same three tests applied to constructive ones: (i) is it justified by a market failure? (ii) does the policy solution fit the problem? and (iii) are enabling institutional capabilities sufficient? Presumably it is in a firm's self-interest to preserve valuable capabilities during a temporary downturn or to reallocate its resources to the best alternative use by selling if a permanent shock makes them nonviable. However, it may fail. For example, viable firms facing a temporary downturn may lack the financial resources (and access to credit) to make the right business decisions to stay in business. If so, a suitable policy could be official lending through development banks; this credit needs to be medium term to bridge the problem but not at concessional terms. Official credit to Brazilian exporters by BNDES during the global crisis of 2009 is an example. Other policies may address the root of the problems more directly. For example, the volatility of the real exchange rate, particularly during episodes of overvaluation, a typical shock in the region, is a serious threat to export sectors; new sectors or those that rely on supporting policies are key for productive development but may be among the most fragile. An exchange rate policy with an eye to productive development would lead to more stability and mitigate the problem. PDPs fostering the use of insurance products to cover some of these risks (such as currency risk) would be perhaps a more orderly way to address them if feasible.

Defensive PDPs would generally take the form of market interventions to isolate firms from shocks. One key aspect to consider is whether to resort to selective, vertical policies. Since policy should help those at the highest risk of failure but leave aside those able to fend for themselves (and those taking excessive risk waiting for a bailout), there is an argument to be made in favor of focalized vertical policies. Since the key driver is the destruction of valuable productive capabilities, the merits for intervention are bound to be sector specific.[20] On the other hand, it is difficult to pick the best candidates, especially under urgent circumstances. Furthermore, these defensive PDPs delivering financial support selectively would be extremely open to the risk of capture. While the benefits from defensive PDPs are potentially enormous under certain circumstances, they require substantial institutional capabilities to be successful.

The Road Map for This Book

The rest of the book is organized as follows: Part II (chapters 3–9) deals with the question of design and implementation of PDPs in different areas. Each of the seven chapters covers policies in a specific subject area, such as innovation and diffusion, financing, or internationalization policies. Rather than assuming that policies are justified, each of them starts by making or questioning the case for policy intervention, along the lines discussed in this conceptual framework. Each presents the fundamental trends seen around the world and in the region in terms of policy design and implementation. Each then focuses on a few specific interventions from the region and elsewhere—some successful and some not—that illustrate the policy issues and may offer important policy lessons. Several chapters also discuss the results of impact evaluations, some of them performed for this book. The hope is that each chapter will inform policymakers in the region, as well as staff of the IDB on the ground, to design and implement better policies.

While the chapters are organized by subject for ease of exposition, in practice quite a bit of connection exists between policies in the different areas. This is most obvious in the case of CDPs, which often involve the identification of obstacles and opportunities for the development of a sector or value chain, and a collection of specific interventions in different areas—innovation, training, financing, internationalization—to address them. Policies addressing failures in the credit system analyzed in chapter 6 are also natural complements of policies that aim to expand investment opportunities, but require a responsive supply of credit to make a difference. Some points of connection between different areas of policy are presented throughout the book, highlighting issues such as the extent to which innovation and export promotion policies complement each other; the successful internationalization efforts of certain clusters in Argentina; or financing programs for innovation activities.

While part II focuses mostly on *what* policies to pursue, part III (chapters 10 and 11) emphasizes *how* to deliver them. The focus of part III is on the institutions for PDPs. Chapter 10 centers on the capabilities required in the public sector in order to appropriately design and implement PDPs, highlighting the overall organizational structure to coordinate its actions as well as the technical, operational, and political capabilities of productive development agencies. In addition to discussing how existing capabilities may constrain the type of policies that countries can implement effectively, the chapter explains how countries can go about building their capabilities. Great emphasis is placed on the need to encourage a learning environment in which there is room for policy experimentation and adjustment over time.

Modern PDPs have become less of a top-down affair, and increasingly involve public-private collaboration in both policy design and implementation. This collaboration is key, as the private sector has information about the sector's challenges and opportunities that is critical for effective policymaking. At the same time, if public-private interaction is not structured appropriately, it can open the door for the type of rent-seeking activities that derailed industrial policies in the past. Chapter 11 discusses in detail how to effectively structure this collaboration, using several examples from the region.

Part II

Sound Policies in Key Areas of Application

3

Investing in Ideas: Policies to Foster Innovation

Since the pioneering work of Solow (1957), technological change has been credited with explaining a substantial share of economic growth. Indeed, recent evidence for the United States shows that investments in R&D—a proxy for the innovation effort of a nation—made up 40 percent of the productivity growth observed during the postwar era (Reikard, 2011). Based on these findings, several Latin American and Caribbean countries have established and implemented public policies aimed at enhancing innovation. In practice, the first explicit interventions to encourage innovation by the private sector emerged even earlier, toward the end of World War II. Although many of these policies were either abandoned or dramatically downsized under the structural reforms inspired by the Washington Consensus, the disappointing results in terms of productivity growth have led several countries in the region to reintroduce policies to stimulate innovation and encourage technology adoption.

Since the early 1990s, a new generation of public programs to encourage business innovation has spread throughout the region. Policy experimentation is already generating new evidence about the effectiveness of these interventions. This chapter assesses the main developments in innovation policies, taking stock of the learning achieved so far.

A Global Perspective: Latin America Lags Behind

Assessing innovation is a very challenging task. Innovation can be defined as the implementation of new or significantly improved products, processes, services, or organizational models (OECD, 2005b). As such, innovation is more than a technological improvement; it includes changes in organizational and marketing models. Innovation encompasses minor changes as well as breakthroughs. Clearly, innovation is a highly subjective concept, as each person may have a very different understanding of how novel a device or a process is. For this reason, comparisons of innovation indicators are colored by individual biases.

However, innovation can be approximated by measuring certain "aspects" of the innovation process. Griliches (1979) suggests that similar to the production of goods, the production of ideas can be explained by a *knowledge* production function, where innovation results from firm investments in R&D and the stock of knowledge. More recent innovation research has expanded the set of inputs to include human capital, training, machinery, licenses, software, and the like. Thus, it is possible to garner a glimpse of innovation by measuring some of those inputs. On the outputs side, approximations for innovation outcomes include productivity indexes, numbers of intellectual property rights, scientific publications, and self-reported figures of innovations collected from innovation surveys (Smith, 2006). Each one of these indicators by itself provides a partial view of the innovation process; however, together they offer a reasonably comprehensive picture of the innovation process of a firm.

Figure 3.1 assesses the performance of Latin America and the Caribbean vis-à-vis developed countries with regard to innovation inputs. Panel (a) summarizes aggregate R&D intensities for a sample of Latin American and Caribbean countries and compares them with a sample of developed countries. This panel highlights several issues. First, R&D intensities in Latin American and Caribbean countries are systematically lower than those in developed countries. Second, according to this indicator, the world's top performers are precisely those countries that have managed to catch up with other developed countries over the last 20 or 30 years: Israel (4.3 percent), Finland (3.9 percent), and South Korea (3.7 percent). Third, in top-performing countries, the private sector finances a large proportion of the R&D effort. While in developed countries firms explain more than 60 percent of the national investment in R&D, this figure is less than 35 percent in Latin American and Caribbean countries. These findings suggest an important deficit in R&D investment in the region, particularly in the private sector.

Panel (b) compares average investment intensities in innovation as a percentage of sales, including not only R&D but also training, purchasing of machinery and equipment, and software licenses and royalties for the use of patented technology for a sample of countries using information from innovation surveys. Even within this broader definition of innovation investment, a significant gap exists. While the average firm in a developed country spends almost 4 percent of sales on innovation, the typical firm in Latin American and Caribbean countries spends around 2.5 percent. The gap is particularly large in intangible investments such as R&D. The pattern that emerges is that technology embodied in machinery, mostly

Figure 3.1 Innovation in Latin America and the Caribbean at a Glance

a. R&D Expenditures as a Percentage of GDP and Source of Performance

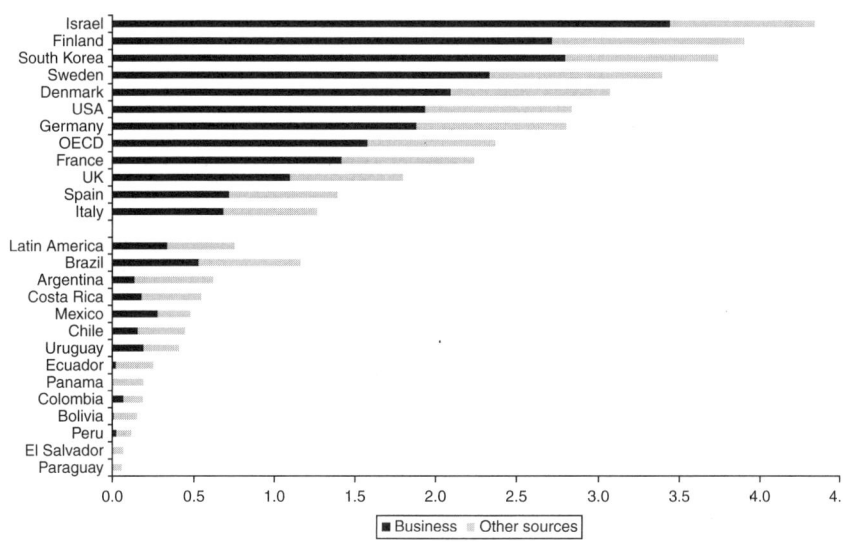

Notes: Data are from 2010 or the latest available year: 2009 for Bolivia, Costa Rica and Peru and 2008 for Ecuador and Paraguay.
Data for Peru are based on authors' calculations using innovation survey data and data from OECD (2011).
Source: Authors' calculations based on OECD (2010) and Red de Indicadores de Ciencia y Tecnologia (RICYT) (2013).

b. Innovation Investment in Firms

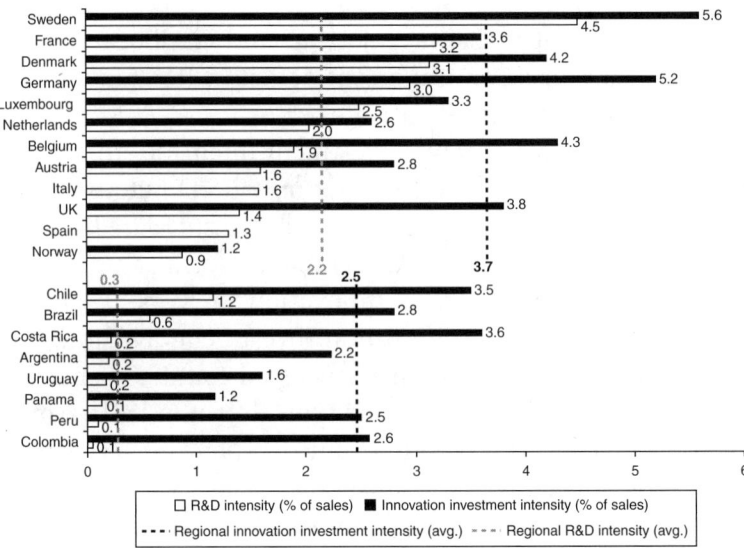

Note: Data are from 2010. Latest available data for Ecuador are from 2008, and for the United States and the OECD are from 2007. Nearest available data for 2000 for Brazil, Denmark, Ecuador, and Sweden are from 2001, and for Costa Rica are from 2003.
Sources: Innovation Surveys for Argentina (1998–2001), Brazil (2005), Chile (2004–2005), Colombia (2003–2004), Costa Rica (2008), Panama (2008), Peru (2011), and Uruguay (2005–2006). Data for OECD countries are from 2009 except for Spain and Italy from Eurostat.

c. Researchers per 1,000 in the Labor Force

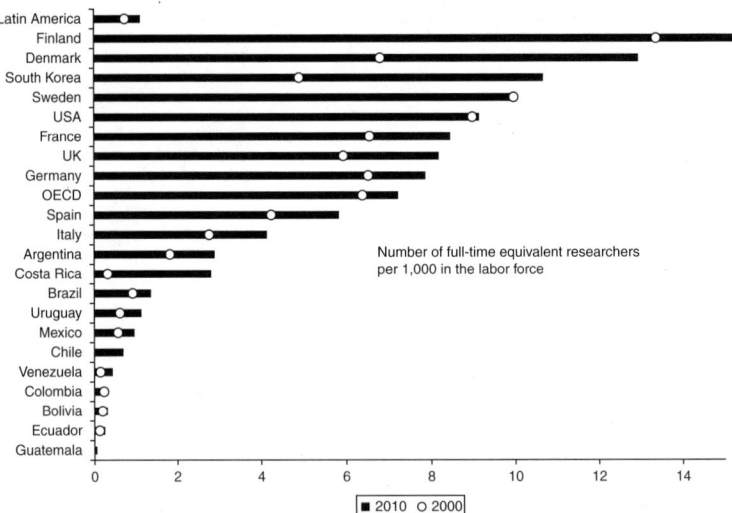

Note: Data are from 2010. Latest available data for Ecuador are from 2008, and for the United States and the OECD are from 2007. Nearest available data for 2000 for Brazil, Denmark, Ecuador, and Sweden are from 2001, and for Costa Rica are from 2003.
Source: Authors' calculations based on OECD (2010) and RICYT (2013).

d. TFP Growth, 1960–2010

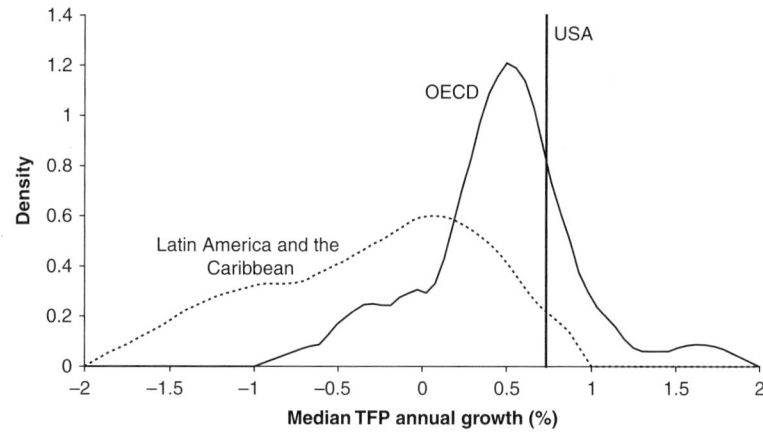

Note: The figure presents the distribution of median productivity growth for each country over the 1960–2010 period. The vertical line represents the United States.
Source: Authors' calculations based on Penn World Table 8.0 (PWT) project.

imported from abroad, is the main force of innovation investment in the region. The evidence from developed countries suggests that relying on imported technology is not necessarily bad if it leads to domestic learning. However, in order for this to happen, technology must be combined with absorptive capacities that allow for further improvements. Absorptive capacities depend on research and development efforts and complementary human capital. According to panel (c), there are on average only 1.1 researchers per 1,000 workers in the region, eight times fewer than in the typical Organisation of Economic Co-operation and Development (OECD) country—even though the average number of researchers in the region increased by 50 percent from 2000 to 2010.[1]

In summary, the Latin American and Caribbean innovation process is based on the adoption and incremental improvement of existing technologies, rather than investment in R&D. Has this pattern allowed the region to catch up to the rest of the world in terms of productivity? The results in panel (d), which shows average productivity growth rates for each county from 1960 to 2010, suggest otherwise. In fact, long-term productivity growth rates in Latin American and Caribbean countries are systematically lower than those in the

OECD countries. Moreover, having a productivity growth higher than the United States—depicted by the vertical line in panel (d)—is the exception in Latin America.

The Rationale for Public Policy

Innovation is the result in large part of investment decisions made by firms; these decisions are affected by the same conditions that affect investment in general. Indeed, the quality of regulation, protection of property rights, tax code, macroeconomic regime, the intensity of competition, and infrastructure development all affect investment decisions on innovation—sometimes even more significantly than for fixed capital investments (OECD, 2013a). However, having the right framework conditions is a necessary but not sufficient condition for innovation. Since most countries in the region have internalized the importance of these conditions and made important progress with them, the focus of this chapter is on explicit innovation policy measures that still need to be implemented.

Although it is generally true that every modern economy needs an innovation policy, a flaw in the design of innovation policy tends to be its focus on symptoms rather than on the actual, underlying causes of underinvestment. Typically, innovation policy is justified on the basis of gaps in R&D or technology adoption when compared with benchmark economies. This focus on symptoms rather than constraints normally leads to poor policy design: low investment in innovation or low levels of technology adoption could also be an optimum response to low returns. In other cases, government justifies innovation policy based on socially desirable objectives, such as job creation or social inclusion, without realizing that the relationship between these objectives and innovation is complex and largely ambiguous.

Theory-Based Justifications

The fundamental premise for innovation policies is that government intervention can be beneficial if profit-driven actors underinvest from a social welfare perspective (Steinmueller, 2010). Broadly speaking, the rationale for public policy in this field can be based on the following considerations:

Spillovers and the "Public Good" Nature of Knowledge
Since the seminal works by Nelson (1959) and Arrow (1962), knowledge has been regarded as a nonrival[2] and nonexcludable[3] good. If knowledge does indeed have these properties, then a firm's rivals may be able to free-ride on its investments. These spillovers may create a wedge between private and social returns and a disincentive against private investment in knowledge production. However, spillovers are not automatic and should not be taken for granted in every circumstance, as not all knowledge enjoys the properties of a public good with the same intensity. Certainly, the "public good" rationale of knowledge applies more strongly to *generic* or *scientific* knowledge than to *technological* knowledge, which is more applicable and specific to the firm.[4] Furthermore, in order for the public good rationale to be valid, there should be some possibility of free riding. If the originator can protect the results of the knowledge generated (through entry barriers or the use of strategic mechanisms, for example), then the potential for market failure declines. On the other hand, knowledge generated through collaboration among different parties might be more difficult to protect and therefore more prone to spillovers than knowledge generated by individual entities.

The Problem of Asymmetric Information and Uncertainty
Innovation projects distinguish themselves from ordinary investments in several ways (Hall and Lerner, 2010). First, the returns to innovation investments are more uncertain and involve longer gestation lags. Second, innovators may be reluctant to disclose detailed information about their projects because of spillovers. Third, innovation investments normally include a large proportion of intangible assets (such as human capital) that have very limited use as collateral. Although the problem of asymmetric information is always present whenever the investor and financier are different entities, this problem may be worse in the case of knowledge investments. This creates a wedge between the rate of return required by an innovator investing his or her own funds and that required by external investors. Unless the innovator is particularly wealthy, privately (and maybe socially) profitable innovation projects may not materialize due to lack of access to financing or to the high cost of capital.

There may also be asymmetric information with respect to the knowledge about available technologies. The most traditional diffusion model—in which technology adoption results from the spread of information about the technology—highlights the fact that diffusion is not automatic. In a world of imperfect information, policy intervention would therefore focus on providing information, such as demonstration projects, advertising campaigns, technology monitoring exercises, and extension services that inform an industry of recent technology advances.

The Pervasiveness of Coordination Failures
Knowledge also has important tacit components that cannot be embodied in a set of artefacts, such as machines, manuals, or blueprints. Thus, firms can benefit from networking with one another and other actors because they need to learn from the knowledge bases of other organizations. However, coordination failures can hinder the effectiveness of these knowledge networks. Coordination failures emerge whenever private and public agents fail to coordinate their knowledge investment plans in order to create mutual positive externalities (Aghion, David, and Foray, 2009). Coordination failures also emerge in the process of accessing technological infrastructure. Firms that alone cannot afford infrastructure can gain access to it if they collaborate with others. Solving coordination problems requires paying special attention to those institutional failures that can affect the linkages between the different actors in the innovation system.

It is argued that one of the few advantages of a developing country is that it can simply free-ride on the innovation investments of developed countries. As is clear from the preceding discussion, the real world is far more complex than this. The returns of a given technology depend on the context in which it is used. Key complementary inputs, such as human capital, institutions, and natural resources, may vary greatly across different locations and affect the performance of the *same* technology in different places. In order to successfully adopt a given technology, firms must discover whether this technology is suitable for each particular context. For that, local investment in learning and innovation is needed. These investments are affected by the same problems of spillovers, asymmetric information, and coordination that affect innovation investments in general. To complicate matters, in developing countries many of these market failures coexist and feedback into each other. So, unfortunately for developing countries, there is no free supermarket of ready-to-use ideas.

Reassessing the Innovation Investment Gap

The evidence so far suggests that Latin America and the Caribbean seriously underinvests in innovation. However, this statement lumps together countries that are very different. The observation that an investment gap in intangibles exists is not enough to suggest that an economy faces an innovation problem. Low investment in R&D can also reflect systemic problems that affect the accumulation of all sorts of assets, including physical and human capital (Maloney and Rodríguez-Clare, 2007). A different explanation for an R&D intensity gap is production specialization. The propensity of firms to invest in R&D varies across sectors (Pavitt, 1984). In an open economy, specialization depends on factor endowments, preferences, and relative productivities across sectors, clearly affecting the validity of the country comparison of aggregate indicators.[5]

Several mechanisms might affect firms' decisions to invest in innovation activities, mostly through their access to generic knowledge, human capital, and finance. The degree to which a society develops institutional arrangements to consistently provide these three complementary inputs affects private investment in innovation. Table 3.1 shows how much these variables explain the gap in innovation investment between Latin American and Caribbean countries and OECD countries. In the period 1995–2010, the business sector of the typical Latin American and Caribbean country invested in R&D 1.18 percent of GDP less than the typical OECD country, and this gap has increased since the period 1980–94, when it was 0.90 percent of GDP.

The factors underlying these gaps have changed. Prior to 1995, low access to generic knowledge explained about 30 percent of the gap, while the absence of dynamic sectors in the production structure explained just 10 percent. The lack of human capital and financial development was in between those figures. After 1995, however,

Table 3.1 Explaining the Gaps in Business R&D: The OECD vs. Latin America and the Caribbean (Percent of the Total Gap)

Time period	1980–95	1995–2010
Business R&D % of GDP (gap between OECD and Latin America)	0.9	1.18
Knowledge[a]	29.7	23.7
Human capital	23.2	25.8
Financial development	26.9	15.3
Production structure	10.7	26.0
Residual	9.5	9.2
Total	100	100

Note: The contribution to the gaps is based on a model, where Y is business R&D as a percentage of GDP, X is a vector of variables described in the text, and LAC is a dummy variable identifying Latin American and Caribbean countries, capturing a residual gap that is not explained by the above-mentioned variables.

a. The main variables are measured as follows: (i) knowledge is built by accumulating publicly performed R&D per worker; (ii) human capital is approximated by average years of schooling in the labor force (owing to data constraints, human capital is not corrected by quality); (iii) financial development is measured by the intensity of credit to the private sector; and (iv) production structure is measured by using the proportion of high-tech manufacturing on value added.

Sources: Authors' calculations based on Lederman and Saenz (2005); OECD (2010); World Bank (2010b); IDB (2010b); RICYT (2013).

human capital increased significantly in importance and, more strikingly, the role of the production structure increased markedly to explain 26 percent of business investment gaps. On the other hand, financial development, and to a lesser extent generic knowledge, have become less important. Clearly, the Latin American and Caribbean business sector suffers from an innovation investment shortfall beyond what would be expected given the financial development and human capital accumulation of the region. Moreover, low public sector investment in the generation of generic knowledge and the lack of sophistication of the production structure explain a significant part of this gap.[6]

Weighing the Social Returns

The evidence of investment gaps is not enough to justify intervention because they could reflect a lack of innovation opportunities. Assessing this possibility requires looking at the social returns rates (SRRs) to innovation investments. A review of more than 50 years of research suggests that social returns to R&D are strongly positive (Hall, Mairesse, and Mohnen, 2010). However, much of this research focuses on evidence from developed countries. Lederman and Maloney (2003) find that the returns to R&D are not only higher for developing countries, but also higher than the estimated return on physical capital. More specifically, for Latin American and Caribbean countries, Maloney and Rodríguez-Clare (2007) find that SRRs calibrated using international data vary between 51 percent in the case of Peru and 16 percent in the case of El Salvador, with a regional average of 33 percent.

To what extent do investments in R&D contribute to productivity growth? Griffith, Redding, and Van Reenen (2004) propose an approach in which productivity growth is the result of innovation and technology transfer, and investments in R&D not only stimulate innovation but also build absorptive capacities for technology

Figure 3.2 Social Returns to R&D, Latin America and the Caribbean vs. the OECD

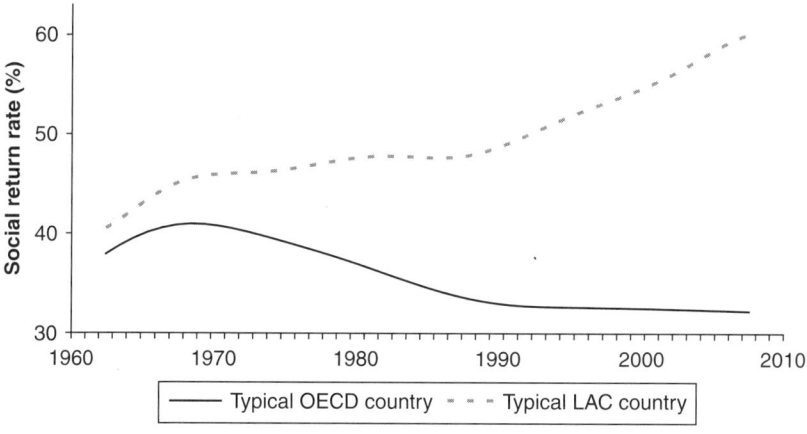

Note: Estimates are based on the following model: $\Delta A_{it} = p_1 \left(\frac{R}{Y}\right)_{it-1} + \delta_1 ln\left(\frac{R}{Y}\right)_{it-1} + \sum_{p=1}^{3} \delta_{2p} \left(\frac{R}{Y}\right)_{it-1} \times ln\left(\frac{R}{Y}\right)_{it-1}^{F}$, where A is total factor productivity, R is research and development investment, and AF is the productivity frontier. In this model, the social return rate to R&D has two sources: its contribution to innovation, which that pushes the technological frontier; and the creation of absorptive capacities for technology transfer. In other words, $SRR_{it} = p_1 + \sum_{p=1}^{3} \delta_{2p} \left(\frac{R}{Y}\right)_{it-1} \times ln\left(\frac{R}{Y}\right)_{it-1}^{F}$. The results are based on OLS estimates. Results using instrumental variables (with the Ginarte and Park IPR protection Index and the Productivity Frontier as instruments) were qualitatively similar. OLS are more conservative than IV estimates.

Source: Authors' calculations based on Griffith, Redding, and Van Reenen (2004).

transfer. The SRRs to R&D are the combined results of these two forces.

In order to implement this methodology, the Pagés (2010) productivity data set is expanded to include data on R&D investments from different sources. Figure 3.2 summarizes the results of this method and suggests that SRRs for R&D investments not only are systematically higher in Latin America and the Caribbean than in the OECD (56 percent vs. 32 percent in 2007) but also have followed a divergent path over time. Indeed, while social returns have declined in the OECD (mostly because of the lower returns from technology transfer as these countries have moved closer to the technological frontier) in Latin America and the Caribbean, social returns to R&D have tended to increase (mostly because of the greater scope for technology transfer as these countries have systematically shifted away from the technological frontier). This increasing trend in social returns, together with growing investment gaps, are consistent with the finding that the Latin American and Caribbean region indeed faces an *innovation shortfall*.

What Works in Innovation Public Policy

Innovation policy covers a broad set of issues that have been in the policy agenda for decades. Although countries vary widely, the experience of successful catch-up economies suggests several key commonalities (OECD, 2005a).

- A long-term, public-private consensus exists on the importance of maintaining public support and continuously updating innovation policies. Indeed, many of the best performers not only boast high innovation investment rates today, but also sustained high rates of effort over long periods of time, even above what was expected given their GDP per capita (see Figure 3.3).
- An early and strong focus on investment in adoption of foreign technology, research infrastructure, and human capital[7] is coupled with support to applied research in key sectors or technologies,[8] and rather weak IPR protection.

Figure 3.3 Star Performers' R&D Investment

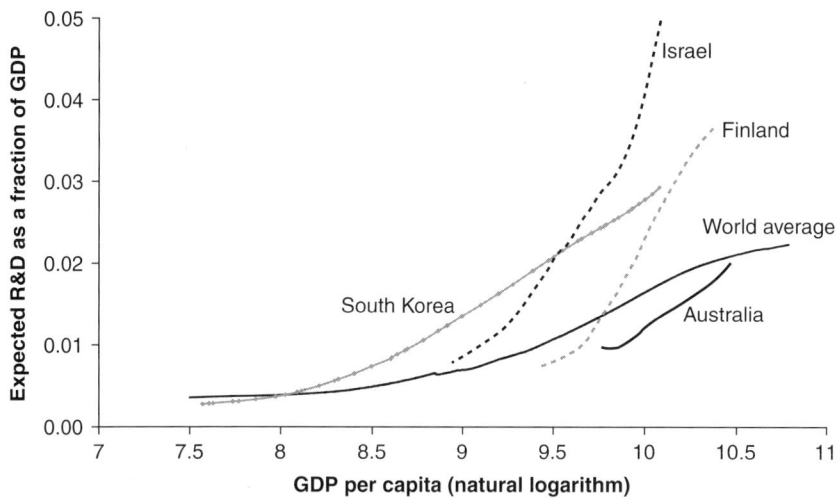

Source: Authors' calculations based on Lederman and Saenz (2005); OECD (2010); World Bank (2010b); IDB (2010); RICYT (2013).

- A continuous effort to improve framework conditions (macro stabilization, trade openness, fiscal balance, competition, regulation, IPR protection, and the like) echoes measures recommended by the Washington Consensus.
- Reforms centered on framework conditions were *simultaneously* accompanied by increasing support for investments in science and technology and business innovation, allowing for a continuous shift of resources toward the most dynamic sectors.
- Policy instruments such as financial entitlements for public technological institutes grants, and tax incentives for business innovation, mission-oriented research funding, and public procurement were used extensively, and refocused continually on the generation of spillovers (research collaboration and technologies that spread across different sectors, such as biotechnology and information and communication technology) (see Box 3.1).
- A continuous focus on institutional capacity building, monitoring, and evaluation fed into policy learning and gradually fostered a more complex and focused policy mix. South Korea

illustrates a typical example of this process of policy building (see Box 3.2).

The current innovation policy landscape in developed countries encompasses many designs. Based on the framework proposed in chapter 2, these multiple policy designs can be organized along two dimensions: scope, depending on whether the policy focuses on the provision of public inputs or market interventions; and type, depending on whether it is horizontal (economy-wide) or vertical (sector-focused). These two dimensions define a 2x2 matrix that reclassifies innovation policies in four quadrants. Table 3.2 presents several examples of scope-type combinations of policy instruments that are commonly found in successful catch-up economies.

Box 3.1   Fostering Innovation through Government-Sponsored, Mission-Oriented Research and Public Procurement: The Case of the United States

Mission-oriented R&D is research funded by public agencies to support their activities. A key feature of mission-oriented research is that policymakers, rather than scientists, choose the fields in which large investments of public R&D funds are made. Allocation decisions are based on assessments of the research needs of specific agency missions in fields ranging from national defense to agriculture, health, energy, and other activities. The R&D investment budgets of most OECD nations are dominated by programs that serve specific government missions. According to a report by the US National Science Foundation, mission-oriented research ranges from 50 percent of total government R&D spending in Germany to 90 percent in the United States, with the budgets of Japan, France, the United Kingdom, Canada, and South Korea falling in between those figures (National Science Board, 2006).

A key feature of mission-oriented research is that the projects being funded are normally of a more applied nature. This has led to the argument that to the extent that research findings are very specific, the scope for spillovers is narrower than in the case of other research. Empirical evidence has shown, however, that this is not the case, as many of the technological breakthroughs currently used by the private sector originated in mission-oriented research programs (including such notable examples as semiconductors, the Internet, GPS, hybrid corn, MRIs, and hydraulic fracturing). Moreover, private sector spillovers can be maximized when mission-oriented research tilts toward funding new bodies of scientific or engineering knowledge that support innovation across different sectors; when it focuses on developments in the early phases of a new technology; when it funds new publicly available technological infrastructure (such as research labs in universities or research centers); and when the procurement rules foster both competition and collaboration among research teams, universities, public labs, and firms.

Mission-oriented R&D is normally complemented by substantial purchases of new technology from one or more public agencies. Placing large orders of early versions of a technological device allows the producer to learn, improve quality, and reduce prices for other private sector users. Procurement rules can also promote technology diffusion. For example, in the US defense sector, public procurement is sometimes accompanied by policies that require the supplier to develop a "second source" for the product: that is, a different domestic producer that could manufacture a functionally identical product in order to avoid supply interruptions.

Mission-oriented research and public procurement, however, are not without risks. Large publicly funded research programs might increase the costs of R&D (such as the salaries of researchers), crowding out private sector R&D investment. Mission-oriented research could also bias the research agenda toward applications that are not easily transferred to the private sector. The United States has solved this institutional challenge by managing mission-oriented research programs through specialized agencies. An example is the Defense Advanced Research Projects Agency (DARPA), set up in 1957 within the Department of Defense to invest in high-risk, high-payoff research. DARPA is a small, flexible, and flat organization, with about 140 technical professionals. It is exempted from the normal federal regulations for civil personnel, providing it with important flexibility for managing talent. DARPA's technical staff are hired or assigned for four to six years. All key staff (office directors and program managers) rotate to ensure a constant infusion of fresh thinking and perspectives. This gives DARPA the flexibility to get into and out of an area without the burden of sustaining staff. DARPA neither owns nor operates any laboratories or facilities. The overwhelming majority of the research it sponsors is done in industry and universities. Project-based assignments are organized around competitions to solve a specific technology challenge. Then the development and production are handed off to the military services or the commercial sector.

Sources: Tether (2008); Mowery (2010); Singer (2014).

Box 3.2 Innovation Policy Building through Catch-Up: The Case of South Korea

South Korea has been one of the most successful latecomer economies in achieving rapid economic growth and is approaching the ranks of advanced economies in terms of GDP per capita. One element of Korea's success has been its emphasis on capability and technological development, which has led to the consolidation of private exporting and R&D capacity. During the catch-up process, Korea went through four phases. In each phase, the government implemented innovation policies using a broad range of instruments.

Initial Efforts (1960s–mid-1970s)

In the 1960s, when Korea began its modernization process, the country faced two key barriers: low technological capabilities of domestic firms and poor human capital (in particular, in applied sciences and engineering). The government focused on encouraging technology imports with licensing, developing a new graduate school of engineering and applied sciences (the Korean Institute of Science and Technology), and setting up key institutions for science and technology infrastructure. These actions facilitated the absorption of imported technologies and attracted technology-based FDI. In this stage, domestic firms participated only in assembling and packaging processes, with very limited investment in innovation. For the Korean firms, this was a learning-by-doing period, without an explicit attempt to develop new capabilities or technologies. During this period R&D investment was never higher than 0.5 percent of the GDP.

More Active Catch-Up Phase (mid-1970s–mid-1980s)

In this second phase, Korean firms more actively adopted foreign technologies through imitative innovation and reverse engineering. They invested more intensively in adapting foreign technology and developing local technological capabilities, mainly through technological licensing and knowledge transfer. The government focused on technological development by funding private R&D through tax incentives, and by conducting R&D activities directly and sharing the results with private firms. In the 1980s, a joint public-private R&D program was set up to support higher-risk projects. Consequently, the R&D/GNP ratio increased from 0.42 percent in 1975 to 1.41 percent in 1985. During this stage, government investment in R&D still exceeded private sector investment.

Rapid Catch-Up (mid-1980s–mid-1990s)

This third phase was a period of rapid catch-up led by the major Korean businesses. Firms increased production of knowledge-intensive products and started to develop new products. Realizing the limits of a strategy based on licensing and embodied technology transfer, Korean firms established their own in-house R&D centers. To encourage this trend, the government eased the accreditation process for setting up private R&D institutes, and a large number of institutes were established. The R&D/GNP ratio increased from 1.41 percent in 1985 to 2.32 percent in 1994. Such active engagement of private R&D activities enabled Korea to absorb the newly emerging technologies. From this period onward, private R&D investment has been a key part of the Korean innovation and technology development process, accounting for more than 70 percent of total R&D investment.

Maturing of the Catch-Up Phase (mid-1990s–the present)

As South Korea approaches the technological frontier, the country is entering a new and critical phase in its development. With the slower growth of labor and capital inputs and increasing competition from new industrializing countries, South Korea faces new challenges. The catch-up model is now under stress, and South Korea is shifting from a "catch-up" to a "creative" innovation system. The creative model requires increased spending on R&D—by both public and private sectors—and improved knowledge flows and technology transfer across the system. This demands stronger support to innovative SMEs and start-ups; increasing the role of longer-term, fundamental research; developing research capacity in the universities; and dealing with lagging productivity in services. This transition toward a creative economy can already be seen in some innovation indicators. Patents owned by Koreans increased from 7 in 1982 to 3,558 in 1999 according to a US register. In 2006, the R&D/GNP ratio passed the 3 percent threshold.

Sources: Lee (2013); OECD (2009).

The Latin American Experience with Innovation Policy

The Latin American experience with innovation policy dates backs to the 1950s, and since then different policy approaches have been tried and abandoned over time. Although country experiences are very idiosyncratic, three broad policy paradigms have been tried: the *supply side approach*, which extended from the 1950s to the 1980s; the *demand side approach*, which reigned from the 1980s through the 2000s; and the (emerging) *systemic approach*, which has increasingly become the focus of policy interest since the 2000s.

The *supply side approach* (1950s–1980s) was based on the idea of linearity from supply to demand: direct production of knowledge and complementary assets—in particular, human capital and information—by public institutions (such as laboratories, research institutes, and universities, mostly funded through entitlements) gave way to a series of instruments in the public inputs/horizontal quadrant of Table 3.2. New institutions—the national research councils—governed the system and were tasked with funding research, supporting human capital formation, and establishing policy frameworks. Technological institutes were established to complement support to research and technical and professional training.[9] Operating at the sector level, these institutes fulfilled a dual role: carry out applied research, and transfer knowledge to firms operating in strategic sectors. Private sector development of technological absorptive

Table 3.2 Innovation Policies in Developed Countries: A Taxonomy

		Type	
		Horizontal	Vertical
Scope	Public good	Higher education/training. Support to scientific research. Intellectual property rights. Research infrastructure. Human capital inmigration. Labor training. Competition policy. Regulation. Technology transfer organization.	Technological institutes (agriculture, industry, energy, fishing, etc). Standardization. Thematic funding. Signalling strategies. Information diffusion policies (extension systems). Technological consortiums. Contests
	Market intervention	R&D subsidies, R&D tax credits. Financial measures (guarantees for technology invesments, intangibles values, etc). Adoption subsidies.	Public procurement. General purpose technologies (ICTS, biotech, nano-tech). Strategic sectors (semiconductors, nuclear energy, electronics, etc). Defense sector.

Source: Authors' compilation.

capacities and linkages between knowledge supply and demand were given far less importance.

The *demand side approach* (1980s–2000s) featured the structural reforms of the Washington Consensus. The diagnosis blamed government failures and argued that keeping intervention to a minimum was the best way to avoid them. This phase had important implications for innovation policy. The majority of the public organizations and institutes designed to promote innovation lost importance within the state bureaucracy. Public budgets were severely curtailed. New incentive regimes were set up to introduce market discipline in technological institutes that had to increase their funding by selling services to the private sector. Human capital formation was deregulated and private universities entered the market while intellectual property frameworks were gradually strengthened. All these changes occurred as productivity growth at the technological frontier accelerated dramatically (Sagasti, 2011). Ironically, just as incentives to innovation on the demand side were enhanced (mostly through product market competition), support to the supply side of the equation was dismantled.

The pitfalls of the reforms became evident toward the end of this phase, when it became clear that spillovers, lack of complementary assets, and financing were important obstacles for firms to adapt to the new scenario. In response, some countries began experimenting with new horizontal/market policy instruments, introducing grants for business R&D, R&D tax credits, conditional loans, and vouchers for technology transfer in the second half of the 1990s. Most of these programs were delivered through technology development funds, which initially worked out of existing institutions such as development agencies or research councils, and later spun off into dedicated agencies or funding units.

The *systemic approach*, which began in the early 2000s, emerged from a growing consensus that business innovation support with a strong focus on the individual firm was not enough to internalize spillovers and solve coordination failures. The diffusion of the idea of an innovation system triggered renewed interest in investing on the supply side, but with increased concern about generating the right incentives to favor closer coordination between supply and demand. New institutions, such as technology liaison offices specialized in linking the different actors, emerged. After many years of inaction, there was renewed interest in supporting technology extension, but now with a focus on building absorptive capabilities in small and medium enterprises (SMEs). Dissatisfaction with purely horizontal policies also grew. Thus, since the early 2000s, the impetus has shifted to vertical programs. Some countries are experimenting with funding schemes in areas where public procurement is important (such as programs in health and energy) and are targeting subsidies to technologies (such as information technologies) that can spread out across the production sector at large. This proliferation of programs with very different designs and implementing agencies has heightened the stress on institutions and highlights the need to improve policy coordination. Currently, the mix of innovation policies in some countries is not very different from that in developed economies, depicted in Table 3.2.

The Innovation Toolbox

The previous analysis offers different justifications for the implementation of innovation policies based on the idea that profit-seeking agents will produce both a level and direction of knowledge that fall short from a social welfare perspective. As David, Hall, and Toole (2000) note, public policy has followed two main approaches: direct production of knowledge by public institutions (universities, laboratories, and public research institutes), most of them under the category of public goods interventions; and fiscal incentives for private investment in knowledge generation.[10]

Issues of governance and funding incentives of public technological institutes are beyond the scope of this chapter; in any case, their public funding is normally far less controversial than market interventions. This section focuses on the second class of policy interventions, in particular, two types of incentives: *fiscal incentives for innovation*, whose goal is to increase private sector investment in innovation and whose focus is the firm as a *knowledge producer*; and *technology extension programs* (TEPs), whose goal is to stimulate firms to acquire or improve their use of technology and whose focus is the firm as a *knowledge user*. Fiscal incentives mostly occur in the form of direct subsidies or tax incentives, while TEPs cover a wider set of interventions. Although other instruments exist, this discussion focuses on these two because they are the most prone to moral hazard and rent-seeking problems, as they imply a net transfer of resources to the private sector.

Fiscal Incentives

Fiscal incentives come in two different forms: *subsidies* and *tax incentives*. *Subsidies* are a type of direct support for business innovation that is project-specific. They transfer cash to firms on the condition that firms execute a series of innovation activities. Subsidies are normally delivered through two different mechanisms: nonreimbursable grants and conditional loans.[11] By contrast, tax incentives are based on firm-level innovation activities and operate through a reduction of the firm tax liability.

Fiscal incentives not only reduce the marginal cost of capital to undertake innovation investments, but can also encourage collaboration with other actors in the innovation system, such as research centers, technological institutes, or firms. Table 3.3 summarizes the main features of both types of fiscal incentives.

Two important differences between subsidies and tax incentives relate to their relative effectiveness to internalize spillovers and their focus on those segments of the population of firms most likely to be affected by market failures. Subsidies, given their project-based nature, can not only target high spillover projects but also direct funding toward firms more severely affected by market failures, such as young firms and innovative SMEs. These features are less clear in the case of tax incentives. In the first place, tax incentives are a fully market-friendly mechanism; the firm decides which projects will be implemented. This might bias the incentives toward projects with higher private appropriability. Moreover, tax incentives are not proportional to the difference between social and private rates of return, as they should be, but instead to total R&D costs (Maloney and Perry, 2005). Tax incentives also suffer from poor targeting as their impacts depend on the fiscal position of each firm—an aspect that normally biases them toward large firms.[12] In the case of subsidies, the fiscal cost is under control, since the resources allocated to the programs are budgeted. On the other hand, in the case of tax incentives, fiscal costs are less certain because the fiscal authority has no control over firms' decisions. Both types of fiscal incentives

Table 3.3 Fiscal Incentives: Subsidies vs. Tax Incentives

	Direct subsidies	Tax incentives
Mechanism	Project-based financing.	Based on firm-level R&D activities.
Impacts	Reduce marginal cost of R&D activities.	Reduce marginal cost of R&D activities.
Collaboration	Funding can be targeted toward collaboration.	Deduction can also target collaboration.
Spillovers	Funding can be targeted toward projects with high spillovers.	Fully market-friendly mechanism. The firm decides. It might be biased toward more privately appropriable projects.
Liquidity constraints	Funding can provide partial cash advances (relaxing liquidity constraints). Funding can provide "signalling" to external investors.	They operate fully ex post, and are less suitable to solve financial constraints. No signalling.
Focus	High (funding can be targeted toward firms with innovation problems, such as innovative SMEs or start-ups).	Low (effectiveness depends on the general tax context of the country, other tax exemptions and loopholes) and biased toward larger firms.
Implementation costs	High ex ante and ex post.	Low ex ante but high ex post.
Institutional capacities	High capabilities in innovation agencies.	Lower capabilities in innovation agencies, but higher in tax authority
Firm capacities	High (to formulate a project)	High (to identify an innovation program)
Fiscal costs	Controlled costs and transparent. Funding targets the marginal project.	Uncontrolled, the fiscal costs depend on decisions taken by the firms. When based on volume, subsidies go to intra-marginal projects as well. They make the fiscal system more complex.

Moral hazard	Financing can go to firms that do not face market failures.	They create an incentive to artificially classify non-R&D expenses as R&D, which may not be easy to control for tax authorities.
	Implementation of cofunding schemes (matching grants) with nominal limits and a list of elegible expenses.	Base the incentives on R&D growth rather than volume or establish a project-based decision-making process similar to subsidies.
Good design practices	Subsidy rate proportional to the size of spillovers (e.g., higher in public goods, generic research, or collaborative projects).	Build monitoring and evaluation capacities in the tax authority
	Implementation of a competitive allocation process (call for proposals).	Include in the deduction a premium for externalities (e.g., collaboration or the hiring of R&D personnel).
	Transparent allocation by a public-private council based on evaluations by external and independent peer reviewers.	Inclusion of carry-forward provisions or cash conversions for new firms.
	Capacity building in firms for project formulation and setting of milestones for funding.	Predict the fiscal cost and inlude it in the budget, setting a transparent mechanism to allocate the credits when the demand is higher than supply.
	Include a sunset clause with a careful monitoring and evaluation system.	Include a sunset clause with a careful monitoring and evaluation system.

Sources: Authors' compilation based on Lederman and Saenz (2005); OECD (2010); World Bank (2010b); IDB (2010b); RICYT (2013)

suffer from moral hazard problems; however, several good practice designs are available to mitigate them (see the bottom panel of Table 3.3). Implementing these good practices requires capacity building in both innovation agencies and tax authorities. The higher administration and compliance costs of the direct subsidies must be compared with the higher policing costs of the tax incentive. In summary, subsidies have a series of nice design features that might make them a preferred choice compared to tax incentives for several Latin American and Caribbean countries, in particular those with very weak tax authorities.

Sometimes subsidies coexist with credit programs that focus on funding the adoption of innovative technologies by firms (particularly technologies embodied in machinery and equipment). The rationale for the credit lines differs from that normally used for subsidies. In the case of the adoption of technology embodied in machinery and equipment, the returns are more likely to be appropriated by the investors, so policy should focus on solving a liquidity constraint problem only through the provision of credit. However, if the purchased technology generates spillovers to the rest of the sector—for example, through demonstration effects by the pioneer adopting firm—the credit could be combined with a subsidy to encourage technology dissemination. The implementing agency must carefully define what should or should not be considered an innovative technology and the potential for spillovers (see Box 3.3).

> **Box 3.3 FONTAR's Toolkit: Basic Rules for Allocating Subsidies vs. Credit**
>
> The Argentinean Technological Fund (Fondo Tecnológico Argentino, FONTAR) was created in 1995 and has been one of the pillars of Argentina's innovation policy. Although the program has expanded its interventions over time, it has focused on providing support to business innovation projects through two main instruments: reimbursable funding, through credit for innovation; and nonreimbursable funding, through matching grants and tax credits.
>
> The assessment of innovation projects usually requires very specific technical expertise. The lack of such expertise can worsen the problem of asymmetric information between investors and the innovator. Programs such

as FONTAR, which assess innovation projects through appropriate review processes, provide valuable signals to financial markets about the technical and commercial sustainability of the investments. Moreover, innovation projects are riskier, more intangible, and more prone to spillovers than technology adoption projects, which are based on more easily collateralized physical investment (like machinery). For this reason, external investors systematically require higher-risk premiums to finance innovation activities, or simply avoid funding them.

Because FONTAR's lines of funding target different kinds of investments with different degrees of risk and lack of tangibility, the instruments used for each line can be sharply differentiated. Thus, their nonreimbursable instruments specifically target R&D projects. By contrast, projects aimed at the adoption of existing knowledge embedded in tangible assets are less risky and the returns are more likely to be appropriated by the innovator. Thus, the policy intervention focuses on solving a problem of asymmetry of information by providing credit. Table B3.1 shows how FONTAR's officers allocate the different projects to the different instruments.

Table B3.1 Basic Rules to Allocate Funding to Innovation Projects: The Case of FONTAR

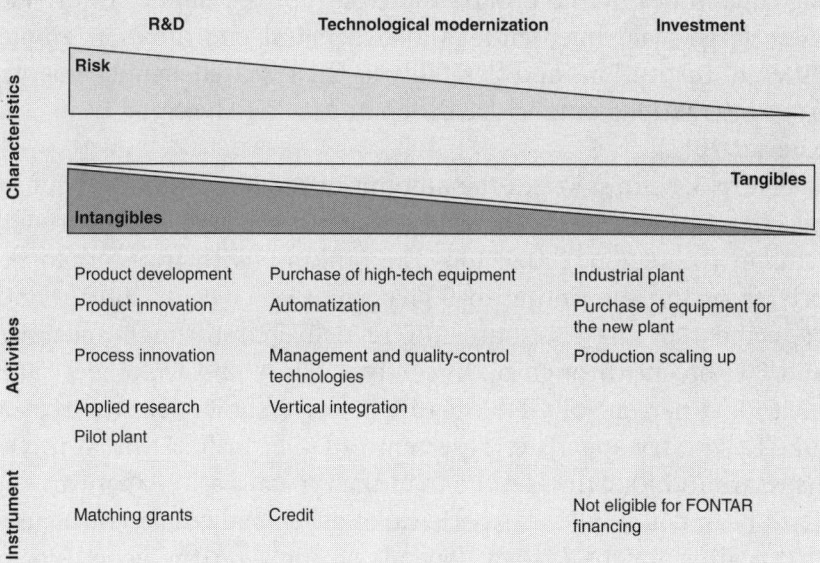

Source: FONTAR (authors' translation): http://www.agencia.mincyt.gob.ar/upload/Presentacion_FONTAR.pdf.

So far in the region, following the trends from developed countries, subsidies have focused increasingly on fostering research collaboration and linkages among the different actors in the innovation system. Indeed, countries are gradually moving from supporting single projects that involve university-industry interaction to more integral programs that involve full sectors by making use of technological consortia. A technological consortium seeks to pool innovation efforts of different firms and to increase their collaboration with universities and research centers, which has been a historical problem in Latin America and the Caribbean. The basic assumption is that these consortia could help internalize spillovers, coordinate complementary private investments, and reduce duplication of competitive research agendas. By solving these multiple failures, consortia should trigger higher returns to R&D investment.[13] Although still too early to make a final judgment on the performance results of these collaborative interventions, early evidence suggests that the results critically depend on correctly aligning the incentives of firms and universities, the absorptive capacities of participating firms, the proximity among participants, and the experience and conflict-solving capabilities by the group's manager. On the public sector side, these large-scale interventions also demand coordination among different institutions and flexibility as the research agenda emerges from interactions among the different actors (Álvarez, Crespi, and Cuevas, 2012).

Figure 3.4 summarizes the amount of public resources spent on business innovation for the countries with the largest support systems in the region. Brazil tops the ranking, with transfers to the private sector amounting to 0.14 percent of GDP in 2008. About 70 percent of these resources were delivered through subsidies, and 30 percent through tax incentives. Chile and Colombia came next (0.04 percent of GDP). Figure 3.4 also shows that the typical OECD country spends 0.11 percent of GDP on R&D fiscal incentives, around four times more than the typical Latin American and Caribbean country. The experience of developed countries suggests that scaling up the system depends strongly on the generosity of the tax incentive component of the policy (the same is true in Latin America and the Caribbean).

Figure 3.4 Direct Government Funding and Tax Incentives for Business Innovation (Percent of GDP)

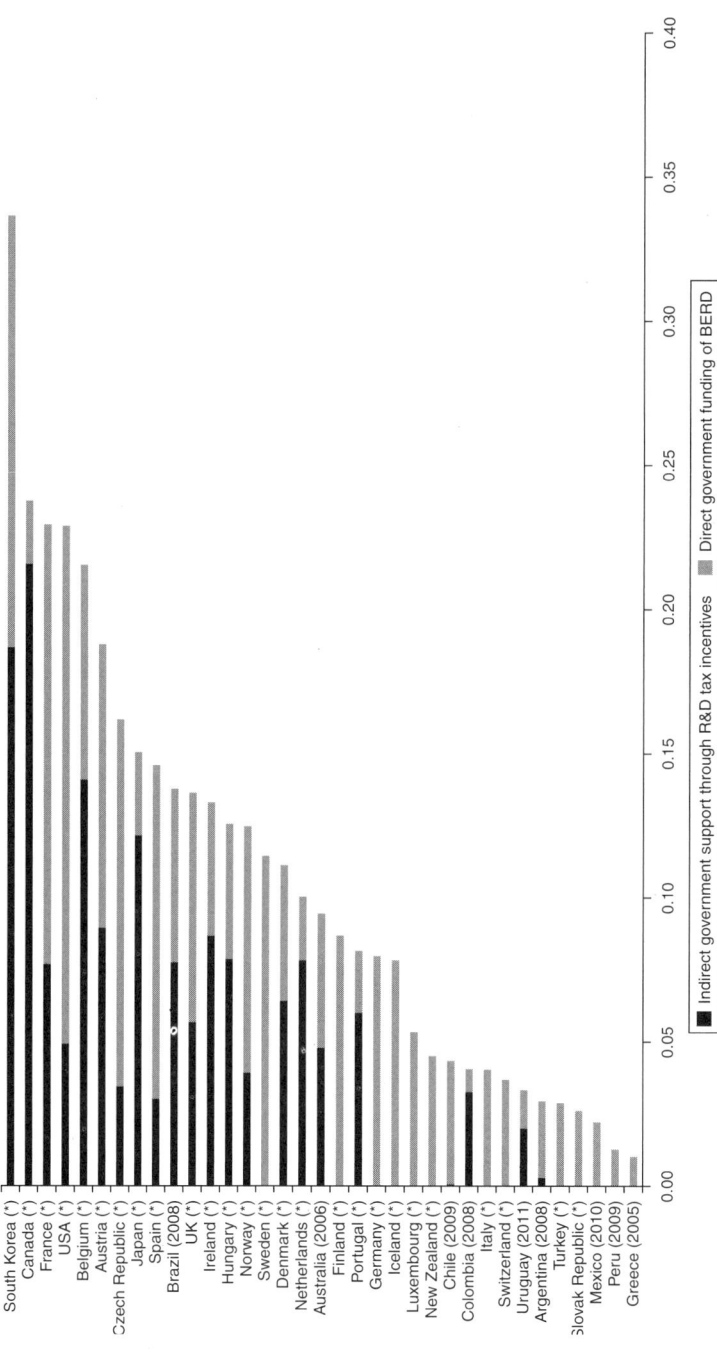

Note: BERD stands for Business Research and Development. Data for Brazil includes grants, sector funds, and loan programs managed by FINEP, as well as the Lei do Bem program and programs managed by FAPESP. Data for Argentina includes several of the lines FONTAR and FONSFOT and some lines of FONCYT and FONARSEC. Data for Chile includes the budget of business innovation programs run by INNOVA, plus CONICYT's FONDEF. Data for Colombia includes the cofunding and loan programs run by COLCIENCIAS, plus the R&D tax credit program. Data for Mexico includes the budgets of the PEI and PROSOFT. Data for Uruguay includes the business innovation programs run by ANII and the R&D tax incentives of the investment law (Parra Torrado, 2011). Data for Peru refers to the business innovation programs run by FINCYT and INCAGRO.
Source: OECD data taken from Wyckoff (2013). (*) Data for OECD are for 2008. Data for Latin America and the Caribbean taken from national sources. GDP and foreign exchange data taken from ECLAC (2013).

Technology Extension

The second type of market intervention to promote private innovation is a technology extension program (TEP). TEPs are designed to facilitate the adoption of existing technologies to improve the efficiency of a production unit. What differentiates a TEP from other innovation policy tools is that the new technology is mostly developed outside the adopting unit.[14] These programs typically have a dual focus. On the one hand, they provide services to reduce the costs of searching for information about new technologies, sometimes matching user needs with appropriate suppliers. They also provide support to enhance firms' ability to absorb new technologies, through hands-on training, pilot production demonstration, and assistance when negotiating with the technology supplier (De Ferranti et al., 2003). In some cases, TEPs are combined with support for incremental innovation (in terms of adaptation to local conditions). As in the case for innovation, cofinancing is a key component of TEPs.

Different models and approaches to TEPs have been developed and implemented over time.[15] The approach in the United States and the United Kingdom—spearheaded by the US Manufacturing Extension Partnership and England's Manufacturing Advisory Service—has traditionally focused on intervening at the firm level by providing field services to enhance the ability of SMEs to adopt new technologies or organizational models. The continental European approach, typified by Austria, Germany, and some Scandinavian countries, focuses more on supporting not only the SME's adoption of existing external technologies, but also improving these technologies through sector-specific research consortia. The Japanese and Canadian approaches borrow elements from both.

Latin American and Caribbean countries have traditionally offered technological extension services to SMEs through national technology institutes (NTIs), in both manufacturing and agriculture, some of them established during the early 1950s. Problems related to funding and incentives have compromised the effectiveness of these institutions. Most of the NTIs have been reformed, and funding through entitlements is gradually being replaced with performance agreements and sales of services. Moreover, the traditional NTI model has been complemented with various programs aimed at creating a market for technological services. Most Latin American and Caribbean governments have introduced programs based on public-private cost sharing, sometimes with vouchers for producers to purchase services from publicly certified private providers and NTIs. These changes have gradually led to the generation of a private supply of technological services for SMEs. Finally, TEPs in Latin America and the Caribbean have progressively moved from targeting individual firms to groups of firms. This change responds to the importance of sharing complementary skills and of accessing certain technological infrastructure. To help overcome potential coordination failures, new TEPs have been developed to promote firm collaboration and networking. Although assessments suggest that these changes are steps in the right direction, as TEPs have effectively improved the performance of their target population, they have also revealed structural limitations in reaching firms that suffer severe financial and technological constraints. For this reason, fully publicly operated services may still be required to satisfy demand for extension services at the base of productivity pyramid. Another limitation of TEPs in the region is that despite the reforms, coverage—in terms of the proportion of assisted firms over target population—seems to be very low (Figure 3.5).

Although fiscal incentives for innovation and TEPs are conceptually different instruments, their performance can be improved by targeting the synergies that might emerge by combining features of both types of instruments. For example, although innovation support programs correct market failures by providing a financial reward to the pioneers, the diffusion of the new discoveries could be further enhanced by linking part of the reward that the pioneers receive to dissemination activities that give followers access to technology (for example, through training workshops, demonstration visits, or pilot productions). Furthermore, in the case of product discoveries, pioneers' rewards could be at least partially linked to followers' sales of the same product.[16]

In terms of the volume of resources invested and number of firms covered, business innovation support in Latin America is still in its

Figure 3.5 Manufacturing Firms That Received Public Support for TEPs (Percent)

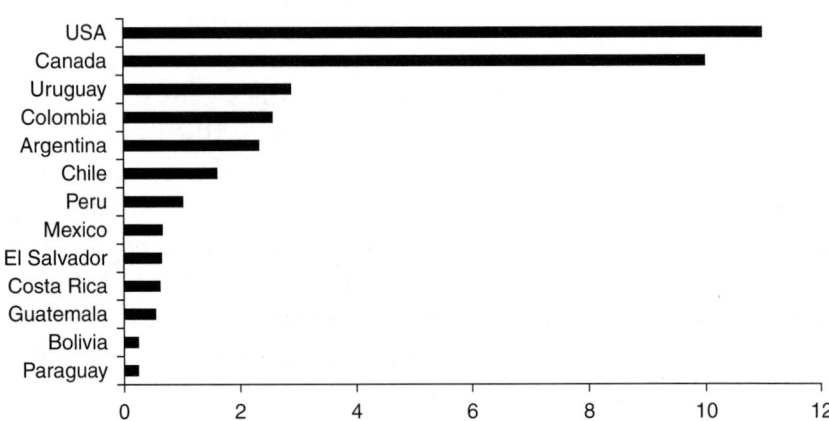

Source: For the United States, data are for coverage of the Manufacturing Extension Program (MEP). For Canada, data are for coverage of the Industrial Research Assistance Program (IRAP). Data for the U.S.A. and Canada are taken from Shapira et al. (2013). For Latin America and the Caribbean countries, data are from the World Bank (2010a).

infancy, as many of the programs are more in the nature of pilots than full-fledged interventions. However, the good news is that the best practice designs outlined in Table 3.3 are gradually being incorporated in their deployment. Of course, the situation is far from ideal, but the trend at least in terms of instrument design seems to be in the right direction. However, before deciding whether to expand the fiscal resources and the coverage of these programs, the effectiveness of the existing programs in solving the aforementioned market failures should be analyzed.

Learning from Impact Evaluations

One of the first issues to be defined in impact evaluation is the set of outcomes of interest. A distinction should be made between input and output indicators. Input indicators are more directly affected by the intervention: for example, total investment in innovation. To the extent that innovation policy reduces the capital cost of firms, it could be possible to identify which innovation policies generate an increase in innovation investment at the firm level (*input additionality*). Therefore, a first-order evaluation question should assess whether innovation policies increase firms' investment in innovation, and the overall contribution of the private sector to this effort: the so-called crowding-in effect. However, just assessing whether innovation efforts increase as a consequence of a subsidy is not enough for evaluation purposes. It is also important to assess the outputs of innovation investments by looking at variables that demonstrate their utility, such as productivity.

The traditional approach in impact evaluations of business innovation policies considers the impact of these programs on direct beneficiaries. However, direct beneficiaries are just one component of the social returns, and perhaps the least interesting one. A key rationale for these policies is based on externalities. Thus, a first-order question of impact evaluation of these programs should be the extent to which they generate spillovers. This can be done by tracing the impact of the programs on indirect beneficiaries (such as through labor mobility or geographical colocation). Although very few impact evaluations to date have explored the relevance of spillovers, some of them have been done specially for this report.[17]

Impacts on Innovation Investment

As in other regions, evaluating the effects on investment has been the most common approach to impact evaluation for Latin America and the Caribbean.[18] Table 3.4 summarizes the results of 16 impact evaluations done in the region. The evidence across the different studies is that fiscal incentives clearly stimulate innovation or R&D investments. In almost all cases, the evaluations found a positive and significant effect on program beneficiaries. Furthermore, in seven evaluations, where the main impact indicator is *private* investment in innovation or R&D, the results for this variable are also positive and significant, suggesting crowding-in. Fiscal support may have a signaling effect on the quality of the projects, allowing firms to leverage additional resources from financial markets (see Benavente, Crespi, and Maffioli, 2007). Comparing across the different instruments, matching grants schemes were not found to have a significantly different multiplier effect on investment than loans

Table 3.4 Effects on Innovation Investment (Input Additionally): Testing Crowding-in/Crowding-out Effects

Country	Evaluation period	Program name	Intervention	Beneficiaries	Indicator	Impact	Crowding in/out	Method
Argentina[a]	1994–2001	FONTAR-TMP1	Subsidized loan	Firms	Ln (total R&D)	0.15**	In	FE-IV
Argentina[b]	1998–2006	FONTAR-ANR	Matching grants	Firms	Ln (private innov exp)	0.18*	In	FE-CS
Panama[c]	2000–2003	FOMOTEC	Matching grants	Firms	Ln (Total R&D)	0.15**	No evidence	FE-CS
Uruguay[d]	2000–2006	PDT-I	Matching grants	Firms	Ln (private innov exp)	0.84**	In	FE-CS
Mexico[e]	2004–2007	EFIDT	R&D tax credit	Firms	Ln (private R&D)	0.25**	In	FE
Colombia[f]	2000–2002	Tax Incentives	R&D tax credit	Firms	Ln (private R&D)	0.06**	In	SM
Argentina[g]	1995–2001	FONTAR CFF	R&D tax credit	Firms	Ln (private R&D)	0.13***	In	FE
Brazil[h]	2005–2010	LEI-DO-BEM	R&D tax deduction	Firms	Ln (R&D employment)	0.07***	in	FE
Brazil[h]	2001–2008	LEI da Informatica	R&D tax deduction	Firms	Ln (R&D employment)	0.01	out	FE-CS
Argentina[i]	1994–2004	FONTAR CFF	R&D tax credit	Firms	(Total R&D $)	1.90**	In	SM
Argentina[j]	2001–2004	FONTAR-ANR	Matching grants	Firms	(Total R&D intensity) %	0.18**	No evidence	DID-PSM
Brazil[k]	1996–2003	ADTN	Subsidized loan	Firms	(Priv. R&D intensity) %	0.66**	In	PSM
Brazil[l]	1999–2003	FNDCT	Matching grants	Firms & UNIV	(Priv. R&D intensity) %	1.63**	In	PSM
Chile[m]	1998–2002	FONTEC	Matching grants	Firms	(Total R&D intensity) %	0.74*	Partial out	DID-PSM
Panama[n]	2006–2008	SENACYT	Matching grants	Firms	(Total R&D intensity) %	0.13**	In	PSM
Colombia[o]	2002–2003	COFINANCIACION	Matching grants	Firms & UNIV	(Total R&D Intensity) %	1.20*	In	PSM

Notes: FE-IV stands for fixed effects, instrumental variable, FE-CS stands for fixed effects and common support, FE stands for fixed effect, SM stands for structural modelling, DID-PSM stands for difference in difference, propensity score matching, and PSM stands for propensity score matching. UNIV stands for universities. *** 1% significance level, ** 5% significance level, * 10% significance level. In the case of the evaluation of SENACYT-Panama, total R&D intensity is computed as R&D as a fraction of total innovation sales.

Sources: Authors' compilations based on the studies noted. [a]Chudnovsky et al. (2006). [b]López, Reynoso, and Rossi (2010). [c]Maffioli, Pusterla, and Ubfal (2011). [d]CENIT and CPA Ferrere (2010). [e]Calderón-Madrid (2011). [f]Mercer-Blackman (2008). [g]Binelli and Maffioli (2007). [h]Kannebley and Porto (2012). [i]Giuliodori and Giuliodori (2012). [j]Chudnovsky et al. (2006). [k]de Negri, Borges Lemos, and de Negri (2006a). [l]de Negri, Borges Lemos, and de Negri (2006b). [m]Benavente, Crespi, and Maffioli (2007). [n]Crespi, Solis, and Tacsir (2011). [o]Crespi, Maffioli, and Meléndez (2011).

or tax incentives. However, matching grants schemes clearly dominate when they provide funding conditioned on collaboration (see cases with "Firms & UNIV" as beneficiaries in Table 3.4) or when they target new innovators.[19] Apparently, matching grants programs are particularly well suited for building linkages among the different actors of the innovation system, addressing both market and coordination failures, and supporting innovation-based entrepreneurship.

The majority of the studies summarized in Table 3.4 use techniques that construct comparable groups of beneficiaries and non-beneficiaries on the basis of observable characteristics of the firms.[20] This provides for an accurate assessment of the programs' selection process, which per se provides valuable information on the programs' targeting. The results show that firms with high levels of human capital or previous experience in managing innovation programs are more likely to be selected. This is not surprising, considering the weight normally given to quality when selecting proposals. However, a system based on past accomplishments might overlook new innovators, which may be more prone to suffer market failures. Ceilings of maximum support per firm could be considered, given the trade-off between fostering excellence, which may require multiple interventions for certain beneficiaries, and variety. The matching grant instrument is particularly well suited to balancing excellence and diversity. It is also important to improve the coordination between innovation support and TEPs, given the focus on the latter on building innovation management capacities in firms.

Impacts on Firm Performance

At the international level, fewer studies analyze the effect of public support on firm performance; the results are mixed. The main difficulty in this type of study is that a longer time horizon is required to detect these effects. While investment effects can be detected almost in conjunction with the receipt of public financing, other effects are detectable only after the innovation has taken place. Thus, rigorous impact evaluations of these effects may require following firms for a minimum of five years after receipt of public financing. In order to fill this knowledge gap, the IDB reassessed some of the programs in

Table 3.4 over a longer period and looked at impacts on productivity. Table 3.5 summarizes the results for the five evaluated programs. All the programs were evaluated using the same approach, with the main output indicator being labor productivity. The results suggest significant increases in labor productivity: from 9 to 12 percent when only individual firms are targeted, and from 10 to 24 percent when joint firm-university projects are supported. Additional evidence shows that strong complementarities could be achieved when the support of different programs is combined in sequences of multiple treatments. Such complementarities are found by evaluating the combined effects of Chile's FONTEC, supporting individual firms, and FONDEF, encouraging university-firm collaboration (Álvarez, Crespi, and Cuevas, 2012), or when innovation support programs are combined with other PDP programs.[21] Complementarities also exist between innovation policies and policies that normally form part of the framework conditions, particularly competition policies (Box 3.4).

The IDB has also evaluated a series of TEPs. Castillo et al. (2014a) evaluate the effect of Argentina's Support Program for Organizational Change (PRE) on employment and wages.[22] The program cofinanced technical assistance to support process and product innovation activities. Using a unique dataset with information for the population of firms in Argentina, the study finds large effects on employment attributable to the program's support, with increases of around 20 percent. For the median firm, participation in the program generated five additional jobs. The program support for process innovation increased real wages by 2 percent, while support for product innovation increased real wages by 4 percent. The evaluation also provided evidence of the program's positive effect on both firm survival and export.

Benavente and Crespi (2003) analyze the impact of the Chilean Productive Development Program (Programa Asociativo de Fomento, PROFO), which promotes joint projects among groups of SMEs to improve access to markets and help them innovate, which sparked productivity improvements of 11 percent vis-à-vis the control group.[23] In addition, the social return rate of the program

Table 3.5 Output Additionality: Testing for Productivity Impacts

Country	Evaluation period	Program name	Intervention	Beneficiaries	Indicator	Impact	Method
Colombia[a]	1995–2007	COFINANCIACION	Matching grants	Firms & UNIV	Labor productivity	0.15***	FE-CS
Colombia[b]	2001–2010	TAX INCENTIVES	R&D deduction	Firms	Labor productivity	0.06***	LDV
Chile[c]	1998–2006	FONTEC	Matching grants	Firms	Labor productivity	0.09***	FE
Chile[c]	1998–2006	FONDEF	Matching grants	Firms & UNIV	Labor productivity	0.12***	FE
Chile[c]	1998–2006	FONTEC only	Matching grants	Firms	Labor productivity	0.06	FE-CS
Chile[c]	1998–2006	FONDEF only	Matching grants	Firms & UNIV	Labor productivity	0.10***	FE-CS
Chile[c]	1998–2006	FONDEF+FONTEC	Matching grants	Firms & UNIV	Labor productivity	0.24***	FE-CS
Panama[d]	2000–2003	FOMOTEC	Matching grants	Firms	Labor productivity	0.13*	FE-CS
Argentina[e]	1996–2008	PRE	TEP	Firms	Ln(employment)	0.19***	FE-CS
						0.22***	
Argentina[e]	1996–2008	PRE	TEP	Firms	Ln(wages)	0.02***	FE-CS
						0.04***	
Mexico[f]	Add	PNAA	TFP-Full subs.	Firms	Ln(wages)	0.05***	FE-CS
Mexico[f]	Add	CIMO	TFP	Firms	Ls(sales)	−0.05***	FE-CS
Peru[g]	Add	BONOPYME	TFP	Firms	Ln(sales)	0.16***	FE-CS
Peru[g]	Add	CITE-Calzado	TFP	Firms	Ln(sales)	No effect	FE-CS
Colombia[h]	Add	FOMIPYME	TFP	Firms	Exports	0.40***	FE-CS
Chile[i]	Add	FAT	TFP	Firms	Ln(wages)	0.09***	FE-CS
Chile[i]	Add	PROFO-PDP	TFP	Firms	Ln(wages)	0.08***	FE-CS
Argentina[j]	2002–2006	PROSAP	TEP-Full subs.	Grape producers	Probability of adopting new variety	0.03**	FE
Uruguay[k]	1999–2006	PREDEG	TEP-Part subs.	Fruit producers	Adoption of new varieties	14** 9.3*	FE-CS
Uruguay[l]	1999–2006	PREDEG	TEP-Part subs.	Fruit producers	Density of plantation	108.5**	FE-CS
Uruguay[m]	2001–2003	LPP	TEP-Part subs.	Livestock producers	Adoption of managerial practices	25.3**/18.74**	FE-CS

Note: FE-CS (

Notes: FE-CS stands for fixed effects and common support, FE stands for fixed effects, UNIV stands for universities, Full subs stands for full subsidies, and Part sub stands for partial subsidies. *** 1% significance level, ** 5% significance level, * 10% significance level.

Sources: Authors' compilations based on the studies noted. [a]Crespi, Maffioli, and Meléndez (2011). [b]Parra Torrado (2011). [c]Álvarez, Crespi, and Cuevas (2012). [d]Maffioli, Pusterla, and Ubfal (2013). [e]Castillo et al. (2014a). [f]López-Acevedo and Tinajero-Bravo (2011). [g]Jaramillo and Diaz (2011). [h]Duque and Muñoz (2011). [i]Tan (2011). [j]Maffioli et al. (2011). [k]Maffioli et al. (2013). [l]Maffioli et al. (2013). [m]López and Maffioli (2008).

was at least 20 percent. TEPs oriented to the diffusion of agricultural technology demonstrated qualitatively similar results (see Table 3.5).[24] Overall, the results confirm that TEPs are effective in achieving their expected results and that different approaches work when applied in the proper contexts. Obviously, evidence on effectiveness should also be complemented by rigorous cost-benefit analysis.

> **Box 3.4   Competition and the Impacts of Innovation Grants: The Case of Chile**
>
> The Chilean government has been experimenting with business innovation policies since the early 1990s, mostly through different direct support (matching grants) programs to stimulate business innovation and university-industry collaboration. Most of these programs have been managed by the National Development Agency (CORFO) and the National Science and Technology Council (CONICYT). More than 6,000 projects have been funded since 1991. This experience has generated rich evidence to learn about a variety of impacts of innovation policies, which can be exploited to maximize the impacts of policy.
>
> One long-standing issue concerning innovation is the relationship between innovation and competition. It has been argued that innovation is at odds with competition because the need to generate innovation rents to reward the innovators normally implies accepting some sort of market distortion (for example, through the granting of intellectual property rights) as the price to pay to obtain more innovation. Recent research on this subject has reevaluated this view, finding that the relationship between these two variables is more complex than previously thought. Aghion et al. (2012) argue that the effects of fiscal incentives to stimulate innovation in a given sector vary depending on the degree of competition among firms: the more competitive the sector is, the more these firms will be encouraged to innovate in order to *escape competition*. In other words, a certain demand for innovation is necessary in order for fiscal incentives to be effective, and competition is the trigger for this demand. Using data from China over the 1988–2007 period, Aghion et al. (2012) report results consistent with this view.
>
> In order to explore whether this argument applies to Chile, the Chilean data on the beneficiaries of business innovation programs were linked to

the manufacturing census over the 1991–2006 period. A difference-in-difference approach tested whether innovation programs have had any positive effect on firms' TFP. To see whether these effects vary across sectors depending on the intensity of competition, the treatment variable was interacted with an index of competition calculated at four-digit industry levels.

The results of these interactions are plotted in the figure below, where sectors are ranked from a very low level of competition on the left to a very high level of competition on the right. As the figure shows, the impacts of business innovation programs clearly grow with the degree of competition in the sector. In fact, the impact may have been negative in sectors with very low levels of competition. These results have strong implications for innovation policy design: *the impacts of the program could have doubled if the fiscal support focused only on those sectors with a high intensity of competition.* This also points to strong complementarities between innovation and competition policies.

Figure B3.1 Innovation Policy and Competition: Evidence from Chile

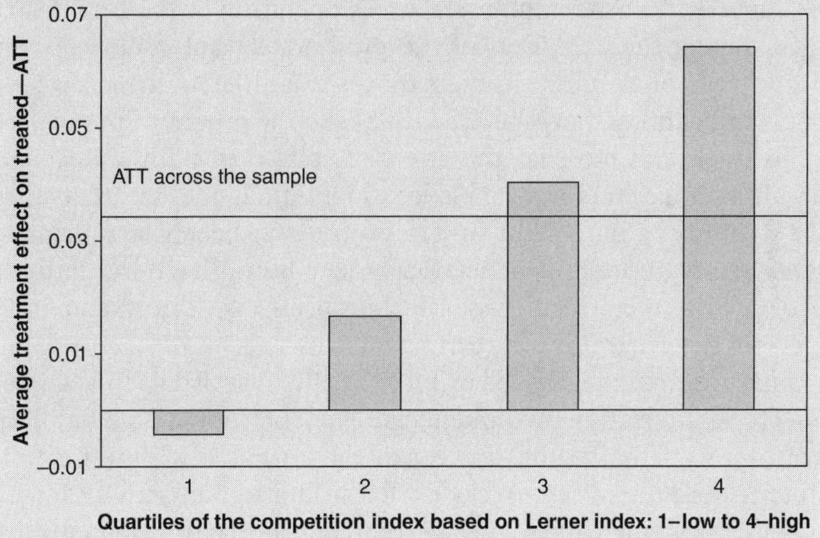

Note: Competition is measured by 1 minus the Lerner index, which in turn is calculated as the ratio of operating profits minus capital costs over sales.
Source: Authors' calculations based on Chile's National Manufacturing Census (ENIA, 1991–2006) and CORFO/CONICYT beneficiaries' registers.

The Search for Spillovers

Although knowledge spillovers are at the core of the theoretical justification for innovation policy, very few impact evaluations measure these potential effects. This omission probably reflects the difficulty of identifying the mechanisms through which spillovers occur. In the context of impact evaluation, measuring spillovers implies identifying the impact of the program not just on direct beneficiaries (firms that received program support) but also on indirect beneficiaries (firms that received benefits from the program through their relation with direct beneficiaries), as well as groups of comparable nonbeneficiary firms.

To fill this gap, the IDB has recently undertaken studies in Argentina (Castillo et al., 2014b) and Brazil (Ingtec and USP Research Group, 2013). The two studies focus on fiscal incentive programs, and define labor mobility as the main mechanism through which knowledge spillovers occur. Because much of this new knowledge is "captured" by the human resources operating in the beneficiary firm during the execution of the project, relevant spillovers may occur when one of these workers moves to a different firm, carrying part of the knowledge generated thanks to the program support.

To track and measure the effect of spillovers, both studies use administrative employer-employee longitudinal data sets that track the mobility of qualified workers from direct beneficiary firms to other firms (indirect beneficiaries). Once both direct and indirect beneficiaries were identified, the causal effects—direct and indirect—of the programs were estimated.

Findings are summarized in Table 3.6. Because of data limitations, effects on innovation investments are available for the Brazilian programs only. The findings for Brazil show positive spillover effects in terms of human resources devoted to innovation activities, with increases ranging from 6 to 17 percent, depending on the programs. Interestingly, the program promoting cooperation between firms and universities produces the largest spillover effects (17 percent), providing evidence that spillovers could be larger when the knowledge generated is more "generic." In terms of spillovers on firm performance, the studies on Brazil and Argentina confirm that the

Table 3.6 The Search for Spillovers

Country	Evaluation period	Program name	Intervention	Beneficiaries	Indicator	Impact	Method
Argentina[a]	1998–2006	FONTAR	Matching grants	Firms	ln(employment)	0.20***	FE-CS
Argentina[a]	1998–2006	FONTAR	Matching grants	Firms	Export probability	0.04**	FE-CS
Brazil[b]	2005–2010	LEI DU BEM	R&D tax credit	Firms	ln(R&D employment)	0.06***	RE-DYN
Brazil[b]	2006–2010	LEI DU BEM	R&D tax credit	Firms	ln(employment)	0.08***	RE-DYN
Brazil[b]	2006–2010	LEI DU BEM	R&D tax credit	Firms	Export/Emeployees	0.16***	RE-DYN
Brazil[b]	2006–2010	Subvention	Matching grants	Firms	ln(R&D employment)	0.15***	RE-DYN
Brazil[b]	2006–2010	Subvention	Matching grants	Firms	ln(employment)	0.06***	RE-DYN
Brazil[b]	2006–2010	Subvention	Matching grants	Firms	Export/employees	0.23**	RE-DYN
Brazil[b]	2000–2010	ADTEN/FINEP	Grants/Credit	Firms-Univ.	ln(R&D employment)	0.17***	RE-DYN
Brazil[b]	2000–2010	ADTEN/FINEP	Grants/Credit	Firms-Univ.	ln(employment)	0.07***	RE-DYN
Brazil[b]	2000–2010	ADTEN/FINEP	Grants/Credit	Firms-Univ.	Export/employees	0.17*	RE-DYN

Notes: FE-CS stands for fixed effects and common support, and RE-DYN stands for random effects with dynamics. *** 1% significance level, ** 5% significance level, * 10% significance level. [a]Castillo et al. (2014b). [b]Ingtec and USP Research Group (2013)

Sources: Authors' compilations based on studies noted.

programs positively affected firm growth (measured in terms of employment), with effects ranging from 7 to 20 percent, and exporting by boosting export probability in Argentina by 4 percent and the ratio of exports/employees in Brazil between 17 and 23 percent.

Overall, these results strongly support the "lack of appropriability" rationale at the basis of innovation policies. They also provide an extremely valuable input for future social cost-benefit analysis of these policies, providing ranges for the potential magnitude of the spillovers. In summary, the evidence is that fiscal incentives for innovation are effective in stimulating business innovation investments and productivity growth. This implies that the programs in general are targeting firms that might be facing some sort of market or coordination failure; when these constraints are relaxed, firms react favorably by increasing their innovation investments. The evidence also shows that the spillovers generated by these programs can be substantial, suggesting that they are effectively correcting for market failures. However, impact evaluation results also suggest that effectiveness can be enhanced by a better focus on market failures (for example, by targeting investments in intangibles rather than tangibles, hiring researchers by firms, or focusing on university-industry collaboration) or on those firms more prone to suffer market failures (such as innovative SMEs and young innovators). Impacts could be improved by seriously considering the interactions between innovation programs and competition, among innovation programs and other PDPs (such as those for export promotion, as discussed in chapter 8), and between innovation programs and TEPs.

Keys to Success

Innovation policies are complex. They require the resolution of complicated market and coordination failures; they involve multiple stakeholders, and require long gestation periods. For these reasons, successful implementation requires significant institutional capabilities, including the ability to engage with the private sector, coordinate across public agencies, and guarantee the continuity of policies. The experience from developed countries and successful catch-up economies suggests that successful implementation of innovation policies requires building four types of complementary institutional capacities (World Bank, 2008).

Strategy-setting capabilities: In successful cases, the fundamental pillars of innovation policy are normally agreed to at a high level within government by a multi-stakeholder organization that sets a long-term national innovation strategy, with clear and measurable objectives and binding recommendations about the policy mix, financing, instruments, jurisdictions, and mandates. Ideally, the institution that assumes this role should not be tied to the political cycle, in order to assure the continuity of innovation policies, and be well staffed with technical resources to make strategic studies and foresight exercises. Several developed countries have established public-private councils that fulfill this function, including Canada, Finland, Germany, Ireland, and South Korea. In Latin America, high-level innovation councils are in place in Argentina, Brazil, Chile, Costa Rica, Mexico, and Uruguay. However, in many cases, these organizations are not fully institutionalized, multi-stakeholder representation is weak, they lack operational resources, and their power depends on the interest of the current administration in power; this violates some of the key principles of these organizations. In many cases, these institutions play only an advisory role, while line ministries still handle the strategic decisions.

Policy-coordination capabilities: Effective innovation policy requires coordination among the different ministries involved in policy implementation. In particular, policy-coordination capacities translate the long-term innovation strategy into specific policy designs and allocate budgets to implementing agencies. Given the multiple ministries involved and the idiosyncratic organization of the public sector, two different models of policy coordination can be identified in the region. Some countries have established "innovation cabinets," where different ministries discuss policy coordination and implementation (Chile and Uruguay). In other cases, this policy-coordination function is concentrated in a specific ministry that leads cross-ministerial cabinets (Argentina and Brazil). Both models have pros and cons. An innovation cabinet is likely to be more inclusive and have better horizontal coordination, but may also suffer from higher transaction costs. A dominant coordinating player could be more efficient at coordinating related agencies, but could lack horizontal reach. Despite these advances, the countries in the region still have a long way to go with regard to policy coordination, in particular regarding the coordination of innovation policies and other PDP policies (Crespi and Tacsir, 2012) and also regarding policies implemented at different levels of government (such as federal, regional, and municipal).

Policy-implementation capabilities: The best practice from developed countries suggests that policy implementation should be carried out by a merit-based technically capable civil service able to partner with the private sector (Devlin and Moguillansky, 2012). Given the current limitations of state organization in many countries, accumulating capabilities in this dimension is not an easy task. Evidence from successful cases suggests that this is sometimes better attained by autonomous agencies, which tend to enjoy higher stability, are more open to experimentation, and more responsive to client needs than centralized ministerial departments (OECD, 2011, and Box 3.1). Autonomous agencies also could have more flexibility to manage talent and hire the human capital required to run their operations. Consistent with this trend, several Latin American and Caribbean countries, such as Argentina, Brazil, Chile, and Uruguay, have created implementing agencies with some of these characteristics, although the exact agency traits vary by country. Whatever the actual institutional configuration of the agency, it should be accountable for the efficiency of its operations at the policy and strategic levels and should be clearly aligned to policy-level decisions. Policy implementation is more than just managing private sector incentives for business innovation; it also encompasses policy capabilities to align the incentives of public research centers and technological institutes to respond to private sector needs and to simulate more pertinent technological research.[25]

Monitoring and evaluation capabilities: Accountability is critical for innovation policies to function well. More specifically, monitoring and evaluation capacities are central not only in order to abort wrong projects early, but also to avoid private sector capture of policy implementation. For effective monitoring, every budgetary line should be linked to measurable outputs so that both outputs and resources can be tracked over time, and deviations from goals can be identified and discussed. Evidence from developed countries suggests that the whole policy system should have an evaluation arm in charge of implementing impact evaluations of the different programs. The evaluation unit should be external (or nested in a different organization within government) so as to assure transparency and credibility. Monitoring and evaluation capacities are severely underdeveloped in the region to date. Although ministerial and agency-level bodies are gradually building the capacity to conduct impact evaluations, they still have a long way to go in order to develop program evaluation plans that incorporate state-of-the-art methodologies and, at the same time, set up information technology systems to produce the data needed to conduct impact evaluations.

In many cases, lack of institutional capacity translates into serious implementation bottlenecks. First, specialized human capital to manage innovation policy is scarce. Training is sometimes done on an ad hoc basis. In some countries, low public sector salaries induce high rotation of personnel, which hinders efficiency and favors capture. Second, public management and financial systems are not adequately set up to manage programs that require regular financial transfers from the public to the private sector and flexible, timely disbursements according to private sector needs. Third, obsolete information systems hinder monitoring and evaluation. Fourth, there is a shortage of external examiners who do not have conflicts of interest, especially in contexts where the research community is small. Finally, low differentiation of functions across multiple governmental organizations results in serious problems of coordination, overlap, and conflicts of interest among the policy actors.

Without giving serious consideration to the institutional arrangements needed for successful innovation policy implementation, government failures could be worse than market failures. Countries in the region have only recently started to build up institutional capacities in some of the above-mentioned dimensions. Not surprisingly, those countries where impact evaluations show the most successful results are also those where at least some of the institutional concerns have been tackled. However, this process of institutional capacity building is still incipient for most of the countries.

One Step Forward, Two Steps Back

Although over the last 20 years, the region has made remarkable progress in improving the framework conditions, this has not been enough to trigger a process of productivity catch-up. Indeed, the market and coordination failures that hinder innovation investment and technology adoption are still pervasive, and governments have notably failed to find a proper policy solution for many of them. Nowadays, the private sector innovation investment gap between Latin American and Caribbean economies and developed or successful emerging economies is larger than it was 20 or more years ago—despite the persistently high social returns to innovation investments. A combination of investment gaps with increasing returns can only be interpreted as a sign of a severe innovation shortfall in the region.

Despite this rather grim scenario, some glimmers of optimism are beginning to appear throughout the region. First, after many years of inaction, several countries have started to invest significantly in education, and in particular in disciplines related to science, technology, and engineering. Some countries have complemented these efforts with additional investments in research capacity and technological infrastructure. Although these efforts are relatively recent and have been insufficient to induce an improvement in business innovation investment, they are a step in the right direction that needs to be sustained over time.

Second, after many swings in innovation policy frameworks, an emerging consensus finds that the new emphasis on building research capacity and human capital needs to be complemented by a consistent stimulus on the demand side (the firms) and on solving the coordination failures that hinder the interaction between supply and demand. In other words, neither a supply push nor a demand pull by themselves are enough; the most likely dividends will come from working on both sides and their interaction. The focus should be on putting in place those policy interventions that can jump-start the region's innovation systems by solving market and coordination failures.

However, in contrast with growing public support to the research base and human capital formation, the fiscal budgets allocated to business innovation programs remain rather meager. To some extent, business innovation policy in the region is still in its infancy. Yet as the evidence presented in this chapter shows, when these programs are correctly designed, they are capable of triggering additional and sustained innovation investment, increasing productivity and employment, and generating spillovers. Although the risks of moral hazard and capture are always present, these problems can be minimized when several basic design principles are put into place (such as program support with a sunset clause, private sector cofinancing, allocation through competitive processes, ex ante evaluation through external peer reviewers, and ex post impact evaluation).

Yet boosting the budgets of these programs will not be enough. In addition to basic design principles, these programs must be specifically designed to maximize their social returns. Issues such as increasing differentiation of the programs according to the basic innovation capabilities of the beneficiaries need to be integrated within the policy mix. Special consideration should be given to programs with clear incentives for collaboration among firms and universities, since programs with such features yield a higher multiplier effect in terms of investment and spillovers. Incentives should aim clearly toward those projects that generate spillovers and technology diffusion.

In addition, many issues with regard to the policy mix are not being tackled properly and need to be given serious consideration, including more experimentation. Among the key issues that require further investigation are the effectiveness of the available instruments to diversify the production structure by encouraging product innovation and enhancing the entry of new innovative start-ups, the role of policy to stimulate innovation in the service sector, and the importance of better aligning incentives with performance (not only by funding investment but also by linking the generosity of fiscal incentives to the outcome of those investments). Finally, and more importantly, far more consideration should be given to institutional arrangements that bring about continuity, good governance, and productive public-private collaboration for innovation. Arguably, reform of these institutional aspects lags the furthest behind in the policy agenda. In particular, important institutional capacities, such as policy coordination, are still weak, and others, such as strategy setting and impact evaluation, are mostly missing. This dimension of institutional capacity building offers an important opportunity for regional cooperation.

4

The Start-Up and Scale-Up of High-Productivity Firms

Economies grow when workers and other factors of production move into projects that have higher productivity. Many higher-productivity projects arise in *existing* firms. These firms can leverage internal capabilities, including internal sources of capital, to help jump-start these new undertakings. But sometimes, these new, higher-productivity projects originate in *new* firms. Such firms could offer advantages, such as greater flexibility or closer supervision, compared to existing firms that may be especially useful when generating products or services or using processes that are more innovative. Yet these new endeavors by new firms could have a harder time getting started because entrepreneurs cannot rely on *existing* firm capabilities, including the ability to borrow cash and collateral from other projects, to attract the right talent, or to secure the required complementary assets for the project to take off.[1]

Reallocating factors of production to more productive projects is not just hampered by problems that beset new firms. In most countries in Latin America and the Caribbean—as in the rest of the developing world—even well-established firms often fail to grow to their potential. As a result, they fail to attract enough factors of production, which remain stuck in firms and sectors with lower productivity. For entrepreneurship to "make a dent" in economic growth, not only the start-up but also the scale-up of the best businesses is needed. This chapter discusses the problems that can inhibit the creation and growth of firms with high productive potential, as well as the policies that can be put in place to address them.

While start-ups are a small fraction of the stock of firms, they can have a powerful impact on productivity and job creation. In the United States, *young* firms—rather than small firms, as sometimes believed—have a disproportionate impact on job creation (Haltiwanger, Jarmin, and Miranda, 2013). Similarly, in a sample of more than 70,000 firms around the world, young firms were found to disproportionally impact job creation (Ayyagari, Demirgüç-Kunt, and Maksimovic, 2011). A recent study of firms in Chile (SEGPRES, 2013) finds a similar pattern. In particular, firms four years old and younger were net job creators, while older firms were net job destroyers (Figure 4.1).

But not all young firms are net creators of jobs, or have a positive impact on productivity. In the United States, the *median* young firm actually has a low growth rate; the reason that young firms have a high *average* growth rates is that the top 10 percent of the distribution grows very rapidly (Haltiwanger, 2012). Eslava and Haltiwanger (2012) find similar results for Colombia. In the United States, the vast majority of new business owners—who operate in sectors such as residential construction, restaurants, legal services, dentistry, physician's offices, automotive repairs, real estate, and insurance

Figure 4.1 Net Job Creation by Age of Firms in Chile, 2006–09 (Percentage)

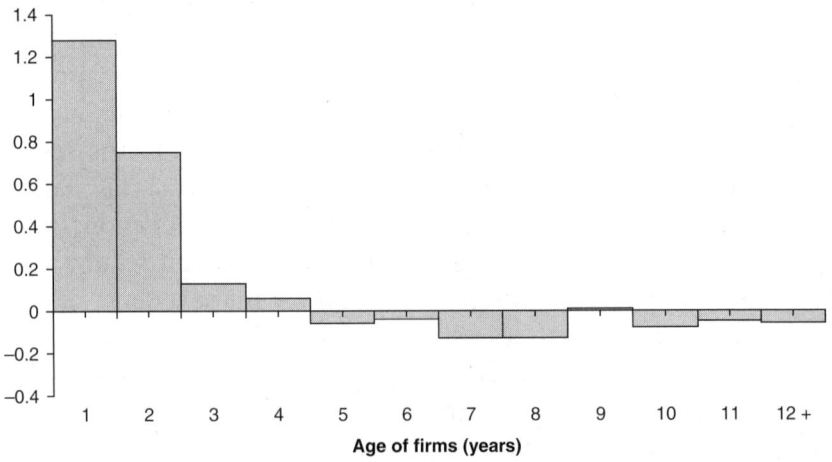

Source: Authors' calculations based on data from SEGPRES (2013).

agencies—did not plan for their businesses to grow substantially, or to innovate in any way (Hurst and Pugsley, 2011). The great majority of new firms were created to remain small by design, and to provide services that were already being provided by other firms. Thus from the perspective of creating jobs, and in particular high-productivity jobs, the efforts to encourage entrepreneurship should not focus just on creating firms, but rather on creating firms with high growth potential.[2]

But how can firms with high growth potential be identified ex ante? While it may not be possible to identify them with any degree of certainty, certain firms are clearly more likely candidates than others.[3] Perhaps the key question, however, is not whether the state can pick the right firms, but rather whether it can put policies in place that either leverage private sector capabilities to screen and identify promising firms (such as incubators or venture capital funds), or in which firms with high growth potential self-select into the programs. At the very least, it is important to avoid spending resources and expending the energy of policymakers on entrepreneurship policies that predominantly impact new firms with marginal productivity.[4]

Is entrepreneurship low in Latin America and the Caribbean? The answer depends on how the universe of firms is defined. In a recent report, Corporación Andina de Fomento (CAF, 2013) uses data from the *Global Entrepreneurship Monitor* to show that Latin America has one of the highest rates of entrepreneurship in the world. However, these data include *informal* firms, which are ubiquitous in the region, and which tend to suffer from low productivity and low growth potential.[5] If the focus turns instead to the flow of new *formal* firms, which have a greater chance of generating employment and becoming productive, Latin America lags significantly behind the average of the high-income member countries of the OECD (Figure 4.2). Furthermore, as discussed in detail in recent reports on entrepreneurship by the CAF (2013) and the World Bank (Lederman et al., 2013), the size of Latin American formal firms at birth tends to be smaller than that in other regions. The region, however, is very heterogeneous. Argentina, Bolivia, Guatemala, and Mexico create less than one new formal firm per thousand people of working age each

Figure 4.2   Number of New Formal Firms per 1,000 People of Working Age, 2004–11

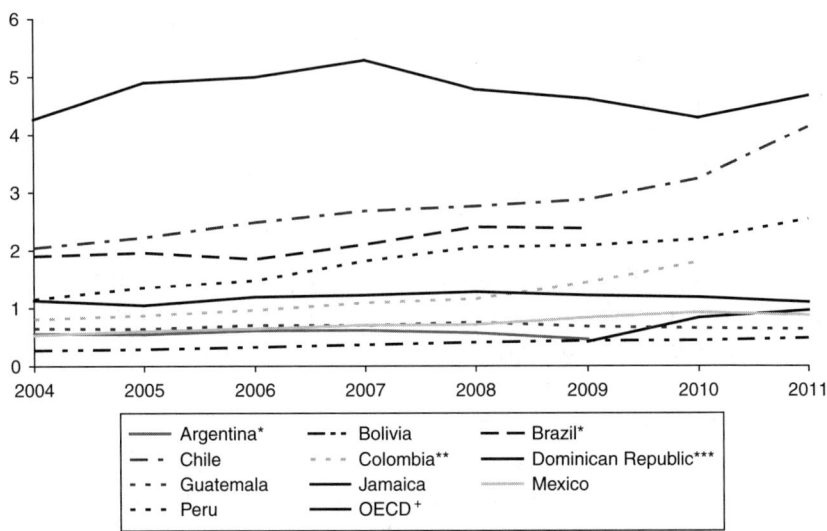

Note: *Data for Argentina and Brazil not available beyond 2009. **Data for Colombia not available for 2011. *** Data for Dominican Republic not available before 2008. + OECD simple average.
Source: Authors' calculations based on World Bank (2012).

year, whereas Colombia and Peru create around two new firms per thousand people of working age, and have made significant strides, as has Chile, which is approaching the mean level of the OECD.[6,7]

While no large-scale comparable data set exists for firms with high productivity and growth potential, Kantis et al. (2013) report that the proportion of firms with high growth potential—so-called gazelles—in Argentina is comparable to that in many OECD countries, at around 3 to 4 percent of formal firms with more than ten employees. If the same were true for the other countries in the region, Latin American countries would also lag behind those in the OECD with regard to the rate of firms with high growth potential.[8] This discussion suggests that in Latin America the gap is not so much in the quantity of entrepreneurs, but in the average quality in terms of innovation and growth potential. The recent World Bank report on Latin American entrepreneurs (Lederman et al., 2014) and a major study by the IDB (Pagés, 2010) reach similar conclusions.

But the fact that gazelles create employment and that Latin America trails other regions with respect to their creation does not in itself provide a sound rationale for policy intervention to encourage entrepreneurship. After all, the freedom of entrepreneurs to start businesses is supposed to be a comparative advantage of a well-functioning market economy. So when it comes to the number and type of entrepreneurs and firms, why doesn't the market achieve the desired outcome?

The answer is that the early stages of a firm are particularly fraught with market failures. Hard-to-insure risks are high, production functions are not well understood, and the standard neoclassical assumptions of efficient markets break down; good firms tend to lack deep pockets, adequate collateral, or a track record that can reassure potential investors and customers that they will produce a high-quality product; and contracting problems are particularly severe. These problems may be especially relevant for firms with high growth potential that are trying to bring a novel idea to market—as compared to the more routine real estate agencies, physicians' offices, or plumbing services.

The next section will explore the rationale for policy intervention in the area of entrepreneurship. Since the type and range of intervention are very diverse, the chapter proposes a classification based on the stage of development of the firm (whether the firm is just starting out, scaling up, or exiting the market), as well as the nature of the intervention (whether related to the real economy or to financial transactions). Finally, the chapter will discuss in some detail specific entrepreneurship policies in the region, from which interesting lessons can be drawn.

The Rationale for Policy Intervention

Policies in support of entrepreneurship are somewhat different from policies to redistribute income or protect the environment. Those policies aim at outcomes—such as distributional fairness or environmental safeguards—that markets are not expected to achieve on their own. The starting point in entrepreneurship policy is different: the presumption is that if there are opportunities to make money, the market will take advantage of them. The idea is brilliantly summarized in a joke usually attributed to Stigler and Friedman about the "efficient sidewalk theory": $20 bills do not lie on the sidewalk, because if one had, it would have been picked up already.

This suggests that when it comes to policies supporting entrepreneurship, policymakers need to be extra careful: without a good diagnosis of the relevant market failures, governments may end up giving out money with low social value. Good diagnosis entails explaining why good business opportunities (like $20 bills) may still lie on the proverbial sidewalk. The market failure may center on problems of appropriability (an undertaking may be socially desirable but lack sufficient private returns because of spillovers or high taxes). Or the market failure may center on coordination problems (where different agents that need to be on board to take advantage of the opportunity fail to coordinate their actions). This section presents the main rationales for policy intervention, building on a very simple conceptual framework that does not aim for completeness.

In an ideal world without spillovers and coordination problems, entrepreneurs would start all projects for which the expected *social* rate of return, $E[R^S]$, is larger than the financial opportunity cost of resources, r. Thus projects would happen when

$$E[R^S] > r \tag{1}$$

In the real world, there are different distortions—on both the real and the financial sides—that complicate matters. The private return for the entrepreneur may not match the social return. Thus expected *private* return would be $E[\alpha \cdot R^S]$, where appropriability, α may be lower than 1 if there are positive spillovers, coordination problems, or even taxation. In this case, the key inequality becomes $E[\alpha \cdot R^S] > r$. Thus, poor appropriability may be one reason why good projects may not be undertaken, or why $20 bills may indeed lie on the sidewalk.[9]

If the entrepreneur has enough wealth to finance the project, or if the project is undertaken by an existing firm with sufficient internal funds, this is the end of the story. But what if entrepreneurs do not have sufficient funding? In this case, they need to credibly promise external investors that they will repay the expected income. The problem is that informational and commitment problems create friction between external investors and the entrepreneur, so only a fraction, π, of the private value of the project may be credibly promised to an external party. This may be because the assets of the project cannot be pledged as collateral, or because protection of creditor or minority investor rights is inadequate. If pleadgeability, π, is lower than 1, then a project financed with external funds will be undertaken only if

$$E[\alpha \cdot R^S] > r/\pi \tag{2}$$

Figure 4.3 illustrates this for the case of π = 0.2, where only one-fifth of the income of the project can be pledged to an external investor, and the opportunity cost of funds, r, is 10 percent. This defines three areas in the figure. To the right, the projects with expected private return above r/π = 50 percent would be undertaken by any type of entrepreneur, regardless of wealth. To the left, the projects with private rates of return below 10 percent would not be undertaken. If this is because social return R^S is low, then there is no inefficiency, since bad projects should not happen. But if it is because α is too low, then there is an inefficiency that would not be solved even for large firms with access to finance. Finally, when projects have an intermediate expected private return between r = 10 percent and r/π = 50 percent, they can be developed only by wealthy entrepreneurs or

Figure 4.3 How Access to Funds Affects the Entry of New Projects and Firms

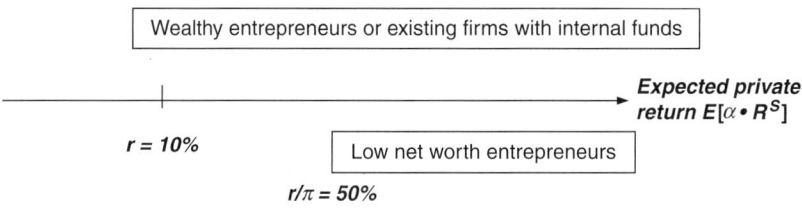

Note: R is social return on a project, while a is the appropriability share; therefore $\alpha \cdot R$ is the private return. Lowercase r is the opportunity cost of funds and p represents frictions in financial markets.
Source: Authors' calculations.

existing firms with sufficient internal funds. In this case, inefficiencies arise in cases in which projects with high enough social and private returns are conceived by entrepreneurs with insufficient funds, since these good projects will not come to fruition.

The discussion that follows is organized around inequality (2). First, real constraints to undertaking projects (associated with the left-hand side of the inequality) are discussed. Then constraints on the financial side, associated with the right-hand side of the inequality, are examined. While separating the constraints on the real and financial sides is convenient for ease of exposition, the distinction is not always clear in practice, particularly at the early stages of the firm.

Constraints to Expected Private Returns (Poor Deal Flow)

On the real side, projects may not be undertaken due to low social returns, R^S, or low appropriability, α.

Lack of Projects with Sufficient Social Returns

Sometimes, it is assumed that if market failures are resolved, good projects will just appear, like mushrooms after the rain. But in some cases, countries simply do not have a good endowment of entrepreneurs or projects with high enough social returns. Some of the problems that may explain the lack of good projects include the following:

- *Poor matching of skills*: Solving some problems may require more than one talent, and these talents are not always allocated to the same people. In order to have a marketable innovation, for instance, a chemist who invents a beauty cream may also need to know about marketing. In that spirit, Lazear (2005) argues that only people endowed with multiple skills may be entrepreneurs because it is not easy to buy the missing talent in the market. Thus, entrepreneurs tend to be "jacks of all trades" rather than specialists.[10] Alternatively, entrepreneurs may need to create teams of people with complementary talents from the pool of people they know and trust. In either case, some features of

Latin America's higher education systems may not be the most conducive to entrepreneurship. In most Latin American countries, in contrast to the United States, students attend universities to become specialists. Thus, the universities typically do not produce as many people with diverse skills. Moreover, since students in the region tend to be grouped according to their specialty, one can conjecture that universities may not provide a natural place for people of diverse and complementary skills to meet and develop entrepreneurial projects.[11]

- *Lack of investments in sector-specific skills*: Another coordination problem is that in small markets, such as those in Latin America, some specialized talents simply do not develop. A salmon parasitologist, for instance, would not develop her expertise without a strong salmon industry and a reassurance that she would be gainfully employed. And the industry would not develop if the specialized talent is lacking.
- *Poor understanding of demand and global markets*: US or Chinese entrepreneurs are in a good position to understand the needs and tastes of very large markets, in the ballpark of 10 trillion dollars each. With markets of such size, there is scope for making money even in non-traded sectors. An entrepreneur from Guatemala or Uruguay will be exposed to tastes and needs of much smaller markets. Many potential buyers of Latin American products are located elsewhere, and one challenge is to understand them well. While this is challenging for existing firms, detecting opportunities for business may be an overwhelming obstacle in the case of start-ups. Export promotion policies, discussed in chapter 8, may help in this regard.

Low Appropriability for Entrepreneurs

Low appropriability for enterpreneurs could be due to the following:

- *Industry-specific public goods and agglomeration spillovers*: Sometimes the unit costs for the first entrant in an industry may be very large, but subsequent entrants may face lower costs and turn a profit. This may be the case if specialized suppliers need to be developed, or collective inputs need to be put in place in order for the industry to be viable. The pioneer may pave the way for later entrants, and thus there will be a spillover. In that case, the social return is high, but appropriability is small for the early entrant, so the firm may never enter (see Hausmann and Rodrik, 2003). In some sectors, branding, patents, supplier agreements, and contracts or franchising may help alleviate these appropriability problems. Grossman and Rossi-Hansberg (2010) argue that this dynamic coordination problem could also be mitigated if pioneers can scale up and internalize part of the externality they create. In practice, though, Latin American firms face problems in scaling up (see CAF, 2013 and discussion below), which reinforces the appropriability problem.[12]

- *Higher wages and tax revenues*: One important benefit of having better business models is that an increase in productivity can raise the wages of workers in a region, which constitutes a pecuniary externality, in the sense that its effects happen through the price system. Also, the more productive the business, the more taxes it pays, which improves the welfare of citizens in the country, through the provision of either public goods or social services and transfers. Each individual entrepreneur does not capture these benefits, however, and may not have enough of an incentive to create a new project.
- *Costs to start a business*: This has been the subject of a great deal of attention, linked to the Doing Business Indexes of the World Bank, which include information on the cost and number of days it takes to start a business. Higher up-front costs may be associated with lower appropriability, in the sense that entrepreneurs do not keep all the returns of their investments, or to a reduction of social return R^S. Importantly, reducing these barriers may have a particularly large impact on marginal firms, since firms with very high returns are likely to start up even if entry barriers are significant.
- *Excessive taxation*: This is an ex post cost that can lower appropriability and affect the decision of whether or not to start a business, as well as the scale of the business. Tax composition may also affect the type of businesses that emerge. For example,

the United States reduced capital gains taxes in 1978 to, among other things, encourage high-risk entrepreneurs.[13]
- *Excessive stigma of failure*: If entrepreneurs are severely punished when they fail, their private costs may be much larger than the social costs. Thus they may expect to appropriate too little of the social value they expect to create, which may prevent them from entering a market. Landier (2005) offers a possible explanation for the self-sustained stigma of failure, which some argue might be a cultural problem in Latin America. Success in a business depends on both luck and ability. In a country in which people engage mostly in low-risk projects (where failures are unlikely to be due to bad luck), then failure is in fact a signal of poor ability. Consequently, some kind of stigma is indeed optimal because failure does help to distinguish good entrepreneurs from bad ones. In this context, a pioneer introducing a high-risk, high-return project where luck matters a lot may suffer the consequences of this stigma. If people regard failure using traditional norms, they could interpret the failure as an indication of poor ability, when in fact the problem might have been bad luck. This self-perpetuating stigma will actually discourage this type of high-risk projects, resulting in a lack of projects of high potential. In this context, educating industry participants (banks, venture capitalists, suppliers, customers, and the general public) regarding the high-risk nature of some projects may help reduce the stigma associated with failure, and encourage the right type of entrepreneurship.[14] Excessive exit regulations that inhibit further attempts at entrepreneurship (such as harsh bankruptcy laws) could also be part of the problem.[15]

Constraints to the Financing of New Ventures

As discussed, the key to financial frictions relates to the imperfect pledgeability of assets. Pledgeability, π, could be particularly low for innovative projects, making the r/π threshold more difficult to overcome. As Rajan (2012) argues, the more novel and differentiated the asset that needs to be created, the worse its pleadgeability. A house construction project can get a mortgage for a large fraction of the value, meaning pledgeability is large. In contrast, the development of a biotech idea is hard to collateralize. The younger the firm, the worse the pledgeability: an established firm may be able to use its shares as collateral for an investment, but a start-up cannot do the same. Savvy fund managers often say that *not all good companies are good investments:* that is, a project with high [$\alpha \cdot R^S$] may not be worth it for an external private investor, due to low pledgeability.[16]

Pledgeability depends not only on the nature of the assets, but also on legal institutions, since pleadgeability depends on whether courts can enforce contracts. Lerner and Schoar (2005) show that in countries with weaker contract enforcement, private equity contracts are much less sophisticated and valuations are lower, suggesting that the limited ability to enforce rules impacts how much an investor external to the firm is willing to commit to a project. Other bottlenecks that could constrain finance for entrepreneurs include the following:

- *Regulatory restrictions*: Sometimes the supply of start-up funding is limited because of regulatory problems. For example, in the past, many pension funds in Latin America were unable to invest in private equity because it was considered too risky, as was the case in the United States until the late 1970s.[17] When regulators understood that diversification protected pension funds from the idiosyncratic risk in private equity, countries started to ease restrictions. Nowadays, for example, pension funds in Brazil, Bolivia, Chile, Colombia, and Mexico can invest in private equity. These reforms can provide an extra supply of funds for entrepreneurial finance.
- *Lack of reliable signals*: Picking the right investments is very difficult and subject to two types of errors: massive investment in projects that ex post were not successful, and failure to invest in projects that were successful.[18] In this context, investors may need signals about which endeavors to finance. In the United States, Lerner (1999) finds that the winners of the government award through the Small Business Innovation Research program had higher returns than the counterfactual, particularly in regions in which venture capital companies were able to read

the signal created by the government. More anecdotally, a few entrepreneurs who have participated in the Start-Up Chile program (discussed below) remarked that after receiving the award from the Chilean government, they were more likely to attract attention from venture capital and other sources of entrepreneurial finance.[19] Providing credible signals about good projects is a public good.

- *Lack of critical mass for human capital specialized in venture capital and other forms of entrepreneurial finance*: Venture capital firms in Latin America have less experience than their counterparts in developed countries. Moreover, in various countries in the region, budding venture capital talent tends to move into later stage private equity, where the deals are bigger.[20] Moreover, in smaller markets with a limited deal flow, the incentives to become venture capital specialists decreases. Without large funds to support specialists working in venture capital full time, and without a large enough flow of projects to be analyzed, it is hard to create specialized knowledge about venture capital.
- *The need to remove multiple bottlenecks to jump-start the system*: Many problems surrounding start-ups require tackling multiple bottlenecks at the same time. For example, pension funds might be hesitant to participate in venture capital because of the low specific capabilities of the potential fund managers; but the best managers would not be attracted to the industry unless there are significant funds in the area. Also, being a high-risk, high-return entrepreneur is not easy when there is insufficient angel investment, and seed and venture capital funding provide a financing continuum throughout the different growth stages of a start-up. To solve this big chicken-and-egg problem, policies need to act simultaneously on various fronts because addressing one bottleneck might not be enough. The case of Brazil, discussed later in this chapter, illustrates this point.

Mapping the Policy Space

This chapter focuses mostly on horizontal policies, which represent the bulk of the interventions to support entrepreneurship. However, some of the policies discussed may disproportionately benefit some sectors and industries, even when they are not specifically targeted to them. For example, policies to foster a venture capital industry will disproportionately benefit those sectors (such as ICT) that use this type of financing intensively. In addition to the public input/market intervention dimension used in the basic conceptual framework throughout this volume, this chapter will classify interventions in this area according to two additional dimensions: the stage of the life cycle of the firm that the intervention targets (entry, growth, and exit); and whether the intervention acts disproportionately on the real or the financial side of a venture.[21]

Policies to increase the quantity or quality of entrepreneurs, foster spin-offs from multinational and other companies, support business incubators, or reduce regulatory barriers to start a business have a direct impact on firm entry, and predominantly affect the real side of a venture. Such policies thus appear in the top left portion of Table 4.1. Some other policies may impact later stages, like scaling-up of the venture—for example, through business accelerators or the professionalization of management. Entrepreneurs may exit, because of either failure or sale of a successful venture—like bankruptcy regulation, regulation of initial public offerings (IPOs) and acquisitions, policies to reduce the stigma of failure, or to improve the prospects of a second chance for entrepreneurs (that is, re-entrepreneurship), such as the NuevaMente program in Chile.[22] These interventions also affect entry, but do so only indirectly, through expectations. For example, if people expect a large stigma if a project fails, projects with potentially high social returns may not be undertaken because of poor expected private returns (once the stigma is factored in). Policies on the bottom row, such as improving the venture capital ecosystem or regulation of IPOs, focus on financial aspects. Some interventions affect both real and financial aspects of the firm. For example, public procurement procedures that are friendly toward young firms may lead to improved sales and profitability; the resulting purchase orders, in turn, can constitute a credible signal for financing (and under some conditions may be pledged as collateral).

Table 4.1 Classification of Policies According to the Stage of a Firm's Development and Targeting of the Real vs. Financial Side of the Venture

	Entry (start-up)	Growth (scale-up)	Exit
Real	Incubators and training	Accelerators (MI/PG) (e.g., TechBA, MX)	
	Reduction of regulatory barriers to start a business (PG) or specific tax reduction for young firms (MI)	Professionalism of family firms	Campaign against stigma of failure
	Foster FDI as a source of spin-offs	Transition of management	
	Public procurement friendly with new firms		Resolving bankruptcy
Financial	Seed funding (MI)	Development of bigger funds and private equity	Acquisitions market, IPOs
	Improve early stage VC ecosystem (PG)	Foster bank funding for high-growth, high-tech firms	Capital gains taxation
	Public VC (MI)		
		Special credit guarantees (MI)	

Notes: MI stands for market intervention, PG stands for public goods, VC stands for venture capital, and IPO stands for initial public offering.
Source: Authors' compilation.

While each of these interventions may improve the environment for entrepreneurship on their own, they are to a great extent complementary. This is true of interventions on the real and the financial sides, as well as for interventions aimed at different stages of the firm's life cycle. For example, a business incubation program may be much more effective if there is a strong venture capital industry that may provide financing for the best business models. Likewise, a strong venture capital industry requires a critical mass of deal flow (that is, business plans that are applying to get venture capital funding)—which a good incubation program helps provide. At the same time, it will be harder for a strong venture capital industry to develop if there is no clear exit strategy for the venture capital investor. They need someone to sell the assets to, in order to realize a return.

It is important to note that the final outcomes—namely, the availability of a good stock of firms that can create good jobs and pay taxes—depends on the entire sequence of interventions throughout the life cycle of the firm. If firms cannot grow, there would be little point in promoting new firms that would remain small. In that case, poor entry dynamics may be endogenous to other problems that appear later in the life cycle of the firm and in the sequence of Table 4.1. While policymakers may want to focus on the most binding constraint, they also need to look for complementarities between policies at different stages of the entrepreneurial life.

Policy Examples

Like the rest of the world, Latin America and the Caribbean has had a long track record of policies targeted at SMEs. In recent years, however, the number of policies for new and young firms has grown. The sections that follow focus on a few emerging policy areas mapped in Table 4.1.

Easing Entry Regulation

Following the pioneering research by Djankov et al. (2002), and the creation of the World Bank Group's Doing Business indicators, many countries have focused their efforts on reducing the bureaucratic burden for doing business. Within this agenda, one indicator has attracted particular attention: the number of days required to start a business. A recent World Bank survey shows that easing entry regulations is the most common type of reform around the world associated with the Doing Business indicators. Between 2005 and 2012, around 180 countries reduced the number of days to start a business. In contrast, in the same period, fewer than 20 countries reduced the number of days to resolve a firm's insolvency. Given the extent to which countries have focused on this one measure, it makes sense to reflect on the expected outcomes associated with these policies, not just in terms of the extent of entry that they may produce, but also in terms of the type of firm entry that it may tend to boost.

Which firms should be expected to enter the market in response to the reduction of entry barriers? The answer depends on how much information entrepreneurs have about the quality of their future business. If entrepreneurs know with certainty the private return of their projects, only those entrepreneurs for which the returns exceed the entry costs will enter. Thus if entry costs are high, only projects with very high return will be undertaken (Figure 4.4). When entry barriers are reduced, the additional entrants are the marginal firms that were previously just left out, which are not as attractive as the existing firms. To put it more clearly, if Bill Gates knew he would be starting Microsoft, he would have entered regardless of the entry costs. In contrast, if entrepreneurs have only a very noisy signal about their potential, founders and backers of many potentially

Figure 4.4 Reducing Barriers to Entry and Rates of Return of Entrants

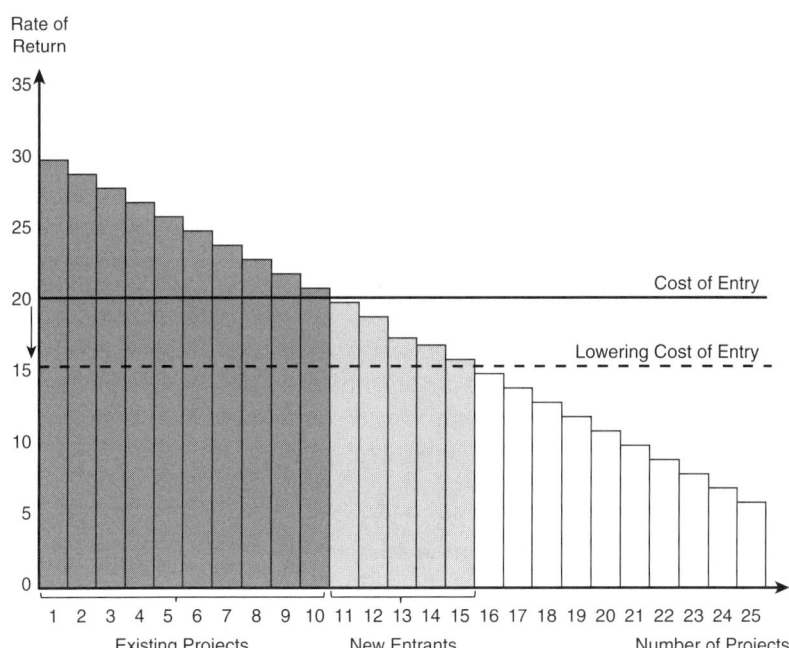

Source: Authors' calculations.

high-return firms—who do not know the firms will ultimately yield high returns—may be discouraged by entry barriers. In the latter scenario, eliminating barriers to entry could have a larger effect on growth.

What has happened in practice? Box 4.1 discusses a few studies that look at this issue, in Portugal, Mexico, and Brazil. Studies tend to find that reduced entry costs do encourage firm entry, but, in general, firms that enter tend to have lower productivity and growth potential. Moreover, the effects, as expected, tend to be associated with one-time jumps in entry at the time the barriers are lowered, rather than large sustained growth of the number of firms.

Box 4.1   Impact of One-Stop Shops in Portugal and Latin America

Evidence from Portugal and Latin America suggests that one-stop shop reforms do have a positive effect on entry, but that the effect of these programs may be short-lived, subject to decreasing returns, and disproportionately affect firms with low growth potential.

Portugal was the world champion in 2006 in reducing legal barriers to start a business. The key intervention was the Empresa na Hora (A Company in an Hour) program, introduced in 2005. It established one-stop shops offering prospective entrepreneurs lower administrative fees and simpler incorporation procedures. The program reduced the time to start a firm from seven months to an hour or so, and reduced associated fees by 80 percent. As a result, Portugal improved its ranking in the Doing Business Index from one hundred and thirteenth (out of 155 countries) to thirty-third. Branstetter et al. (2010) evaluated the program, and found that in the short run it led to a 17 percent increase in the number of start-ups. Firms that entered, however, disproportionately had lower productivity and lower growth potential, as depicted in Figure 4.4. The proprietors of marginal entrants had less schooling than proprietors of existing firms, and their firms were less likely to be in high-tech sectors, and less likely to survive the first two years. The authors conclude that "the social impact of entry deregulation may be limited by the quality of the firms it creates." They do not claim that the program did not work. However, their results temper expectations about what these kinds of programs can deliver. The evidence for Latin America points in a similar direction.

Two papers focus on Mexico, and explore the effect of the Rapid Business Opening System (known as SARE, for its Spanish-language acronym) around 2005; its staggered entry across municipalities facilitated impact evaluation. SARE reduced the number of days to start a business from more than 30 to less than 2 days. Bruhn (2011), using data from the Mexican labor market survey, finds that the total number of registered firms increased by 5 percent in eligible industries. Moreover, the effect came from new firms started by previously employed workers, rather than from registration of existing informal firms. Kaplan, Piedra, and Seira (2011) look at the same reform, but use social security data rather than the labor survey. Exploiting differences across time within municipalities between eligible and ineligible industries, they find effects that are much smaller in firm creation—less than one-seventh of those found by Bruhn (2011). The authors conclude that "the estimated effect is much smaller than World Bank and Mexican authorities claim it is, which suggests attention on business deregulation may be over-emphasized."

The different data sources used in these studies may be important in explaining the different results. Given the high level of informality in Mexico, not all firms report their workers to the social security system. Thus the social security database used by Kaplan, Piedra, and Seira (2011) may include a higher proportion of formal firms, with higher growth potential. If this is the case, the larger results in Bruhn (2011) may be consistent with a disproportionate effect on entry by firms more likely to be informal and to have less growth potential, in line with the findings of Branstetter et al. (2010) for Portugal. Moreover, the results of both papers seem to be consistent with a one-time jump in economic activity, rather than a permanent effect on growth.

In a study on Brazil, Bruhn and McKenzie (2013) explore the Minas Fácil Expresso program in the state of Minas Gerais, which aims to reduce the legal burden to start a business in more remote municipalities. However, they find that business registration *decreased* as a result of the program. After considering different potential explanations for this surprising result, they argue that the one-stop shop reform took away the flexibility of registering a business with one government agency but not another. Presumably, in contexts of informality, some firms that would have preferred to register partially—a preference that is common in Brazil—decided they would rather not register at all. The authors raise the question of whether governments should extend simplification efforts to firms in more remote areas, where many of the benefits of registering may be small.

Improving the Productivity of Start-Ups

In order to sound great, an orchestra needs high-quality musicians. But a good orchestra also needs a good conductor. Many policies focus on improving the quality of the workforce, which would be akin to improving the talent of each musician. But countries may also need to improve the stock and quality of the entrepreneurs and managers (conductors) that employ them.[23] When market forces do not naturally produce these entrepreneurs, they can be created through incubation or even by bringing them from abroad, in the form of a global incubator (see the case of Start-Up Chile in the next section), or as FDI. Existing companies, including multinationals, may serve as additional training grounds for entrepreneurial spin-offs.

In theory, incubators or accelerators ease the contracting problems that prevent entrepreneurs from either starting up or scaling up. To be effective, incubators should start by selecting a pool of promising entrepreneurs, but incubators should also add value. In recent years, there has been a recognition that incubators should focus relatively less on providing a shared roof, a printer, or a secretary—which are things that markets can now provide—than on things that markets are less apt to generate, like good-quality mentoring, as well as matching the young firm with complementary ideas or assets that could help it grow. The following sections explore a number of emerging policy issues related to business incubation.

Aligning Incentives of Incubators (CORFO in Chile)

Incubation policies typically involve a government agency (the principal), which is tasked with the responsibility of encouraging business incubation but does not deal directly with entrepreneurs, and a network of incubators (the agents), which carry out the selection process and directly provide incubation services to aspiring entrepreneurs, with a high degree of discretion. As in any program involving a principal and an agent, the key to achieving the desired results is to put in place the right scheme so that the incentives of the agents are aligned with those of the principal. Unfortunately, in most of the incubation programs in Latin America, this has not been the case. In most cases, incubators are paid according to the number of firms being incubated, regardless of whether these firms survive beyond the incubation period, whether they attract private financing, or whether they ultimately become successful. Thus the incubators do not have the right incentives to select the right firms, or to provide the incubated firms with high-quality services. Such was the case until recently of the incubator program run by Chile's development agency (CORFO). CORFO's payment to the incubator was a flat fee per firm incubated, whether the business succeeded or not.

In 2010 CORFO reformed the system, incorporating some pay-for-performance criteria. In a paper written for this report, Álvarez, Benavente, and Price (2013) discuss the reform in detail. Incubators now get up to $420,000 a year that can be extended for up to six years. But the renewal year by year, as well as the size of the subsidy, depend on a series of criteria that include factors such as the quality of the incubator's corporate governance, management, selection process, and services, as well as more objective criteria such as the sales performance of the incubated firms, the degree to which firms have been able to internationalize, or the extent to which they were able to obtain financing.[24]

Rather than receiving a flat fee per incubated firm, incubators now have the option of retaining up to 7 percent of ownership in the incubated firms. Thus they get a substantial upside that depends on firm performance; this means that they have the right incentives not only to select firms of high potential, but also to provide them with high-quality services.[25] An additional but related CORFO program, the Flexible Seed Capital Fund (Subsidio Semilla de Asignación Flexible, or SSAF) allows incubators to provide seed capital to incubated firms, and to be rewarded on the basis of the success of the firm with respect to sales growth and private funding raised.

While no impact evaluation has been performed on these reforms, Álvarez, Benavente, and Price (2013) report some preliminary conclusions based on extensive interviews. The general perception is that the changes have enhanced the quality of the incubated firms and the incubation services. In particular, those interviewed agree that the awards and the reasonable profit-sharing incentives have helped good incubators succeed and forced some bad ones to exit. The new incentive scheme has also motivated changes in hiring practices. For instance, instead of hiring former officials of CORFO as general managers (a common practice before these changes took place, because incubators earned a fixed amount of money per project approved by CORFO), the incubators are now hiring people from the banking and retail sectors, with commercial expertise. The manager of one incubator noted that they now have incentives to send their incubated entrepreneurs to Silicon Valley to close important sales deals, since incubators are rewarded for the sales of their incubated firms.

Nevertheless, interviews suggest there is still room for improvement: incubators allege that the SSAF resources are insufficient, and the corresponding transfers are not always timely. While the methodology with which incubators are being evaluated is generally sound, there are concerns about the timing of evaluations and the quality of the professionals in charge of the evaluation process.

Attracting Foreign Entrepreneurs (Start-Up Chile)

Start-Up Chile is a program launched in 2010 by CORFO. The idea was to bring entrepreneurs from abroad as a way to increase the deal flow of projects with high growth potential, and to promote a culture of entrepreneurship by example. In order to become viable, the emerging venture capital industry in Chile needed to build up a critical mass of entrepreneurs with good ideas looking for finance. Moreover, it was thought that bringing people with entrepreneurial attitudes into Chile would generate positive externalities, as the change in culture would result in more start-ups by local entrepreneurs.

Candidates apply through a quick Internet-based business plan competition. Once in Chile, selected entrepreneurs receive $40,000 in nonrefundable seed money, with almost no strings attached, as well as physical space for their business. They are required to stay in Chile for at least six months. The program ensures that the process of obtaining a work permit is fast and efficient. Entrepreneurs receive training and feedback from both peers and other advisors. Ideally, during their stay, they should move their businesses into the prototype stage, and maybe start selling, but this is not required. As payment, they are asked to give a few talks in places like universities, to spread the culture of entrepreneurship. Despite its relatively modest budget, the program has received massive attention from applicants as well as from the international media.[26] The last application round attracted 1,600 applicants from more than 50 countries. While some firms left without leaving a footprint, others stayed or created real links by hiring local workers.[27] While it is too soon to tell whether the program has been successful, and no impact evaluations have been performed, other countries like Peru and Brazil have launched programs with similar names, and Uruguay and Jamaica are planning to emulate them.[28]

Whether or not it has been successful, Start-Up Chile is interesting because it represents a good case of what Charles Sabel would call "experimentalist policymaking."[29] The program was started with a budget of $15 million spread across four years—less than one-third of 1 percent of CORFO's budget—but it was subject to a pilot implementation. Juan Fontaine, the minister responsible for the program, noted that sometimes there is uncertainty about the actual constraints to entrepreneurship, as well as the type of program features that are effective in addressing those constraints. Thus, rather than implementing a fully specified program after a lengthy and costly design process, Chile opted instead to come up with and pilot a "minimum viable product," which was ready and implemented in just a few months. An innovative program does not have to get everything right from the beginning. The idea was that the early implementation would allow the government to learn and adjust the program along the way.

The management team at CORFO was new, and eager to try new things that would help communicate the ideas of the new government. In this context, the perceived political cost of restructuring existing programs was lower, and the willingness to take risks higher. Fontaine hired Nicolás Shea, a Chilean entrepreneur working in Silicon Valley, as an adviser on entrepreneurial issues. The time was ripe for some disruptive ideas.

Thus Start-Up Chile was born. It was managed by people who did not see themselves as remaining public employees for a long time, which helped create a flexible environment. Management decided to start small; in the first round, they selected only 24 entrepreneurs from 14 countries. They engineered the process in order to minimize the nonessential administrative burden. For example, preselection of the business plans was made by Younoodle, a California Web-based company that specializes in scoring business plans. This decision freed up the scarce time of managers, who retained the final approval decision. Starting small allowed them to jump-start the program quickly using discretionary funds, rather than having to wait for the next fiscal budget process.

There were political challenges along the way. Giving away money to foreigners is not an easy sell, even if socially profitable. The initial restriction on local participation was politically unpalatable, and the program adapted by allowing Chilean residents to apply. After the first round, one-fifth of the grants have gone to local entrepreneurs, not because of a hard quota, but because locals competed successfully with foreign participants. The "no strings attached" nature of the grants goes against the standard ethos of bureaucracies, which are designed to prevent others from stealing public funds. But the team understood that this feature was key to the success of the program, as it helped insulate entrepreneurs from the administrative burden of the state. Attaching strings (for example, by asking for shares of the new start-up or requiring even more detailed accounting of expenses) could have derailed implementation.

Summing up, even if Start-Up Chile had a general idea of the market failures it wanted to address, there was uncertainty about how best to tackle them, so the program started as an experiment. This experimentalist approach also facilitated the program's implementation, as the attention and the quick wins it generated, together with the flexibility to adjust along the way, helped create the political space to consolidate the program. In spite of these quick wins, however, it is still too early to ascertain whether the program has been successful in attracting high-quality entrepreneurs, and whether these will have a lasting impact on attitudes toward entrepreneurship in Chile.

Spin-Offs and Spawning: Firms as Incubators
Sometimes ideas are not incubated in an incubator, but in a previous job. Such spin-offs could be important as a source of start-ups in the region. Moreover, since spin-offs usually originate in highly productive companies, they can generate the type of high-impact start-ups that policies should seek to encourage.[30] Muendler, Rauch, and Tocoian (2012) use a comprehensive employer-employee database in Brazil to show that at the moment of entry, spin-offs are larger and more likely to survive than new firms without parents. Overall, their results suggest that a fraction of the productivity of firms is embedded in firms' employees, and thus is portable.[31] Employee spin-offs are also pervasive. Depending on the definition, they account for between one-sixth and one-third of the new firms in Brazil's private sector in the period under study.

In Costa Rica, Monge-González, Leiva Bonilla, and Rodríguez-Álvarez (2012b) show that around 4.2 percent of the former employees of tax-exempt multinational companies in the country start a new venture. When compared with the other new firms in Costa Rica, these new ventures owned by former employees of multinationals tend to have higher survival rates, employment, and sales growth—although not higher output per worker. While these differences are partly driven by self-selection—since an employee will need a better prospect in order to resign from a high-quality job at a multinational company—Monge-González, Leiva Bonilla, and Rodríguez-Álvarez (2012b) document an important channel through which policies to attract multinationals may generate entrepreneurship.[32]

While working in a firm, an employee can learn about new projects that the parent firm may not want to pursue: for example, because the employee and management disagree about the value of the project—as modeled by Thompson and Chen (2011) and Klepper and Thompson (2010). Also, by working in certain types of firms (those backed by venture capital, in clusters, or in high-tech sectors) workers can become more entrepreneurial and may be more likely to start a firm. Gompers, Lerner, and Scharfstein (2005) call this process "spawning."

In short, spin-offs are an important source of new firms. Unfortunately, most countries in the region do not monitor spin-offs, making it hard to compare how well existing firms perform their job as incubators. Addressing this measurement gap might be an important step toward identifying good policies in this area.

Venture Capital in Latin America

In the developed world, venture capital has been a crucial source for financing new firms with high-risk projects that make intensive use of new ideas that are hard to collateralize. While venture capital is relevant for a very small share of firms, when it comes to startups with high growth potential and overall productivity, this form of financing can have a powerful impact. In the United States, for example, the share of new firms backed by venture capital is less than 0.2 percent (Hall and Woodward, 2010). Yet these firms represent a large fraction of initial public offerings (IPOs), and comprise 8 percent of the US stock market capitalization. Moreover, according to the National Venture Capital Association, they account for nearly 11 percent of private sector jobs, and 10 percent of total sales in the United States.[33]

Because ideas cannot be collateralized, venture capital uses other contractual mechanisms and monitoring to align incentives between the owner of capital and the entrepreneur. First, venture capital funds are truly active investors that closely monitor firms and participate in some of their business decisions. They sit on the board of directors, provide strategic counsel, help establish connections that may lead to sales and financing, and assist in hiring management. Moreover, their role usually becomes more important when the business underperforms, with venture capital investors often getting more seats on the board, increasing control rights beyond cash flow rights. Second, venture capital funds tend to use convertible securities that resemble debt, and are thus safer, if the return on assets is poor, but can turn into equity if return is high. While providing some safety, this feature gives investors a lot of upside potential, making them willing to invest in projects with high risks but high returns. While venture capital can provide financing to risky projects that are not easily bankable, it requires smart managers with strong monitoring capabilities and knowledge of the business. These capabilities are hard to develop in an economy without previous experience with venture capital and limited deal flow.[34]

In a background paper for this report, Stein and Wagner (2013) describe some features of venture capital investments in Latin America. As expected, venture capital in the region is orders of magnitude smaller than in the United States and other developed countries. It is also much smaller than in other developing countries such as China and India (Figure 4.5). The average Latin American economy has just one-tenth of the venture capital relative to GDP that China and India have, despite having twice as much income

Figure 4.5   Venture Capital as a Share of GDP in Various Countries

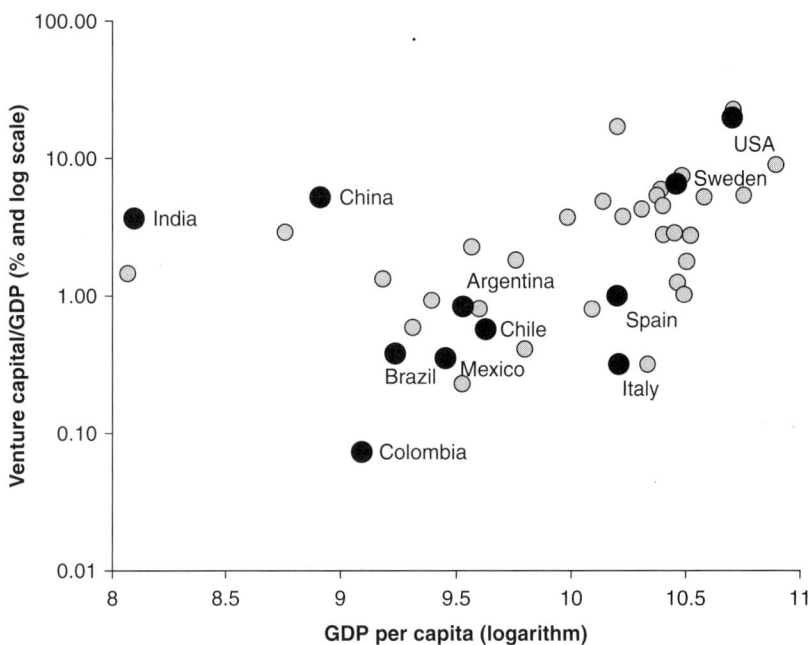

Note: Data are circa 2011. Data on GDP per capita in terms of purchasing power parity (PPP) in US dollars are from the World Bank's World Development Indicators. Venture capital is naturally lumpy. In countries with few players and low amounts, a few investments could strongly impact the relative ranking among Latin American countries. Therefore, it is best not to focus too much on differences among countries in the lower half of the figure. A similar figure using data from Thomson One (available in Stein and Wagner, 2013) shows different orders among Latin American countries; however, the big picture with respect to developed economies, China and India, remains the same.
Source: Data from the Latin American Venture Capital association (LAVCA), EMPEA, and other regional venture capital associations, compiled by Lerner, Leamon, and García-Robles (2013).

per capita. This difference could point to the lack of critical mass in Latin America, in both funding and deal flow.[35] Nonetheless, since 2005, venture capital investments in Latin American companies have been growing by more than 30 percent per year, on average. Foreigners are playing an important role in this growth, accounting for around 40 percent of investments. While venture capital is smart money, investment behavior in Latin America looks relatively less sophisticated than in other regions. The share of high-tech companies backed by venture capital as a proportion of all firms backed by venture capital is smaller, and investments are made by less-experienced venture capital firms.

Policies to develop a venture capital industry are not just about pumping public money into the system. Very good ideas and skilled fund managers that can add value to the companies are in short supply and are slow to develop. And when too much money is pumped too quickly, the additional entrants might be disproportionally fund managers with lower skills associated with companies with lower growth prospects. Making progress in this front may take time, and may require acting on several fronts at the same time, as the case of INOVAR in Brazil will illustrate.

Jump-Starting a Venture Capital Ecosystem (INOVAR in Brazil)

The early stages of a venture capital industry are fraught with spillovers and coordination problems. In the absence of a good venture capital ecosystem, making the first deal is much more expensive than making the hundredth deal. Moreover, spillovers within the industry imply that no firm has the incentive to devote enough effort into jump-starting the system. Many of the benefits would be appropriated by others. To overcome this coordination problem, the Brazilian Agency for Innovation (FINEP) developed INOVAR, a support program for venture capital, in cooperation with the IDB's Multilateral Investment Fund (MIF). This section follows the discussion in Leamon and Lerner (2012).

The diagnosis of Brazilian ecosystems for venture capital was not promising before INOVAR was established. Despite some entry into private equity in the late 1970s and until the 1990s, various macroeconomic barriers constrained the use of venture capital in Brazil. Toward the 2000s, however, problems became more industry-specific. In particular, very few venture capital fund managers had significant experience. Pension funds, which represented more than 13 percent of GDP, barely invested in private equity, despite the fact that regulations allowed them to invest up to 20 percent of their assets in this asset class. There was no national organization of venture capital or private equity firms to provide "industry-specific public goods," such as sharing lessons or even sharing the burden of due diligence in venture capital. Companies that needed venture capital or private equity financing did not know how/where to find the venture capital or private equity firms. The legal framework for venture capital and private equity investments was underdeveloped. The few fund managers that accumulated some knowledge of venture capital quickly wanted to move into later-stage private equity (such as buyouts) that had greater money flows. Overall, the stock of experts available to manage venture capital funds was relatively inexperienced.

In this context, FINEP, with the financial support of the MIF, launched INOVAR, a program to provide public goods to foster a venture capital ecosystem. INOVAR, which aimed at the development of the venture capital industry through a "big push," worked simultaneously on various aspects of the ecosystem.

On the one hand, it facilitated the creation of venture capital funds by matching investors with fund managers, and also facilitated the training of venture capitalists. A crucial component was the INOVAR Funds Panel. This was not an investment vehicle, but a consortium of investors that analyzed funds together, and later independently decided where to invest. In a few hours, a fund manager could meet with many potential limited partners to obtain money.[36] Initially, the MIF played a key role in training FINEP employees on due diligence and other matters. Soon, FINEP/INOVAR's staff helped in the due diligence process, reducing the burden of starting the first deals. INOVAR also facilitated visits of managers of Brazilian pension funds to the United States to meet with their US counterparts, who had more experience investing in the private equity industry. A crucial step was to convince Petros, one of the largest pension funds in Brazil, to invest in venture capital and private equity funds more aggressively, which they did since 2006. Getting Petros on board convinced other pension funds that investing in venture capital was worth attempting, and thus facilitated the whole process.

On the other hand, INOVAR facilitated the matching of entrepreneurs and venture capital investors. First, INOVAR staff, aided by junior officers from Brazilian seed and venture capital funds, pre-screened the entrepreneurs who would pitch in front of the evaluation board, which would decide which firms would participate in a focused incubation stage. During that incubation period, entrepreneurs received training on how to run a start-up and how to improve their business plans. At the end of this process, entrepreneurs presented to a panel of venture capital funds and angel investors that could potentially finance them. This arrangement amounts to the provision of a public good for the entire private equity/venture capital industry in the country, which was instrumental for the development of the industry.

Overall, to jump-start the venture capital ecosystem, INOVAR worked on many aspects to address coordination problems. They did so while avoiding direct subsidies, focusing instead on the provision of public goods. Given the success of the program, the MIF has adapted the INOVAR model for Peru and Colombia. In turn, FINEP has advised Argentina, Chile, and Mexico on the potential for replicating INOVAR.[37]

Scaling Up High-Productivity Firms

Firm growth after start-up is very important for both entrepreneurship and aggregate productivity. The greater the expected growth of a firm, the more willing entrepreneurs will be to start the business because they can recover the investment more easily. Moreover, once a business has achieved high productivity, the economy's aggregate productivity can grow *if* that firm has the capacity to expand, absorbing workers and other resources that were previously employed in low-productivity activities. This is productivity growth by reallocation. For entrepreneurship to "make a dent" in economic growth, not only the start-up but also the scale-up of the best businesses is needed.[38]

Just as physicians study the physiology of healthy people before they study diseases, a benchmark is needed in order to study whether the scaling-up of businesses and the process of reallocation suffer from pathologies. The natural benchmark would be to start with three standard assumptions in economics: that there are perfect factor markets, so firms are competitively bidding for workers and other factors; that firms have U-shaped average-cost curves with a single minimum or optimal scale, rather than a W-shaped curve with different local minimum cost scales; and that firms are price takers. For purposes of this discussion, these assumptions are selected not because they are true—like physicians, we know they are unlikely to be true for our patient—but because they provide a baseline thought experiment that is useful for understanding why economies differ from it.

If the assumptions that markets are competitive and cost curves have a single minimum indeed apply, then the additional revenue generated by the last worker would be equalized across firms (see Hsieh and Klenow, 2009).[39] Firms would be hiring up to the point at which one additional worker would generate enough additional revenue to pay for his or her wage. Having fewer workers than the benchmark would mean firms are leaving money on the table because an extra worker would increase profits. If the optimal scale is exceeded, the additional revenue generated by the last worker would be lower than the wage, in which case the firm would be inefficiently large. This argument does not imply that all firms would be of similar size. Some firms—namely, those that are more productive—would operate with many more workers than low-productivity firms. In that benchmark world, a high-productivity firm that increases its productivity further would expand its scale, pushing factor prices up and forcing some low-productivity firms to exit. This analysis suggests that while competitive markets have many features, the love for low-productivity firms is not one of them. The discussion that follows will briefly explore departures from this benchmark, on both the financial and the real sides.

Financial constraints preventing scale-up: Since revenues typically do not show up as quickly as the wage bill and capital bill, financial constraints may prevent the firm from scaling up. Some authors argue that these borrowing constraints could be a major impediment to reallocation into higher-productivity firms.[40] Having said that, under many conditions one would expect that if firms are hitting their borrowing constraint, then over time this problem could be mitigated, since the internal cash flows created by revenues could be reinvested, thus gradually increasing their scale of operation. In this scenario, the best projects eventually bypass the borrowing constraint. [41] Therefore, financial constraints should matter more for relatively young firms. Using data from the World Bank's Enterprise Survey, Wagner (2014) shows that the share of profits reinvested decreases over time, from approximately 15–20 percent for firms younger than 5 years old to an average of 10 percent for firms that are 15 years old. These findings are consistent with the story that firms use retained earnings to gradually address their financial constraints, and that these constraints become less binding as firms become more established.

Production and cost constraints: Firms are smaller, on average, in Latin America than in the United States. In part, this is because firms are smaller at birth. But this smaller size could in part be the result of a lesser ability to scale up compared to US firms. Hsieh and Klenow (2012) show that firms in the United States that have survived for 40 years employ nearly eight times as many workers as firms that are 5 years old or younger. In contrast, they observe that the same scale-up factor for Mexico was only two times (Figure 4.6). Interestingly, firms in India show a minimal amount of scale-up.

Financing constraints may not be the culprit in the comparison between the United States and Mexico, since the differences become large for firms 25 years of age and older, at which point financing constraints are probably not binding. Many other factors could explain Latin America's relatively low scaling up. One potential explanation has to do with firm ownership. In Latin America, to a greater extent than in developed countries, firms tend to be family businesses. In a context of strong market failures in early stages of a business, as tends to be the case in the region, the family could

Figure 4.6 Firm Age and Size in the United States, Mexico, and India

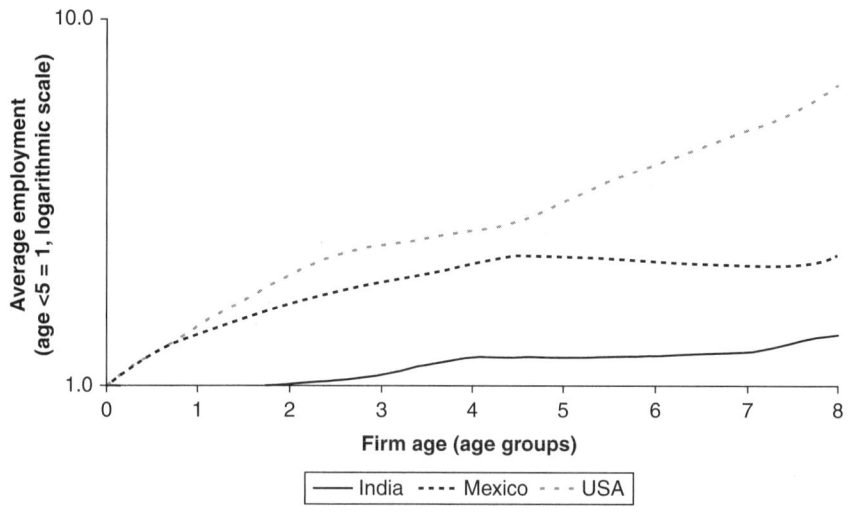

Note: Age groups: 0 = (<5 years); 1 = (5–9 years); 2 = (10–14 years); 3 = (15–19 years); 4 = (20–24 years); 5 = (25–29 years); 6 = (30–34 years); 7 = (35–39 years); 8 = (>40 years).
Source: Hsieh and Klenow (2012).

be a very useful device to bypass contractual failures, enabling the start-up of a business. But the same family structure that facilitates start-up could be an impediment to scale-up. As firms scale up, a cousin or brother-in-law may no longer be well suited for a management position. Moreover, firing them may generate important personal costs, and finding middle managers in the market to replace them may be difficult.[42] Some of these problems may also arise in firms that are not family owned; as noted by Wasserman (2012), the optimal skills for the CEO of a start-up may not be the same as the skills required to successfully scale up a firm.

One related problem has to do with management practices. In particular, there is evidence from Aghion, Bloom, and Reenen (2013) that there is little managerial delegation in Latin America, in comparison to developed countries.[43] Whether this is due to cultural differences or to the difficulty of finding middle managers, in a context in which delegation is lacking, scaling up may be more challenging, and may imply important personal costs and trade-offs for the entrepreneur in terms of time spent with the family.

In this context, entrepreneurs may be less willing to expand their operations.

These constraints of start-up management to scale-up are mitigated in countries like the United States by the existence of an active private equity industry that invests in companies and improves their management practices, restructuring the organization so it can operate at a higher scale. Failure to develop a healthy private equity ecosystem could be part of the reason why some high-productivity firms do not scale up in the region.

Older firms can also contribute by acquiring start-ups with growth potential and synergies with their existing assets. Looking at innovative companies, Hall and Woodward (2010) document that most of the successful exits of venture capital-backed firms in the United States are acquisitions by other firms—usually older ones. Bernstein (2012) shows that when companies get access to public stock markets, they decrease their direct level of innovation, but they increase the acquisition of innovative technology, exploiting their new financial comparative advantage. To the extent that public stock markets in countries in Latin America are underdeveloped, this alternative channel for high-productivity firms to scale up is curtailed.

Overall, little is known about why firms scale up relatively poorly in Latin America. Another possibility is that the U-shaped average cost curve assumption is violated, so that a small expansion is inefficient, even when a large expansion may be profitable. If this is the case, firms may need critical mass to scale up. This could be the case when scaling up requires making a large indivisible investment, like a machine or the creation of a new layer of organizational structure (see Caliendo, Monte, and Rossi-Hansberg, 2012).[44] As shown in Figure 4.7, a firm producing a small quantity, q_1, would not want to scale up unless it has a very large purchase order that could lower its marginal cost. Obviously, these problems are less relevant in the larger markets in developed countries, where it is more likely that firms will naturally attain the optimal scale given by the global minimum average cost.[45] In smaller settings, as Hausmann and Wagner (2014) argue, a large purchase order by the government or any other large customer (such as global mining companies in Chile or Intel in Costa Rica) could make the firm jump to the next

Figure 4.7 Average Cost Curve for a Firm with Multiple Local Minimum Costs

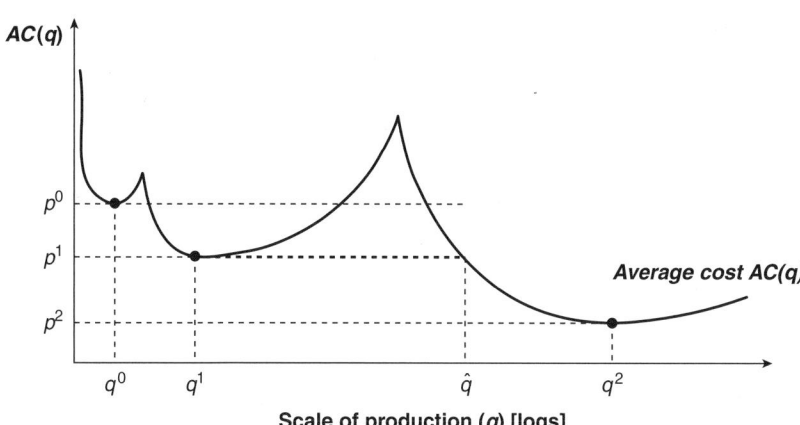

Note: p^1 = local minimum cost. $\hat{q}$ = minimum scale to make profitable investing in an upgrade when starting at q^1. p^2 = global minimum cost.
Source: Authors' calculations.

scale of production, $\hat{q}$. Thus from a policy perspective, government procurement could be an important tool to allow high-productivity firms to scale up. This, in turn, may help drive low-productivity firms out of the market, leading to a virtuous reallocation of factors of production.

Marketing constraints—understanding demand: A related potential constraint to the scaling up of Latin American firms has to do with marketing and the size of the domestic markets. If marketing products abroad is more costly and requires fine-tuning of the products in order to adapt them to foreign demand, firms in smaller markets could get stuck below the optimal scale. They may know how to sell to their initial customer base, which is typically domestic, but they may not know how to expand their customer base effectively beyond borders. Internationalization policies such as export promotion, which help connect local producers with the demand in international markets, can be important in this regard; they are covered in detail in chapter 8. One example of a policy that combines internationalization with business acceleration services is Mexico's TechBA program. It was launched in 2004 to help Mexican small and mid-sized tech companies meet the challenge of penetrating the rest of the North American Free Trade Area (NAFTA) and position Mexican firms as providers of world-class technology. It has locations in five cities in the United States and two in Canada, as well as one in Spain (Madrid), as a stepping stone for the European market. The program brings Mexican entrepreneurs to these locations and facilitates their interaction with local actors, leading to sales, strategic alliances, and investments. TechBA is financed by the Mexican Ministry of the Economy and the Mexico-U.S. Foundation for Science.[46,47]

How to Encourage High-Productivity Firms to Start Up and Scale Up

New firms have the potential to be a disproportionate source of productive projects and jobs in the economy. However, the early stages of a business are among the most difficult. At this stage, firms do not yet fully understand their production possibilities, and they have a hard time making credible contracts with clients and suppliers, financiers, employees, or even cofounders. All these factors can prevent socially efficient projects from happening.

The goal of policies to support entrepreneurship and early scale-up is to prevent these constraints from holding back projects with potentially high social returns. Some of these constraints are related to the real side of new ventures, and others to the financial side. But in all cases, it is paramount to identify the market failures, and to design interventions that address them. Simply spending more money on entrepreneurship policies because the region does not create enough firms will not do.

Another crucial challenge relates to selectivity. Given that the typical new firm is not particularly productive and has a low probability of surviving, it is important to think about (self) selectivity criteria in the allocation of public funds. This does not necessarily mean that the state should pick winners. Rather, it means that it should put in place policies that either leverage private sector capabilities to screen and identify promising new ventures (such as incubator programs with the right incentives, or venture capital funds), or in which firms with high growth potential self-select into the programs. At the very least, it is important to avoid spending resources and expending the energy of policymakers on entrepreneurship policies that predominantly impact new firms with little marginal productivity. The fact that policies to reduce the barriers to start a business seem to predominantly impact these marginal firms suggests that the overwhelming attention that these policies have received in the region and the world has been misplaced, at least to some extent.

While this chapter has focused largely on individual policies, it is important to understand that some of the interventions in this area have strong complementarities. For example, efforts to develop the venture capital industry may not succeed without good incubation programs that provide the requisite deal flow. Incubation may not reach its potential without a venture capital industry that offers a potential exit from the incubation stage to the most promising ventures. And in the absence of both, the capabilities required to effectively manage venture capital funds and incubators will not naturally emerge. As should be clear, entrepreneurial systems may need consistent and multiple interventions in order to break a vicious cycle. Policymakers should think about these complementarities, and should consider individual interventions not just on their own merits, but also with respect to the way they impact the ecosystem as a whole.

As in any other field, public policies in the area of entrepreneurship need new evidence that can support their rationales and help separate policy failures from successes. Despite important recent efforts to compile data on entrepreneurship and its financing in Latin America and the Caribbean, there are still too few bodies of data to answer too many questions. Hopefully this modern push toward policies for young firms will spur additional efforts that will produce new waves of data in order to learn from existing policies and improve them for the future.

5

Beyond the Classroom: Preparing People to Produce

Few subjects have been more studied in the social sciences than the role of human capital in economic development. The consensus is that education—broadly understood as the continuous process of acquiring skills and/or capacities—determines the productivity of workers, their income levels, and, ultimately, the overall welfare of society. In turn, a better-educated population boosts the innovative capacity of an economy, speeds up the development of new technologies and products, and facilitates the dissemination of knowledge and adoption of new technologies developed by third parties. Through these diverse channels, higher individual levels of human capital result in higher levels of economic growth and development (Hanushek and Woessmann, 2008).

Not surprisingly, nations on five continents have been working hard for decades to boost investment in education and job training. For example, between 1980 and 2008, public investment in education doubled in real terms in Latin America and sub-Saharan Africa, almost tripled in the Middle East, more than quintupled in East Asia, and increased eightfold in South Asia (Glewwe et al., 2011).[1]

But not all the efforts have produced real progress. Evidence shows that successful countries in this area have known how to transform investment in education and training into a workforce with appropriate levels of relevant skills for productive development. These countries have also understood that the education process does not end with a high-school diploma or even a college degree; it simply never ends. Thus successful cases emerge from continuous training models that integrate education systems with the labor market and promote lifelong learning, ensuring stimulus for production. In these systems, workers continuously transit from the labor market to the education or training system throughout their working life cycle.

Latin America and the Caribbean does not belong to this select group. Countries in this region have significantly expanded coverage in primary and secondary education, but have not progressed to a continuous training model and have not paid enough attention to integrating schooling and training for work systems. Efforts have been disproportionately concentrated on expanding education systems and creating isolated niches of training for work with limited coverage, leaving little room to review and improve their quality assurance mechanisms and the relevance of the skills taught, to better meet the demands of the productive sector. Latin American countries seem to have simply assumed that a population with more years of education is synonymous with a better-educated population.

Education and training for work in Latin America and the Caribbean have been running on separate tracks. Various countries of the region have institutional systems that support training for work, but they are typically focused on technical education and training systems. Both these systems are very heterogeneous in terms of institutions and scope, but they are generally outdated, discredited, and disconnected from the needs of the productive sector. General education, in turn, is seen as the path for providing young people with academic skills to enter college and then the labor market. Various indicators suggest that the region has not even made progress in this dimension. Based on the results of international tests, Latin America lags significantly in academic knowledge.

The result of this situation is a cause for concern. The workforce in Latin America is deficient in basic knowledge and lacks other competencies or skills that the productive sector needs in order to operate competitively, innovate, and grow. The disconnect with the needs of the labor market is reflected in a significant skills gap, which has been sporadically addressed in some sectors and countries with piecemeal strategies.

This chapter proposes that only a quality lifelong learning system connected to the needs of the labor market can ultimately breed a population that drives and supports the productive development of a country. The evidence presented herein suggests that this has not been the case in Latin America—a very diverse region where neither common efforts in coverage nor isolated sectoral targeting have significantly enhanced the productivity of the population. Without sweeping reforms, starting at the base of the education system, it will be difficult to achieve general and sustainable improvements in human capital for the region's productive development. However, this type of reform transcends the time frames linked to political cycles; for this reason, such efforts often face problems of political economy that make their implementation difficult. Consequently, discussion of policies to improve human capital and close the skills gap needs to consider complementary actions to speed up change, albeit in specific areas.

In this context, this chapter aims to answer the following questions:

- Why, despite the recognized efforts of the region in building human capital, are the skills required for productive development not being generated?
- What have other countries—developed and developing—done in the policy area to build human capital in order to effectively improve the productivity of their people?
- What conditions are necessary to promote the development of a country based on the capabilities of its population? What can be done in the short term?

Five key messages result from the analysis:

- *The countries of the region need to adapt their goals.* Advances in coverage without improvements in quality or relevance have not been effective in promoting productive development. The future costs of not implementing an agenda that improves quality and relevance will be significant—which is why it is essential to propose a new structure based on a work-oriented system of education and training.
- *The process of human capital accumulation is continuous, and the education and training system must respond to this reality.* The accumulation of human capital must be conceptualized as a lifelong process that does not end with an education diploma

or certificate. It is a sequential process where the quality of each level either facilitates or holds back the future process and extends beyond the transition from school to the world of work. This has practical implications when defining public policies and institutions associated with building human capital.

- *Acquisition of relevant skills and/or capacities must be the backbone of the education and training for work systems.* Giving priority to skills and competencies will have a stronger impact on the economic welfare and productive development of countries than years of training. These skills and competencies change rapidly and are increasingly complex. The labor market and society now require not only academic knowledge but also other socioemotional skills less commonly associated with the traditional education system. Similarly, these skills are not linked to a specific stage early in people's lives. This reinforces the importance of considering education as a lifelong learning process in which the school has a central but not exclusive role.
- *There is no single model of education and training for work, but the active participation of the productive sector is indispensable for improving relevance and quality.* Supporting the new public policy agenda requires a system that involves the productive sector in identifying required skills, developing the content of education and training for work, and assessing skills. A system oriented to relevant quality training needs a sound institutional framework that facilitates coordination of the productive sector with the state, education agencies, and institutions that train people for work. The system must also be compatible with a funding scheme that offers appropriate incentives, and include a monitoring and evaluation system to assure quality.
- *Reforms that lead to sustainable improvements require a medium- to long-term view that is not subject to political cycles. However, remedial policies can help bridge specific gaps in human capital in strategic productive sectors.* The problem of the lack of quality and relevance of human capital in the region starts early in the education system. Without sweeping reforms that strengthen the skills acquired by children and young people from school, and that promote the continuous updating and improvement of the skills of the workforce, no substantial and sustainable change is

possible. However, targeted public policies that complement and coexist with medium-term strategies can help bridge skills gaps in key sectors.

Human Capital in Latin America

The Traditional Building Blocks: Education and Skills

Public investment in education has grown in Latin American countries, although less so than in developing economies outside the region. The efforts of most countries in the region in education and training have resulted in an increase in public spending on education from an average of 3.87 percent of GDP per year in the 1990s to about 4.7 percent today—more than in past decades, but still well below the investment in countries with good results in education. Average public spending by OECD countries, for example, is over 12 percent of GDP.[2]

This investment has focused on expanding coverage by building schools to make the education offered accessible to families outside the system. It has also aimed at strengthening access by providing incentives to increase demand, through conditional transfer programs such as Bolsa Escola in Brazil and Progresa-Oportunidades in Mexico. These efforts have succeeded in significantly expanding the coverage of primary and secondary education. For example, access to primary education grew from 86 percent in the early 1990s to the current level of 95 percent, while secondary coverage expanded from 60 percent to 76 percent in the same period. However, in a region facing the challenge of consolidating its growth and development, concentrating efforts on simply expanding coverage is not enough. Wider coverage and more years of education of the population have not measurably improved workforce productivity.

Illustrating this point, Figure 5.1 shows the trend in the number of years of education of the population aged 15 years or over and the increase in workforce productivity in one country in Latin America (Brazil) and one country outside the region (China). Unlike China, important advances in education in Brazil were not accompanied by similar improvements in worker productivity. A very similar trend is generally found in the rest of the region.

Figure 5.1 Expansion of Years of Education of Adult Population and Workforce Productivity, 1970–2012

a. Brazil

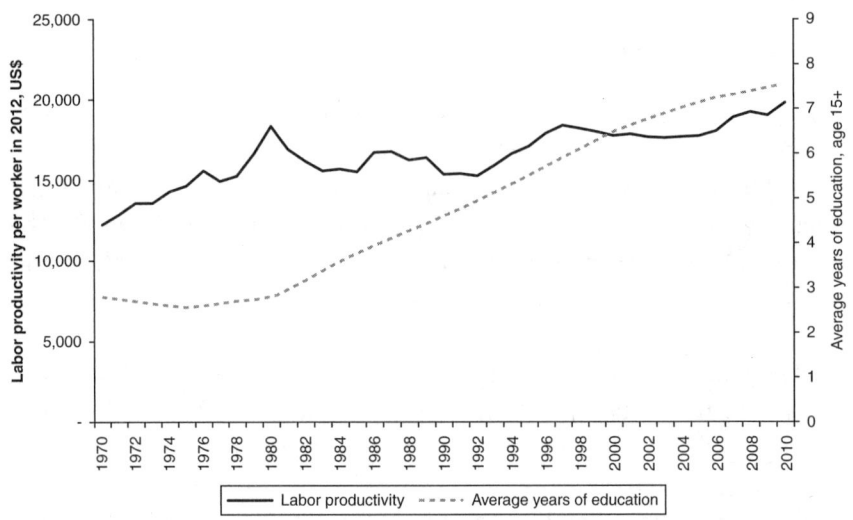

b. China

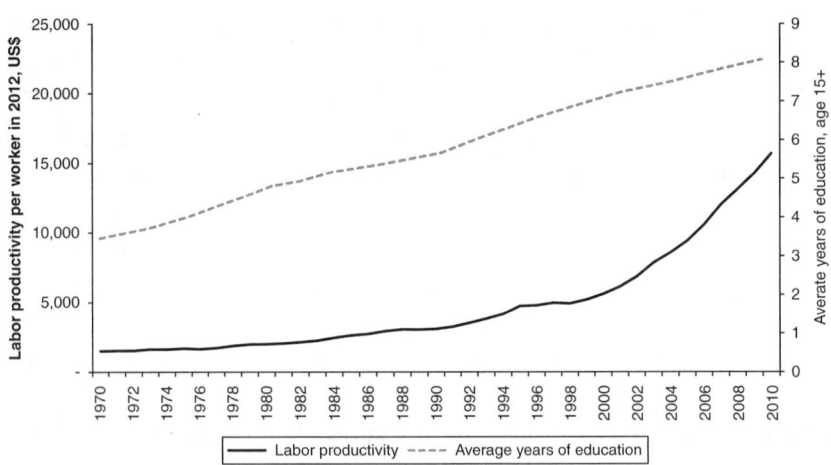

Source: Authors' calculations based on data from UNESCO Institute for Statistics (2013), The Conference Board (2013), and Barro and Lee (2013).

Why have the important advances not helped boost Latin America's disappointing economic growth in the last 50 years? Why has the rapid convergence of the region with developed countries in terms of education coverage and years of education of the workforce not contributed to a similar convergence in terms of productivity, income, and economic welfare? While not ignoring the other important factors that affect economic growth, the hypothesis presented in this chapter is simple: years of education and training (or education in general) have not resulted in the specific types of learning or skills relevant to the labor market, comparable to those achieved by other countries in similar conditions (see Box 5.1).

> **Box 5.1 How Much Does the Status Quo Cost? How Long Can the Reforms Take to Show Results?**
>
> The most recent literature on the impact of education on growth emphasizes the distinction between *quantity* and *quality/relevance* of education in the country: that is, it distinguishes the coverage of a system or the years of education of the population from the cognitive skills acquired. In several studies, Hanushek and Woessmann (2008, 2010, 2012a, b) show that it is the quality of training of the workforce that affects economic growth. In turn, quality depends on the skill levels acquired both inside and outside the education system (through the family, informal training, work-based learning, and so on). These authors show that if measures of educational attainment are included, the years of schooling variable no longer has a significant relationship to growth.
>
> In Latin America, human capital measured by international tests can explain between one-half and two-thirds of the differences in per capita income between the countries in the region and the rest of the world (Hanushek and Woessmann, 2012b). In contrast, only about one-quarter of the changes in the income of the countries can be explained by measures of school attendance without considering differences in acquired skills. The conclusion is that skill levels, rather than educational attainment, explain individual wage differences, income distribution, and economic growth.
>
> But how expensive is the lag in knowledge skills of the region's workforce? Following the methodology proposed by Hanushek and Woessmann (2011) for the OECD, the analysis presented below estimates the economic

loss suffered by Latin American and Caribbean countries as a result of this lag. Two scenarios are considered:

1. Education reform that improves the average PISA (Programme for International Student Assessment) score of each country by 50 points (0.5 standard deviations) in 10 years.
2. Education reform + training: a 50-point improvement of PISA in 10 years, supplemented by a similar effort for each cohort of workers already in the labor market.

The exercise assumes that a working life extends for 40 years (the workforce includes 40 age cohorts), that the reforms are gradual (affecting one cohort per year), and that GDP growth without reform is 2 percent, on average, for Latin America. The increase of 50 basis points in PISA is ambitious, but similar to the increase achieved recently by Brazil and Mexico (30–35 points in reading between 2003 and 2009).

The results are summarized in Table B5.1 and Figure B5.1 (which present data for Chile). Under the assumptions of the exercise, in the first scenario, GDP per capita 40 years after the reform would be 17 percent higher than GDP per capita with no reform. In the case of supplementing the education reform with training for the active workforce, GDP per capita would be 37 percent higher than the scenario with no reform. Although the results are the product of the assumptions, they highlight not only the important difference that can be achieved through these reforms, but also the time frame involved. As illustrated by the example of Chile, because of the gradual nature of the change, consistent with the current context of education reforms, it would take about 15 years to begin to identify marginal effects. This underscores the importance of designing supplementary policies to education reforms to deal with skill gaps in the active workforce.

Table B5.1   GDP per Capita in 2050 under Different Reform Scenarios

Country	GDP per capita, 2010	GDP per capita, 2050		
		No reform	Scenario I	Scenario II
Argentina	14.8	23.2	27.1	31.8
Brazil	10.1	15.7	18.4	21.5
Chile	15.6	23.8	27.9	32.7
Colombia	8.6	10.9	12.7	14.9
Mexico	13.3	18.0	21.1	24.7
Peru	9.0	12.9	15.1	17.7
Uruguay	13.4	25.8	30.3	35.4

Source: Authors' calculations based on Hanushek and Woessmann (2011).

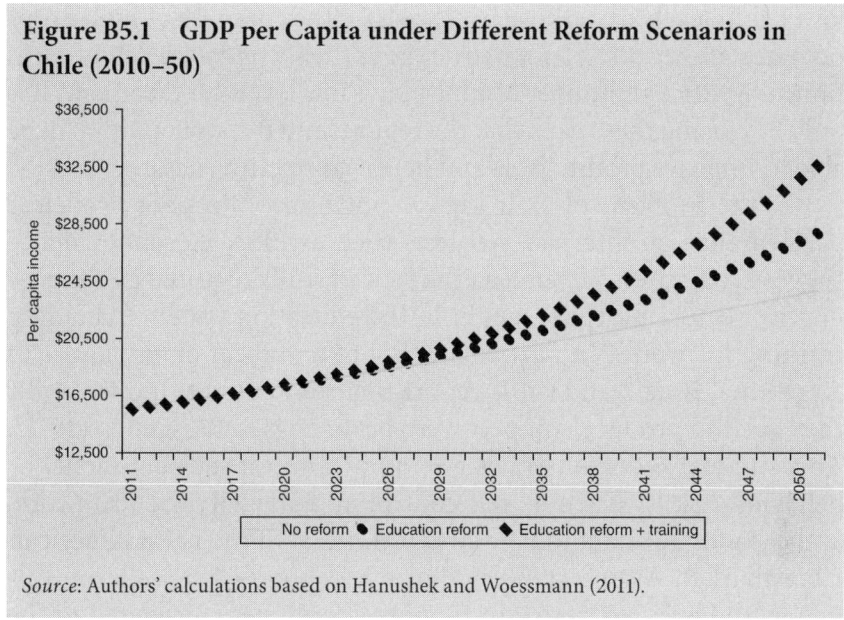

Figure B5.1 GDP per Capita under Different Reform Scenarios in Chile (2010–50)

Source: Authors' calculations based on Hanushek and Woessmann (2011).

This hypothesis explains why the most critical educational deficiencies of the region are in the areas of relevance and quality. These deficiencies manifest themselves, for example, in the results of international tests such as PISA (administered by the OECD), which measures not only basic academic skills (math, reading, and science) in samples of 15-year-olds, but also their ability to use this knowledge in solving real-life problems. In the 2012 test (the latest data available), all eight Latin American countries that participated came in the bottom fifth of the total of 65 countries in the three disciplines.

Moreover, the results show that 46 percent of Latin American students do not understand a basic text, well below the 18 percent in the OECD average and 3 percent in China (Shanghai). In math, 63 percent of students from Latin America cannot solve basic mathematical problems that could arise in everyday situations, compared with 23 percent in the OECD and 4 percent in China (Shanghai).

The scenario is even more serious considering that in Latin America and the Caribbean, a high proportion of young people remain outside the education system (and presumably have even lower skill levels than those in schools), either because of high dropout rates[3] or because of poor coverage at the secondary level. In addition, a significant number of adults have low levels of education.[4] It is only by closing these gaps that the region (and its population) will be able to improve productivity and hence competitiveness.

But the problem of skill gaps is not limited to poor academic performance on international tests such as PISA. Recent evidence suggests a disconnect between the type of skills required by the productive sector and those taught in the education system (including training for work). In particular, about 90 percent of employers in Argentina, Brazil, and Chile report that they cannot find the skills they need to produce competitively, according to Bassi et al. (2012). This study also demonstrates the importance of socioemotional or behavioral skills (such as self-control and capacity for teamwork, and capacity to adapt to new circumstances) in the Latin American labor market. As an example, Figure 5.2 shows what skills are valued by the business sector in the three countries considered in the same study. The survey asked 1,200 business respondents to give a total of 100 points to three skill sets according to their importance for their productive activities. The results show that, on average, employers assigned 15 points to technical skills or skills specific to the activity, 30 points to knowledge skills, and 55 points to behavioral skills. These results are repeated after disaggregating the data by country (as shown in Figure 5.2), economic sector, firm size, or other dimensions.

These findings are particularly relevant given that currently, education and training in the region are focused largely on knowledge or technical skills, rather than on the development of what are known as "soft skills." Without questioning the importance of technical knowledge or skills in the education process, the evidence suggests that other skills relevant to the job market are needed to build human capital.

In the same vein, a World Bank Enterprise Survey (2010a) shows that companies in the region report that shortages of man power with appropriate capacities are the main obstacle to their productive development. On average, one-third of companies in Latin America and the Caribbean identify inadequate training

Figure 5.2 Survey of Skill Demand in Argentina, Brazil, and Chile (Average Points Assigned)

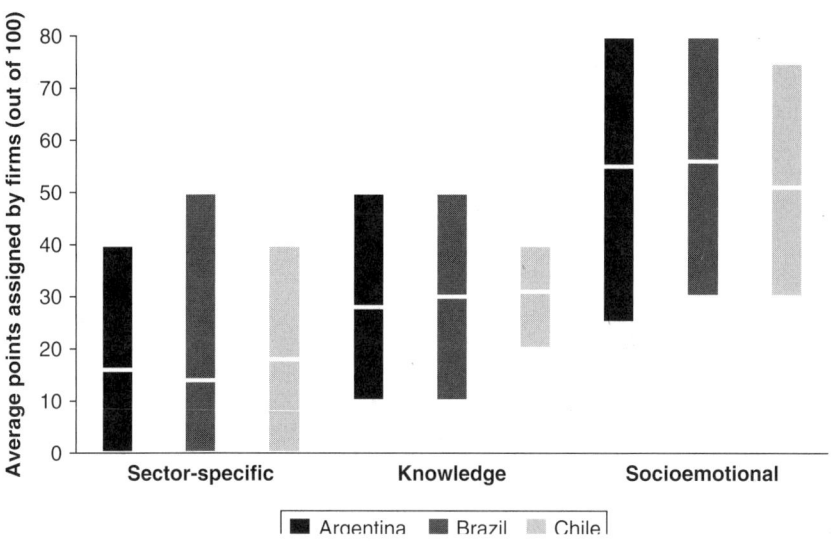

Note: The horizontal break in each bar indicates the average. The upper limit corresponds to 90% of the skills distribution and the lower limit to 10%.
Source: Bassi et al. (2012).

of workers as the most serious obstacle to their operations and as an important constraint on innovation: the share is much higher in Brazil and Argentina—69 percent and 56.6 percent, respectively (see Box 5.2). This finding is confirmed by the results of the Productivity and Human Resources Survey (IDB, 2012) in the Bahamas, Honduras, Panama, and Uruguay, which finds that the workforce lacks skills and experience, and the capacity to perform well in job interviews.

However, it is important to bear in mind that demand for skills can change rapidly, which makes the challenge of closing the skills gap—and designing a system of relevant training for work—even more complex. The results of the Demand for Skills Survey (IDB, 2010a) show that 50 percent of firms in Argentina, Brazil, and Chile consider that their production needs have changed in the past five years and they now require workers with more extensive and different skills compared with five years ago.

Box 5.2 Does Higher Education Respond to Market Demands? The Montevideo Software Cluster

The development of software and services has been marked by very rapid growth and export orientation in several Latin American countries.[9] The emergence and expansion of knowledge-based service sectors has highlighted the bottlenecks in the required labor supply. There is simply not enough highly qualified talent, especially in the ICT sector.

Universities and ministries of education—even of science and technology—have reacted slowly to the need to expand the workforce of knowledge-based sectors, especially information technology, the most dynamic sector.

The recent experience of the Montevideo software cluster is a good example of high-level technological development in a developing country whose expansion is constrained by the lack of highly qualified workers. The cluster has 150 small, medium, and large enterprises, dynamic in terms of technology and economic performance, which produce mainly for the global market.

In Uruguay, the supply of high-level computing skills was provided initially by the academic system, with the University of the Republic playing an important role. This strong initial impulse was followed by the creation of enterprises that were largely export oriented due to the almost total absence of local demand for the services they offered. This external demand provided the impetus for the industry to expand. However, educational institutions could not keep pace with the industry's expansion and were slow to shift from a predominantly scientific to a more professional orientation capable of satisfying market demand more directly. Moreover, the creation of intermediate careers, which could have partially compensated for the scarcity of engineers, did not take place, and any incentive to enter the critical professions for the software industry was absent.

Public policies in Uruguay and in other countries of the region have struggled to resolve the tension between the short-term needs of businesses for qualified staff and investment in education and training, which tend to be changed or adapted only in the long run (Didier and Pérez, 2012). A variety of market and government failures underlie this mismatch between the demand and supply of highly skilled human capital, most notably:

- The failure of families to steer their children into technical fields. The private returns to a diploma in ICT-related fields remains high but is apparently ignored by many families that have a strong say in the choice of postsecondary programs for their children who continue to enroll more in traditional liberal professions over engineering and more

technically oriented fields. This suggests an informational problem that may need to be addressed by an intervention.
- Both private and public tertiary institutions have, for different reasons, encountered difficulty adapting supply to visible changes in the demand for skills. In the case of UDELAR, the dominant public university, no well-defined channels are in place for incorporating the business perspective in decision making. In addition, the rigidities in the publicly financed yearly budget make it very hard to produce quantum leaps or drastic reforms in faculty hiring or infrastructure, which weakens the ability to provide short-term responses. Private universities have indeed responded, particularly in the case of ORT, yet the exclusively private pattern of financing, based on tuition fees, makes it hard to finance large-scale growth in any field, particularly in technical areas that require investments in equipment, laboratories, and faculty with high opportunity costs in the labor market.

As a result, the shortage of qualified human resources has clearly affected development of the sector over the past two decades. The number of university graduates from IT careers in 2012 was practically the same as in 2004. In the meantime, the sales of the software sector in only one year—between 2009 and 2010—grew by nearly 10 percent. Clearly, the growing demand from business for technical and professional profiles—in this case at the postsecondary level—has had a limited impact on decision making by government and universities.

Given this failure of government, the business sector has adopted measures to "recycle" professionals from other disciplines by training them in specific areas as needed. In this respect, the State along with LATU (the Uruguayan Technological Laboratory, a private-public technology institute) and some private companies have set up the Knowledge Development Center, a training center for human resources in the IT industry, whose main objective is to focus on areas not covered by the academic sector (González and Pittaluga, 2007). Initiatives like this, however, tend to generate short-term actions with insufficient volume to counteract the inadequate response of the mainstream educational system and universities.

Technical Education and Training for Work

The solution to adapting the levels and types of skills in the workforce may lie in improving the training for work systems, commonly called on to correct the deficiencies of the education system, update skills, and provide new ones based on the actual productive situation of the economies. But are such systems efficient in Latin American countries? Do they close the skill gaps between demand and supply in the labor market? Unfortunately, the answer is no. Even though substantial public resources are directed to these systems, the evidence suggests that their operations are ineffective, coverage rates are deficient, and levels of quality and relevance are poor. In the 1980s and 1990s, most governments in the region set up mechanisms to promote job training for people who had left the education system in an effort to encourage them to continue training—especially the disadvantaged. Most countries are now allocating funds from specific national or sectoral payroll taxes or tax exemptions that can be used only to train workers, and are implementing the training through national training services. This investment ranges from 0.01 percent to 0.37 percent of GDP.[5,6]

Table 5.1 shows the percentage of GDP that governments invest in training and the percentage of trained workers versus employed workers.

Public spending on training (at least the portion allocated to national training institutes) averages no more than 0.4 percent of regional GDP. Colombia has the highest investment in this area (although it is concentrated on short courses). The results also show that despite large skill gaps, only a small percentage of workers

Table 5.1 Share of Trained Workers to Employed Workers and Cost of Training

Country	Trained/employed (%)	% of GDP for training
Chile	14.8	0.1
Colombia	24	0.37
Dominican Rep.	10.1	0.08
El Salvador	–	0.12
Honduras	5.5	0.19
Panama	4.3	0.29
Uruguay	0.3	0.04

Sources: Questionnaire to training institutes in each country; household surveys in each country; and authors' calculations based on Huneeus, de Mendoza, and Rucci (2013).

receive some type of training in the region. This results in a deficit stock of skills and portends a bleak future for the productive potential of the population.

Reversing this situation is one of the main challenges for the productive development of the region. In this context, it is important to pay more attention to providing technical education in a framework of continuous training for productive development.

Technical education in Latin America and the Caribbean—which is generally administered by the ministries of education—was originally conceived as a type of secondary-level education that could also offer postsecondary education through the provision of technical diplomas. A feature of secondary-level technical education in the region, unlike other regions, is that the programs are not generally terminal: that is, students are eligible to continue to higher education.[7] Technical education systems in Latin America are heterogeneous in their institutions and coverage. They range from models of secondary technical education parallel to general secondary education, whose curricula differ only in the final years of middle school (as in Chile and Argentina), to more complex systems where different subsystems and possible education pathways coexist (as in Brazil and Mexico).[8]

On average, about one-third of secondary school students in the region attend technical schools (Székely, 2012), although enrollment varies considerably from country to country. While in Chile and Mexico technical education at the secondary level represents about 35 percent and 40 percent of the student population, respectively, in Brazil only about 11 percent of students attend this level (Ñopo and Bassi, 2013).

For decades, secondary technical education has been the choice for young people with fewer resources and those unable or unwilling to continue to higher education. This is the case even though, on average, graduates of secondary technical education earn about 10 percent more than their counterparts who graduate from general education in Latin America and the Caribbean and do not go on to higher studies in higher education (Ñopo and Bassi, 2013). Although on average technical graduates earn less than college graduates, the dispersion of earnings is large, and the return from some technical specialties exceeds that from some university courses (Bucarey and Urzúa, 2013).

Why, despite the returns, does technical education not have a greater presence in Latin American and Caribbean countries? Although there are several possible explanations, on both the supply side and demand side, the absence of a link with the requirements of the productive sector and the obsolescence of technical education systems in the region contribute to its limited role in training for productive development. The absence of a link with the productive sector is also reflected in significant gaps in technical profiles between the requirements of the labor market and training in the education system. As an example, Figure 5.3 shows the distribution of enrollment in secondary-level technical education by specialty in the case of Chile. A comparison of these figures with job creation by sector between 2010 and 2012 reveals significant shortfalls in key sectors, such as mining and construction, which created on average more than 23,000 and 27,000 jobs per year, respectively. In the

Figure 5.3   Enrollment in Secondary Technical/Vocational Education by Specialty Sector, Chile, 2010

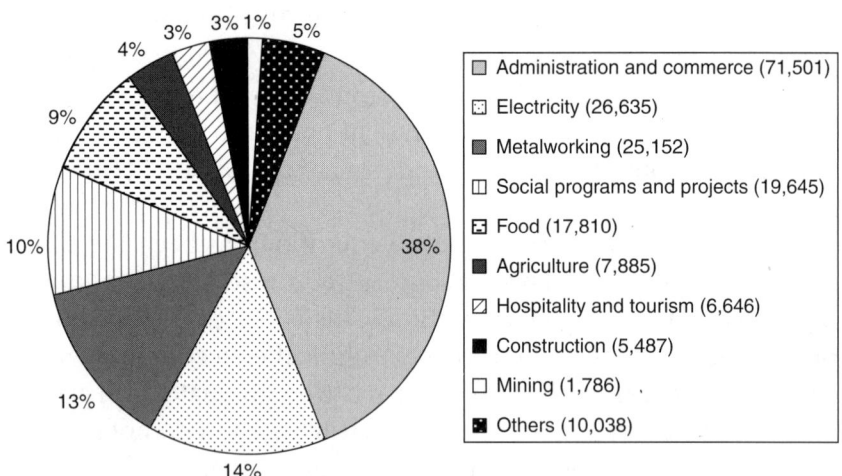

Note: The number of students enrolled appears in parentheses.
Source: Data from the Ministry of Education of Chile (2010).

case of mining, the third section of this chapter describes how sector companies organized to make up the shortage of technical workers in order to fill vacancies available in this expanding sector.

The challenge for Latin America and the Caribbean is to offer attractive, relevant, and quality training that contributes to the sustained growth of economies, higher productivity levels, better wages, and, ultimately, the greater welfare of the population. This challenge is relevant to all economies in the region, irrespective of their level of development.

The conventional justification for public sector involvement in the process of investment in human capital is based on the existence of market failures and externalities that affect stakeholders, leading to investment levels that are lower than the socially optimal level. These include imperfections in the capital market because the credit for investments in education must be granted against acquisition of knowledge and future income. Market failures also occur due to incomplete contracts: for example, cross-cutting skills acquired by a worker through training are potentially beneficial to other employers, which discourages employers from investing in education and training. Various forms of information asymmetries also play a role. For example, students and parents are often unaware of information about the returns on education for different education career options. Thus identifying the most important market failures impeding the promotion of productive development through human capital will have a fundamental impact on the design, implementation, and effectiveness of the design of public policies.

The countries that have best overcome these challenges have been successful in providing certain basic inputs. These inputs are the pillars of a lifelong training system, based on work skills and competencies, which continuously promotes development of the productive economy. This suggests that government efforts to improve the human capital of their populations must focus not only on building schools or promoting training programs, but also on ensuring that training systems (in or out of school) provide students and workers with adequate skills relevant to the world of work.

International evidence reveals that no ideal or single model guarantees that training for work responds to the needs of productive development. Although the engineering of mechanisms and instruments will depend on various factors in each country, certain factors ensure that human capital contributes to development: the coordinated participation of various actors, especially those in the productive sector; a sound institutional framework and functional institutions with clear roles, precise objectives, and consistent national and regional strategies; resources and transparent cofinancing mechanisms, and the adoption of incentives to achieve better results; rigorous mechanisms for quality assurance; and a continuum of coordinated and flexible options that operate effectively as a system, promoting portability and lifelong learning for the workplace.

These basic factors are relevant for Latin America and the Caribbean. Although several attempts have been made in the region to adapt interventions or models from other countries, they have not taken into account the cross-cutting elements inherent in a medium-term view; consequently, they have not achieved significant results at the country level. However, those attempts have resulted in promising sectoral initiatives, as illustrated below, which show that short-term differences could speed up changes that supplement long-term structural reform. Short-term initiatives can also have a demonstration effect of learning and validation, before the reforms are expanded to a large scale. However, the general experience in the region suggests that skills training has not been approached as a productive development policy at the national level (see Box 5.2).

To achieve training that is relevant for work, the productive sector must be actively involved in education and training. This link (or its absence) significantly affects the performance of the workforce of a country in pursuit of productive development. Countries have usually made the connection through public-private partnerships, but there is no single model. Globally recognized technical education systems include cases where learning of basic content is mostly through traineeships in companies (dual systems such as Germany and Switzerland), or mostly in schools (as in the Netherlands), or where both components are separated by skills certification systems (as in Australia, New Zealand, and England), or where two years' work experience is required after completing two years of general education (as in Norway) (Cuddy, Leney, and Ward, 2010;

Hoffman, 2011). The common element in these technical education models is the central role of the productive sector—usually in a legal framework—in defining the qualifications required for the various economic sectors and in developing curriculum content and skill assessment systems. For its part, the state—in coordination with the productive sector—is responsible for defining standards and supervising the system, as well as guaranteeing that the training includes adequate development of general and academic skills (Hoffman, 2011).

Schemes to provide training for work after formal education also come in a variety of arrangements around the world, including partnerships between industry and higher education institutions, training by the productive sector financed by payroll taxes, or skills certification by leading international companies.[10] South Korea offers an example of the first modality. This country has fostered partnerships of productive sectors with universities, where large companies (such as Samsung, Hyundai Steel, and Mobis) provide technical knowledge (curriculum), experts, and equipment; clusters of small- and medium-sized enterprises and suppliers of large companies participate with their workers; and the technological university provides facilities and equipment maintenance.

Training by a specific sector to develop the skills it requires financed by payroll taxes is the model used by the Chamber of Construction in England. This sector is very cyclical and is made up of many small firms and self-employed workers; it requires manual activities; most workers have only a secondary education; and the workforce displays high turnover rates. This level of rotation exacerbates the problems of appropriability for an individual firm that decides to train its employees. The solution is to fund training through payroll taxes at the sectoral level; companies pay in proportion to their employees' payroll. This arrangement solves the problems of free riding that would otherwise be difficult to resolve, in the context of a sector as atomized as construction. The objective is to develop a demand-driven set of skills that are flexible and innovative; training is focused on low-skilled adult workers. The service offers advice and training in both classrooms and workplaces. The system also has instruments to identify skills in demand, define the occupational standards of the industry, and calculate internal rates of return for each investment to ensure proper use of public funds.

Finally, some leading international companies offer skills certification through virtual programs. For example, an initiative by Microsoft operates in 70 countries, including Colombia. The training program in computer science and software operates in coordination with public and private sponsors. The objective is to equip the urban population with the technical skills in demand, assuring quality and relevance. Microsoft forms partnerships with schools, universities, and technical institutes to give students access to Microsoft programs online and certify their skills. The program mainly involves three services: legal and free access to its packages for young people in affiliated institutions; job portals, as a way of linking young people with skills with the "Microsoft seal" with potential employers, retailers, and distributors of Microsoft; and online education and training in various areas. Microsoft certifies the learning and works with institutions to incorporate changes to the courses and receive international accreditation.

These examples illustrate the wide variety of specific initiatives available to connect training to work with the productive sector, thereby making the training relevant. The next section analyzes a case of reforms at the country level in New Zealand. The case is relevant for Latin America for several reasons. New Zealand is a small economy abundant in natural resources. It adapted elements of the traditional English model to its situation and needs. In a relatively short time, New Zealand implemented a robust system with evident results. The other cases analyzed are sectoral experiences in Latin America that have arisen from the shortage of labor force with the skills required by industry. The first case is the mining sector in Chile, which has expanded enormously in recent years and is a key component of the economy. The shortage of workers with the necessary skills was a serious bottleneck to the ambitious expansion plan of the sector. The second case is the construction sector in Uruguay, whose problems were caused by a workforce with a high proportion of inexperienced young workers and high turnover. The last case centers on an automobile company, Volkswagen, in Argentina. Faced by shortages of technical staff with the required skill level, the company implemented a dual education program in coordination with a public school near the plant.

These sectoral cases show that the participation of the productive sector is indispensible to close existing skill gaps by making training relevant to work. The jump to the country level, however, is achieved in the long term through structural reforms aimed at a national system of continuous training for work, where education and training are a continuum, and where institutions, (co)financing, and monitoring and evaluation for quality assurance and relevance are basic pillars connected to this framework.

A Continuous Training System for Productive Development: The Case of New Zealand

New Zealand is an interesting case study at the national level. As a small young country with a developed economy, it has made building the skills of its workforce in response to the needs of production a national strategic objective for the last 10 years. The country has developed a system of lifelong learning with long-term horizons, where the formal educational system, job training, and training for work constitute a single integrated market of training providers. The system is based on certifications (under the New Zealand Qualification Framework, or NZQF) and is offered by ten levels of skill packages.[11] The basic governing principle is the *portability of qualifications.* The schemes are flexible with respect to how skills are acquired, but focused on developing those in demand in the labor market. The emphasis is on public and private participation and funding, in the belief that this interaction promotes effective training in a dynamic and evolving system based on precise institutional arrangements, including rules for funding, as well as monitoring and evaluation. These elements are the fundamental pillars of quality assurance and relevance. As a result, the system operates in an integrated way.

The institutional structure of the New Zealand education and training system is clearly coordinated so that each entity performs key connected functions, as part of a national qualifications system. The Department of Labour, the Ministry of Education, and the

Qualifications Authority all work together. Technical schools and training institutes form a single, transparent, and competitive market of training providers. The productive sector participates through the Industry Training Organizations and Sector Councils. The Industry Training Organizations are training providers grouped by sector, with recognition and partial funding by the government. They design skill standards, which the New Zealand Qualifications Authority (NZQA) then registers. They lead the process of identifying training needs for active workers in industry, and develop mechanisms for the provision of training. The Sector Councils are nonprofit, independent, industry-led institutions but funded by the state. They act as intermediaries, providing intelligence on industry needs, maintain and update skills, and connect companies' training needs with providers. In parallel, an independent and institutionally strong quality regulatory agency follows individual workers, their learning process and job performance, and the resources invested.

As mentioned, the funding for training for work in New Zealand is mixed. The aim is to ensure that the lifelong learning process has incentives aligned with industry and well-defined priorities that guarantee relevance. Only qualifications recognized in the national qualifications system receive public funding. The system is moving away from a scheme based on the results of learning to one aligned with the results of work performance.

The New Zealand scheme of quality assurance and relevance has a strong focus on results, emphasizing at the institutional level accreditation, regular independent assessments, and monitoring of identified risks. Currently, the country is evaluating the impact of both training and tertiary education qualifications on wages.

The NZQA is an independent agency that regulates and monitors quality at the national level. It operates the Qualifications Framework (NZQF) and defines the rules to assure quality at all levels of the system, including university and nonuniversity education, and even has powers to close courses or institutions. The authority guarantees that a qualification has national recognition and quality assurance, and allows different training pathways to the same qualification. Only those qualifications approved by the NZQF can receive public funding. The competency standards and national qualifications framework also assure relevance since they are the result of the needs of each sector, validated by industry advisors or the national quality authority. Based on the framework of qualifications and projections of the demand for skills, estimates of skill shortages are used to monitor and adapt the system.

National Certification Systems in Latin America and the Caribbean

Countries like New Zealand are successful examples of the development of a national training system that builds human capital as a productive engine, with clear and stable rules for the medium term, institutional capacities, established funding arrangements, and effective control mechanisms. Obviously, the possibility of implementing mechanisms and instruments for monitoring and evaluation aimed at improving the effectiveness of policies depend on the country's institutional capacity.

Some Latin American and Caribbean countries have also made significant efforts to develop national certification systems for qualifications or work skills. For example, more than a decade ago, Chile initiated a Continuous Competency-Based Training System, known as Chile Califica. The first pilot experiments began in 1999, and in 2002 Chile implemented Chile Califica, with a mandate to develop competency profiles to form the National Qualifications Framework. In 2008, the National Work Skills Certification System (known by its Spanish-language acronym, SNCCL) was set up, and in 2009, a commission was set up to begin to coordinate its work. Despite recent progress, the initiative has not yet succeeded in reaching a systemic or national level, and still faces significant challenges, including delineating the elements that prefigure the operation at the system level; linking with the productive sector; designing the institutional, operational, and financial structure; and defining the business model (Rucci, 2010).

In Mexico, a federal entity, the National Council for Standardization and Certification of Work Skills (CONOCER) has been promoting and coordinating the National Skills System for workers since 1994. Its objective is to contribute to the economic growth, educational development, and social progress of Mexico. CONOCER's mandate also includes overseeing education and training for work assuring pertinence of the system. Despite efforts to develop occupational standards with industry, the scope of these standards and the participation of the productive sector remain limited. The ongoing challenge for CONOCER is to put its mandate into practice (Kappaz, 2013).

Sectoral Initiatives in Latin America and the Caribbean

The development and strengthening of national systems do not exclude sectoral initiatives. On the contrary, successful national experiences create incentives and coexist with different sectoral arrangements based on different needs, which leverages incentives and the individual characteristics of each case. In England, for example, arrangements such as the one by the Chamber of Construction are part of a national qualifications system that provides clear and consistent rules (institutional, funding, quality assurance, and relevance) and that permits and encourages a range of combinations. This is the case in all successful countries.

Although Latin American and Caribbean countries have not yet managed to establish systems of technical education and job training that substantially impact the quality and relevance of the skills of their workforce, the region boasts a variety of sectoral cases where the public and private sectors have managed to coordinate efforts to correct gaps in the productive development of that specific sector: in general, an important productive sector. These are cases such as mining in Chile, construction in Uruguay, and the manufacture of automobiles in Argentina. Although rigorous impact evaluations have not yet been conducted, these examples suggest there is room for sectoral public policies that promote joint action by the state, the education system, and the productive sectors, with the objective of achieving relevance and quality in worker training. These policies should accompany deep structural reforms with medium-term impact and strengthen the base for a sustainable system designed to build human capital for productive development.

The Mining Sector in Chile: Closing the Skills Quality-Quantity Gap by 2020

Mining companies in Chile currently produce 34 percent of the world's copper and 16 percent of the world's molybdenum. On average, since 2003, these activities have represented 7.4 percent of Chile's GDP and 58 percent of total exports. Copper mining is carried out by nine large companies. Global growth in demand for copper and the consequent increase in price encouraged companies to undertake ambitious expansion plans. While in 1989 about 1 million tons of copper were produced annually, by 2020 this figure is projected to reach about 7 million metric tons. To successfully implement these plans, the companies will face major challenges, including the need for a trained workforce of sufficient quantity and quality. It is estimated that all the large mining companies and contractors together will need to increase their manpower by 53 percent between 2012 and 2020, considering only their mining, processing, and maintenance operations. Worse yet, there is currently a relative scarcity of skilled labor, which is reflected in the steady rise in wages and growing difficulty filling vacancies within the scheduled time period.

To quantify the extent of the challenge, the large copper and gold producers provided information on all their projects to Fundación Chile (the entity responsible for the analysis), which resulted in an almost census-like calculation of staffing needs. On this basis, demand for human capital was projected in 15 key entry profiles for the processes of mining, processing, and maintenance (Figure 5.4). The results suggest that over the next few years, the industry will need 37,638 skilled workers, including 12,373 to replace workers reaching potential retirement age. This figure far exceeds the projected flow of graduates and workers in training programs in different levels and schemes. The most important human capital gaps identified include profiles associated with the maintenance and operation of mobile and fixed equipment (which do not require postsecondary studies). This gap is due to a combination of factors resulting from the lack of relevance of existing training and the small number of training programs.

Figure 5.4 Human Capital Gaps in the Mining Sector in Chile, 2012–20

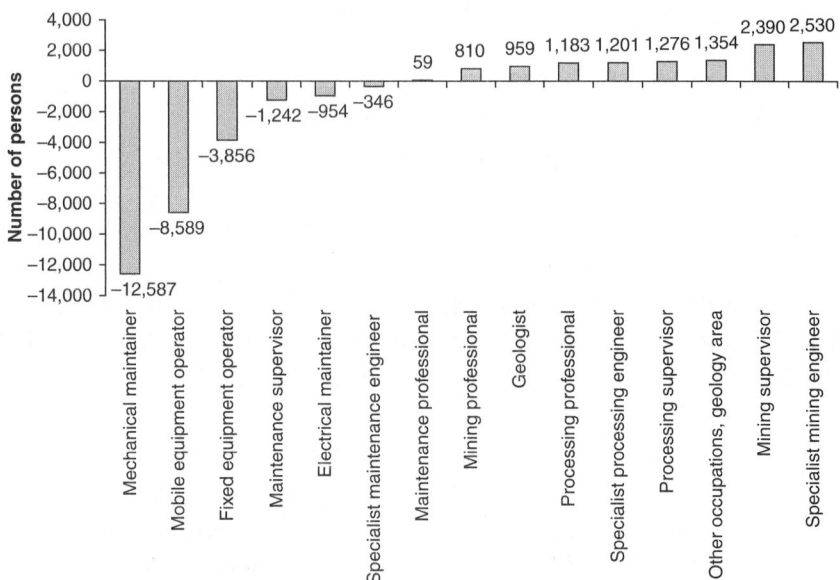

Source: Fundación Chile (2012).

Among its first measures, the mining council commissioned Fundación Chile (2012) to prepare a study, entitled *Workforce of the Chilean Mining Industry: Diagnosis and Recommendations 2011–2020*, to measure the shortages of human capital during this period. Fundación Chile played an important role in coordinating and acting as intermediary among the participants. The study was the starting point for dialogue in the sector, and setting up the Mining Skills Council (CCM) in 2012. The CCM is a private entity that—working in coordination with the ministries of labor, education, mining, and economy—has the task of creating the conditions for generating the quantity and quality of workers required through training and qualification opportunities.

The model is based on the Australian system and works through skills councils, including one for mining. The CCM is Chile's first skills council. Other economic sectors, such as construction, transport, the salmon industry, and agribusiness, are expected to replicate this experience. To meet the challenges facing the sector, the

CCM prepared the Qualifications Framework for Mining, which contains the training requirements for each profile, with qualification levels corresponding to technical training levels. The goal is to match training with the demands of the industry.

Aside from the strategic initiative of improving the quality and quantity of workers at the sectoral level, the case offers an interesting model for improving education and training for work, and thus the employability of graduates from training organizations and the productivity of firms in the sector. The case also demonstrates the importance of coordination and intermediation between the participating companies in a sector and the role that private sector players can have in overcoming the lack of coordination within the private sector.

Construction in Uruguay: A Promising Cofinancing Initiative

The construction sector accounts for 6.5 percent of GDP and 9 percent of formal jobs in the private sector in Uruguay. The number of workers formally employed in construction has tripled between 2004 and 2011. About 35 percent of workers are aged 24 years or under and 20 percent have entered the sector with no prior experience.

In 1997, employers and employees signed an agreement to set up a fund to train workers in the sector. Its functions include funding training actions and instruments and issuing industry certifications for the sector. In 2010, the training of workers, middle managers, technical staff, and construction officers was assigned high priority and a sectoral committee was set up in cooperation with the National Institute of Employment and Vocational Training. Sources of funding consist of private bipartite contributions (from employers and workers), and public funds from the Institute (from a payroll tax).

A pilot scheme was implemented in 2010, along with an investment plan for 2010–13, which calls for investments of $6 million and training of 5,000 new workers in the period. Courses and profiles were designed with the Work University of Uruguay and highly qualified national and international instructors were recruited. To date, no impact assessments have been conducted, so results are preliminary.

Volkswagen in Argentina: Dual Training in the Automotive Sector[12]

In Argentina, the Dual Training Plan is a mixed system of secondary technical education that works through agreements between companies and public schools. Students receive theoretical and practical training at the company, in direct contact with advanced technology, while at school they receive basic general education.

At Volkswagen, students receive training as automotive, electronic, and metalworking technicians. An example is the system in place since 2005 at the Pacheco Industrial Center, where cars are produced for the domestic market and for export. Students in Don Torcuato in Buenos Aires province, who are specializing in automotive studies at Technical Education School No. 4 (known as EET No. 4, for its initials in Spanish), complete their workshop training at the Volkswagen plant.

The teachers of workshop subjects are recruited, trained, and qualified by the company in the same way that Volkswagen trains its own human resources. In the in-plant training, section heads who have received teacher training act as tutor-guides. A coordinator and three teachers hired by the company give theoretical and practical classes. Teachers from EET No. 4 participate in training courses provided to company staff, and have access to sophisticated advanced technology training facilities. The technical training lasts three years. Students enter the third year of secondary education and attend the program throughout high school. A (still small) group of students is selected every year to receive full workshop training at Volkswagen. These students may come from any school, but if selected they transfer to EET No. 4.

Students attend workshops every morning at the company's training facilities. The students return to school in the afternoon to receive the general components, along with the other students who take part in the school workshop. Training in the plant is one day a week, rotating through 12 sections during the year.

Volkswagen also participates in and promotes training of other students at EET No. 4 by donating equipment and machines to the school, organizing plant visits, and inviting teachers to attend training courses for company employees. Although there have been no impact assessments, the program appears to be producing satisfactory results. Of the graduates from the Dual Plan, about two-thirds are employed by Volkswagen. The rest have gone on to university. Promotion rates of students training with the Dual Plan are 100 percent, while only about 15 percent of students who pursue technical studies in EET No. 4 graduate (although these students have different characteristics). According to the company, the program has been effective in integrating Dual Plan graduates into the plant in an optimal way.

In conclusion, sectoral initiatives are necessary but not sufficient to provide the economies of the region with the flow and stock of skills required in the medium term. Even if the various productive sectors of a country are organized to align training for work with the skills needed, the absence of a systemic national development program of continuous training for work limits the efficiency and effectiveness of these initiatives. The absence of a country-wide framework creates a low ceiling for human capital for productive development. This does not mean that countries like New Zealand, England, Norway, or Germany do not also have a varied range of successful sectoral cases. They do, and they are doubly successful simply because they are part of national systems of training for work. This successful combination goes hand in hand with a good business climate based on stability and clear regulations, along with a political economy aligned to the medium term.

Is the Region Ready to Accept the Challenge?

The analysis in this chapter clearly points to the need to establish a new order in the field of education and training for work in Latin America. It is necessary to create awareness that the process of human capital accumulation is continuous; the quality of each level facilitates or holds back future advances, and the entire process extends beyond the transition from school to workplace. In this context, the acquisition of skills and/or relevant capacities must be the central focus. This new order is the fundamental basis for improving the economic welfare and productive development of countries.

There is no single or best model of education and training for work anywhere in the world. Countries must identify their own strengths and weaknesses and build on the progress made. Embarking on poorly designed structural reforms may in the long run entail higher costs than those associated with the status quo. The prevailing short-term view largely explains the problem facing the region. Without sweeping reforms that strengthen the skills acquired by children and young people in school, while promoting the continuous updating of skills in the workforce, substantial and sustainable change will be difficult to achieve.

However, sectoral public policies that complement medium-term reforms can help close skill gaps in strategic sectors. In this respect, it is possible to combine short-term and long-term efforts in different dimensions. A strategy for developing a sectoral reform with short-term and medium-term impacts should promote both technical education and training for work. This strategy should identify, first, the problem of skills and the market failures (coordination, appropriation, information) underlying them. Next, it must assess institutional capacity, funding (who funds what and for whom), and quality assurance and relevance (monitoring and results measurement).

Undoubtedly, sectoral policies will have a greater impact if developed in the context of robust national frameworks, with clear long-term rules, and consistent promotion of skills as the engine for productive development. The national systems of training for work in turn will be more successful if they develop and strengthen certain fundamental capacities—including institutional and financial capabilities, quality assurance, and guarantees of the relevance of the training. Building these capacities will also encourage and promote the coexistence of a menu of cost-effective sectoral arrangements.

If policymakers in the region really want to stimulate the development of their countries in terms of human capital, they must begin the transformation as soon as possible—a transformation that begins by looking beyond the classroom to train the workforce. Without this fundamental change in the vision and understanding of education, the region will likely fall further behind.

6

Giving Credit to Productivity

Productivity and financial development go hand in hand. Unfortunately, credit is scarce, volatile, and expensive in Latin America and the Caribbean (IDB, 2004). Average credit to the private sector in the region, at about 40 percent of GDP, is much lower than the averages for the advanced economies (112 percent of GDP) and for East Asian developing countries (64 percent of GDP) (Figure 6.1).[1] A GDP-weighted average presents an even bleaker picture, with credit to the private sector at 33 percent of GDP in Latin America, compared to 156 percent for the advanced economies and 98 percent of GDP for developing East Asia. Given this lack of financial development, it is not surprising that productivity in the Latin American and Caribbean region is low.

If small credit markets resulted from low demand for investable funds because of limited investment opportunities, the financial sector would not be a bottleneck to economic development. Productive development policy could then focus on improving the structure of the real economy, by providing public inputs or altering private returns through market interventions, under the assumption that the financial resources would flow to the best projects and to the most productive firms and sectors. However, small credit markets in Latin American countries are also due to distortions and bottlenecks in the supply of credit—which in turn explains high and heterogeneous lending rates. At about 8 percent, the region's average real lending rates are much higher than those of most developing regions (only Sub-Saharan Africa has higher average lending rates).[2] High lending rates, which tend to be associated with credit rationing, cutting off supply at low levels of credit, are especially high for small firms (Figure 6.2). Beck, Levine, and Loayza (2000) suggest

Figure 6.1 Credit to the Private Sector, 2005–10 Average

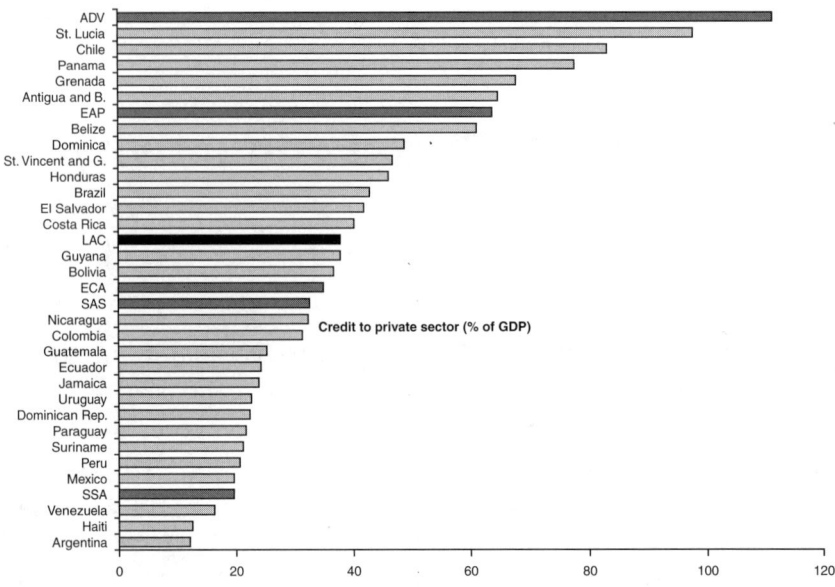

Note: ADV = Advanced Economies; EAP = East Asia and Pacific; LAC = Latin America and the Caribbean; ECA = Europe and Central Asia; SAS = South Asia; SSA = Sub-Saharan Africa.
Source: Authors' calculations based on data from Beck et al. (2012).

Figure 6.2 Interest Rates on Loans with Maturity Greater Than One Year, 2011–12 Average

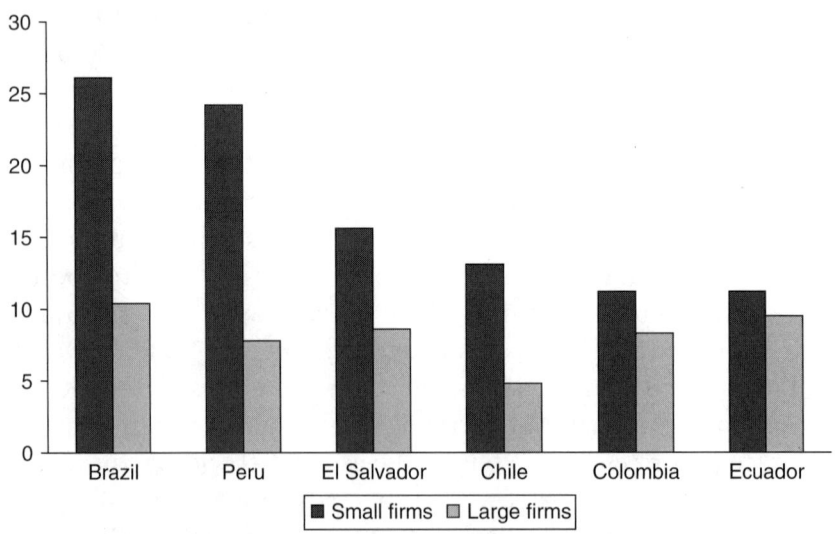

Source: Authors' calculations based on data from OECD/ECLAC (2012).

that an improvement in Latin America's financial depth to the levels prevailing in East Asia would have increased the region's annual average productivity growth by 1 percentage point, closing 60 percent of the gap between the two regions (Figure 6.3).[3]

To the extent that the financial sector is a bottleneck to development in the region, policies addressing it are key aspects of productive development policy. A deep financial system is crucial for new ventures to emerge and displace older, less productive firms, as well as for resources to be rapidly reallocated from less productive firms and sectors to more productive ones that may lack access to financial backing to grow. Schumpeter had this process of creative destruction in mind when he stated that the banker "is the ephor of the exchange economy" (Schumpeter, 1934: 74) PDPs reviewed in this report often require firms to have easy access to finance in order to take advantage of the investment opportunities opened up by those policies. Accordingly, financial development is also a vital complementary productive development policy. This chapter analyzes credit policies as PDPs, applying an analytical framework similar to the one used in previous chapters.[4]

Figure 6.3   Financial Depth and Productivity Growth

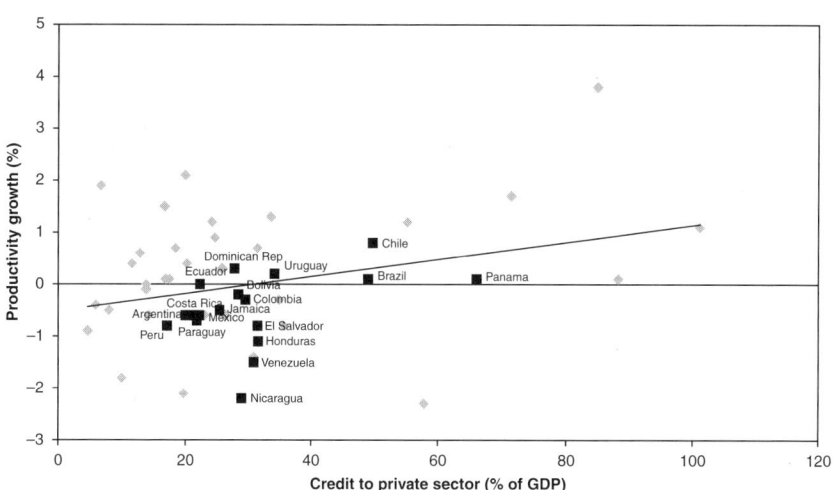

Note: Productivity and financial depth are measured over the 1965–2003 period for a cross-section of 51 developing and emerging markets.
Source: Authors' calculations based on data from Beck, Levine, and Loayza (2000).

Inadequate legislation and institutions that reduce the ability to post and enforce credit collateral and, more generally, weaken creditors' rights, are a fundamental cause of financial underdevelopment (IDB, 2004). While horizontal public inputs are not the focus of the report, it is clear that addressing government failures should be a priority. Nevertheless, information asymmetries and economic spillovers may lead to insufficient private lending even under an optimal legislative and regulatory framework, let alone under imperfect ones that resist reform. Therefore, besides trying to advance in institutional and legal reforms, financial policies may be needed to improve the performance of private credit markets. Furthermore, productive development may also benefit from utilizing state-owned development banks to fill gaps of the commercial credit system. This chapter focuses on these policy issues.

Market Failures and the Rationale for Intervention

A useful starting point for discussing the costs and benefits of possible areas of intervention is a simple analytical framework that highlights the main market failures that limit financial depth and stunt productive firms in Latin America (for a formal model, see Fernández-Arias and Panizza, 2014). Consider a set of firms that seek credit to implement projects and face a competitive credit market. For the sake of simplicity, assume that project returns are certain and known by all parties, so there are no concerns about uncertainty or information. However, limitations on contract enforcement prevent banks from recovering any amount that exceeds the collateral pledged by the firm, and possibly less due to poor legal enforcement.[5] In this simple setup, defaults are always due to loans beyond the legally pledgeable collateral. The lender will thus set the lending limit at a level at which the borrower always repays. In this extreme case, there are four reasons for curtailed lending levels or excessively high lending rates that may merit policy intervention: low pledgeable collateral; poor enforcement of creditors' rights; excessively high funding rates; and an inefficient banking system with high intermediation costs.

The first two reasons (collateral and enforcement) relate to the fact that if investors cannot commit to repay, lenders may lend too little because of concern that borrowers will decide they are better off by not repaying, after the project is realized. Commitment problems may be allayed by posting collateral and by strong creditors' rights to enforce the agreement. The legal ability to post and enforce collateral are thus necessary conditions for a well-functioning credit market.

The third reason (funding cost) relates to circumstances such as macroeconomic instability causing pervasive risk aversion and excessive risk premiums. In that case, funding rates of financial intermediaries (for example, bank deposit interest rates) may be much higher than the social opportunity cost of funds and drive up excessively high lending rates. This reason may justify policies that temporarily support credit during macroeconomic downturns or banking crises in order to avoid the unnecessary adjustment of viable firms due to lack of liquidity. As to the fourth reason, intermediation costs are inversely related to the efficiency of the banking system and to the availability of resources such as quality credit scoring technology and credit reporting systems or credit bureaus. As competitive banks pass on these costs to their customers, high intermediation costs result in a high lending rate and lower investment.

Thus, impediments to credit can exist even when firms have projects with known high returns. These reasons for intervention can be extended to a more realistic setting in which firms repay beyond the value of collateral if project return is high and they are interested in continuing to borrow, so that collateral is not the only factor affecting creditworthiness. In this more realistic case, uncertainty over returns and repayment prospects discourages risk-averse lenders and adds a fifth reason why lending may be unduly curtailed. Presumably the lender has inferior information about return prospects, which leads to a sixth reason for market failure associated with moral hazard and adverse selection that may justify policy intervention. In the presence of asymmetric information of this kind, credit will be rationed even in the presence of perfect enforcement of creditors' rights (Stiglitz and Weiss, 1981).[6]

The six rationales discussed above assume that project returns are the true measure of investment values. Since firms continue investing until the return of the marginal project in their portfolio is equal to the interest rate they face, policy intervention in these cases aimed to ensure that the interest rate remains undistorted—meaning that it reflects the true or social cost of lending. However, private returns are not a good measure of value if the project generates spillovers to other agents. In that case, policymakers ought to consider social returns, which may deviate from private returns. Therefore, a seventh reason for policy intervention has to do with the spillovers of private investments. Contrary to the previous rationales, this one does not reflect a problem in the financial system. If a given investment project generates positive spillovers, the social return of this project will be higher than its private return, and firms will underinvest—even in the presence of perfect capital markets.[7] Policies may target these spillovers, rendering socially profitable projects attractive from the point of view of individual investors by distorting credit markets (for example, by giving a subsidy) to align the private cost of capital with social return.[8]

Last but not least, in designing the optimal policy response to a given market failure, policymakers must navigate the various trade-offs between market and government failures. Take the case of direct lending by state-owned banks. On the one hand, state-owned banks can be a powerful tool for directing financial resources, bypassing undue obstacles that impede the market from making such allocations. On the other hand, public banks managed by incompetent or captured agents—let alone corrupt ones—can quickly turn into fiscal and economic disasters. Some of these issues are reviewed in the last section of this chapter.

Financial Policies as PDPs: How and Where to Intervene

Rule of law, strong creditors' rights, and macroeconomic stability are necessary conditions for a well-functioning financial market (Pagés, 2010). However, these enabling conditions are not sufficient to produce deep and efficient financial markets. The process of financial development to support productivity requires policies that are specifically designed to alleviate the market failures discussed in the previous section.

Public Inputs and Market Interventions

Public inputs that can improve productivity through better access to finance include setting transparent and enforceable ground rules for supervision and regulation of financial markets; lowering barriers to entry in financial markets; reducing asymmetries that distort the allocation of capital or lead to credit rationing; and establishing (or improving) the legal basis for credit bureaus, secured transactions, land registries, registries of moveable property, and bankruptcy laws.[9] As mentioned, the ability to pledge collateral is key.

Insolvency laws that do not establish clear priority rights or allow for quick restructuring of going concerns in the case of default amplify problems related to the lack of pledgeable collateral. Given time-consuming court procedures and high fixed administrative and legal costs, creditors are discouraged from lending, especially to small enterprises, because they know that the cost of collection can exceed the amount of the original loan plus interest. Unfortunately, reforms of bankruptcy laws to strengthen creditors' rights are often opposed by political actors who want to protect those who, paradoxically, are more likely to benefit from these reforms. They often argue against reforms by pointing to the case of a small business owner that could have her property seized by creditors. They seem to forget the additional financing that would be available to grow productive small firms and the additional firms that would be created by such a reform process. The idea that borrowers, and especially small and poor borrowers, can greatly benefit from strong creditors' rights is counterintuitive, and for that reason falls prey to populism.[10]

Market interventions are policies that attempt to counteract market failures by altering the market conditions under which financing can be obtained. Some of these policies are hybrid, blending public and private participation. Consider the case of contractual arrangements in which a third party guarantees the repayment of a specific loan to promote access to credit by constrained firms and sectors (for a survey, see OECD/ECLAC, 2012). Multilateral reciprocal guarantee schemes (MGSs) are cooperative arrangements in which certain partners (participating members) receive and offer guarantees, while other partners (sponsoring members) only offer guarantees. Although most of these guarantee schemes are fully private—for instance, out of the 24 MGSs that operate in Argentina, only one receives public funds (OECD/ECLAC, 2012)—MGSs often benefit from tax advantages aimed at providing incentives for the sponsoring members to participate. Other models utilize financial incentives (such as subsidized long-term loans by CORFO, Corporación de Fomento de la Producción, to Chilean MGSs) to promote ample coverage and horizontal development of MGSs. These interventions address market failures on three fronts. First, they allow borrowers to commit to repay (because the related party that guarantees the credit may be a large firm that has substantial leverage over the borrower). Second, they reduce information asymmetries (because the party that guarantees the credit has better information than the borrower because both parties have a long-term commercial relationship). Third, they increase the stock of information about creditworthiness because they allow previously credit-constrained firms to build credit histories.

Purely public credit guarantees can directly reach credit-constrained firms by reducing the lender's risk of repayment.[11] However, while credit guarantees relax credit constraints, they do not increase borrowers' willingness to repay. Such credit guarantees reallocate, but do not reduce, overall risk. As a consequence, borrowers will be able to borrow more, as intended, but the guarantee exposes the public agency to the risk of large losses. As guarantees are risky, either they need to be realistically priced or their intended subsidy component explicitly recognized.[12]

Alternatively, one way to induce financial institutions to reduce their lending rates without directly reducing the risk of the loan through guarantees is for second-tier development banks to provide cheap funding to commercial banks. However, lower lending rates applied to all firms across the board may fail to yield much additional productive lending. First, firms with full access to financing and investment returns already in line with the cost of capital would end up investing in projects with returns that are lower than the social costs of funds. Second, cheap funding may be insufficient to induce substantially more lending to firms that are perceived to be too risky by the private commercial banks that assume the full risk of the credit operation. This is why lending programs by second-tier banks are most effective when they come with conditions that direct the cheap funds toward projects with positive spillovers, which would turn profitable because of the lower cost of capital and lead to substantial new investment.

Both types of interventions, guarantees and funding, presumably have (implicit or explicit) fiscal costs if they are conducted at below-market prices.[13] To maximize the development effect of a given type of fiscal resource devoted to these policies, these interventions must be correctly matched to each type of distortion. Guarantees are better suited to tackling credit constraints, and are particularly efficient when private banks are excessively risk averse and the guarantor has superior enforcement capacity or information about collateral value. By contrast, cheap funding is ideal for targeting firms that generate positive spillovers but do not face tight credit constraints impeding borrowing, so that once the cost capital is low enough to match their private returns, investment will naturally follow at the appropriate scale.[14]

Why should subsidized lending be provided instead of grants, which would more transparently reflect the costly nature of the promotional policy? Consider, for instance, a firm that could invest $100 to finance a project with a social return of $6 and a private return of $5. Further assume that the going lending rate is 6 percent. While implementing the project would be socially optimal, the firm will not invest because the private return is lower than the interest rate. Subsidized lending at 5 percent would achieve the socially optimal level of investment. This, however, would be equivalent to letting the firm borrow at 6 percent and providing the firm with a $1 grant conditional on the firm making the investment. If the investment condition is enforceable, the latter policy has the advantage of being fully transparent.

Special Policies for Small Firms?

Small and medium enterprises (SMEs) absorb nearly 50 percent of formal employment in Latin America and the Caribbean (OECD/ECLAC, 2012), but often face precarious access to credit.[15] Given the pervasiveness of credit impediments to SMEs, it is not surprising that financial interventions often target SMEs, and that direct credit to SMEs has been a standard practice in many developing and advanced economies.[16] However, are these interventions justified on productivity grounds?

Some of the aforementioned market failures hurt SMEs more intensely and would thus justify special attention for SMEs. For example, the range of assets that can be effectively used as collateral is particularly important to equity-scarce SMEs. Collateral could be expanded by developing registries of movable assets that allow lenders to track what collateral has been pledged and on what terms (Pagés, 2010).[17] However, is there a case for special policies for SMEs beyond the generic market failure justifications reviewed above? The case is often made that SMEs deserve special treatment because fixed lending intermediation costs lead to higher lending rates as the size of the loan becomes smaller. As firms with more pledgeable collateral enjoy higher credit limits, the presence of fixed costs means larger firms or wealthier entrepreneurs can borrow at a lower rate, even if they are not more productive. However, the fact that SMEs face more problems accessing credit markets because of their scale does not necessarily justify SME-specific interventions. Aside from social objectives concerning this important segment of the economic structure, which are beyond the scope of this report, it is difficult to make a case for special policies for SMEs on productivity grounds based on an argument of diseconomies of scale. Higher intermediation cost per unit lent is a real cost associated with interacting with small firms, and a real cost to an economy based on small firms. Unavoidable financial intermediation costs are part of the productivity equation, and on this count artificially sustaining funding for small firms would simply be burdensome for the economy.

Furthermore, SMEs are on average less productive than large firms (Pagés, 2010), and therefore promotional policies that target SMEs may reduce overall productivity.[18] Presumably, small firms with high productivity will naturally experience rapid growth through retained earnings and reach a level of equity at which the credit constraint is no longer binding (Albuquerque and Hopenhayn, 2004). If unworthy firms cannot be screened out reliably, as high-productivity firms grow, special SME policies would end up sustaining economically unviable firms that fail to grow for the most part (Hallberg, 2000).[19] Chapter 4 discusses the prospects of venture capital to finance selected start-ups and new firms that this instrument may be able to screen. However, blanket easy credit to young firms, let alone to SMEs in general, would have a very large failure rate.

In that case, it would be better to abstain from helping SMEs with promotional credit and let the productive ones self-finance and grow at their own pace. Short of inaction, SME credit programs aimed at increasing productivity should have built-in mechanisms that prevent them from continuously supporting inefficient enterprises that are only viable in the presence of subsidies.[20]

However, it could be argued that institutional and structural factors linked to the region's poor business climate may lead to stunted firms trapped in a low-productivity state (Chrisney and Prats Oriol, 2012). In that case, policies that help these small firms evolve into more productive medium-sized enterprises could have a large positive effect on productivity growth.[21] Targeted interventions could be second best if the underlying impediments cannot be removed. Such an argument could apply to fledgling firms whose operations are in transition and not yet scalable. For example, Midrigan and Xu (2014) show that financial frictions can negatively impact productivity because they prevent credit-constrained entrepreneurs from entering the modern sector. They also show that financial frictions have little effect on the productivity of producers in the modern sector. However, it is not clear how relevant this case is in practice. Empirical findings for Colombia in Eslava and Haltiwanger (2012) suggest that for productive firms, being small is not an important constraint to growth.[22] Alternatively, a more fruitful policy approach may be to focus on new and young firms, as analyzed in detail in chapter 4, rather than small firms in general. Fledgling firms are more likely to be trapped in a credit constraint impeding their development to reach critical mass or even their emergence in the market.

From Theory to Practice

This section presents illustrative cases studies of policy interventions aimed at relaxing collateral constraints, offering credit guarantees, and combining financial and nonfinancial services.

Relaxing Constraints on Collateral through Factoring

One way to access credit beyond available collateral is to sell accounts receivable to a factoring company. Factoring is a type of supplier financing in which firms sell their accounts receivable at a discount and receive immediate cash. Factoring is not a loan and is often "without recourse," meaning that no additional liabilities appear on the firm's balance sheet, and the agent that purchases the receivables assumes the credit risk of these assets. Hence, factoring is a comprehensive financial service that includes credit protection, accounts receivable bookkeeping, collection services, and financing. One drawback is that in the presence of limited competition and uncertainty about the creditworthiness of a firm's accounts receivable, factoring operations may carry high implicit interest rates.[23]

A successful example of a policy that creates the legal and logistical framework to facilitate factoring services to SMEs by creating "chains" between large buyers, including the government, and small suppliers is Cadenas Productivas (Productive Chains), a program put in place by the Mexican state-owned development bank Nacional Financiera (NAFIN). By using receivables from large creditworthy buyers to obtain cash, small suppliers implicitly enlarge their collateral (they "borrow" collateral from large, creditworthy firms), and in this way can effectively reduce their credit risk. NAFIN provides the financial infrastructure for the program—a public input—thereby ensuring competition among the lenders enrolled in the program and giving national reach to regional banks. NAFIN also acts as a second-tier bank and refinances the participating financial institutions. Furthermore, NAFIN encourages the participation of large buyers in the program and provides training for SMEs enrolled in it.[24] Importantly, Cadenas Productivas required critical public inputs of supporting laws that allow secure and legally binding factoring transactions, including electronic factoring.[25]

Cadenas Productivas relaxes credit constraints for small suppliers because risk is linked to well-known large buyers, instead of suppliers with little collateral and credit history. Furthermore, the electronic platform reduces the fixed costs of providing credit to SMEs and transaction costs by eliminating collection costs. This works to the advantage of suppliers, which obtain working capital financing at favorable interest rates and instant liquidity against previously illiquid receivables.[26] All parties benefit from increased efficiency, not only suppliers. The program benefits large buyers by reducing their administrative and processing costs (because the lender settles their accounts payable) and by allowing entry of new suppliers, thereby potentially lowering the price or increasing the quality of goods they purchase. Finally, the program allows lenders to make new clients without increasing risk-taking and uses the information acquired through the factoring operations to market new financial products.

As of December 2012, Cadenas Productivas covered 550 large buyers, more than 100,000 small and medium firms, and more than 50 domestic lenders. Since the inception of the program in September 2001, NAFIN has brokered more than 17 million transactions, amounting to more than $131 billion in financing. One advantage of Cadenas Productivas is that it targets firms that, by supplying large international producers, have passed many market tests and thus proved to be competitive. In a sense, the large buyer plays the role of identifying productive firms, providing a screening service, and Cadenas Productivas relaxes the financing constraints for these selected firms.

Offering Credit Guarantees

Credit guarantees are another instrument to relax credit constraints. Providing a partial guarantee reduces the financial institution's risk of lending. This allows credit-constrained firms to obtain more credit, effectively expanding collateral. Partial credit guarantees may have additional benefits. For example, by increasing the number of firms with access to credit, a credit guarantee program creates credit histories and also expands the available information for lenders to estimate and assess firms' ability and willingness to pay. With the expanded number and diversity of firms with access to credit, more accurate credit scores can be developed.

Using average rates for Latin America, for every dollar publicly guaranteed, a credit guarantee program generates $7.3 of credit (the effective leverage rate) to their target markets. However, these guarantee schemes generate contingent public liabilities, whose size depends on how the program design establishes incentives for prudent risk analysis for guaranteed loans. If realistic contingent liabilities are not made explicit, free credit guarantees may look cheap but lead to sizable fiscal losses.

It is crucial that the financial terms offered create the incentive for participating financial intermediaries to avoid offering overly risky loans. Perhaps the most significant incentive is the fraction of the loan obligation being guaranteed, or the rate of coverage of the guarantee. The lower the coverage, the greater the financial risk assumed by the financial intermediary—and thus the greater the incentive for safe loans. However, if the coverage rate is low, the incentive for financial intermediaries to lend to enterprises facing the greatest credit shortage is also reduced. Therefore, when setting the coverage rate and pricing the guarantee, policymakers should strike a balance between the goal of credit additionality (effectiveness) and financial sustainability.[27] The risk of the guarantee should be realistically assessed. The price of the guarantee may be concessional, as long as the implied subsidy is clearly identified and funded.

A program in Chile, FOGAPE (Fondo de Garantía para el Pequeño Empresario), administered by Banco Estado (a state-owned commercial bank), offers an innovative way to balance these goals and achieve increased market participation.[28] Rather than setting a fixed coverage rate and guarantee fee, these parameters are flexible. First, access to guarantees is auctioned in such a way that financial institutions bidding lower coverage levels obtain larger quotas of guaranteed amounts. This creates market incentives to reduce coverage rates, but in line with loan demand. Banks with the greatest demand, presumably based on more profitable projects, will be willing to accept lower coverage. Moreover, to ensure that the resulting risks are internalized, the guarantee fee is determined in such a way as to create market incentives for the conduct of prudent credit analysis and selection of creditworthy firms in the loan portfolio. When the past due rate of the portfolio of a financial institution exceeds an established ceiling, the guarantee fee on its whole portfolio is increased in line with the deterioration of the portfolio's quality. These mechanisms have contributed to the success of the FOGAPE scheme in terms of not only strong and sound financial performance but also high levels of credit additionality and firm performance.[29] Also, it has proven to be effective in maintaining access to financing during periods of external shock. During the period ranging from the end of 2008 to the end of 2010, the value of guaranteed loans in Chile increased fivefold and the number of beneficiary firms tripled (de Olloqui, 2013).

Combining Credit with Nonfinancial Services

Credit programs are sometimes needed to complement nonfinancial services (NFS) to address market failures (López-Acevedo and Tan, 2011). For example, clusters and value chains represent forms of industrial organization in which financial services may also usefully accompany the provision of NFS. In particular, traditional firm-based credit analysis may fail to capture the synergies of financing entire cluster operations. A proper analysis of a cluster and its firms demands a full understanding of the market, the interrelation with suppliers and clients, production and market cycles, the relevance of a firm within a chain, its associative capacity, and related factors. This is costly information. Public policies to ensure cluster financing imply additional evaluation of credit; the cost of this extra evaluation may need to be defrayed.

A good example of this type of public intervention is the productive development program in San Juan province in Argentina. It includes financing, as well as technical assistance components, totaling $53 million to support 11 identified value chains. These value chains represented 76 percent of the province's exports and 32 percent of the local economy as of 2007. The program was coordinated by Agencia San Juan de Desarrollo de Inversiones, an agency created specifically to facilitate the public-private linkages needed to alleviate the market failures that had prevented the financing of productive investments (IDB, 2011). Financing was funded through the Central Bank of Argentina, operating as a second tier-institution providing medium- and long-term financing. The funds were auctioned among private and public banks through a transparent process. Beneficiaries of the program increased sales by 69 percent and exports by 29 percent, compared to firms in the province that did not participate in the program.

Technology loans offer another example. Because they may lack technical expertise, banks may be unable to evaluate investment projects by firms interested in improving their technology. In these cases, banks can delegate the task of carrying out the analysis of the technological risk surrounding such projects to public agencies (Rivas et al., 2012). Examples are the partnership between agencies of innovation promotion and banks in Argentina and Colombia. The challenge for public policy is to make sure that these services are structured so as to support the financial intermediary's need to learn about the firm's repayment capacity.

A New Generation of Public Development Banks

Public development banks appear to be natural instruments for conducting both horizontal and vertical market intervention based on either lending or guarantees. Depending on the circumstances, the development bank may choose to deal directly with the beneficiary (first tier) or indirectly through a private financial intermediary, which on-lends to the beneficiary (second tier). In all cases, a development bank that aims to promote more financing must grant financial enticements or advantages to ease market financial conditions and make lending to the productive sector more attractive.[30]

The enticements provided by development banks need not lead to visible fiscal costs, depending on their size and budget accounting, but they always have a fiscal opportunity cost and in that sense are subsidies. In its mildest form, the subsidy may consist of passing on funds raised at regular public funding rates. Normally, the government is able to raise funds cheaply because the sovereign power carries a strong balance sheet. The government also has a natural advantage over the private sector in its ability to spread risk across space and time (Arrow and Lind, 1970), which provides a clear rationale for the provision of guarantees (Anginer, de la Torre, and Ize, 2011). Nevertheless, in both cases, cheap public financial support entails renouncing the revenue from lending at a profit or from charging the insurance premium the market would bear—a fiscal (opportunity) cost. The natural financial advantages of the public sector in relation to development bank activities are maximized during cyclical macroeconomic downturns, when development banks often expand to protect production as private banks retract. In stronger forms, the subsidy entails an actual transfer of resources from the Treasury to cover below-market financing terms. This transfer may be implicit, as in funding rates below public debt yields. Brazil's development bank, BNDES, is a case in point of implicitly subsidized funding put to the service of massive long-term lending at below-market rates.

The bottom line is that as a PDP instrument, development banks are a mixed bag. They are potentially key instruments for financial productive development policy because they are in a position to implement market interventions with enticements or subsidies. But at the same time, they are risky instruments precisely because they offer subsidies—meaning, valuable financial benefits given for free—and they can leverage these subsidies at the risk of creating contingent liabilities. If a development bank lacks the right institutional capabilities, it may fall prey to private capture and political abuse, leading to unsound operations and unjustified fiscal costs. In fact, development banks have a controversial, checkered record in the region—which serves as a reminder of the risks entailed and, hopefully, a source of lessons.

Some history is in order. As discussed in chapter 1, in the 1960s and 1970s there was strong intellectual support for government intervention in the banking sector and direct state ownership of banks. The "development view" of public banks recognized that in poor countries with incipient financial markets, interest rates can be inefficiently high because private banks may have monopoly power or may not internalize the value of strategic investments.[31] The idea that state-owned banks can promote economic development came under attack in the 1980s and 1990s, when the "political view" replaced the development view of state-owned banks. This change in views led to a wave of rapid privatization. Average state ownership of banks went from 46 percent of total bank assets in 1970 to about 30 percent in the mid-1990s and reached 15 percent in 2010 (Figure 6.4). In Latin America and the Caribbean, state ownership of banks plunged from nearly 70 percent of total bank assets in the 1970s to about 30 percent in the mid-1990s, and reached a trough of 15 percent at the beginning of the new millennium, when Latin American state-owned banks started becoming more active (de Olloqui, 2013).[32]

The situation in the region now contrasts with that of the 1970s. The typical Latin American development bank now enjoys good capitalization levels and prudent risk management, and is unlikely to become a fiscal burden (de Olloqui, 2013). This kind of financial performance demonstrates that these institutions can be managed soundly to achieve set financial targets. Some development banks can count on a strong and technically competent bureaucracy that allows them to be effective agents of their governments and follow

Figure 6.4 Government Ownership of Banks

a. All Countries

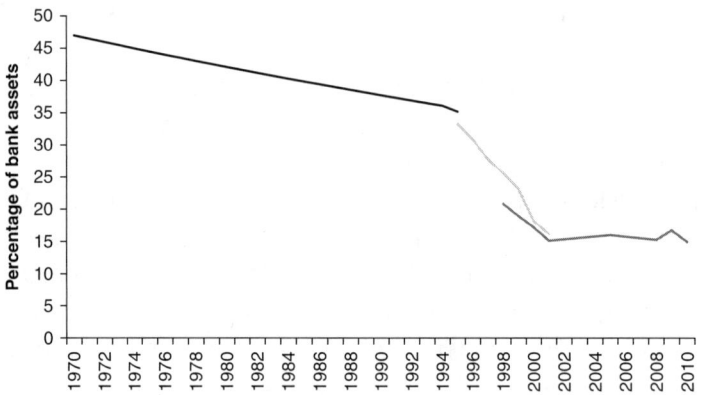

b. Advanced Economies

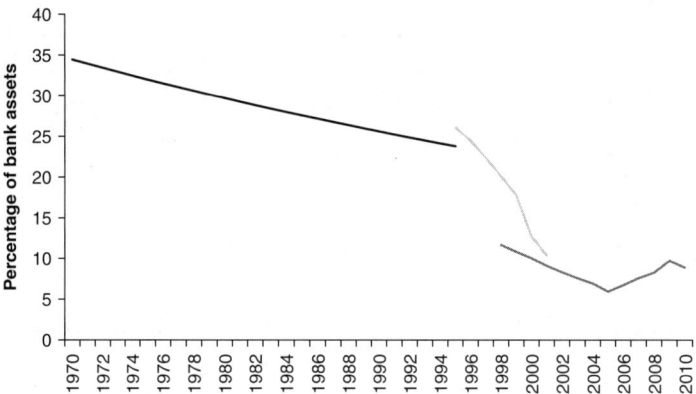

c. Latin America and the Caribbean

d. Other Developing Countries

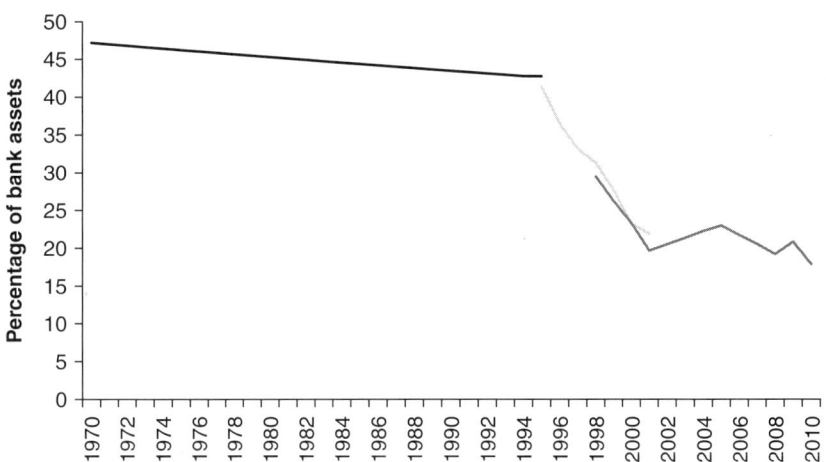

Note: Data covering select years between 1998 and 2010 are available from Barth, Caprio, and Levine (2013).
Source: Data for 1970 and 1995 are from La Porta, López-de-Silanes, and Shleifer (2002). Data for the 1995–2001 period are from Micco, Panizza, and Yañez (2007).

the mandate set by their principals, actively targeting sectors in accordance with the development priorities defined by the national government while avoiding undue political pressure.[33] BNDES, for instance, was built as a silo of bureaucratic efficiency (Colby, 2013). Selective hiring criteria and the fact that most employees spend their entire career within the Bank generate an *esprit de corps* and strong incentives to resist outside pressures.[34] Bank staff have the ability to reject individual loans and have at their disposal procedures to defend technical and financial soundness.[35]

To some extent, the backlash against development banks threw out the baby with the bathwater. The development and political views of state-owned banks are not necessarily incompatible (Levy Yeyati, Micco, and Panizza, 2007). While in many countries the expansion of the private credit system has rendered inapplicable some of the traditional rationales for development banks, modern productive development policy may involve new roles. A constructive reform agenda would work on building the institutional capabilities required to reduce political economy distortions, rather than discarding an instrument that may be well suited to address financial market failures and support strategic policies (de Olloqui, 2013).

While the stronger operational capabilities available today are not necessarily a guarantee of good programs, the viability of sound institutional capabilities is enough reason to rethink the roles of development banks to put them to the best use.

For starters, the dismissal of development banks was and is partly based on the incorrect premise that state-owned banks can be evaluated on the basis of their financial returns like commercial banks, and that fiscal costs necessarily indicate weak or misguided management. Certainly, excessive operational costs and poor management are bad and tend to be reflected in losses. But, as discussed, development banks cannot be too useful without subsidies of one kind or another. For development banks to make profits would amount to leaving unused subsidies that could support their mandate. The misconception that a good development bank makes profits continues to this day in many quarters and arguably hamstrings the potential of these development agencies. The result for development banks that are set up under this wrong premise is repressed scope of action in order to do without fiscal costs as well as hidden or covered losses to appear that way (for example, subsidized funding that is not transparently recognized as a fiscal cost). In practice, many development banks seem to be more concerned with showing financial strength than with their development mandate; in the extreme, this may make these banks sustainable from a financial point of view, but not as useful from a development perspective.[36,37]

A good development bank uses well the subsidy it receives to further its development objectives. Subsidy transparency, properly recorded in the government's budget, is key. Hidden subsidies distort policy justification and may lead to a corrupt system. Implicit subsidies (for instance, access to cheap financing) should be made explicit. Ideally, the subsidy would be approved through the budgetary process and be subjected to the same parliamentary scrutiny as other types of public expenditures. A bank that creates contingent liabilities oversteps its authority to spend. Cumulative contingent liabilities often lead to disastrous fiscal shocks (similar to those resulting from private bank bailouts in times of crisis in systems whose financial risk is not well regulated). Bank regulation and supervision can avoid contingent liabilities by making sure that banks properly evaluate and report the risks they take. In this sense, there is nothing special about state-owned banks.[38] As long as the subsidy is transparent and state-owned banks are properly regulated, supervised, and audited, the risk of contingent liabilities arising from state-owned banks should be similar to that from private banks.

In summary, an effective development bank would fulfill its development mandate to its maximum extent within the subsidy envelope authorized, and therefore needs specific appropriate metrics to assess performance. Like commercial banks, it should operate efficiently minimizing operational costs. But unlike commercial banks, it should not strive to maximize revenue but, rather, maximize development impact. Therefore, profit is not the measure of success; assessing development banks requires complex performance evaluation. First and foremost, evaluation needs to detect evidence of capture, such as directing loans to favorites.[39] But it also needs to detect lack of focus or effort in pursuing operations with high development impact, such as "easy" lending to creditworthy firms that are sound but do not need much support. Development banks are supported by subsidies not to fish in a fishbowl but in the wild seas. Performance evaluation of development banks is therefore complex because it involves non-financial metrics and strong institutional capabilities to apply them with skill and independence. Similar complexities go for the special governance needed for their goals, which is beyond the scope of this report (for a discussion, see Rudolph, 2009 and de Olloqui, 2013).

Recent evidence suggests that development banks supported by larger subsidies and tasked with more ambitious mandates could contribute more. Eslava, Maffioli, and Meléndez (2012a, b) find that the lending activity of BANCOLDEX in Colombia has a positive impact on exports, production, and productivity, and that firms that benefit from BANCOLDEX lending programs are able to borrow more and at better terms from other sources. Also, there seems to be a demonstration effect, and firms that access BANCOLDEX credit are able to start credit relationships with a larger number of intermediaries. This suggests that BANCOLDEX could go further with more financial muscle than its ordinary public sector funding. Similarly, other successful banks such as NAFIN could do more with a larger subsidy allocation and a mandate to take advantage of it, rather than return it as profit. Coelho and de Negri (2011) show that credit lines managed by BNDES and FINEP (the Brazilian agency for innovation) have had a mixed impact.[40] These mixed findings are consistent with those of Colby (2013), who argues that when BNDES acts as the primary supplier of long-term credit, it places limited importance on spillovers. Thus, there may be room for improvement within existing development banks along the lines of the PDPs favored in this report, rooted in addressing market failures and giving priority to spillover effects.

First-Tier and Second-Tier Development Banks

Development banks can operate as first-tier institutions, as second-tier institutions, or as dual institutions that operate both as first-tier and second-tier banks.[41] When many of them were founded, private credit markets were underdeveloped, and they tended to fill a gap with first-tier operations. As private banking systems developed, the role of development banks became less clear-cut, and the question of whether they help or hurt financial development became critical. In this context, skepticism grew concerning the traditional roles of development banks in general and first-tier banks in particular. For example, the massive nature of BNDES's participation at below-market terms in the lending market has sparked criticism that its activity stunts the development of credit markets (see, for example, OECD, 2013b), especially because a substantial share of BNDES lending goes to large corporations that could have access to market funding.[42] The alternative view is that if BNDES reduced its first-tier long-term lending, the Brazilian private banking system would not be prepared to fill the gap and productive investment would suffer (or borrowing abroad would create balance-of-payments risks). This issue of the potentially negative effects of first-tier development banks on financial development is beyond the scope of analysis of this report. Nevertheless, clearly a second-tier modality would be an attractive alternative if first-tier development banks cannot be constrained to supplement the reach of commercial banks and crowd them out.

At the end of the 1990s, second-tier development banks were considered more efficient and less risky than first-tier development banks. As a consequence, many Latin American first-tier development banks were transformed into second-tier institutions in order to sever their links with beneficiary firms (de Olloqui, 2013).[43] As they were in direct contact with beneficiaries, first-tier banks were more exposed to arbitrary lending and attendant financial risks, and therefore mounting fiscal contingent liabilities. Second-tier institutions can be more efficient than first-tier development banks because they leverage the resources, and credit screening capacity, local knowledge, and distribution network of private financial institutions.[44] They are safer because the intermediary banks, which are creditworthy institutions, keep the underlying loans on their own balance sheets.

However, second-tier development banks have their own limitations. By relinquishing full control of the credit allocation process, they let private banks—whose profit motivation may be at odds with the objectives of development banks—make credit decisions. Consequently, private banks may fail to channel public resources to support investments with high social returns, and perhaps lend to projects with high private returns that they would have financed anyway—thus rendering lending programs ineffective. They may even fail to pass on subsidies to borrowers if funds are not subject to competition through auction mechanisms of some kind, which adds an additional level of complexity. The performance of a second-tier development bank is maximized when the development bank can closely monitor the performance of its agent (the intermediary private bank). For this purpose, second-tier lending programs include guidelines that condition credit allocation in order to target certain classes of final borrowers, as well as procedures for allocating financing with the aim that any subsidy is passed on to the final borrowers.[45] It is unclear how tight these controls can be made to align the incentives of all parties, in terms of being able to contractually stipulate the conditions for loan allocation and pricing as well as to enforce them.

More research is needed at the country level to properly evaluate the relative advantages of these different institutional setups under current conditions. Lately, there has been a change in views, and some policymakers now believe that second-tier institutions are lacking substantially in terms of development impact. Some second-tier banks with solid financial footing have begun to change their operational mode in order to reach more beneficiaries, allowing or strengthening first-tier operations (de Olloqui, 2013).[46] First-tier lending, which had contracted by 0.3 percent from 2000 to 2005, expanded more rapidly than second-tier lending from 2005 to 2010 (21.5 percent versus 17 percent) (de Olloqui, 2013, Table 1.8).

It is also possible to think of hybrid institutions that mix first-tier and second-tier characteristics. For example, first-tier development banks could establish institutional arrangements addressing some of the political and managerial failures that have plagued them in the past by subcontracting part of the credit process to a commercial bank (such as credit analysis and administration), thereby benefiting from the commercial bank's distribution platform and analytical capacity, in exchange for a commission. At the same time, the development bank would control loan eligibility and assume the financial risk.[47] In an interesting example of this sort, the Spanish development bank, Instituto de Crédito Oficial (ICO), channels first-tier lending through the branch network of commercial banks without being charged any commission. Commercial banks are willing to provide this service for free because they can sell complementary services to ICO's first-tier customers (Gutiérrez et al., 2011). The Mexican development bank NAFIN is at the forefront in developing innovative hybrid credit guarantee schemes with both first- and second-tier components. For example, it is developing a first-tier credit guarantee system in which it preapproves a total or partial guarantee for firms that satisfy certain requirements and then let firms use this guarantee to shop around different commercial banks for the best possible credit conditions (*garantía engrapada*). This process will be complemented by the development of regional funds aimed at evaluating firms that can obtain such guarantees.

Problems related to poor risk evaluation and political lending could be attenuated by requiring first-tier development banks to enter into suitable cofinancing arrangements with private banks to introduce the market test into allocation and pricing decisions, thus controlling contingent liabilities. Alternatively, they could be required to sell their loans to private banks after a prespecified period of incubation. This will generate incentives to carefully select these loans (good loans will increase in value with time) and, by exonerating the bank from the onerous task of collecting loans or enforcing collateral, also exploit the superior credit enforcement ability of the private sector. (In certain institutional environments, public banks may face political obstacles in collecting loans and enforcing collateral.)

The time is ripe for rethinking the modalities for development bank operations.

A New Role for Development Banks: Economic Intelligence

Arguably, if the government has good knowledge of the market failures that need to be addressed by a development bank, a second-tier institution with strong procedures for allocating funds would be superior to a first-tier development bank if detailed first-tier lending guidelines describing the rules for lending to address the market failures can be specified and enforced.[48] Things can be different in the presence of uncertainty concerning the precise nature of the market gaps that need to be addressed. Sufficiently precise lending guidelines may be impossible to specify before acquiring the knowledge of social returns that accrues only from direct contact with real projects of the kind that first-tier development banks have (Fernández-Arias, Hausmann, and Panizza, 2013).

In this context, Fernández-Arias, Hausmann, and Panizza (2013) go one step further and suggest that development banks may play another useful role because they can actively exploit complementarities between lending and the design of PDPs. Specifically, rather than assuming that the government has a list of market failures and uses development banks to treat them, the development bank could assume the job of identifying these market failures and using its knowledge to propose possible policy solutions. First-tier development banks, as opposed to second-tier ones, would be in a better position to exploit these complementarities because they are in closer contact with firms and thus, in principle, better suited to collect information on market gaps.[49]

This intelligence role of development banks is similar to the role that modern theories of financial intermediation assign to banks as institutions with a comparative advantage in producing and processing information (Leland and Pyle, 1977; Fama, 1985). However, while private banks focus on information on private returns, development banks would potentially produce and organize information about social returns. For this reason, private intermediaries in second-tier systems could not be successfully instructed to do this public interest service. Through their loan screening and lending activities, first-tier development banks could gather information such as what type of goods and services existing firms need in order to develop a viable national industry; what the undue bottlenecks are in a given sector; which sectors could benefit from the experiences already acquired in other sectors; and which economic sectors can generate positive spillovers. If banks can learn by lending, or more generally, by screening loan applications, development banks can become an instrument for formulating public policies aimed at promoting productive development (and not only executing those policies). [50]

The interviews summarized in Fernández-Arias, Hausmann, and Panizza (2013) show that several development banks implicitly play the intelligence role described in Box 6.1. Some of these banks (such as BNDES and the German development bank KfW) have well-established mechanisms and channels for providing policy advice to their national governments (see Box 6.2).

Box 6.1 Development Banks as Agents of Economic Intelligence: The Opinion of Bank Managers

Bank managers from 16 development banks interviewed by Fernández-Arias, Hausmann, and Panizza (2013) almost unanimously agreed that development banks can be an ideal tool for providing economic intelligence. They cited two main reasons. Not only do development banks have the capacity to generate information, but they have qualified personnel with well-remunerated jobs and meritocratic career paths that are often independent from the political cycle. Only one bank manager expressed the view that it is not desirable to mix lending with policy advice. He feared that close interaction with the government would bring more costs than benefits, as it would limit the independence of bank managers, push the bank toward politicized lending, and ultimately lead to large losses for the bank.

When asked about possible trade-offs between first- and second-tier development banks, most bank managers identified greater efficiency and less political pressure as the main benefits of operating as a second-tier institution. However, all but one respondent stated that second-tier development banks have an information disadvantage with respect to first-tier banks.

Box 6.2 The Cases of BNDES (Brazil) and KfW (Germany)

Two banks (BNDES and KfW) interviewed for this report said their institutions have a structured system for collecting and analyzing information and providing inputs to the design of economic policies.

BNDES: BNDES is primarily a first-tier bank. It gathers economic intelligence by favoring a continuous exchange of information between project managers in the operational departments and the Bank's research department. BNDES has four operational sectors that target different segments of the Brazilian economy (industry, infrastructure, trade and services, and agriculture). Each operational sector has its own small research group that gathers information from project managers and feeds it to the Bank's main research department, which aggregates all information flows and disseminates them to the rest of the Bank. Economists are also encouraged to conduct research projects and submit research notes or papers to an internal refereed journal, called *BNDES Sectorial*.

To facilitate this exchange of information, BNDES uses a uniform methodology to evaluate sector-specific firm capabilities and intangible assets. Developing such a methodology required a large initial investment in research capacity, but affords BNDES a common language and methodological approach for evaluating different firms and activities and quantifying the challenges faced by different sectors of the Brazilian economy.

BNDES uses this internal intelligence to design and adjust its strategy, with the ultimate objective of achieving its government-defined mandate. Besides having considerable autonomy in deciding how to implement and shape its development mandate, BNDES plays an important role in defining the mandate and the government's overall development policy. Ideas originated in the research department of BNDES have set the economic agenda of several presidents and become the main drivers of Brazil's productive development policy. The most prominent examples of the intellectual leadership of BNDES are the Plano de Metas implemented by President Kubitschek in the second half of the 1950s, and the Plano Nacional de Desestatizacao of 1990–97 (Colby, 2013). More recently, the Productive Development Policy (PDP) program implemented by President Lula led BNDES to work closely with the high-tech sector and allowed the Bank to gain a better understanding of what niches are well suited for Brazilian firms. This, in turn, allowed the Bank to fine-tune its lending strategy and provide the government with inputs for implementing the PDP program. Along similar lines, BNDES provided key inputs for the design of Plano Brasil Mayor (PBM) implemented by President Dilma Rousseff.

BNDES has both formal and informal channels for communicating with the government. As BNDES staff members have a good reputation in Brazil, government officers often informally seek staff opinions and views on a wide variety of policy and technical issues. At the formal level, BNDES management has seats on various ministerial-level committees that provide inputs to the design of Brazilian economic policy. Specifically, in Brazil productive development policy is organized along 19 sectors (and multiple themes); BNDES has representatives in each of the 19 competitiveness committees in charge of designing sector-specific policies. Six out of nineteen of these committees are chaired and coordinated by BNDES staff.

KfW: Unlike BNDES, KfW operates only as a second-tier bank. While lack of direct contact with the ultimate borrower leads to some loss of information, KfW has a close relationship with its first-tier agents and can collect data on all the German SMEs that have accounts with first-tier banks that receive KfW second-tier funding. This data set covers more than 100,000 SMEs. In addition to standard indicators on capacity to pay, it includes information for forecasting future production and evaluating some of the constraints faced by German SMEs. One of KfW's priorities is the promotion of green economy. This is a field in which the Bank has a vast amount of information because KfW is the main market-maker in emission trading in Germany.

KfW uses survey data to guide its own lending strategy, to provide advice to German policymakers, and to produce (in cooperation with various German think tanks) periodic reports on different sectors of the German economy. While KfW's research activity was originally fully financed with the Bank's general budget, research now generates a substantial amount of its own resources because KfW sells a large number of indicators and analyses to the German government and Eurostat.

KfW provides inputs to the design and implementation of federal and regional economic policy in Germany by supporting government officials who conduct bilateral negotiations with the private sector and by participating in advisory meetings with the Ministry of Finance and the regional governments.

7

More Than the Sum of Its Parts: Cluster-Based Policies

In a market economy, firms constantly interact in a variety of market transactions with other firms and organizations. They buy and sell goods and services as well as production factors in markets where prices convey essential information. In the course of doing business, they forge linkages that may yield important benefits to themselves, other firms, the economy, and even society at large.[1] These benefits may include reducing information asymmetries, generating knowledge spillovers, strengthening economies of scale, and facilitating the generation of public goods. However, these linkages do not occur at random; firms located in a given geographic area or within a specific value chain or cluster are more likely to interact. And even within these geographic and production neighborhoods, linkages are not automatic and may lack the depth to reap all the benefits.

Despite the obvious potential benefits, coordination cannot be taken for granted, and in many cases market incentives actually inhibit coordination. As a result, the industry may underperform from a social point of view, encouraging the government to intervene to help these latent linkages materialize. Public policies and programs can strengthen coordination among firms that are in the same geographic area or value chain while internalizing spillovers and facilitating the production of public inputs. This chapter addresses the logic, evidence, and lessons learned from cluster development programs (CDPs) and related programs, which are increasingly widespread in both developed and developing countries.

These programs vary in form and name from country to country, but for purposes of clarity they may be classified in two major categories:[2]

1. *CDPs*, in a strict sense, typically focus on subnational areas where firms in specialized productive activities, often identified as *industry clusters*, tend to agglomerate. Their challenge is to remove or compensate for the obstacles to firm coordination within these areas in order to guarantee provision of the public inputs needed for production and to help internalize within the cluster the knowledge spillovers required for product and process upgrading. In the extreme, programs may also induce the formation of clusters by providing a tailor-made environment in which firms cooperate and capitalize their synergies, as in industrial or technology parks.
2. *Value chain programs*, where linkages among firms tend to be both vertical and horizontal, and firms perform various functions along various segments of the chain. Conflict and cooperation among firms typically emerge, for example, over the price buyers pay suppliers or over the setting and fulfillment of common quality and sanitary standards. Value chain programs—also briefly discussed in chapter 8 on internationalization with regard to global value chains—share some similarities with CDPs; however, they also differ remarkably because of the marked governance and power asymmetries that often prevail when large buyers and lead firms work together with a large group of small-size suppliers or customers (Pietrobelli and Staritz, 2013).

Why Public Policies Make Sense for Interlinked Firms

Firms tend to colocate in a given geographic area. Many forces of attraction can induce colocation, the most obvious one being natural resources. Thus, steel plants tend to locate near iron mines and pulp mills gravitate to forest regions. Sometimes colocation is inspired by transport costs; this explains why some industries that produce consumer goods set up shop near large urban areas. Other motivations for colocation or agglomeration, such as externalities, are more subtle, yet are equally relevant for productive development (Marshall, 1920; Ellison, Glaeser, and Kerr, 2010; Moretti, 2012).

First, agglomeration may occur in areas where skilled workers trained in a specific field are available (Becattini, 1989). Because in thick labor markets it is easier to match workers with employers, firms and workers joining a cluster enjoy direct benefits in terms of productivity and higher earnings, but they also generate a benefit for other firms and workers in the cluster, which are made more productive by the new entrants (Giuliani, Pietrobelli, and Rabellotti, 2005). This externality is a market failure that may require government intervention.

Similarly, firms may flock around specialized service providers that are important for a particular activity, such as advertising, legal support, technical and management consultancy, shipping, and repair and engineering support. These services let firms focus on what they are good at, without having to worry about secondary functions. For providers of these specialized services, being close to their clients helps them assess what they need and demonstrate how they can help. Thus, specialized providers locate in the cluster because their clients are there, and their clients are there because their specialized providers are also there (Schmitz, 1995).[3]

Third, new ideas rarely emerge in a vacuum; they most likely result from social interaction among skilled workers. The empirical evidence on patenting suggests that innovators are significantly more likely to cite other innovators living nearby than innovators living farther away (Jaffe, Trajtenberg, and Henderson, 1993). Innovators are more familiar with the knowledge produced by those who work near them, presumably because they share ideas and information through informal conversations and interactions. Thus, firms willing to innovate have an incentive to locate near other innovative firms because this improves the creativity of their own employees and makes them more productive (Feldman and

Audretsch, 1999; Glaeser, 2010). Localized knowledge spillovers are another source of market failure that might require government intervention.

Similar market failures occur along a value chain. The market transaction between a large firm (buyer) and its suppliers typically involves large information asymmetries: the buyer usually does not know ex ante the efficiency, quality, and compliance capability of its suppliers, and in turn the suppliers are not sure of the reliability of the buyer's demand, willingness to pay, and the like. Moreover, if intellectual property protection is inadequate, the buyer may fear the spillover of core knowledge, and prefer vertical integration or reduce the amount and quality of knowledge transferred together with the transaction. In summary, information asymmetries, delays due to imperfect contracting, and knowledge spillovers might affect the performance of an entire value chain and the distribution of benefits within the chain (Pietrobelli and Rabellotti, 2006), where success often depends on effective linkages among a variety of providers, buyers, and other intermediate firms and institutions.

Most of these market failures are idiosyncratic and specific to the agglomeration or value chain in which they are generated. So, why don't firms cooperate and organize in order to correct these failures, if they realize the importance of knowledge spillovers or the provision of key complementary inputs? Coordination failures are often to blame. Coordination failures are a widespread and well-known problem in development economics that inhibit proper resource allocation if not adequately addressed (Rosenstein-Rodan, 1943; Hoff, 2001). Obviously, sometimes the agents can organize themselves and internalize the benefits of these externalities. When the market itself generates a solution, public policies and interventions are unnecessary. For example, export business associations or credit cooperatives may emerge as spontaneous private solutions to a coordination problem. The role of Asocolflores, the Colombian flower growers' association, in solving issues such as air transportation and market access to the United States is an excellent example of this and is presented in Box 11.1 in chapter 11.

However, in many cases, transaction costs are too high and an appropriate institutional arrangement to help organize collective action is necessary.[4] For example, although firms may recognize the importance of cooperation for production of a public input, they may be on the defensive if they think greater collaboration might make them more vulnerable (by losing skilled employees to competitors, for instance) or expose them to free-riding behaviors. In this context, collaboration does not occur and the public input never materializes. Obviously, this scenario is more likely when firms in the group compete intensely in the same product markets. Moreover, as agents gain experience and develop a sense of mutual trust, transaction costs decline considerably and increase the benefits of linkages (Granovetter, 1985; Nooteboom, 1992).

In the extreme, agglomeration could be induced by public policy, for example creating industrial or technology parks and offering subsidies and inputs to entice firms to join. Once participating firms benefit from agglomeration, subsidies would be discontinued and inputs charged or outsourced. However, according to Rodríguez-Pose and Hardy (2012), parks in the region frequently fail owing to the government's lack of investment and clear strategic vision. This kind of policy to induce agglomeration is significantly riskier than to just facilitate coordination of firms already producing in established or fledgling market-driven agglomerations in which the value of synergies is already tested and proven. For this reason, this chapter focuses on the latter.

Nevertheless, an intermediate route that may be worth exploring is the creation of Special Zone regimes in which the *private* offer of collective inputs for coordination is promoted by offering assurances of protection from tax hikes and government interference through "investment contracts" (Hausmann, Rodríguez-Clare, and Rodrik, 2005).[5] Long-term protection of this kind requires a strong rule of law to make these promises credible. This policy approach of facilitating private-sourced collective inputs may be particularly fruitful in countries in which regular public services and inputs to businesses are limited or unreliable. Zonamerica, born under the auspices of the Uruguayan Free Zone regime, illustrates the potential of schemes of this sort (Box 7.1).

Box 7.1   Zonamerica: An Island of Excellence

Uruguay has a generous corporate tax regime for Free Zones originally intended to export manufactured goods to Argentina and Brazil within a MERCOSUR Free Trade Zone that never materialized.[6] However, despite its failure as a tool for MERCOSUR trade, the Free Zone regime has been very useful in attracting foreign investment in Uruguay and fostering exports to the world. One of its offsprings was Zonamerica.

Free Zones in Uruguay allow corporate tax-free operations to firms in all activities, including services. Firms pay only labor taxes and contributions; they are exempted from income, value added, or import taxes, both current and in the future. Besides these tax advantages, free zones can access privately supplied energy and telecommunications services that are usually under public monopolies and regulations. Mr. Orlando Dovat saw this special regime as an opportunity to build a private space, a private "island of excellence," within which to attract foreign investment as tenants to provide services to the world. And Zonamerica was born in 1989.

Zonamerica provides a campus with the infrastructure needed to conduct business at world standards in a way that is tailor-made and scalable according to the needs of tenants. It includes office and business centers, warehousing and associated services, and personal security services. It provides redundant energy connections to ensure safe and continuous energy supply, and powerful computing and information technology with a variety of connectivity options, with the safety of redundant data centers and cloud computing to ensure service reliability. Zonamerica also offers services of human resources hiring, training and management, and a campus with attractive amenities for the talented workforce it brings. This model may provide a private-based solution to the provision of collective services for clusters that may be particularly effective when the public provision is not up to par.

Over time, Zonamerica has attracted a good number of world-class firms to operate in campus to provide regional or world services. Once star firms such as Tata Consultancy Services or Merrill Lynch, the first large bank to join, demonstrated the viability of the model, others followed. Services now include a select roster of firms in information technology and software development, biotechnology labs, financial services, consulting and professional services, and call centers, as well as regional logistical operators. Firms share campus resources and form a functional ecosystem, fostering synergy benefits. In fact, despite the fact that the Software Law provides the same tax exemptions to software companies established anywhere in the country, many of them choose to pay rent and do business in Zonamerica in order to benefit from its campus business environment (and legal certainty going forward).

The extent to which the full exemption of corporate taxes is necessary to sustain a mature park like this is not clear. In any event, subsidies would not be justified unless there are larger spillovers beyond the firms operating within the campus to the benefit of the rest of the economy. Can this model be more than an island? While Zonamerica is an island in the economy in a spatial sense, the skilled labor it employs is an important bridge. Zonamerica demands better educational offers in specialized fields and contributes to a better labor force that may find employment elsewhere, bringing high productivity practices to the rest of the economy. Whether productive arrangements such as Zonamerica's can be scaled up with an acceptable fiscal sacrifice is worth exploring.

In sum, coordination failures represent the guiding principles and justification for productive coordination programs that aim to strengthen and improve linkages among firms. In many cases, clusters offer an ideal place to address these coordination issues and improve business linkages. They represent models to reveal and focus policy needs and achieve better policy coordination. The focus of most of these coordination policies is the provision of public inputs. In many cases, the setup of a mechanism to induce coordination—for example, through sector councils or business associations—is itself the most important contribution of these programs. In terms of the 2 × 2 matrix presented in chapter 2, most of the policies reviewed in this chapter can be classified within the quadrant of public inputs/vertical policies.

CDPs in Advanced Countries

Although policy measures to improve production coordination date back to the early days of the industrial revolution, the academic literature on the importance of interfirm collaboration and linkages for productivity growth grew quickly during the 1980s, and even more rapidly during the 1990s. The new ideas traveled fast from academia to policy circles. Many policymakers working on regional development or industrial policy soon perceived the potential of these new ideas to tackle challenges that were harder to address when the only focus was the individual firm (Schmitz and Nadvi, 1999). Multiple case studies of industrial districts in Western Europe showed how interfirm cooperation, and their linkages to other local institutions such as universities, research facilities, and training centers, helped cluster firms compete globally. Many pioneer CDPs were launched in Western Europe, and focused mostly on strengthening existing clusters.[7] By the early 1990s, several programs were using a cluster approach in the Basque Country, Italy, and Denmark. Some states in the United States also experimented on a limited basis (OECD, 2007). Most of these programs continue to operate, and have adjusted to new demands, but many more have been set up since then. By the late 2000s, more than 130 cluster programs were in place in 31 European countries at the national or subnational level—demonstrating that this policy instrument had become a key element of productive development policies (PDPs) in Europe (EC, 2008).

This is still a growing policy area. A survey conducted in 2012 by the European Cluster Observatory (2012) identified 578 "cluster initiatives" in the continent, some of them involving a single cluster, and several involving a group of clusters. In the United States, beyond the several state-level CDPs already in existence, in 2010 the Small Business Administration, together with several other federal agencies, launched a series of cluster initiatives that support the growth of more than 40 clusters across the country. In Japan, the combined efforts of the Ministry of Economy, Trade, and Industry and the Ministry of Education, Culture, Sports, Science and Technology support over 100 clusters, mostly in the high-tech sectors. CDPs are also widespread in many emerging economies, notably China and India (Lin, 2011; FMC, 2007, 2008; Yusuf, Nabeshima, and Yamashita, 2008; UNIDO, 2010; Zeng, 2010).[8] In developing countries, the focus is largely on value chain programs.

Some programs in OECD countries use multiple instruments, while others are more narrowly focused. However, sometimes these differences respond more to the general policy context than to the actual focus of the programs. CDPs frequently serve as an umbrella instrument under which other policy interventions can be coordinated. In contexts where several microeconomic intervention tools are available, these programs provide support only in those areas that lack instruments, while encouraging cluster participants to use the readily available instruments. In other contexts, where other tools are less available, CDPs deploy more instruments. This distinction is important for the discussion of CDPs in developing countries and in Latin America and the Caribbean in particular, where other policy tools are often unavailable. Thus, programs in these settings must offer instruments beyond what are normally found in more advanced countries.

An interesting trend is the change in the nature of the sectors supported by CDPs. In the beginning, these programs focused on traditional sectors such as textiles, ceramics, furniture, and automotive. While more recent initiatives still support some of these sectors, the composition has shifted toward emerging or innovation intensive sectors including eco-energy industries, ICT, microelectronics, biomedicine, or knowledge-intensive business services, which are typically plagued by coordination failures or the need for public or collective inputs. These are precisely the type of sectors that may benefit the most from this type of intervention.

A Long-Term Approach to CDPs: The Case of the Basque Country

The Autonomous Community of the Basque Country (known as CAPV, by its Spanish acronym) was one of the first regions in the world to adopt a cluster approach to industrial policies, together with Catalonia and Scotland (Aranguren and Navarro, 2003). The PCP emerged to help industries in the Basque Country face the challenges of the new competition that arose when Spain joined the European Union (EU). The 1980s had been a decade of swift economic restructuring shaped by industrial policy from the central government—a process that increased unemployment to 25 percent in the region. That policy sought to salvage the remnants of the old heavy industry of the Basque region, which was closely linked to traditional steel-related industries (del Castillo and Paton, 2010). In 1991, in the context of the growing delegation of policymaking authority from Madrid, the CAPV established the 1991–1995 Industrial Policy Framework, which supported nine prioritized clusters[9]. The size and growth potential of each cluster, determined by variables such as number of firms and jobs, degree of internationalization, and technological level, constituted the selection criteria for the program. The chosen clusters represented 31 percent of the region's industrial GDP. The policy marked a shift from the typical top-down industrial policies in place until then; the new framework proposed a degree of public-private cooperation that, although timid at the beginning, would become a hallmark of the Basque model. In one of its first actions, the CDP helped each cluster set up its own governance mechanism through cluster associations (Asociaciones Cluster). Members are mostly private firms, and frequently include one or more public agencies. The collective governance structure introduced checks and balances in the system to control public capture or attempts at rent seeking.

The Basque CDP included three types of actions: generation, capture, and management of strategic information; identification, evaluation, and prioritization of synergies to be obtained by collective action; and creation of collaborative groups. In each case, the key issues were related to technology, quality, and internationalization. For each of these areas, the program offered to cofinance collective activities identified in medium-term strategic plans (three to four years), and set up an annual monitoring system. The program worked bottom-up with the firms in each cluster, it identified clear and concrete demands from them, and the public sector then used these demand signals to reshape its innovation promotion tools to meet the demand (del Castillo and Paton, 2010).

The program is now more than 20 years old. Although it has been remarkably stable, it has evolved to follow the structural changes of the Basque economy. As for the results of these industrial policies—although no impact evaluations allow for a clear attribution of causality—the general transformation of the Basque economy over this period has been impressive. In almost all relevant indicators, the area has outperformed the rest of Spain, and to some extent Europe. The per capita GDP of the Basque Country is now above the EU15 level—increasing from 15 percent above that level in 2000 to 21 percent above in 2011—and 34 percent above the EU27 average. Unemployment declined from 25 percent in the 1980s to full employment before the crisis. In the area of innovation, results are even more impressive: R&D expenditure as a percentage of GDP went from negligible levels in the early 1980s, to 1.11 percent in 1998, to 2 percent in the late 2000s—slightly above the EU average, and well above the 1.4 percent average for Spain as a whole.

CDPs in Latin America

Latin America has been experimenting with interventions to solve productive coordination failures at least since the early days of the industrialization process.[10] Although CDPs started a few years later than the pioneering programs in Europe, their spread in Latin America has accelerated recently (Maggi and Dini, 2012). As in OECD countries, these programs can be found at different levels of government: local, regional, and national. Several international institutions—notably the IDB—financed many of the earlier CDPs, contributing to a sort of technology transfer as they helped disseminate this new approach to industrial policies within Latin American policy circles. In some ways, these institutions fulfilled the role that the EU had assumed for several European countries when they launched their early versions of CDPs.

Some of the earlier CDPs in Latin America aimed only at reducing the transaction costs of inter-firm collaboration, generally promoting networks of small and medium enterprises (SMEs) in the same sector to cooperate and achieve specific goals: increase economies of scale in buying/selling, access difficult markets with high entry costs, engage in joint innovation processes, and generate strategies for the industry as a group, among others. Examples of these early programs are the business networks of the United Nations Industrial Development Organization (UNIDO, 2010), CORFO's Programas Asociativos de Fomento (PROFO) in Chile, and the productive integration programs of the IDB's Multilateral Investment Fund (MIF).

PROFO was the first instrument of this kind to be implemented as a national policy in the region. It emerged as one of the new tools designed by CORFO under the new democratic government in Chile in 1992, and has continued with minor changes until today. It promotes joint projects among groups of at least five SMEs to improve their access to markets and, to a lesser extent, to help them innovate. Over the years it has reached about 10,000 SMEs (Maggi and Dini, 2012), and several evaluations since 2001 have shown its positive impact on numerous policy outcomes such as beneficiary management capabilities, willingness to innovate, and ability to reach foreign markets.

CDPs in Latin America encompass two types of coordination-enhancing programs described in the first section. Many emphasize vertical collaboration among different stages of a value chain. These chains exist everywhere, but in Latin America they receive special attention for two reasons. The first is the importance of agro-industrial chains in the region. These chains tend to be plagued by market failures such as information asymmetries and oligopsonies/oligopolies. The second is the importance of enclave-type activities, such as mining, in which large firms produce for foreign markets, practice global sourcing, and create few local economic linkages. Policy objectives typically include improving the linkages among the different stages of an existing value chain (Pietrobelli and Staritz, 2013), and developing local suppliers to improve the spillover effects of certain firms/industries in a given region/country.

While CDPs in Latin America started in the 1990s, they became much more widespread in the 2000s. Most of them follow a similar structure, particularly those supported by international institutions.[11] Typically, a public institution receives funding to implement these programs with activities designed to strengthen selected clusters in the country (or the state/province). The activities usually involve four stages: mapping and selecting clusters to be supported in the targeted territory; identifying challenges and needs for policy intervention in individual clusters with the participation of both public and private sector actors; implementing actions identified in the second stage; and monitoring and evaluation.

One of the key objectives of these programs is to solve coordination failures. In order to do so, they create formal and informal institutional arrangements and frameworks to facilitate private-private, public-private, and public-public collaboration. To induce more collective action among private firms in a given cluster, the programs generally strengthen a local business association, or help generate a new one, or generate a new "cluster association" that firms may join, as the common interest of firms in a cluster may not coincide with existing business chambers. These institutional arrangements have also proven useful to deal with traditional problems like free riding, sometimes by enforcing a formal membership in the cluster association, with an annual fee that provides access to certain services for free or at a reduced price.

Public-public coordination has been the most difficult of the three types. This is a problem, since microeconomic interventions of this kind require extensive collaboration among multiple public agencies. In most Latin American countries, in any given territory where a new CDP starts operating, several national, regional, and/or local public agencies and ministries have the responsibility and mandate to contribute to improve cluster performance. Originally, these programs were expected to generate a detailed diagnostic of the cluster's strategic needs, and once missing public and semipublic inputs were identified, then public agencies would find it easy to coordinate interventions. However, conflicting mandates, bureaucratic processes, strategic views, and short-term political considerations among public actors trumped the collaborative opportunities of the programs. Even though public-public collaboration increased in many cases at the cluster level, its scale and scope were lower than expected, and the higher the level at which collaboration was sought (between national ministries, for instance), the lower the degree of success.[12] The probable reasons for the disappointing outcomes were, first, public-public coordination for PDP at a macro-level is extremely difficult and successes are rare, and second, cluster policies are not the core of the PDP in any country in Latin America and the Caribbean, meaning a cluster program could not have sufficient clout to overcome turf politics. The difficulties of implementing policies that involve coordination across multiple agencies are discussed in detail in chapter 10.

This difficulty relates directly to the issue of which agencies are best placed to carry out CDPs. These programs cut across sector barriers and have a hard time dealing with the traditional state apparatus with its line ministries. There seems to be a trade-off between horizontal ministries (such as the economy, planning, and development ministries), which deal with horizontal programs and coordination issues, but have little industrial policy expertise, and the large, powerful sectoral ministries, which have considerable capacity to execute policies but are unable to operate beyond sector boundaries. In this context, development agencies, such as Chile's CORFO, are well placed to oversee CDPs: they are horizontal, have implementation capacity, and tend to be less constrained by the political cycle of line ministries. However, few developing nations can count on truly effective general development agencies.

CDPs can also finance sector-specific worker training, which requires strong coordination among closely located firms and training service providers. In those places where a government training agency already exists, like the Industrial Workers Training Service (SENAI) in Brazil (see case analysis below), CDPs help redesign local labor training programs so they can more closely match the needs of the cluster. Where those agencies are not present, the programs support ad hoc labor training activities to cater to human capital constraints identified during the diagnosis process.

CDPs in Action

Since CDPs occur in so many different forms and are so specific to their contexts, a review of four individual programs serves to illustrate the variety of interventions. The first supports a traditional manufacturing cluster in the Brazilian state of São Paulo. The second deals with a service sector cluster (tourism) in Uruguay. The third works with a vertical value chain in Chile. The fourth examines a supplier developing program in Chile. Finally, Box 7.2 discusses the internationalization efforts of the agricultural machinery cluster in Santa Fe, Argentina.

Box 7.2 CIDETER: An Agricultural Machinery Cluster Engaged in Internationalization Policies

In Santa Fe Province, Argentina, a dense network of economic activities has evolved around the farming of the fertile Pampas, creating a complex agro-industrial cluster. The group of mostly SMEs in this cluster dedicated to agricultural machinery and parts production in Santa Fe has a long tradition of cooperation. Over the past decade they decided to internationalize, and for that they needed to formalize their cooperation and create an institution to face the necessary scale that opening new foreign markets demand. In 2000, they created the CIDETER (Regional Technological Research and Development Center) Foundation. Since then, it has consolidated and grown increasingly sophisticated. In 2006, with the assistance of a cluster promotion initiative of the national government, they created the Agricultural Machinery Business Cluster (known as CECMA, by its acronym in Spanish), which groups together the region's firms, universities, technological institutes, and local governments. Currently, the CIDETER Foundation is CECMA's executing arm. It has three main functions: it administers a technological center that serves all firms in the cluster; manages a unit that puts together collective projects and searches for funding from local, regional, national, and international sources; and manages the cluster's search for new export markets.

Since the evolution of the agricultural machinery industry is directly linked to farming technology, the cluster soon realized that accessing foreign markets required exporting the new no-till farming techniques, of which Argentina is a technological leader, as a complete technological package. Thus, they innovated in two joint actions that proved very successful. First, they began organizing what they called Agro Showroom, a "reverse" trade fair where they invite foreign buyers to Santa Fe to see local farming activities and their machines in action. With the support of INTA, and national and provincial export promoting agencies, they organize an annual event that welcomes buyers from over 20 different countries, where all the cluster's firms can demonstrate their products while agronomists from the local INTA center explain their advantages.

However, the fact that machines work well in the soil and climate of the Pampas does not mean that they will perform equally well under different conditions. For this reason, the second joint activity targeted specific foreign markets with the aim of exporting the whole farming model. In 2011, they set up their first experimental agricultural field in South Africa to show how the farming techniques and the machinery work, and also make any necessary adaptation to local agro-ecological conditions. They expect to use this as a platform to reach other Sub-Saharan African countries. In 2013, they finalized the formal agreements to launch a similar initiative in Australia. The results of this internationalization drive are quite impressive. While exports were negligible at the beginning of the last decade, during 2010–12 they averaged 25 percent of sales and reached more than 50 countries. In 2013 alone, one of its member firms, Apache S. A., exported to South Africa more than 20 seeding machines designed for no-till farming at around $200,000 each. Since transportation of agricultural machinery is costly—as the machines are very bulky—they are now considering exporting the more complex components, and setting up a production facility in South Africa to produce other components and assemble the finished product.

Case 1: Cluster Policies in São Paulo

General context: The state of São Paulo in southeastern Brazil covers only 3 percent of the country's territory, but generates about one-third of the country's GDP. Many companies in São Paulo participate in value chains linked to large industrial companies, or in specific industry clusters, known as local production arrangements, or, in Portuguese, Arranjos Produtivos Locais (APL). Traditional sectors with mature technology are prevalent in areas outside the capital, and it is in these areas where clusters are most common.

Policy and institutional context: The shift in the 1990s in Brazil from import substitution and state-led industrialization toward a more open, market-led economy opened the way to experimenting with new types of industrial policies. At the state level, this process began very early—and in a large country organized along federal lines, state-level policies play an important role. São Paulo's APL became the focus of some of the state's industrial policies, although their main promoters, remarkably, were not strictly public agencies. The leaders were two semiprivate state-level organizations: the Federation of Industries of the State of São Paulo (FIESP), and the agency promoting micro, small, and medium enterprises (MSMEs) in São Paulo (SEBRAE-SP).[13]

The cluster program: Based on the lessons learned from early experiments, FIESP and SEBRAE joined the Secretary of

Development (SD) of the state of São Paulo to create a tripartite program to support clusters in the state. The IDB provided financing. The $20 million project, launched in 2009, supports 15 clusters and has four components: mobilize local firms and business chambers of the selected clusters; identify challenges and obstacles to cluster development, and prepare action plans; execute activities identified in action plans; and perform monitoring and evaluation.

The program aimed to solve coordination failures and improve the effectiveness of existing industrial policies. It emphasized public-private collaboration and bottom-up decision making, a departure from the more top-down, state-led nature of traditional policies. FIESP and SEBRAE-SP are part of the governing body of the program, and are co-executers of several activities; SEBRAE-SP contributes 50 percent of the funding.

The 15 clusters to be supported were selected based on quantitative and qualitative criteria. Favored quantitative factors included a location outside the São Paulo Metropolitan Area, large numbers of businesses and jobs, heavy sector concentration in a single municipality, high growth in jobs and businesses, comparative advantage, and a high percentage of MSMEs. Priority qualitative criteria included a preexisting institutional framework, connections to the local market, sector diversification, and a well-defined geographic concentration.

A key element of the program was the definition of a strategic plan for each cluster. For this purpose, an international consulting firm, together with program officials, worked with local businesses in each cluster to develop a cluster strategy for the short, medium, and long term. This plan identified key challenges for small groups of participating firms, as well as missing public or semipublic inputs. In both cases, the plan had to provide a guide to policy intervention. The international consulting firm used a methodology that departed from the "laundry list" style used until then by public agencies. The firm conceptualized the cluster as a business unit, identified its core business, contacted key global buyers for that business, and analyzed the most relevant global market trends. Then, it contrasted those trends with the strengths and weaknesses of the local cluster, and set out a course that would allow the cluster to meet current and future market challenges.

This emphasis on global market dynamics was new to many firms, especially to MSMEs. Some of them highly valued the approach, while others considered it too disruptive. The role of the public agencies led to a mixture of government interventions that provided some support to increase local firms' general capabilities to compete, and other support to change the sector's strategy in targeting global markets. The former comprised actions such as quality certifications, or labor and management training, whereas the latter involved helping firms work together in order to offer combined products from the cluster sold as integrated packages ("building solutions" instead of red tiles, for example, in the case of the red tile cluster discussed below). The political support from the SD dwindled after the initial enthusiasm, while the program enjoyed more stable support from the private sector through SEBRAE-SP and FIESP. Beyond the impact of this program on jobs and exports, analyzed in the next section, some of the results may be better understood by looking at the experience of a specific cluster, as described below.

The Red Tile Cluster in Tambaú

The city of Tambaú in the province of São Paulo is home to a large concentration of producers of ceramic products, mostly red roof tiles. The origin of this cluster is a large deposit of red clay that has been mined since the early twentieth century. The sector consists of 67 firms, mostly SMEs, which represent 48 percent of all manufacturing firms and 66 percent of manufacturing employment in the district (IDB, 2013). Various small firms extract the clay to supply these firms, mostly in the informal sector.

The intervention can be divided into three stages, which somewhat mimic the evolution of cluster policies in the state described above (IDB, 2013):

- 2004 to 2006: FIESP chose Tambaú for its cluster project in the state. It was a modest start, but significant, as firms in the region began thinking in terms of their collective needs for the first time.

- 2006 to 2008: The SD incorporated the Tambaú cluster into its cluster program and used the local SEBRAE-SP to mobilize local actors and help create an interinstitutional governance mechanism that proved to be effective and sustainable. The new program financed the preparation of an Action Plan that addressed several local demands. At the same time, the city government prepared a Territorial Development Plan focused mainly on the environmental problem created by informal clay mining firms. The program set up a governance body for the cluster, with representatives of the city government, the local business association, the Ceramic Center of Brazil,[14] FIESP, SEBRAE-SP, and SENAI, the government training agency managed by the federation of industries that provides labor training and technical service facilities.
- 2008 to the present: The program built on the previous experiences and institutional development to create a more sophisticated cluster business plan. The new one proposed that local firms move from being "tile suppliers" to "building solutions suppliers," integrating their business with others from related sectors and catering directly to end-consumers. This entailed the development of building models that use ceramic tiles intensively, and offering them in several markets including individual homes, schools, hospitals, etc. With strong local governance, this high-level strategy was integrated with more down-to-earth local needs. Participants finally agreed on a set of interventions that in time would allow these clusters to provide a more sophisticated supply of building solutions while taking concrete, short-term steps to improve collective efficiency and solve environmental challenges. For example, the first common challenge identified was the environmentally damaging activities of local informal clay mining firms. The city government commissioned the local technological institute to analyze the problem and propose solutions. The cluster governance, having identified a problem, and now equipped with technical information, shared it with the partner institution in the cluster and the local SENAI branch. This last agency offered to build a new facility in Tambaú to train mining workers in the sector's best practices, and provide

laboratories and testing facilities to help local mining firms upgrade their technologies and environmental standards.

Case 2: The Cluster Program in Uruguay

The cluster program in Uruguay was designed in 2005–06 and launched in 2007. The program began by mapping the country's clusters and promoting its value to potential beneficiaries. Then, clusters were selected through calls for proposals from business groups and on the basis of competitive bidding according to criteria that included social indicators of the territory where the cluster is located, its dynamism (in terms of exports and global trade), local impact, size, kind of intervention needed, quality of governance, and strategic relevance for the country.

The selected clusters received support to strengthen collective governance, prepare a participatory strategic action plan, create governance mechanisms to foster public-private and public-public coordination in each specific cluster, and finance strategic actions identified in the plan, with emphasis on public inputs.

This method of intervening, relying heavily on the private sector to help decide the scope and characteristics of the program's intervention in each cluster, was clearly new in Uruguay (Rius, 2013). It was also unique in its emphasis on supporting formal and informal schemes to promote multi-actor coordination.

The Tourism Cluster in Colonia

Colonia is a small town in southwestern Uruguay. Its historic downtown boasts a unique mixture of Spanish and Portuguese colonial structures that reflect the city's change of hands in colonial times. Declared a World Heritage Site by UNESCO in 1995, it was already well established as a tourist destination when the program got underway.

The cluster participated in the second call for proposals. The Tourism Department of Colonia headed the initiative. The head of the Tourism Department was a well-trained technocrat, knowledgeable in the field, who earned her job in open competition. The local hotel association, which participated in the bidding, had promoted inter-sector collaboration in previous years, and had developed a strategic plan—albeit a rudimentary one. The private-private interactions at the time the program was launched were intense, complex, and often conflictive. Among other things, the arrival of new international hotel chains was disrupting the traditionally family-owned hotel sector. The company that managed the monopoly of ferries connecting Colonia with Buenos Aires, its main market, refused to become involved. And it took time for the chamber of restaurants to join the initiative. Another challenge was that the sector was experiencing a demand boom, so businessmen were focused more on capitalizing on the favorable short-term conditions than on the medium- and long-term perspectives for the sector as a whole. The Tourism Department deserves much of the credit for overcoming these initial obstacles and mobilizing key actors behind the initiative.

To overcome the problems of fragmented private sector representation and improve cooperation among public agencies, the program created a cluster association, the Tourism Association of Colonia (known as ATC, by its Spanish acronym). This association brought together local private and public actors, and proved resilient through the whole process, even in the face of several conflicts among its members. The Tourism Department proved to be a key actor, not only to facilitate interaction with other local stakeholders, but also to ensure that national-level actors, such as the Ministry of Tourism, participated in the cluster initiative and channeled its interventions in a way consistent with the cluster's strategy (Rius, 2013).

The strategy developed with the program's support proposed several lines of action to enhance the town as a tourist destination. In order to do so, the ATC reached a consensus on 12 initiatives involving over $500,000 in resources. The program on average funded 70 percent of the 12 initiatives. These initiatives ranged from the very basic (like developing a web page for the town) to more demanding ones in terms of collective action (such as developing a common brand for the destination, commissioning an international benchmarking exercise, and strengthening the ATC). The program is still being implemented. Formal evaluations will be carried out during 2014, when international financing for the program ends.

Case 3: CDPs That Promote Agricultural Value Chains in Chile

In 2008, the government of Chile launched a program to decentralize part of its industrial policy. This program created regional development agencies in each of Chile's 15 regions. Each of these agencies selected at least three groups of firms in their region to support. The program refers to these groups of firms as "clusters," but the definition was very lax, encompassing traditional clusters, as well as value chains and even some supplier development programs. A coordinating unit at the central offices of CORFO in Santiago led the program. Each region received support to create a local development agency with public-private governance, which in turn selected the three business groups to receive program support. For each of these groups, the program financed a strategic plan, a broad governance structure (a cluster manager, and a public-private cluster board), and selected public inputs (either directly, or by taking identified demands to other public programs available in that region). Unfortunately, just as the agencies and the actions with the clusters were beginning, a new government took office in 2010 that lost interest in the program. As a result, many of the agencies closed and several cluster initiatives have been cut back.

The Fresh Grape Value Chain in Atacama

The Atacama Regional Development Agency selected the grape industry as their first beneficiary group. This sector was one of the most important economic activities in this region in northern Chile, and the Atacama region produces 12 percent of the countries' production of table grapes; because of its latitude, it enjoys one of the first grape harvests in the Southern Hemisphere, allowing it to fetch high prices in export markets in the Northern Hemisphere. The program created informal governance mechanisms with the participation of private firms from the grape industry, local universities, the regional government, and the local representatives of national ministries, in particular agriculture. The region's grape growers export mostly through big exporting firms whose headquarters are not in the region, and sell ultimately to large importers (mostly big supermarket chains) in Europe and the United States. The large exporting firms were never active participants, mostly because they are not local actors, but also because growers wanted to strengthen their own understanding of and role in the value chain; the most pressing demand of most growers was for help in lessening the information asymmetries between them and exporters regarding destination markets. An international consulting firm worked with all these local actors to develop a strategy for the whole chain that began by creating consensus around a few goals and proposing a set of joint actions for the next two to three years. The strategy centered on adding value to local production through a marketing effort to create a local brand (a kind of protected designated origin) that could help differentiate its grapes in destination markets. For that, it included initiatives in three areas: a marketing strategy to position its products in foreign markets, developed jointly with other actors in the chain, including foreign distributors and retail chains; labor training and skill development to increase the overall quality of the final product; and a joint initiative to identify new markets for the whole chain.

The program itself financed part of these initiatives, while it managed to leverage funds from other public programs. One of the cluster managers led trips to destination markets with growers, who for the first time had direct contact with end-clients, especially procurement managers from leading retail chains in the United States and Europe, and thus were able to gather valuable information. The training and marketing initiatives were financed mostly by other agencies based on the demands identified in the strategic planning exercise. After a new government ended the agencies' program, this particular initiative remained active thanks to the funding of other public agencies and the private sector support and participation organized under the previous programs. It retained the same name with which it was launched under the agencies program, FreshAtacama.

Case 4: The Supplier Development Program in Chile

In the 1990s, Chile signed several free trade agreements with other countries and regions in the world. In order to take advantage of the new market opportunities that those agreements presented to Chilean firms, their products had to meet the standards (technical, sanitary, quality) required by those markets. This issue was most obvious for emerging agricultural exporters that complained that the produce (mostly fruit) they were receiving from growers was not up to standards. Producers did not invest to upgrade their production by themselves because they lacked information about foreign market requirements, financial resources, and/or certainty about the potential individual returns they would get from such investments. The exporters (or potential exporters) would not help them because they were uncertain as to how much of their efforts they would capture, as upgraded suppliers could switch buyers. CORFO, following the example of a similar program in Singapore, set up a supplier development program aimed at solving precisely those problems. The program accepts proposals from anchor firms to help upgrade their SME suppliers. It partially covers the cost of a diagnosis carried out by an independent consultant that determines the needs for upgrading, and presents a plan. Then the program covers up to 50 percent of the costs of activities, including technology transfer, professional services, and technical advice, that help upgrade the group of participant SME suppliers.

The sponsor firm must be large, with annual sales of at least $42 million, and must involve at least 20 supplier SMEs. The large firm is responsible for implementing the action plan and contributing counterpart funds. The program grew rapidly during its first decade to reach almost 7,000 firms per year in over 300 projects by the end of the 2000s (Dini, 2009). Given its nature, it became particularly attractive for agricultural value chains, which were the main beneficiaries. The participation of the firms in the program lengthens their time horizons, and increases their certainty regarding the potential future benefits they might reap by increasing their investment in upgrading. Some of the results of this program are discussed in the next section.

Effectiveness and Evaluation of Productive Coordination Programs

The trend that led many countries to implement CDPs has generated a remarkable amount of literature that discusses the justification and rationale of these programs, as well as the different approaches to their design and implementation. Unfortunately, little of this literature has focused on measuring the effectiveness of these interventions. Hence, the evidence on their real impact is still scarce and hardly generalizable.[15]

Although several reasons may have contributed to this deficiency—including a bias in the policy evaluation literature toward social topics—some specific factors have played a role in generating this knowledge gap.

- CDPs are complex. They do not consist of a unique standardized treatment, but usually include a menu of possible interventions—often not precisely outlined ex ante—that can be implemented in different mixes and sequencings.
- Gold standard impact evaluation techniques, such as randomized control trials (RCTs), are hardly applicable in this area because CDPs always imply a strong selection of beneficiaries, often based on motivational characteristics.[16]
- Because their most important effects are likely to occur over a long period of time, impact evaluations of CDPs require collecting data several years after the program's inception,[17] making the political economy of impact evaluations quite challenging.
- CDPs aim at fostering firms' performances through the creation and strengthening of linkages among firms. Ideally, these effects should be measured through social network analysis (SNA) techniques, which require the construction of complex datasets based on relational data.[18]
- CDPs always imply effects beyond those on their direct beneficiaries, in the form of either spillover effects or other externalities. Both spillover effects and externalities are serious threats to the validity of impact evaluations, and dealing with them is particularly challenging.

These challenges notwithstanding, impact evaluations of CDPs can and have been performed (Pietrobelli, Maffioli, and Stucchi, forthcoming). As could be expected, the complexity of CDPs has been addressed by simplifying the intervention models to allow for econometric analysis. However, econometric analyses have increasingly been complemented by a qualitative approach. Indeed, a clearer understanding exists of the contribution that each approach can provide to assess the effectiveness of CDPs. Impact evaluation provides credible estimates of the magnitude of the CDP's effects on some key outcomes, such as employment generation, productivity, and exports. More heuristic approaches, such as the narratives adopted by the case studies reported in this chapter, complement the findings of impact evaluations, facilitating better understanding of why and how these effects depend on the specific characteristic of each program. The data and methodological problems have been addressed by applying nonexperimental techniques and expanding the use of administrative and secondary data. Increasingly, studies have used panel data techniques applied over longitudinal administrative data sets, which also allow for effects to be identified over long periods of time.

The measurement of linkages through SNA techniques has also evolved significantly, and some studies have started integrating SNA and econometric techniques. The impact evaluation of the PROFO program by Maffioli (2005) provides an example of how to combine SNA and econometric methods. The study confirms a strong correlation between the innovativeness and industrial cooperation of firms that participated in the PROFO program, proving the existence of an interactive learning process among participant firms. The case of the Córdoba ICT CDP in Argentina has also been recently evaluated using SNA techniques and shows that networks have changed structure, becoming less dense and more hierarchical over time. This means that local firms have become more strategic about their linkages and more selective of their partners (Giuliani, Matta, and Pietrobelli, forthcoming). Furthermore, the analysis shows that the program has led to the strengthening and creation of new technology transfer ties between the electronics firms in Córdoba and local universities.[19]

Finally, an increasing number of impact evaluations include measures of spillovers. In this area, the most common measurements are constructed on the concepts of labor mobility and geographical proximity. Labor mobility is useful for determining whether firms are linked and if spillover effects may have occurred because the mobility of skilled individuals is probably the most crucial factor behind knowledge transfer.[20]

In an effort to evaluate the programs supported by its operations, the IDB has recently launched a series of initiatives aimed at generating rigorous evidence in this area. This effort has generated methodological and applied studies and produced encouraging results on the effectiveness of CDPs. Figal Garone et al. (2012), for instance, analyze the case of the APL in Brazil using geographic proximity to define linkages among firms and spillover effects. The study sheds light on some important features of the APL policy. First, the study finds clear positive direct effects on employment, the value of total exports, and the likelihood of exporting, with a constant or increasing pattern over time. This signals that the program produced significant efficiency gains, given that simultaneous effects on export likelihood, export volume, and employment would hardly be achievable without an increase in productivity. The study also finds strong positive spillover effects on exports measured in the medium and long term, as well as a negative temporary indirect effect on employment—and only during the first year after the program's implementation. The strong indirect effects on exports seem to confirm the existence of knowledge spillovers—in this case, knowledge of external markets—which in the absence of the program could have led to severe coordination failures and limited exports for both direct and indirect beneficiaries. The temporary dip in employment is probably due to the difference in timing between direct and indirect effects. Because direct beneficiary firms received the program's benefits before and more intensively than the indirect beneficiaries, in the very short run they may have attracted employees from the local pool of specialized workers, at the expense of the other firms in the APL. Over time, this effect faded away, most likely because the benefits of the APL policy started to spread to indirect beneficiaries, and additional qualified employment was either attracted from outside the APL or trained within.

A second study by Boneu et al. (forthcoming) on the impact of a CDP on the ICT sector in Cordoba confirms and expands the findings on the APL programs. Using both labor mobility[21] and geographic proximity to account for spillover effects, this study also finds that the program not only was effective in promoting sales, employment, wages, and exports of the direct beneficiary firms, but also had positive spillover effects in terms of sales, employment, wages, and exports.

Finally, a couple of evaluations of the Chilean supplier development program discussed above provided evidence on the potential effectiveness of the value chain approach. In this case, the evidence comes from a combination of qualitative and quantitative approaches. A qualitative evaluation carried out four years after the start of the program pointed out that the program helped the beneficiary firms and producers to establish a complex and long-term relationship within the value chain. It also helped producers increase yields and prices (Dini, 2009). These findings were expanded and complemented by Arráiz, Henríquez, and Stucchi (2013), who performed a quasi-experimental study on the program's effects on different types of beneficiaries. The study finds that both small and medium providers and large clients benefited from the coordination efforts. In particular, the program increased sales, employment, and the sustainability of suppliers, while it boosted the sales of the large client firms and enhanced their ability to become exporters.

Lessons Learned

Solid impact evaluations of CDPs are possible and are beginning to emerge. These evaluations reveal that these programs often have important (and measurable) effects on firms' productivity, sales, exports, and employment. These analyses have also shed light on the indirect impact through externalities on other firms that do not participate in the programs directly.

Given the complexities of evaluating CDPs, several studies have complemented formal evaluations with detailed analyses of specific cases. These studies have revealed some policy lessons, which can help improve program design. In particular:

- CDPs tend to have longer maturation periods than policymakers think, as they depend on emerging trust among actors, which takes time to build. This may lead actors subject to the political cycle, and thus with short time horizons, to become frustrated or withdraw support prematurely. Strong private sector involvement seems to provide some protection against this tendency.
- The programs are useful for supporting practical ways of coordinating microeconomic interventions. However, the programs' potential to become platforms from which to coordinate other PDPs is limited when the executive agencies lack sufficient political influence to convene and coordinate other public agencies. Unlike successful cluster policies in advanced countries, CDPs have not yet become a central feature of the governments' PDPs in Latin America. They work mostly on the margins, and this weakens their effectiveness.
- Given the heterogeneity of their target population, CDPs work better when they are flexible and adapt to local needs.
- As CDPs tend to be implemented increasingly at the subnational level, central-level governments need to guarantee consistency and regulation in order to avoid a "race to the bottom," with regions stealing resources from surrounding areas.
- Most CDPs analyzed managed to create the conditions at the local level for increased private-private, public-private, and public-public collaboration that could not have happened spontaneously. The emerging collaborative governance structures have the potential to become a platform on which more sophisticated collective actions can occur.
- Although the cases analyzed here concentrate mostly on traditional sectors characterized by high geographic agglomeration and mature governance, a stronger focus on emerging sectors—which usually suffer more acutely from weak productive linkages and lack of key public inputs—has great potential. This trend is already occurring in advanced economies.

- Participatory strategic planning at the cluster level was a very useful tool to identify missing public inputs and create consensus around interventions associated with the CDP.
- Capture and rent seeking seem to be lower than expected thanks to the "checks and balances" introduced by the participation of several actors at multiple levels.
- Rigorous impact evaluations are feasible and should become part of a standard practice to foster necessary and continuous processes of experimentation and policy learning.

8

A World of Possibilities: Internationalization for Productive Development

Openness and diversification can be beneficial for economic growth (Brainard and Cooper, 1968; Frankel and Romer, 1999).[1] Openness to trade can foster growth by making it easier to import goods that embody new technology, by reaping economies of scale, and by facilitating the process commonly known as learning by doing through exporting, among other channels (Harrison and Rodríguez-Clare, 2010). Export diversification, in turn, reduces sensitivity to sector-specific shocks. Furthermore, deeper participation in global value chains (GVCs) facilitates access to international flows of knowledge and technology, and thus increases the potential for learning and productivity improvements in local firms.

A number of studies suggest that what countries export matters: foreign sales are more likely to lead to economic growth if they mainly involve manufactured or skill-intensive goods or if the composition of their exports is closer to that of higher-income countries (Hausmann, Hwang, and Rodrik, 2007). Similarly, the growth effects of foreign direct investment (FDI) appear to be larger for sectors that are skill-intensive (Alfaro and Charlton, 2007). However, skill or knowledge intensity cannot be considered an intrinsic feature of sectors. Goods in the same sector could be produced with a backward technology that is not skill-intensive in one country, but with a modern, skill-intensive technology in another country (Rodríguez-Clare, 2007). Rather than the sectors themselves, the way that goods are produced and their quality may be what matters (Lederman and Maloney, 2012).

Given the importance of internationalization, the picture that Latin America and the Caribbean presents is not satisfactory. Exports from a number of Latin American and Caribbean economies—despite improvements in recent years—still remain below their potential and the level that would be expected given their levels of development. The same holds for their degree of export diversification (Figure 8.1). In addition, while countries do not lag significantly in terms of total inflows of foreign direct investment, their participation in GVCs, as captured by the number of vertically linked subsidiaries they host, is also relatively limited.

For these reasons, countries around the world—including those in Latin America and the Caribbean—have designed and implemented a range of policies to favor the internationalization of their economies. These policies mainly take the form of promoting exports,

Figure 8.1 Trade, Vertically Linked Subsidiaries and Level of Development, Latin American and Caribbean Countries, 2010

a. Exports and Level of Development

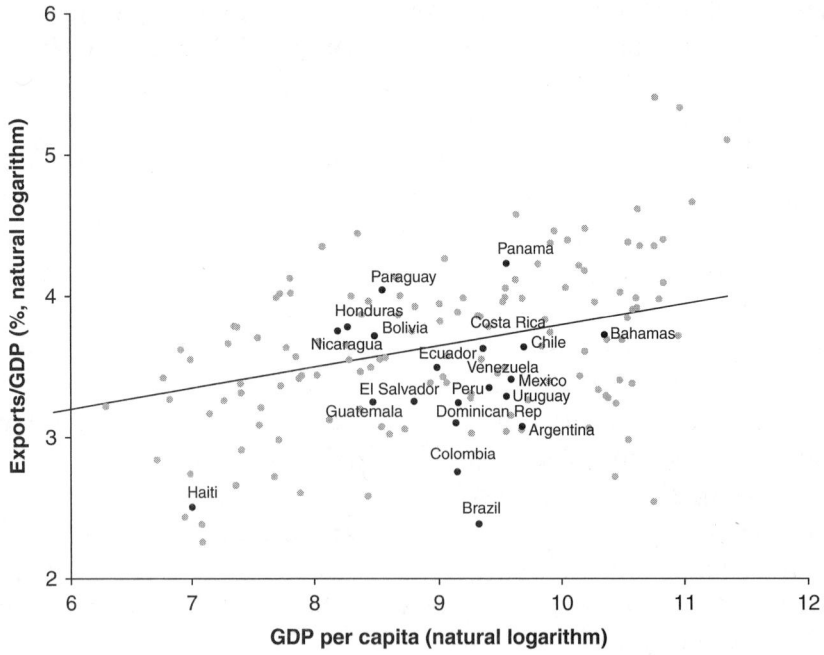

b. Export Diversification and Level of Development

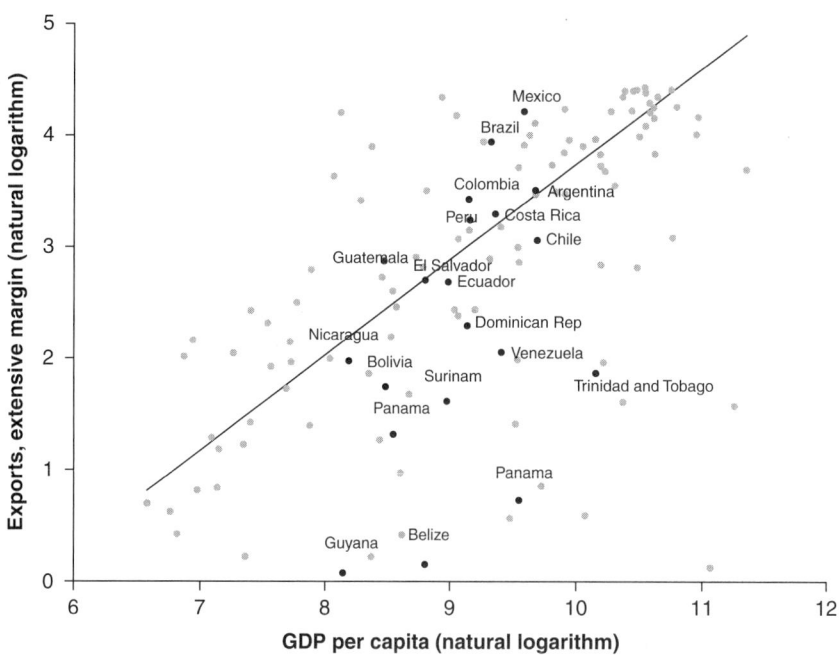

c. FDI and Level of Development

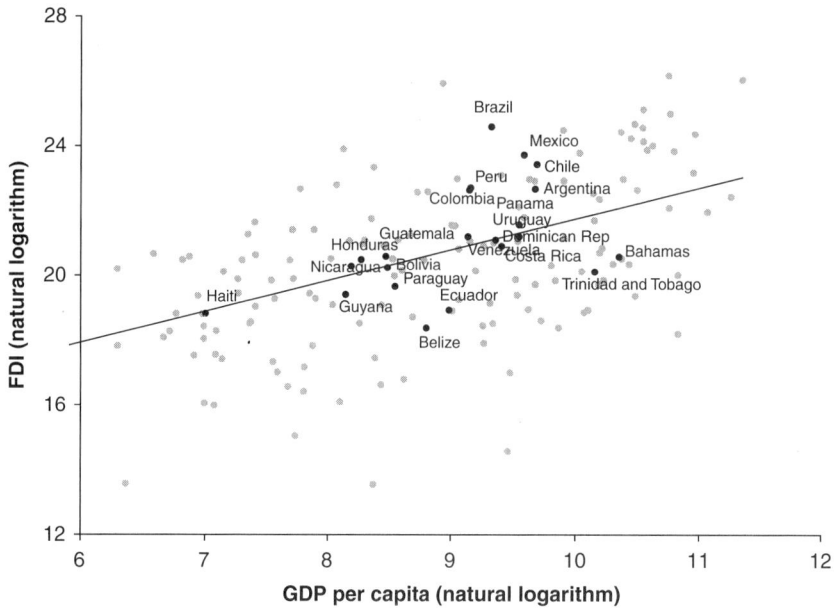

d. Number of Subsidiaries and Level of Development

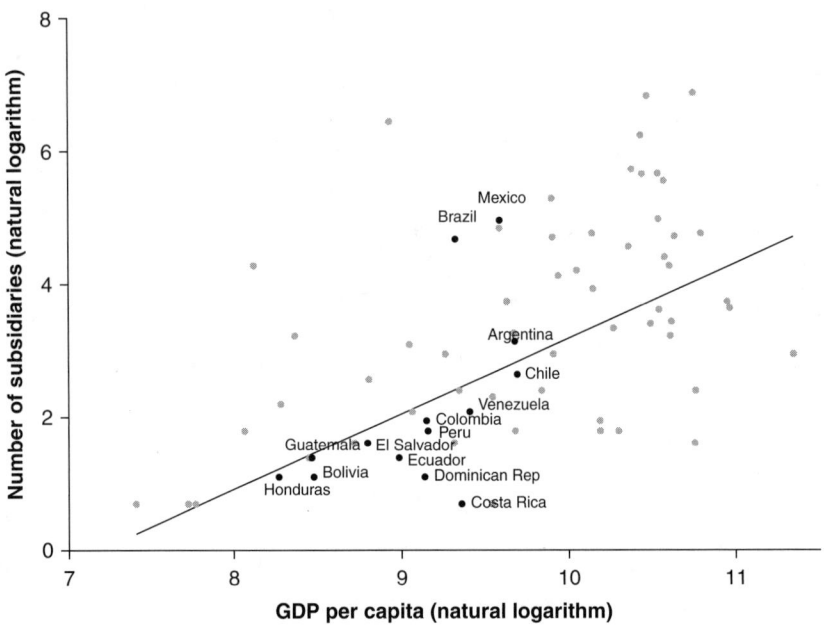

Note: All variables are expressed in natural logarithms and contrasted with the natural logarithm of countries' respective GDP per capita as a proxy of their level of development. The straight line shows the relationship between these variables as obtained from a robust regression, to account for the presence of outliers. The estimated coefficients on GDP per capita and the respective t-values (in parentheses) are: for exports, 0.20 (5.98); for export extensive margin, 0.63 (7.86); for number of subsidiaries, 1.02 (5.59); and sectoral concentration of subsidiaries, -0.73 (6.67).

Exports to GDP: Percentage share of exports in GDP; Extensive margin: Extensive margin indicator proposed by Hummels and Klenow (2005), which is a weighted count of the products exported by a country relative to the products exported by the rest of the world using the relative importance of the latter as weighting factors. Foreign direct investment: Net foreign direct investment flows. Number of subsidiaries: Number of vertically linked subsidiaries of multinational companies as identified by Alfaro and Chen (2012): that is, a subsidiary is considered to be vertical if the direct requirement of the subsidiary's primary product category in the parent firm's final good production measured by the input cost share exceeds a threshold value of 0.1 (similar patterns are observed when more liberal criteria are used).

Source: Authors' calculations based on data from World Development Indicators and COMTRADE.

attracting investment, and facilitating linkages between domestic producers and multinational companies (MNCs). This chapter examines the rationale for public intervention in this area, the institutional and policy trends both within and outside the region, and the impact of some of these interventions in Latin America and the Caribbean.

The Rationale for Public Intervention

In policy circles, the evidence that economic growth is correlated with the sectoral composition of exports is sometimes wrongly interpreted as indicating that interventions aimed at fostering the production and trade of certain goods are warranted. If at all, public interventions focused on internationalization should instead be economically justified on the basis of market failures such as externalities and coordination failures.

For example, firms searching for foreign buyers through customs documents, customer lists, employee exchanges, and informal information transfers across firms that are located close to one another may unwittingly generate information that benefits other firms (Rauch, 1996). As long as it is difficult to exclude third parties from this information, the potential exists for free riding on these searches. Followers may eventually imitate the pioneering firms without incurring the pioneers' costs. In doing so, the followers obtain important benefits from the leader's initial investments (and devalue the potential benefits from their searches). This is particularly true when companies attempt to enter a new market or produce or trade a new product, as in the case of "discoveries," so named by Hausmann and Rodrik (2003). The same thing occurs when companies join GVCs. Once a firm has landed a contract with a lead firm and establishes a good track record, it is easier for other firms in the same sector to follow. Thus, the returns accruing to the firms carrying out these new activities (private returns) would be lower than the corresponding returns for the economy as a whole (social returns), and investment in their development would then be suboptimal—thereby potentially providing a rationale for public intervention. Spillovers can also take place among buyers (Egan and Mody, 1992). A buyer's "discovery" of a well-qualified local supplier may also benefit other buyers, and thus the private returns associated with the investment in developing the business relationship may be lower than the social returns.[2]

Externalities may also stem from business, organizational, and managerial practices, training activities, production methods and technologies, and, in particular, production linkages with exporters and multinational companies (MNCs). For example, MNCs are likely to adopt efficient and competitive management practices and provide employees with higher-quality training, which may potentially benefit local firms via demonstration/imitation and turnover of managers and technical employees (Keesing, 1967; Bloom, 1992; Glass and Saggi, 2002). Moreover, externalities related to technological development may be extensive due to the imperfect appropriability of technology (Westphal, 1990). In addition, multinational exporting companies may transfer knowledge, provide suppliers with technical assistance, and allow for access to new (or improved) inputs by firms in downstream industries (Rodríguez-Clare, 1996). In particular, interactions between MNCs, foreign buyers, and local firms in the context of GVCs can be a conduit of knowledge that may foster processes of learning and acquiring capabilities, leading to process and product innovation and industrial upgrading—which, in turn, may spill over to other firms that are not participating in the same global supply chain (Gereffi, 1999; Javorcik and Spatareanu, 2009).[3] These spillovers, however, are generally not included in the foreign buyers' and MNCs' private assessment of the costs and benefits associated with doing business overseas and investing abroad; thus they may invest less than what would be socially optimal. This gap between private and social returns might also provide a rationale for intervention (Blomström and Kokko, 2003).

In addition to externalities, coordination failures might also potentially provide a rationale for public interventions with implications for internationalization (Hausmann, Hwang, and Rodrik, 2007). The productivity and internationalization of firms may depend on providing certain public goods such as infrastructure and regulation, as well as on the actions of other firms (see Rodríguez-Clare, 2007, and chapter 7 of this report). In clusters at the local level, coordination among firms and the public sector may be necessary to provide collective goods—such as storage facilities at the airport in the case of flower exports from Colombia—in order to facilitate access to international markets. Coordination among firms may also be needed for industries related through backward and forward linkages. For example, an assembly plant might not start operations in a given location because it lacks local suppliers of a particular component, but a potential supplier of that component might not initiate production because there is no local downstream demand for its product (Trindade, 2005).

Is There Really a Case for Intervention?

What the Evidence Says about Exports

The existence of a rationale for intervention associated with potential spillovers does not automatically imply that intervention is warranted. It is important to establish first whether spillovers associated with exports do in fact occur. A number of studies present evidence of export spillovers associated with employee turnover (Mion and Opromolla, 2013) and spatial agglomeration (Koenig, Mayneris, and Poncet, 2010; Mayneris and Poncet, 2013).[4] Data from Peru indicate that—after conditioning by time-invariant, firm-product-destination factors and year-specific factors—firms located in municipalities with larger numbers of firms that were already exporting a given product to a given destination are more likely to start exporting the same product to the same destination. These export spillovers are stronger for specific product-destinations than across all product-destinations and for more narrowly defined spatial areas (municipalities) than for broader spatial areas (departments). These external effects appear to be generally small, however (Figure 8.2).[5] By contrast, some studies fail to identify export spillovers (Barrios Cobos, Görg, and Strobl, 2003; Bernard and Jensen, 2004).

Spillovers are far from automatic and generalized, which explains these contradictory results. Based on data from four countries, this point is informally illustrated in Table 8.1 and Figure 8.3, using the number of firms that followed peers that introduced a new export product as a proxy—an admittedly imperfect one.[6] For most new export products, the few pioneering firms (usually only one) have a limited number of followers, whereas for a few of these products, the first movers were followed by several companies.[7] Some of these followers are new-to-export firms, represented in the figure by the light-gray bars.

Clearly, there are sectors in which pioneering firms enjoy a first-mover advantage and virtually no followers; this is typically the case

Figure 8.2 Local Export Spillovers, Peru (2000–11)

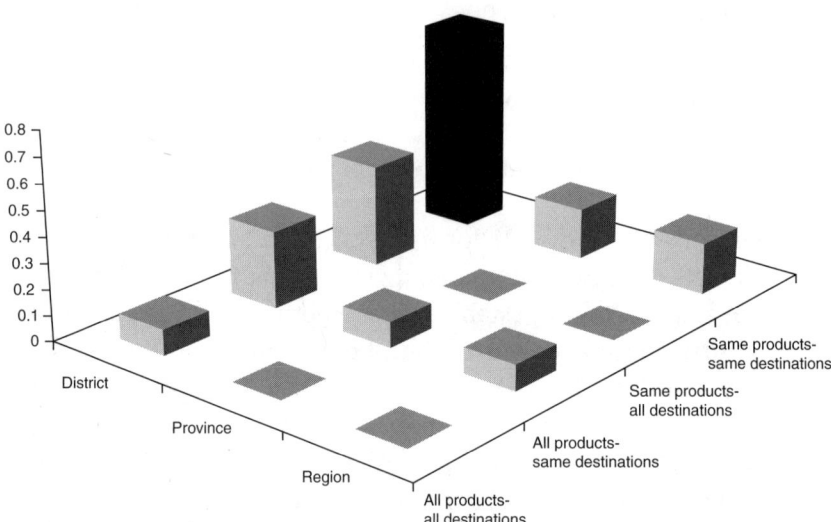

Note: The figure reports the estimated percentage increase in the probability that a firm will export a given product to a given destination, associated with an increase of 100 in the number of firms that exported from the same region, province, or municipality (district) any product to the same destination, the same product to any destination, or the same product to the same destination. Estimates have been obtained from a linear probability model that includes firm-product-destination fixed effects and year fixed effects. Control variables include time-specific firms' number of employees, total imports of the destination country, and export assistance status. Alternatives available for the firms—and accordingly, the estimation sample—have been constructed following Koenig, Mayneris, and Poncet (2010).
Source: Author's calculations based on data from PROMPERU.

Table 8.1 New Products Introduced in 2003–06: Pioneers and Followers

Country	Number of new products	Share with followers
Chile	236	52.5
Costa Rica	534	56.2
Colombia	301	60.5
Peru	365	57.3

Note: The table reports the number of products at the HS 6-digit level of classification that were not exported in the 1997–2002 period (or the 1998–2002 period, in the case of Costa Rica) and started to be exported in the 2003–06 period. It also presents the percentage share of the products that had followers: that is, firms that started to export them after the pioneer.
Source: Authors' calculations based on data from PROCHILE, PROCOMER, DIAN, and PROMPERU

Figure 8.3 Distribution of the Number of Followers and Share of New Exporters for New Products Introduced between 2003 and 2006

a. Chile

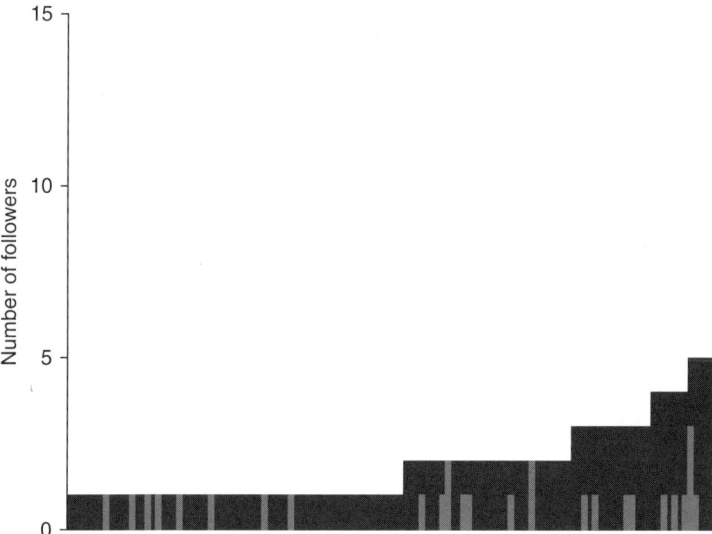

b. Colombia

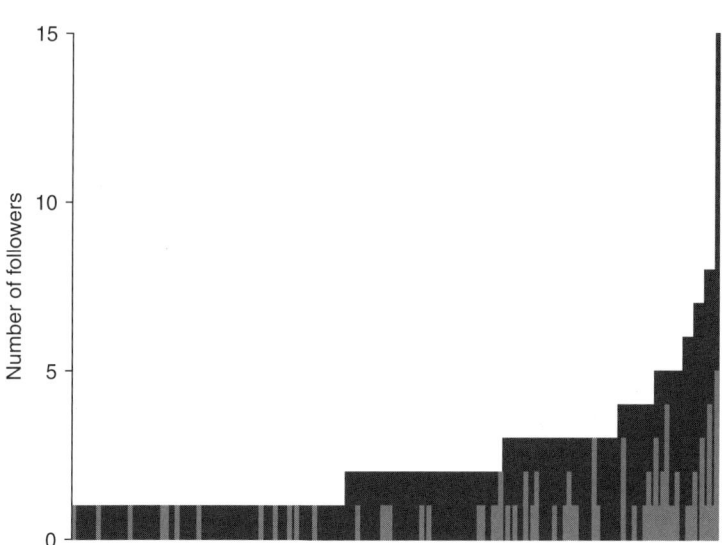

c. Costa Rica

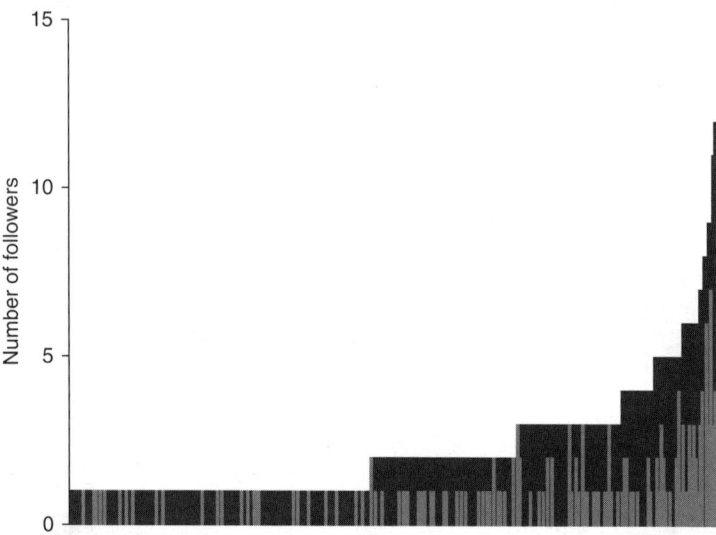

d. Peru

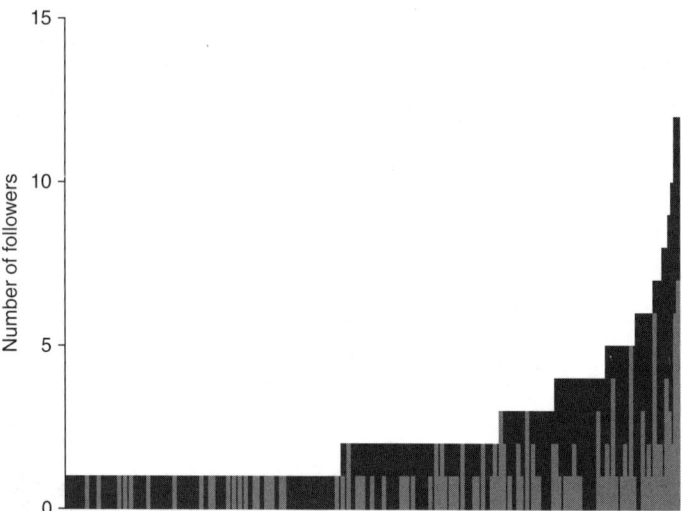

Note: The darker-gray bars depict the number of firms that started exporting those products introduced by pioneering firms between 2003 and 2006, from the year after their introduction, to 2010. The light-gray bars depict the number of followers that are new-to-export firms. Only products with a positive number of followers are included.
Source: Authors' calculations based on data from PROCHILE, DIAN, PROCOMER, and PROMPERU.

of goods produced on a large scale by a small number of producers (Wagner and Zahler, 2013). Recent evidence further shows that pioneers whose new products survive in foreign markets have more followers, which are generally larger than the pioneer. These companies either learn from the successes or avoid the failures of their predecessors (Wagner and Zahler, 2013). Moreover, not all exports create the same external effects. Some preconditions need to be met. For instance, firms that succeed in international markets prepare by investing in new technologies, hiring workers from other exporting companies, and upgrading their products (Álvarez and López, 2005; Iacovone and Javorcik, 2012). As pioneers, these firms are more likely to be successfully imitated than firms that are less prepared to export (Artopoulos, Friel, and Hallak, 2010).

What the Evidence Says about FDI and GVC

According to the literature, FDI generates spillovers through labor turnover, particularly of highly skilled workers (Balsvik, 2011; Poole, 2013), and among former employees of MNCs who start their own businesses in their home countries (Muendler, Rauch, and Tocoian, 2012). There is also evidence of productive vertical spillovers from FDI to local firms in upstream sectors of the supply chain (Aitken, Hanson, and Harrison, 1997; Javorcik, 2004; Alfaro and Rodríguez-Clare, 2004). Moreover, FDI enhances export activities in host countries, in terms of both increasing the export orientation of domestic firms (Aitken, Hanson, and Harrison, 1997; Greenaway, Sousa, and Wakelin, 2004) and upgrading the quality of their export baskets (Harding and Javorcik, 2012). In contrast, FDI spillovers to local firms within the same industry appear to be more elusive (López-Córdova, 2002; Damijan et al., 2003).[8]

As with exports, spillovers are not ubiquitous. The externalities from FDI may be uneven across sectors, as some activities have stronger and more diversified linkages with the rest of the economy, and these linkages may differ across countries (Volpe Martincus and Gallo, 2009). Even within sectors, such externalities may arise only when "modern technologies" are used (Glass and Saggi, 1998; Harrison and Rodríguez-Clare, 2010). In this vein, for spillovers to occur there should be some technological gap between MNCs and domestic firms (Findlay, 1978; Blalock and Gertler, 2002). If this gap is too large, however (Lipsey and Sjöholm, 2005), the superior technology of the MNC may be out of reach for domestic firms that lack sufficient human capital. More generally, the national absorptive capacity needs to be above a certain threshold (Lipsey and Sjöholm, 2005).[9]

Balancing the Social Costs and Benefits of Intervention

Externalities (or coordination failures) are a necessary condition for intervention. Spillovers may be present, but they are far from common: the potential for these external effects is likely to differ across groups of firms and activities. Moreover, there may be complementarities. The question becomes: What are the relative payoffs of intervening to correct a specific market failure without correcting other market failures, compared to correcting these market failures in a more comprehensive fashion? In addition, the magnitude of spillovers is not well established (Pack and Saggi, 2006). For these reasons, market failures alone are not a sufficient condition. In fact, most interventions must factor in costs and are advisable only if their potential social benefits exceed the corresponding social costs.

Internationalization Policies: Past and Present

The degree and profile of countries' internationalization are shaped by the interplay of different factors. A first set of factors covers the macro dimension, and includes the macroeconomic policies and business climate. A second set of factors can be generically bundled as *trade costs* and their determinants (Anderson and van Wincoop, 2004).[10] A third set of factors encompasses the availability of human capital, innovation efforts, and access to finance, which are the subject of policies that are reviewed in other chapters of this report.

Over time, Latin American and Caribbean countries have resorted to different mixes of policies to promote the internationalization of their economies, varying in their degree of alignment with the criterion of correcting market failures. Specifically, internationalization policies are not new in the region; they date back at least five decades. The first initiatives focusing on nontraditional exports appeared in the 1950s, complementing the import-substitution strategies of the time in a context of high import tariffs and restrictive quotas. These policies relied heavily on fiscal incentives and special credit packages to firms and, to a large extent, were based on the idea that diversifying away from primary products would be conducive to sustained growth. Thus, for instance, in Colombia, the equivalent value of export promotion subsidies as a percentage of total nontraditional export values was above 20 percent between 1967 and 1974, and peaked at approximately 27 percent in 1972–73 (Meléndez and Perry, 2010).

Starting at the end of the 1980s and as a consequence of the new regulations associated with the multilateral and regional trade agreements signed at that time, fiscal incentives and other instruments that represented direct subsidies became much more restricted, particularly on the trade side. The extensive public sector reforms enacted at the same time also put a cap on these instruments. Accordingly, internationalization policies shifted away from heavy-handed state interventions. Current productive development policies (PDPs) aim to correct market failures and focus primarily on improving the competitiveness of domestic producers in generally more open economies—thereby making them subject to the "discipline of the international market" (Melo and Rodríguez-Clare, 2006). In terms of the conceptual framework presented in chapter 2, today's policies are softer forms of horizontal public inputs and horizontal market intervention. In particular, relative to their predecessors, they emphasize subsidized information, counseling services, and matching grants to participate in international marketing events, while downplaying instruments that create strong distortions in market mechanisms (Jordana, Volpe Martincus, and Gallo, 2010).[11] These policies are mostly carried out across a wide range of sectors. Still, there is sectoral targeting and thus there are vertical elements. Moreover, emerging GVCs and foreign buyers operating in developing countries are inducing some countries to adopt more targeted, vertical interventions to deal with the specific challenges posed by these international actors (Cattaneo et al., 2013; Gereffi and Sturgeon, 2013; Pietrobelli and Staritz, 2013).

The rest of this chapter will focus on export and investment promotion policies, along with their respective organizational arrangements. Such policies are the core of these new PDPs, addressing market failures—primarily those associated with information problems. Other policies directed at macroeconomic conditions, the overall business climate, or traditional barriers to trade such as tariffs and transport costs, which can also affect countries' specialization, will not be covered here (IDB, 2002; Moreira, Volpe Martincus, and Blyde, 2008).

Export and Investment Promotion: Who, What, and How[12]

The first Export and Investment Promotion Organizations (EIPOs) were created during the import-substitution period to manage the fiscal incentives and special credit packages granted to firms. The overall assessment of these initial organizations was clearly negative (Keesing and Singer, 1991). The strong antitrade bias associated with the prevailing import-substitution regime helps explain their poor performance and assessments. Most of these EIPOs became nonoperative and even disappeared as a consequence of public sector reforms and changing economic conditions. A new generation of EIPOs has emerged since the beginning of the 1990s, featuring diverse and innovative organizational designs. This ongoing process of institutional development involves substantial experimentation and is still the subject of an intense policy debate. EIPOs provide firms with a range of services, which will be examined in depth below.

Export and Investment Promotion Services

What is export promotion today? Export promotion organizations (EPOs) offer exporters training in export procedures, marketing, and business negotiations; analyses of country and product market trends; information about trade opportunities abroad as well as specialized counseling and technical assistance to take advantage of these opportunities; coaching through peers; coordination, support, and cofinancing of firms' participation in international trade missions and trade shows; and assistance arranging meetings with potential foreign buyers.[13] Most of these services effectively subsidize searches, which counter the disincentives arising from potential free riding (Rauch, 1996).[14] EPOs also support initiatives to promote associations, such as sponsoring exporter consortia and sectoral trademarks (PROCHILE's exporter committees and *marcas sectoriales*), which can address coordination failures.[15] Most EPOs offer a similar basic portfolio of services. However, they vary in terms of their quality, the scale and scope of different activities, and the delivery process, including whether or not they are coordinated with one another.[16]

What is investment promotion today? Investment promotion activities can be grouped into five categories. National image building encompasses actions aimed at improving the perception of the country as an attractive location for FDI. Investment generation entails identifying and approaching potential investors. Investor servicing provides assistance to investors in analyzing business opportunities, obtaining permits for establishing a business in the host country, and disseminating information on available incentives, as well as support in accessing those incentives (Box 8.1). Policy advocacy encompasses all activities aimed at improving the investment climate, identifying the public inputs needed by the private sector, and coordinating with the rest of the public sector to deliver those inputs. Investment aftercare for already established MNCs consists of facilitation services and development support in tandem with the corporate evolution of these companies (UNCTAD, 2007; Harding and Javorcik, 2011).[17] While the services are similar, they differ across organizations along several dimensions, and these differences seem to matter for their effectiveness. To cite a notable example, investment promotion organizations (IPOs) that handle investors' inquiries in a more professional manner and have higher-quality websites tend to attract larger volumes of FDI (Harding and Javorcik, 2013).[18]

Box 8.1 Incentives for FDI

Most countries around the world offer incentives to attract MNCs as part of their investment promotion initiatives (UNCTAD, 2000). Fiscal incentives such as tax holidays and breaks lower certain taxes on a temporary or permanent basis (such as decreasing the base rate of the corporate income tax) or even exempt companies from certain taxes. Financial incentives such as grants and preferential loans act as direct subsidies that can reduce the MNC's fixed and variable costs. Financial incentives are more prevalent in developed economies (Blomström and Kokko, 2003; OECD, 2012a). These incentives can be combined with one another and with other measures, such as subsidized infrastructure and land, as is typically the case with export-processing zones. These instruments also have a sectoral/spatial dimension, as certain activities (mainly high-tech manufacturing) and certain regions (notably poorer areas with above-average unemployment) tend to be targeted (see chapter 5).

Competition among countries to attract FDI has intensified along with the surge in FDI in recent decades (Fernández-Arias, Hausmann, and Stein, 2001). Both the number of countries offering incentives and the range of incentives offered are significantly larger than in the mid-1980s (UNCTAD, 1996). While there are no publicly available systematic data on the form and amount of subsidies to FDI and hence on the costs of these programs, anecdotal evidence suggests that subsidies per FDI-related job are substantial and have even increased over time. In the United States, for instance, incentives per job directly created in the automobile sector increased from $4,000 in the late 1970s to $168,000 in the early 1990s, whereas in Brazil this ratio ranged between $54,000 and $340,000 in the mid-1990s.

Tax policy and investment incentives can affect the location of MNCs across countries and within countries. While evidence points to externalities linked to FDI by these companies, difficult questions arise about the magnitude of the incentives relative to the size of these externalities, and how long the incentives should remain in place. Moreover, competition between governments to attract firms can make incentives ineffective. This "fiscal war" scenario is particularly likely in federal countries.

Last but certainly not least, all empirical studies consistently indicate that fundamentals such as location, market potential, relative factor costs, and agglomeration of related economic activities play a key role in determining the geographical distribution of FDI, along with macroeconomic policies and the institutional context. The Costa Rican experience is illustrative in this regard. While the role of the export-processing zone regime can hardly be overlooked, several attributes of the country help explain the larger inflows of FDI in more sophisticated manufacturing sectors in recent decades. These include the country's political, social, and macroeconomic stability; rule of law; low levels of corruption; relatively high levels of economic freedom, especially regarding trade and capital flows along with a pro-business environment; appropriate transport logistics; an attractive location, close to a large market such as the United States; quality of life; and, importantly, a labor force with relatively high levels of education and good knowledge of English—the result of continuous investments in education over several decades. On top of this, all accounts of the Costa Rican experience highlight the role played by the country's IPO, CINDE—even though there are no econometric assessments. The relative importance of determinants like these will differ across countries. Thus, while the use of incentives can be a tool for attracting FDI, implementing such incentives requires dealing with challenging issues like their magnitude, timing, and balance with the role of the fundamentals.

The Specialization-Coordination Trade-Off

Policies and specific services tend to be more integrated than in the past. For example, EPOs facilitate production linkages with MNCs. IPOs attract foreign investors as well as foreign buyers and facilitate matchmaking with local suppliers, and sometimes even extend their support to their learning process to comply with the standards required by the foreign counterparts. These developments have an institutional dimension. The trend is toward integrating promotional activities (export, investment, business development, and even tourism in a few cases) into single organizations (Australia's AUSTRADE, Colombia's PROEXPORT, Finland's FINPRO, Germany's GTAI, and the Republic of Korea's KOTRA). In a few cases, notably Enterprise Ireland (EI) and New Zealand Trade and Enterprise (NZTE), the mission of the organizations also encompasses the design and implementation of programs to favor business development in general. This creates an integrated support chain for firms that aim to increase their overall competitiveness and thereby facilitate their participation in international markets. The incipient convergence of the policies and institutions addressing these issues is also clearly related to the integration and complementarity between exports and FDI, with a large portion of exports coming from MNCs, and with GVCs as the main conduit for the exports of local firms.

In general, there may be a trade-off between having specific organizations that provide specialized support in particular areas (which require more intense coordination efforts), and having a centralized organization (which would ameliorate coordination problems, but potentially at the price of being less specialized in the distinct areas) (ECLAC, 2008).[19] Between these extremes are alternative arrangements for achieving coordination, such as the cross-membership of officials of relevant entities in their respective boards. The optimal organizational arrangement depends on several country-specific factors.

EIPOs and the Private Sector

The private sector can be organically integrated into EIPOs by participating on their board of directors, if they have one; the board defines the EIPO's overall strategy and oversees their activities. In Latin America and the Caribbean, representatives from this sector are typically authorities of national sectoral chambers or business associations, such as the Chambers of Exporters of the Argentine Republic in EXPORTAR; the National Association of Exporters and Importers (ANIERM) in PROMEXICO; the National Society of Industries (SNI) in PROMPERU; and the National Chamber of Commerce and Services in URUGUAY XXI. In other EIPOs (EI, FINPRO, Jamaica's JTI, and NZTE), staff members of individual companies directly represent the private sector. This representation should allow for a more formal incorporation of firms' preferences into trade and investment promotion policymaking. In reality, however, the degree of control retained by the public sector in many Latin American and Caribbean countries tends to be substantial, particularly when the public sector funds the EIPO. Whether or not it is formally represented in the governing bodies, the private sector can collaborate with EIPOs by carrying out joint promotional activities (Jordana, Volpe Martincus, and Gallo, 2010).

Size Matters

The resources available to EIPOs vary greatly. In developed countries, annual budgets exceed $100 million, and even top $300 million in some cases, and their employees number more than 300. In Latin America and the Caribbean, only two organizations have annual budgets close to or exceeding $100 million (PROMEXICO and APEX-Brazil) and only three entities in the region have more than 300 employees (PROCHILE, PROMEXICO, and PROMPERU). Many EIPOs in the region have limited allocated resources, even after adjusting for the size of their GDPs. A few notable exceptions include the Foreign Trade Promoter (PROCOMER), PROCHILE, and PROEXPORT (Figure 8.4).[20]

This relatively low level of funding might reflect the low priority assigned to export and investment promotion, or a backlash due to the disappointing experience with EIPOs during the import-substitution period. However, if a minimum critical mass is required to operate effectively, the allocation of limited resources may lead organizations to underperform relative to needs and expectations, which

Figure 8.4 Absolute and Relative Size of EIPOs, Latin America and the Caribbean vs. the Rest of the World, 2007–10

a. Absolute Size

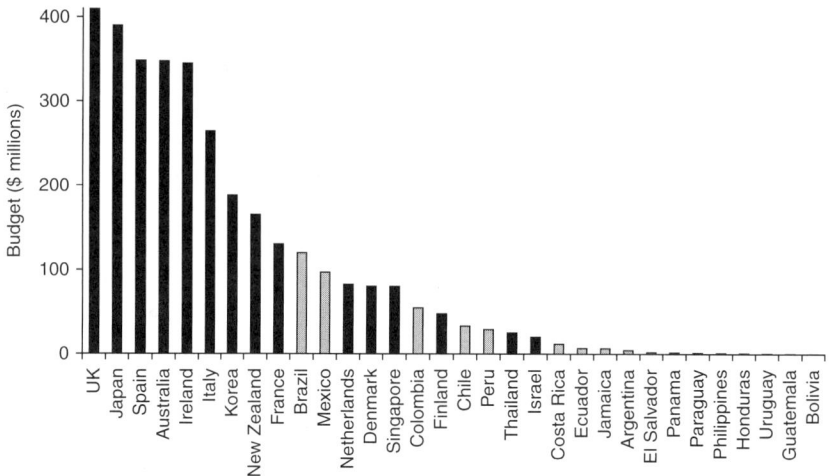

b. Relative Size

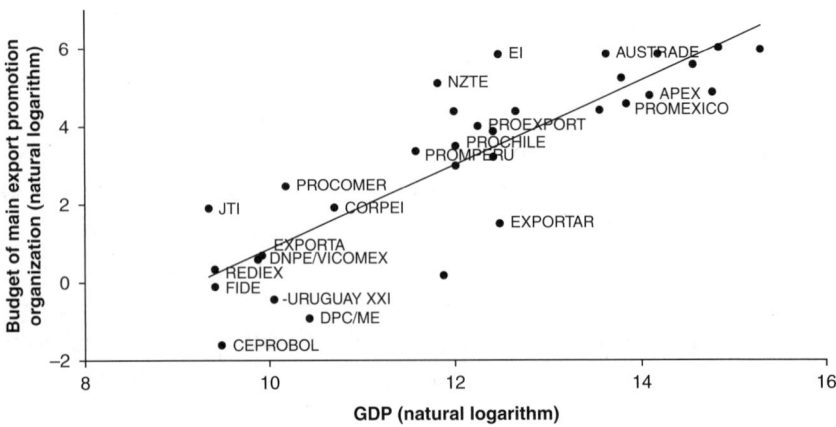

Source: Authors' calculation based on data from Jordana, Volpe Martincus, and Gallo (2010), and Volpe Martincus (2010).

would damage their reputation, negatively affect their weight in the states' power structure, and shrink their constituencies—thereby triggering a vicious circle of tighter budget constraints, worsening performance, and deteriorating reputation (Melo and Rodríguez-Clare, 2006).[21] The evidence points to a positive relationship between the budget of the EPOs and their economies' total exports, although strong diminishing returns seem to prevail (Lederman, Olarreaga, and Payton, 2010). In short, while rigorously establishing how the level of resources affects the organizations' performance is far from easy, size seems to matter.[22]

Merit Pay Is the Exception in the Region

In several entities of countries outside Latin America and the Caribbean, including EI, NZTE, and KOTRA, personnel remuneration consists of a fixed wage plus a variable component based on individual performance. The setup is substantially different in the region. With only a few exceptions (notably PROEXPORT), most organizations pay fixed wages that are not tied to performance.[23] The use of a variable pay scheme is generally limited in the region by the public recruiting systems to which EIPOs must adhere. While according to PROEXPORT's lead officials the variable remuneration system has made a difference in terms of motivating personnel, strengthening an institutional culture of goal achievement, aligning the organization's missions and priorities, and establishing the precise way in which this pay scheme influences organizational effectiveness require additional research.

To Be or Not to Be Abroad?

Many EIPOs from developed countries have numerous offices abroad that give them a presence in many countries. Entities from Latin America and the Caribbean, on the other hand, have a very limited presence abroad (Figure 8.5), with a few exceptions (PROCHILE, PROEXPORT, and PROMEXICO). Several organizations do not have foreign missions and must rely on the support of diplomatic personnel at embassies and consulates (diplomatic missions, DMs) to assist exporting companies.

Figure 8.5 Presence Abroad of EIPOs, Latin America and the Caribbean vs. the Rest of the World, 2007–10

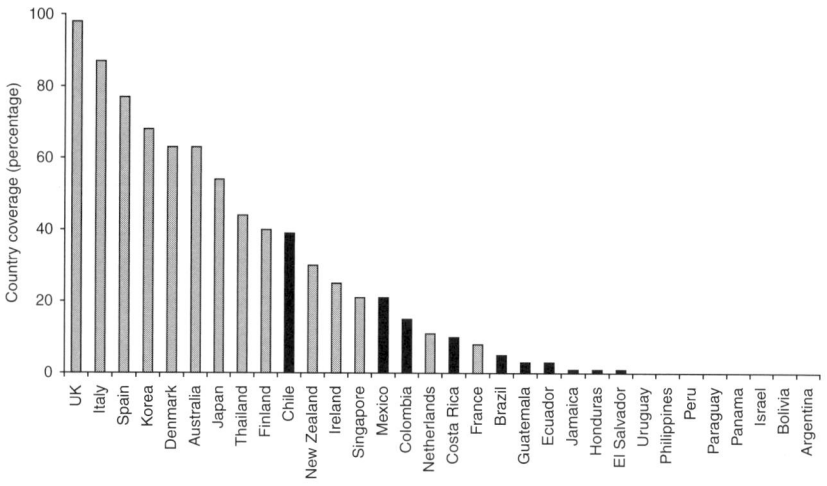

Source: Authors' calculations based on data from Jordana, Volpe Martincus, and Gallo (2010), and Volpe Martincus (2010).

Evidence from Latin America and the Caribbean indicates that offices of both EPOs and DMs seem to positively affect countries' exports, by primarily favoring their diversification (that is, along the product extensive margin, here proxied by the number of products exported). However, their effects are not uniform. In general, the establishment of a foreign office of an EPO has a greater effect on exports, and makes a greater contribution to export product diversification than opening a new DM (Figure 8.6). Moreover, the addition of a foreign office of an EPO favors the expansion of the extensive margin of exports of more differentiated goods, while the increase in the number of products because of a DM is mostly linked to homogeneous goods (Volpe Martincus, Carballo, and Gallo, 2011; Volpe Martincus et al., 2010; Gil-Pareja et al., 2011). Thus, whereas EPOs help countries diversify into new sectors, DMs tend to promote

Figure 8.6   Impact of Foreign Missions on Countries' Intensive and Extensive Margins of Bilateral Exports, Latin America and the Caribbean, 2000–07

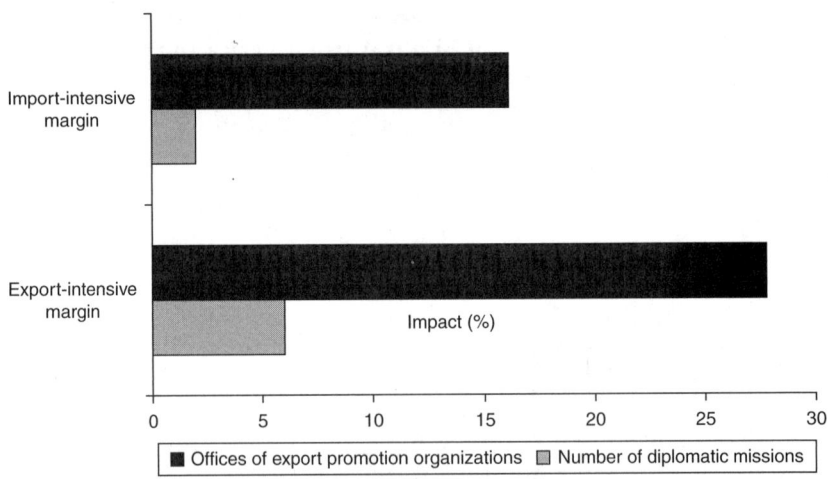

Note: The figure reports the estimated effects of both an office of the export promotion organization and the number of diplomatic representations (missions) of the exporter country in the importer country on the average exports per product (intensive margin) and the number of products exported (extensive margin). These effects have been obtained by estimating a gravity equation that includes the typical enhancing/hindering factors and export-year and importer-year fixed effects.
Source: Volpe Martincus (2010).

foreign sales of the same kinds of goods in which these countries are already specialized.

These results highlight the importance of specialized export-promoting services abroad to increase export diversification. EPOs are specialized entities, staffed with personnel experienced in international marketing who are specifically tasked with helping firms do business abroad. In many cases, EPOs are managed according to private sector practices. In contrast, DMs do not always have a commercial section or personnel with expertise in export promotion, and spread their activities among a wide variety of tasks. Moreover, mechanisms for coordinating EPOs and DMs tend to be informal and weak, or even nonexistent.[24] In addition, diplomatic officials formally responsible for export promotion usually do not have any incentives, such as career progression, to perform the required activities.

This does not mean that EPOs must open their own offices abroad. The same result could be achieved by properly strengthening trade competencies in DMs, increasing incentives of the officials tasked with export promotion, and improving the coordination of these representations with their countries' EPOs.[25] Of course, making these moves would require addressing major institutional challenges. If, as expected, the costs of these alternative strategies differ, then the implied cost-benefit relationships should be computed and compared to one another.[26]

Does Targeting Make a Difference?

Most EPOs perform some kind of geographical or sectoral targeting, and even certain combinations of both, although to different extents. This targeting introduces a vertical dimension in policies that otherwise tend to be horizontal, and is based on selection processes that have different levels of "rigor." The most rigorous type of targeting uses both demand orientation (specific market prospects, as established by research conducted by staff in foreign offices) and domestic supply potential (the domestic potential to take advantage of these prospects). As long as more than one firm is pursuing the activities in question, these activities might be seen as proxy for potential for spillovers, under certain conditions.[27]

Despite targeting, firms operating across the entire product-destination spectrum that request assistance generally receive some form of support. Targeting can be accomplished largely through the level of support provided. Thus, data from PROCHILE indicates that, on average, firms active in targeted product-destinations are assisted with a larger number of instruments.[28] While priorities tend to persist, these are likely to be adjusted over time (Figure 8.7).

Targeting seems to make a difference. The analysis suggests that, conditional on firm-product-destination and year-specific factors, export values from those firms assisted by PROCHILE to targeted product-destinations tended to grow more than those from their counterparts to product-destinations that were not targeted. In addition, product-destination pairs in which the country did not initially register exports were more likely to be introduced if they were targeted.[29] Moreover, targeted product-destinations that were

Figure 8.7 PROCHILE's Export Promotion Instruments

a. Number of Instruments

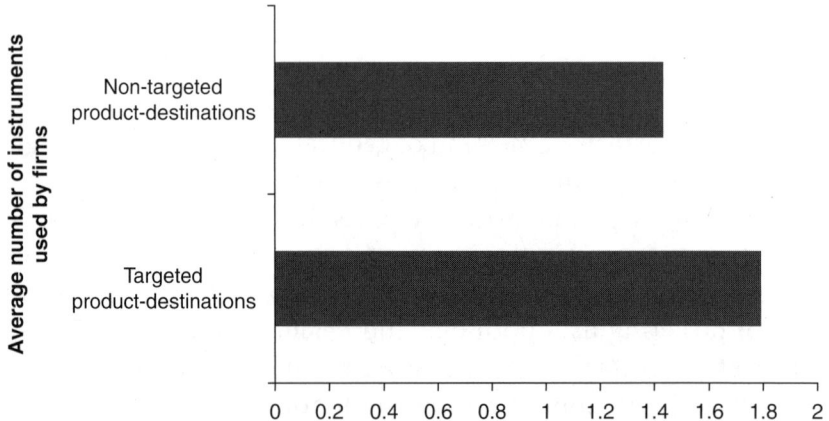

b. Persistence of Targeting

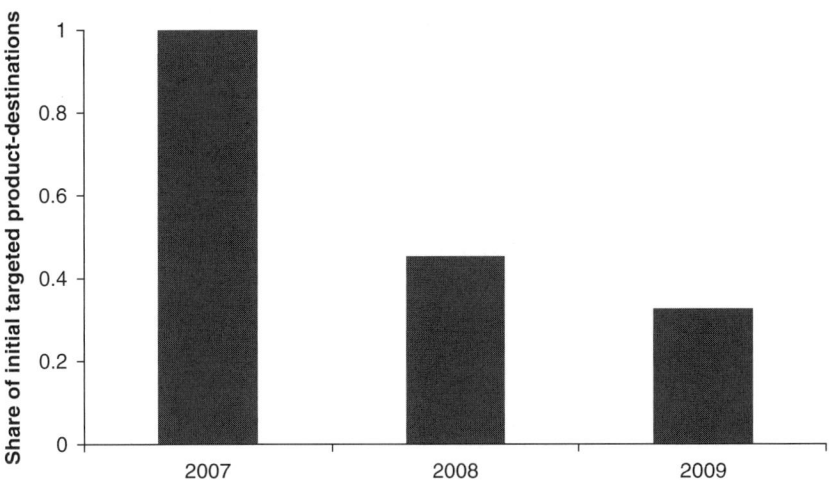

Note: In panel a, averages are computed over three possible instruments: specialized information services, support to participate in international marketing events, and assistance to develop commercial strategies and export capabilities. Panel b shows the share of targeted product destinations in 2007 that remained as such in 2008 and 2009.
Source: Authors' calculations based on data from PROCHILE.

introduced have more followers than their counterparts that were not targeted.[30]

Regarding FDI, a survey conducted in the mid-2000s indicates that more than 70 percent of the IPOs target some sectors (Charlton et al., 2004).[31] Among practitioners, targeting is considered a best practice because it allows for messages to be more focused and tailored, and delivered to a more narrowly interested audience, which tends to increase the effectiveness of promotional efforts relative to those that are general and emphasize countries as good places to do business across sectors (Loewendahl, 2001; Proksch, 2004; Harding and Javorcik, 2011). In particular, IPOs tend to concentrate on sectors in which their countries have comparative advantage and sectors that allow for diversification, thereby bringing new technologies and skills to their host economies (Alfaro and Charlton, 2007) (Box 8.2).[32]

Box 8.2   Two Cases of Sectoral Targeting to Attract FDI

The experiences of Ireland and Costa Rica illustrate the different strategies that countries might follow to attract FDI.

Ireland: Promoting Entirely New Sectors

Foreign ownership of firms operating in Ireland was strictly prohibited until the late 1950s, as part of a broader policy to protect domestic manufacturing. In the late 1950s, economic crisis led to the abolition of the Control of Manufactures Act, and marked the beginning of an explicit policy of cultivating FDI. Under different guises, this policy has remained in place until today (Barry and Bradley, 1997). Initially, the efforts to attract FDI did not involve sectoral targeting. Many firms came to Ireland looking for a location within Europe with low labor costs. As these costs increased and new locations emerged in Eastern Europe, some sectors—primarily textiles, electronics, and assembly—lost competitiveness and foreign investors left the country. In response to these developments, the country's IPO, the Industrial Development Agency (IDA), decided to start targeting sectors that reflected Ireland's characteristics and comparative advantages: it is a small country located on the periphery of Europe. The country had invested heavily in education, but many graduates left the country because of lack of opportunities; and it had low corporate income taxes. Given these country characteristics, Ireland targeted sectors based on some specific criteria: sophisticated sectors, to take advantage of the availability of skilled labor; products with high value-to-weight ratios, owing to the peripheral location in Europe; and products that had high profit margins, to take advantage of low corporate tax rates. Naturally, efforts also focused on sectors with high growth potential. Based on these criteria, four sectors were chosen: information and communication technologies, pharmaceuticals, financial services, and other services (technical support, consumer services, and consulting). While two of these sectors were already present in the country, the other two were entirely new. Projects in other sectors were also given consideration, but the promotion efforts focused on these four.

Costa Rica: Supporting Sectors That Were Already Promising

Like Ireland, Costa Rica has also attracted substantial amounts of FDI. The crowning moment came in 1997, when the country's IPO, CINDE, helped attract Intel. While fiscal incentives for FDI in Costa Rica are available for all sectors, nowadays CINDE focuses its promotional efforts on

> a few specific sectors: electronics, medical services/devices, and business services. CINDE's policy advocacy is also concentrated on these sectors, and has led to the provision of some vertical public goods. The development of a mechanical engineering career at the public university to attract firms in the electronics sector is an example. There is an important difference between the Costa Rican style of targeting FDI and that of Ireland. In particular, unlike Ireland, at the time sectors were targeted in Costa Rica, they were not entirely new. Those sectors had started to reveal themselves as competitive and at the very least, they had been the subject of interest by perspective firms.

In practice, and consistent with what is observed in EPOs, targeting is implemented by adopting organizational structures and staffing policies designed around the targeted industries. This implies having discrete management units for each targeted sector, staffed with specialized personnel who focus their promotional efforts on the respective sector (as done, for example, by Invest in Sweden). Potential investors in targeted sectors are offered special services, and responses to their inquiries are given priority (Alfaro and Charlton, 2007).

Harding and Javorcik (2011) use targeting and their timing to estimate the impact of investment promotion efforts to attract FDI from the United States from 1990 to 2004. Their results suggest that promotional efforts led to higher FDI inflows to developing countries. In particular, priority sectors received 155 percent more FDI after being targeted, which translated into an additional annual inflow of $17 million for the median country-sector observation.[33] Furthermore, targeted sectors that received more FDI upgraded their exported products relative to their counterparts that were not targeted (Harding and Javorcik, 2012).

Evaluation: The Weakest Link

Consistent periodic evaluations of program effectiveness are necessary components of the process by which EIPOs adjust to their clients' evolving needs. While some EPOs in developed countries carry out (or commission) careful assessments consisting of both rigorous econometric analyses and detailed surveys to firms, most EPOs in Latin America and the Caribbean assess the effects of their actions merely by taking into account measures of client satisfaction. Many also base output evaluations on the value of exports achieved by supported firms or on the change in their export values, as computed either from customs data or from information gathered through questionnaires sent to firms participating in the activities they organize—typically missions and fairs. Substantive methodological problems amount to serious flaws in all of these evaluation strategies, making it impossible for them to generate reliable indicators of impact—and hence of the actual contribution of EPOs and their programs to their countries' exports. Despite their limitations, these assessments are frequently used as the basis for important decisions about strategies, budgetary allocations, and other matters.

Dosage, Sizing, and Coordination of Export and Investment Promotion: Evidence from Three Cases

This section presents evidence from three specific interventions in the region: a number of trade promotion programs and their combination in Colombia, to investigate whether the dosage of trade assistance (that is, how much support is provided to operate abroad) makes a difference; a program in Costa Rica linking MNCs to local suppliers, to explore the conditions under which such programs can work; and the interplay between trade and innovation promotion programs in Chile, to examine whether there are synergies between PDPs that could be better exploited through appropriate institutional design and policy implementation.

Dosage Makes a Difference

In recent years, a series of rigorous studies has assessed the overall impact of export promotion activities on export outcomes. These studies use quasi-experimental methods on firm-level data in several countries, thereby substantially improving knowledge of these effects. These studies generally conclude that trade promotion boosts firms' export performance, particularly in terms of the number of products exported and the number of destinations reached (that is, along the product and destination extensive margins (Volpe Martincus, 2010).[34] Most of these studies evaluate the effects of export promotion as a single, overall program. However, public policies in this area consist of a variety of programs that tackle the different information gaps across the various stages of the export-development process, from the early exploration of exporting—and specific markets in particular—to the identification of, contact, and negotiation with possible individual buyers. Despite a common purpose of addressing market failures and improving export outcomes, these programs and their alternative combinations may differ significantly from one another in terms of their effectiveness. PROEXPORT's experience from 2003 to 2006 provides interesting insights in this regard.[35]

The services that this organization provides exporters can be broadly aggregated into three fairly homogeneous groups: counseling (C), which consists primarily of training and information services; trade agenda (A), which refers to the arrangement of appointments with potential customers through the commercial offices of the organization; and trade fairs, shows, and missions (M), which are international marketing events in which firms may gain experiential knowledge, display their products, establish contacts, and close deals.[36]

Firms can and do participate in more than one of these activities in the same year. Hence in each year, firms can be assisted with different—and mutually exclusive—bundles of services, as formed by alternative combinations of the basic services (A, C, M, AC, CM, MA, ACM) and with different intensities of trade promotion assistance: (1 service [A, C, M] vs. 2 services [AC, CM, MA] vs. 3 services [A, C, M]). Bundling of services is a relatively recent phenomenon among EIPOs, and is far from widespread. PROEXPORT is one of the agencies that are moving toward this strategy. Between 2003 and 2006, more than 55 percent of the assisted firms received more than one service, and 24.5 percent of them were supported with all three.

Firms using these different bundles of services may differ along relevant dimensions. A key variable to understand a firm's demand for specific types of assistance is the firm's degree of export development. Firms' awareness of the available promotion instruments, as well as their obstacles and needs, tends to differ across the various stages of the internationalization process. On the supply side, EIPOs' services are also targeted to firms depending on their stage of the internationalization process (for example, training in the export process is mainly intended to support beginners). As expected, program usage is closely related to the extent of preexisting engagement in export activity as measured by total exports, previous number of destinations, and previous number of exported products.[37] Firms that are more engaged in international trade tend to participate in various activities, thus making a more intensive use of PROEXPORT services (Figure 8.8).

Once differences among firms are properly accounted for, it is possible to explicitly evaluate whether combined services are more effective in promoting exports than individual ones.[38] This implies identifying the differential effect of joining a program consisting of more than one service instead of a comparison program consisting of only one service for firms participating in the program bundling more than one service. These pair-wise program comparisons indicate that higher trade promotion intensities tend to be associated with larger, positive effects on export outcomes, and thus systematically perform better than other programs. Firms combining A, C, and M have significantly higher export growth (17.7 percent), both along the country-extensive margins (11.7 percent) and product-extensive margins (11 percent), than if they had used each of these services separately (Figure 8.9). Furthermore, these firms exhibit a higher increase in the number of destinations (on average, 9.4 percent), when compared to a situation in which they had used alternative combinations of two of these three services.[39]

To sum up, EPOs are likely to be more effective—and probably encourage greater spillovers—when they bundle services. Bundled services provide exporters with integrated assistance throughout the export development process, which is more effective than isolated

Figure 8.8 Some Measures across Groups of Firms Participating in Different Export Promotion Programs in Colombia

a. Distribution of Total Exports

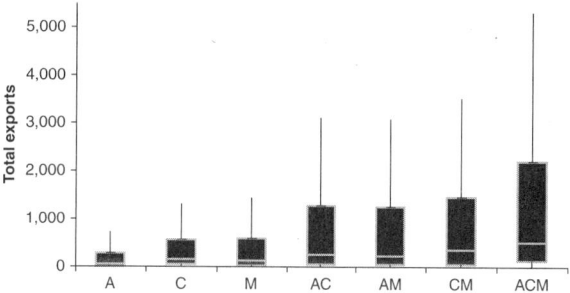

b. Number of Export-Destination Countries

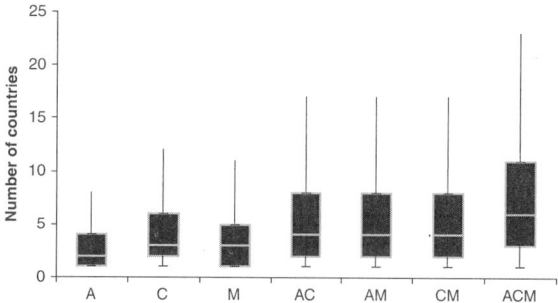

c. Number of Products

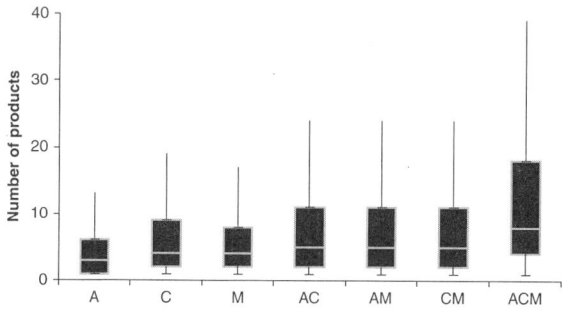

Note: Horizontal axis: A – trade agenda services; C – counseling services; M – trade fair, shows, and mission services.
Source: Volpe Martincus and Carballo (2010), based on data provided by PROEXPORT.

Figure 8.9 Average Effect of Export Assistance Programs in Colombia

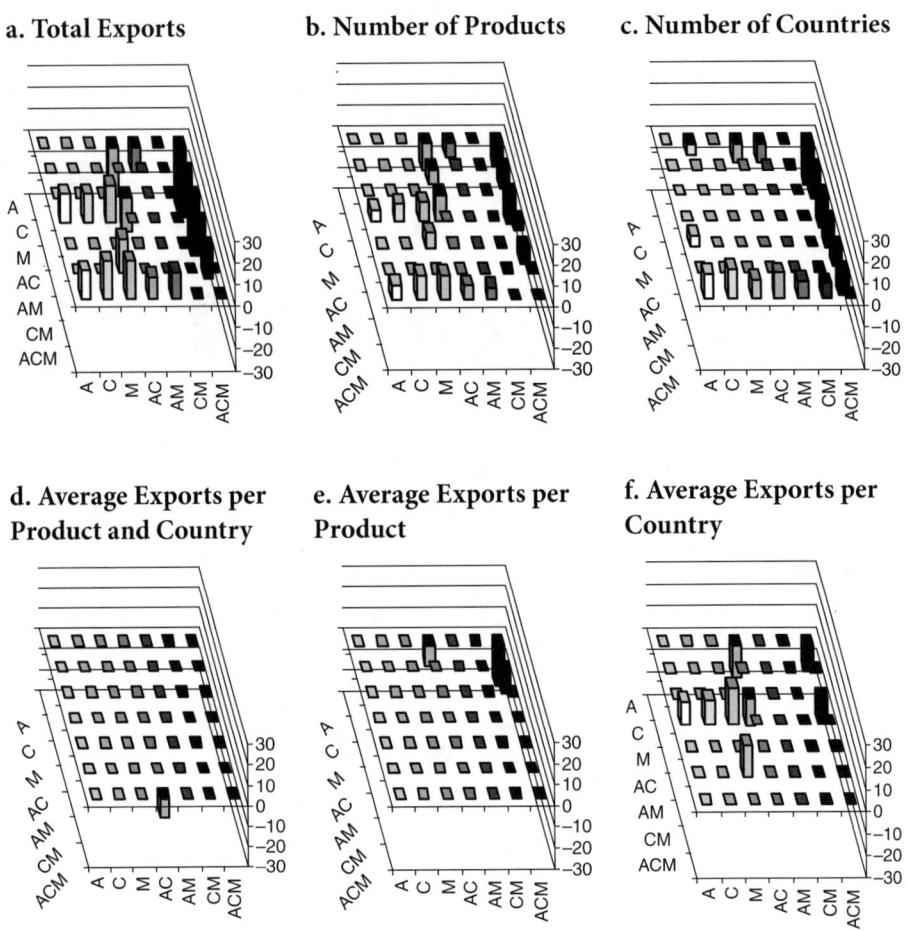

Note: The figure reports the effect of each export promotion program relative to each other. Sample period is 2003–06. Statistically insignificant effects are reported as zero. The figure should be read as follows: a positive number m indicates that the effect of the program shown in the row on its participants compared to that if they had joined the comparison program given in the respective column is an [e^m-1]*100 percent additional growth rate of the export variable being considered.
Source: Volpe Martincus (2010), based on data from PROEXPORT.

support. The costs of these different export support strategies are likely to differ. In particular, programs that combine various services are predictably costlier. Hence, cost-benefit ratios should be computed and compared to decide on the allocation of a given budget across these support strategies.[40]

Linkage Programs and FDI

As discussed, successfully attracting MNCs or lead firms in GVCs does not automatically mean that positive spillovers will occur. Whether and to what extent such spillovers take place depend primarily on the technology with which MNCs operate in the host country and the gap relative to that of domestic firms, as well as the absorption capabilities of the host countries (such as availability of relevant human capital and a well-functioning innovation infrastructure). The existence of positive spillovers may also hinge upon policy efforts aimed at removing information barriers that impede the emergence of production linkages between MNCs and local companies. This point is illustrated using the experience of the linkage program in Costa Rica, formerly known as Costa Rica Provee (CRP hereafter), and currently known as Encadenamientos para la Exportación (Linkages for Exports). This program is designed, administered, and monitored by the country's national EPO, PROCOMER.

FDI has increased substantially in recent decades in Costa Rica and led to a major shift in the country's export specialization profile toward high-tech manufacturing. Moreover, FDI in Costa Rica has already generated training and education spillovers.[41] Nonetheless, the consensus is that overall production linkages with MNCs located in export-processing zones have been weak, thereby limiting the benefits that could have been reaped from their presence. These linkages have been a long-standing matter of policy concern.

After various previous initiatives in this area, CRP was established in 2001 to increase the domestic value added from high-tech MNCs and to improve the technological capacity of SMEs to help them become local suppliers of MNCs and, eventually, direct exporters.[42] The program has operated primarily as a business matchmaking service based on the demands of multinational firms for inputs and raw materials. These needs are identified and then matched with local suppliers that comply with the production, technical, and quality specifications and characteristics required. CRP therefore mainly addressed market failures associated with information problems (Monge-González, Rivera, and Rosales-Tijerino, 2010).[43]

In terms of targeting, CRP initially focused on high-technology MNCs, but later broadened its focus to include ICTs, and the electronics, electrical, and metalworking sectors; the medical, chemical, and pharmaceutical sectors; and agribusiness and textiles (OECD, 2012a). Further, the program has focused mainly on SMEs with greater capabilities and a higher likelihood of becoming successful suppliers to MNCs. Firms that already had export experience and higher real wages, were expanding in terms of the number of employees, and were located in the main cities were more likely to join the program (Monge-González and Rodríguez-Álvarez, 2013).

From 2001 to 2012, CRP created 1,355 linkages between more than 400 local companies and 301 exporters, primarily MNCs.[44] The annual number of backward linkages sponsored by the program increased from less than 10 to more than 200, and sales jumped from $0.8 million to $12 million from 2001 to 2012. The average number of products sold by domestic companies reached 1.5 in most recent years, compared with 1.0 in the first half of the 2000s (Figure 8.10). The average annual exports of participating SMEs reached $283,000 in 2009, more than double the average of $132,000 at the beginning of the period (MIF, 2010). These data, as well as interviews with both SMEs and multinational corporations, suggest that the program has been an effective matchmaking mechanism (Paus and Gallagher, 2008; Monge-González, Rivera, and Rosales-Tijerino, 2010; MIF, 2010).

A recent econometric evaluation of CRP that carefully accounts for differences between participating and nonparticipating firms reveals that the program has had a positive impact on real wages, employment, and exports (export status) of participating firms. These effects go beyond the year in which firms join the program; this could suggest that assisted firms continue to derive benefits from the knowledge acquired through their commercial relationships with the MNCs (Monge-González and Rodríguez-Álvarez, 2013). Interestingly, the magnitude of the impact increases with the dosage of assistance, as proxied by the number of participations in the program (Monge-González, Leiva Bonilla, and Rodríguez-Álvarez, 2012a) (Figure 8.11).

Figure 8.10 Costa Rica Provee: Sales, Links, and Products Sold, 2002–12

a. Sales

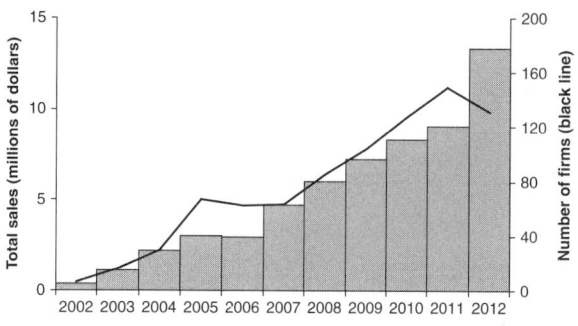

b. Links

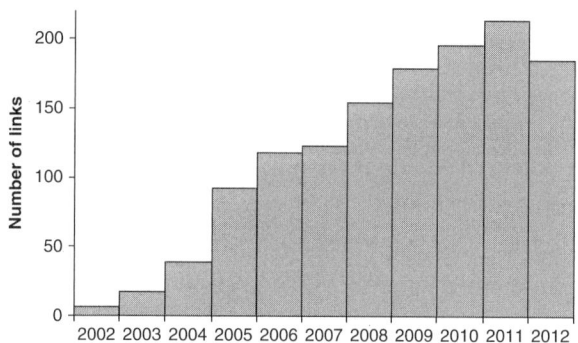

c. Products Sold

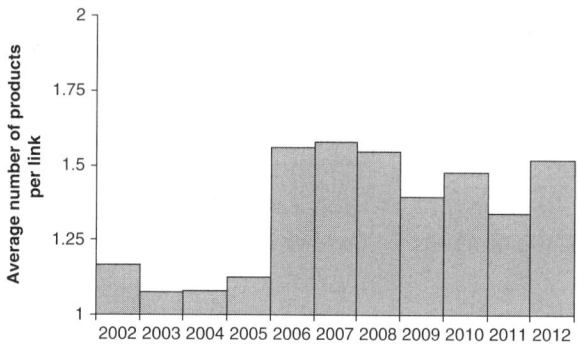

Source: Authors' calculations based on data from PROCOMER and Encadenamientos para la Exportación.

Figure 8.11   Estimated Impact of Costa Rica Provee on Exports

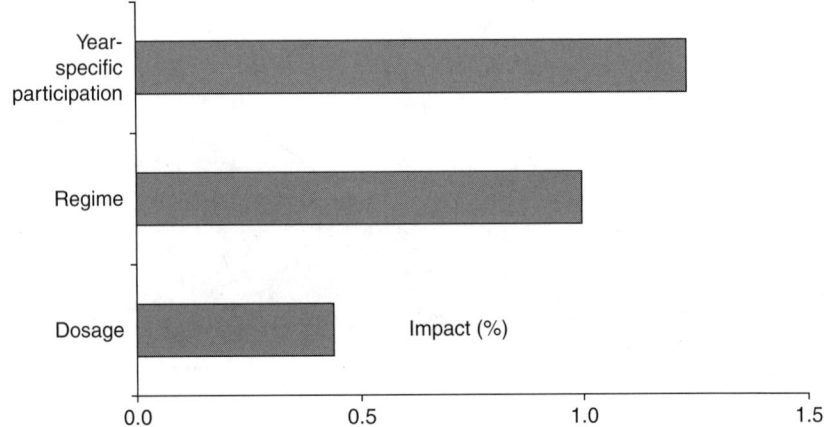

Note: The figure reports the estimated direct impact of participation in Costa Rica Provee on participating firms' export status. Year-specific participation is captured through a binary indicator that takes the value of one if the firm participated in the program in the year in question and zero otherwise. Regime is a binary indicator that takes the value of one since the first year the firm participated in the program and zero otherwise. Dosage is a count variable that takes the value of one for the first year of participation, two for the second year of participation, and so on, and zero otherwise.
Source: Authors' compilation using data from Monge-González and Rodríguez-Álvarez (2013).

Despite these positive effects, the scope of the program appears to have been limited. Purchases associated with participation in CRP accounted for a very small share of the total local purchases by MNCs in Costa Rica from 2001 to 2011, amounting to less than 1 percent in 2007 (Monge-González, Rivera, and Rosales-Tijerino, 2010; MIF, 2010). Furthermore, less than 20 percent of the linkages under the program were actually incorporated into the high-technology final products of the MNCs, suggesting that most of these linkages involved nonspecialized inputs (de Groote, 2005).[45] Overall, observers agree that while certainly valuable as a first step, the program has fallen short of making a substantial difference, as linkages between MNCs and domestic firms and spillovers are still limited (Paus and Gallagher, 2008; OECD, 2012a).

A possible explanation is the interplay between limited potential for spillovers from the specific FDI in the country and limited, domestic absorptive capacity (Paus and Gallagher, 2008). Although the situation has been changing over time, a significant portion of FDI has not been intensive in technology. Moreover, some of the key inputs may not be currently bought in Costa Rica because of insufficient scale or technological sophistication. Lack of local capabilities not related to size also seems to play an important role. The case of Baxter is illustrative. At least until recently, Baxter's affiliate in Singapore sourced some key parts from local firms because there was essentially no quality difference relative to those produced in-house. In contrast, Baxter's plant in Costa Rica kept their production in-house for quality-control purposes.

A second explanation is that CRP does not have the proper size and has not coordinated properly with other public support programs to meet the important challenges associated with the development of linkages with MNCs. The unit running the program has had seven employees and an annual budget of roughly $300,000 over the last five years. While the evaluation referred to above suggests that CRP has positively affected the employment and exports of participating firms, these resources seem to be too small to change the country's linkage capability qualitatively and quantitatively.

In addition, while CRP has concentrated on correcting the market failure associated with information barriers, other relevant market failures remained unattended, such as those linked to access to technology and financing. What is needed goes beyond the initial contact between a local supplier and a MNC. Lack of technical know-how, certifications, and human resource training and difficulties in accessing financing have been identified as obstacles to expanding sales to MNCs in Costa Rica and elsewhere in the region (Beltrán and Gutiérrez, 2007). Moreover, the learning and upgrading via integration in GVCs is influenced by the characteristics and effectiveness of the local innovation and business support system (Morrison, Pietrobelli, and Rabellotti, 2008; Pietrobelli and Rabellotti, 2011, 2012). In this regard, CRP and other public programs dealing with these other market failures in Costa Rica—such as PROPYME, a matching grant scheme to promote R&D and other forms of innovation—have not been well interconnected (Monge-González and Rodríguez-Álvarez, 2013).[46] Further, coordination with investment promotion efforts has been relatively weak. Thus, in general, the absence of institutional cooperation and program coordination has limited the impact of public interventions on efforts to upgrade the quality of local suppliers. The Government of Costa Rica has taken steps to correct this situation. First, the directorate in charge of CRP has begun to provide assistance to develop suppliers; this is an interesting case of institutional learning (Dobles Madrigal, 2012a). Second, the Commission of Linkages for Exports (Comisión de Encadenamientos para la Exportación) was established in 2010 to improve the coordination of programs administered by member organizations (Dobles Madrigal, 2012b).[47]

Various countries around the world, particularly those that have attracted large amounts of FDI, have also implemented programs targeted at local firms to support their efforts to become suppliers of MNCs and particularly their insertion into GVCs. A well-known example in this regard is the National Linkages Program (NLP) in Ireland, established in 1985 and managed initially by Ireland's IDA. The program consisted of two components; the first one targeted MNCs to assist them in finding potential firms within Ireland. The second component targeted local firms to build capabilities and capacity. Through an initial screening process, companies seeking to participate were assessed on their potential to improve their technical, financial, and managerial capabilities. Then, assistance was given to the suppliers selected in specific areas targeted for development, including operational management and control, quality systems, finance, and marketing. Eventually, the NLP evolved from the exclusive support of linking local firms with MNCs in Ireland to a more general program that helps incorporate Irish companies into GVCs.

Another program was Singapore's Local Industry Upgrading Program (LIUP) implemented in 1986 and administered by the Economic Development Board. The distinctive feature of the LIUP was that the training of local firms fell to the MNCs, which in turn received incentives from the government. In particular, the LIUP went beyond matchmaking and procured partnerships between specific MNCs and potential suppliers. Multinationals were encouraged to choose local subcontractors and assist them in improving overall operation efficiency. An employee from the multinational was seconded to the local supplier and in return, the program paid the salary of the employee. In 1994, there were 32 buyer companies and 180 SME suppliers (Battat, Frank, and Shen, 1996). By then, the LIUP had already reported some positive impacts. According to studies by the LIUP and reported in Battat, Frank, and Shen (1996), the suppliers' productivity in the early years of the program increased by 17 percent, while the value added per worker rose by 13.7 percent. The program continued to expand over the decade, and by 1999 the number of suppliers that benefited from the program had risen to 670. Eventually, the LIUP was subsumed in a more general partnership program, which in 2012 was endowed with $250 million over five years.

The experience of Malaysia is particularly interesting because it provides elements of both success and failure. An early initiative was created in 1988 with the Vendor Development Program, which aimed at assisting local SMEs to become suppliers of MNCs and other large companies in the country. For the most part, the program was restricted to SMEs owned by indigenous people from Malaysia, leaving aside those firms not owned by this ethnic group.[48] The selection of SMEs based on such noneconomic criteria resulted in many suppliers failing to meet the needs of the MNCs (UNCTAD, 2011). For example, in 1996 there were 54 anchor companies signed up, but only 27 had developed any vendors under the program (Karikomi, 1998). The largest anchor company, Proton, the national carmaker, had 17 vendors under the program, but that represented only 12 percent of all of its vendors (Suyderhoud, 1999). The main concern was the poor quality of the products developed by vendors (UNCTAD, 2011). In the mid-1990s, a new linkage program—the Industrial Linkages Program (ILP)—was created. Unlike its predecessor, it introduced more merit-based selection criteria, gave MNCs a more active role in selecting suppliers, and provided more complementary assistance for the supplier to access finance and build capabilities. The main policy tool of this program consists of a series of tax relief measures to both the supplier and the MNC. The program seems to have fared better than its predecessor. By 2007, a total of 906 SMEs were registered under the ILP, and 128 of them were linked to MNCs and other large companies (UNCTAD, 2011).

In Latin America and the Caribbean, Mexico has considerable experience supporting the creation of business linkages between MNCs and local suppliers. During the 1970s, the Mexican government created an information-exchange system called Bolsas de Subcontratación, which consisted of a database of businesses in Mexico that was made available to multinationals seeking local suppliers. Another initiative, the Centros de Articulación Productiva, helps foreign firms identify and select potential suppliers, mainly through matchmaking services. Establishing matchmaking mechanisms, however, has had limited effects on fostering successful linkages relative to other initiatives with a more comprehensive range of services (UNCTAD, 2010). Accordingly, Mexico has also experimented with other actions beyond simple matchmaking. The initiatives in the Guadalajara electronic cluster are an interesting example in this regard. This cluster has been supported by a set of active policies to promote the emergence of favorable spillovers from FDIs and the upgrading of local firms into more sophisticated segments and niches of the electronics value chain (Dussel Peters, 2010; Dussel Peters, Galindo Paliza, and Loría Díaz, 2003; ECLAC, 2008; Padilla-Pérez, 2005, 2008). Such policies have been co-funded by the state government and the private sector, and include the support of innovation and R&D activities, the support of highly specialized training programs, and the creation of high-tech incubators.

Discerning the effectiveness of all these programs is a difficult task because rigorous impact evaluations are rare. Nonetheless, these experiences provide some general lessons regarding their design. First, programs based exclusively on matchmaking services foster fewer linkages between lead firms and local suppliers than programs that also provide suppliers with complementary support to upgrade. Second, proper coordination with other programs addressing other barriers to internationalization related to market failures is a necessary condition for greater effectiveness. Third, most successful programs use merit-based selection criteria. Ineffective selection of the supplier based on noneconomic factors may not only waste valuable resources, but also jeopardize the sustainability of the program and discourage further FDI flows into the country. To ensure that the linkages are mutually beneficial, the merit-based selection can be based on criteria designed both by the government and by the MNCs, as in the Malaysian ILP program. This calls for the involvement of the multinationals from the early stages of the process. Fourth, assistance should be based on a transparent diagnosis and auditing of the supplier, so critical areas of improvement can be addressed. The particular assistance might vary depending on the program's design. Examples include soft loans provided directly to the suppliers, cofinancing, tax relief to the suppliers and/or multinationals, or contributions to the salary of the employee seconded to the supplier from the MNC, as in the Singapore LIUP program. Finally, before committing significant resources for a full-fledged program, a pilot program may be undertaken to fine-tune objectives, strategies, targets, and action plans. After the program is initiated, periodic reviews allowing for feedback into future policy design are desirable (UNCTAD, 2010; Potter, 2002; IFC, 2007; Axèle and Delane, 2008; Pietrobelli and Staritz, 2013). During this process, the program should reach a minimum scale to make a difference.

PDP Interaction to Shape Internationalization

By paving the way for increased productivity and lower marginal costs through better processes or through the introduction of new varieties (or the improved quality of existing varieties), innovation can help firms enter and expand in foreign markets.[49] Hence, policies promoting innovation—as well as other policies improving productivity—may affect firms' and their countries' internationalization (see chapter 3). Under certain conditions, the extent to which these other PDPs contribute to self-sustained internationalization might be seen as a measure of their relative success in open economies, and they can also interact with and condition the outcomes of PDPs aimed explicitly at increasing internationalization.

In general, existing evaluations of PDPs implicitly assume a single program and ignore public programs in other areas. However, in practice, firms receive assistance from different organizations, and these other forms of assistance can affect the outcomes of interest. Failure to account for interventions other than those being focused on has direct consequences for estimated effects.[50] Ignoring other interventions also implies leaving relevant policy questions unaddressed. For example: To what extent does it pay to intervene to correct a specific externality without properly taking into account other externalities that may also affect the relevant outcomes, compared to working on these externalities in a more comprehensive manner? Are there specific complementarities among programs that could be explicitly exploited by adequately designing, coordinating, and sequencing policy instruments? What would be an appropriate institutional organization of public support to the private sector to maximize potential synergies (single agencies with divisions vs. umbrella arrangements)?

The implications of the existence of multiple programs will be addressed by examining the interplay between Chile's export and innovation promotion programs in affecting export outcomes, primarily along the intensive margin. In particular, two groups of interventions are considered: export support by PROCHILE, and innovation support by FONTEC/INNOVA and FONDEF (Álvarez et al., 2013). PROCHILE is a well-established EPO that provides exporters with the services described above. Both FONTEC/INNOVA and FONDEF cofinance private initiatives primarily to improve firms' innovation capabilities and productivity. FONTEC/INNOVA focuses on alleviating the financial constraint that harms business innovation, whereas FONDEF operates to mitigate coordination failures that hinder collaboration and interaction between public research organizations and firms.

Firms supported by PROCHILE are larger than their counterparts supported by FONTEC/INNOVA/FONDEF in terms of their total exports, and their number of products and destinations prior to receiving support. As with the case of the different export promotion programs in Colombia, larger exporters tend to use more instruments: in this case, both (Table 8.2).

Variation across groups of users along these dimensions needs to be accounted for to properly identify the impact of the programs and their combination on export outcomes. This is primarily accomplished by comparing outcomes of firms with the same export value in 2012 and 2013, along with conditioning on additional firm char-

Table 8.2 Characterization of Exporters Participating in the Different Programs: Median Export Indicators and Test of Differences in Medians

Program	Value	Median test (p-values)			
		NP	IP	EP	EP/IP
Exports					
NP	13.7				
IP	109	0			
EP	160.4	0	0.017		
EP/IP	425.3	0	0.006	0.03	
Number of products					
NP	1				
IP	3	0			
EP	3	0	0.32		
EP/IP	5	0	0.001	0.001	
Number of countries					
NP	1				
IP	2	0			
EP	2	0	0.038		
EP/IP	4	0	0.002	0	

Notes: The first column of the table reports the median exports, number of products, and number of destinations for the different groups. For those firms participating in a program, figures correspond to periods before participation. The remaining columns present the p-values of the nonparametric tests of differences in the medians of these export outcomes across groups. Exports are expressed in thousands of US dollars.
NP stands for no participation, EP stands for export promotion, IP stands for innovation promotion, and EP/IP stands for export and innovation promotion.
Source: Authors' compilation using data from Álvarez et al. (2013), which is based on data provided by CORFO, PROCHILE, and CONICYT.

acteristics, such as export experience and the main export sector (Álvarez et al., 2013).[51]

The results of the evaluation reveal that both export and innovation promotion favorably impact firms' exports. While simultaneous participation in the respective programs does not seem to affect foreign sales contemporaneously, there is evidence of complementarity between previous innovation assistance and current export assistance (Table 8.3). Thus, firms that have participated in FONTEX/INNOVA/FONDEF programs and that are likely to have innovated

Table 8.3 Complementarity between Export and Innovation Promotion

PROCHILE and FONTEC-INNOVA/FONDEF, 2002–10

		Innovation promotion		
		t	t-1	t-2
Export promotion	t	-0.056 (0.704)	**0.190*** **(0.062)**	-0.114 (0.848)
	t-1	-0.025 (0.630)		
	t-2	-0.036 (0.732)		

Note: The table reports the complementary test statistics between the programs at different points in time, along with the respective p-values.
Source: Authors' compilation using data from Álvarez et al. (2013), which is based on data provided by CORFO, PROCHILE, and CONICYT.

either in terms of processes (thereby becoming more productive) or in terms of products (thereby improving existing goods or introducing new ones) and later participated in PROCHILE programs have reaped more benefits in terms of export outcomes than their counterparts that used only trade promotion services (or have resorted to assistance to both innovate and export simultaneously, thus not allowing innovation to mature). On the other hand, previous export support does not appear to have led to enough additional gains from innovation support in terms of foreign sales outcomes. Clearly, exporting is a complex process that requires previous accumulation of technological capabilities (Lall, 2001). The specific sequencing of the programs is also important in terms of their effects: in order to maximize their synergies, assistance to innovate should come before assistance to export.[52]

These findings provide preliminary evidence indicating that there may be complementarities among PDPs, and that their impact on internationalization could be reinforced if they were properly articulated and sequenced. Further research is needed not only to overcome the limitation of the previous analysis but also to explore the possible interplay between internationalization policies and other specific PDPs, such as those concerning human capital, financing, and linkages.[53]

Lessons Learned

Past and recent experiences of Latin American and Caribbean countries with interventions directed at internationalization should be a reminder of the importance of the macroeconomic context, institutions, and the trade regime. Policies aimed at addressing market failures that might potentially hinder internationalization are likely to be powerless under conditions of macroeconomic instability or in closed economies. In particular, there is no justification for substantially distorting the allocation of resources across sectors through high and variable tariffs or heavy subsidies.

In today's context of more open economies, there is clearly room for public interventions to favor internationalization, as long as these are strictly focused on addressing market failures and have the potential to generate spillovers.

Moreover, given the very integrated nature and intense complementarities between exports, FDI, and GVCs, policies and programs need to be consistent and integrate efforts and functions as much as possible. Thus, beyond explicit policies for productive development to promote internationalization, relevant interventions should be coordinated to take advantage of their complementarities and potential synergies, and avoid the suboptimal outcomes that might arise when market failures in different areas are not addressed in a comprehensive way. Assessments should specifically address which interventions would be best to coordinate with and how. This type of assessment involves both the organizational dimension (single organizations vs. separate organizations that are linked through certain institutional arrangements) and the program dimension (sequencing of instruments). Consistent and comprehensive evaluations are also needed. The increasing emergence and presence of GVCs in developing countries pose new policy challenges that will need to be addressed adequately and that further require clever policy coordination.

In order to carry out these interventions and pursue their goals, an appropriate institutional arrangement must be established. This requires considering the institutional context, and involves determining the proper role of the private sector, sound internal structures, and adequate staffing and compensation. Funding should not be too high (as diminishing returns seem to prevail) or too low (as below a certain threshold, there would be no critical mass, and results are likely to be ineffectual). In terms of strategy, the assessment of assisted firms should be refined and based on objective criteria. Assistance should be fine-tuned to be provided in the right dosage, always taking into account the cost-benefit ratios of the different alternatives.

The definition of appropriate organizational arrangements and programs is a moving target, as economic conditions differ from country to country and change over time. Experimentation is therefore a key part of the process. In this sense, it is wise to start with (relatively) small pilot projects, and review, adapt, and scale up to a reasonable degree. In particular, this involves continuously monitoring institutional practices around the world to identify those that could be applied with proper adjustments to the local circumstances. (Several EIPOs carry out such benchmarking.) It also requires continuous and periodic impact evaluations, along with rigorously designed surveys (which presupposes a more systematic shared use of the data gathered by the public and private sectors, and collection of new and relevant data). The private sector should be properly involved in the process; the customary cautions against rent seeking apply in this regard.

Last but definitely not least, the important conditioning role of other policies cannot be overemphasized. For instance, given the existence of strong policy complementarities, trade promotion will be predictably more effective in fostering exports if properly combined with additional policies that remove other trade costs. This is particularly the case with domestic infrastructure and trade facilitation actions (see Volpe Martincus and Blyde, 2013; Volpe Martincus, Carballo, and Graziano, 2013). Thus, for trade promotion to actually lead to exports of new, locally produced goods, it is necessary to have routes that allow them to be transported to the exiting ports economically. Similarly, promoting trade may be worthless in terms of additional exports if goods sit for days while companies deal with customs procedures or port operations.

9

Selecting Priority Sectors for Productive Transformation: An Elephant in the Room?

The process of economic development does not just center on the ability of countries and their firms to make more of the same goods and services they already produce. Most of the successful cases of development around the world have been associated with the capacity of countries to produce new and better-quality goods and services—that is, to engage in processes of productive transformation that stimulate economic development. As important as it is, focusing on increasing the efficiency with which production is carried out—characteristic of a static approach to economics of "doing more with less"—is not enough; catching up with advanced countries may require a dynamic process of productive transformation.[1]

To some extent, productive transformation occurs "naturally," as countries leverage the productive capabilities used to produce their current products in other sectors that require similar capabilities. But productive transformation does not always happen spontaneously. In practice, most countries that have successfully gone through these processes have rarely done so without deliberate development strategies and active policies that enhance their capacity to expand and upgrade the basket of products they produce.

What are the policy lessons from successful countries? What types of policies stimulate healthy processes of productive transformation? Unfortunately, no recipe or blueprint exists for countries to follow. Productive transformation may require a combination of productive development policies (PDPs), from horizontal ones, encouraging the emergence of new things without any specific sectoral aim, to selective policies seeking to develop specific sectors, products, or processes that are perceived to have high development value. How best to combine these policies in each country depends on how well positioned the country already is with its existing basket of products, how favorable its opportunities are for productive transformation, and the extent to which it naturally takes advantage of those opportunities. It also depends on the country's ability to design and implement policy (as will be discussed in chapters 10 and 11), as some policies in the policy toolbox demand more advanced institutional capabilities than others.

Horizontal policies that can support productive transformation—such as policies to stimulate export pioneers, encourage the emergence of new firms of high growth potential, attract foreign investment, or educate a flexible labor force well adapted to innovation—have been covered in previous chapters. This chapter focuses instead on what some consider the elephant in the room: the selection of sectors for the application of vertical policies. In other words, it focuses on the controversial topic of sector selection.

These policies are controversial for good reason. While they can contribute to processes of productive transformation, they also involve important risks. Particularly risky are vertical policies in the form of market interventions, in the lower-right quadrant of the framework developed in chapter 2. They involve tax breaks, protection, or subsidies that affect firms' bottom lines without necessarily affecting productivity, effectively becoming rent transfers to possibly unproductive firms. They generate high stakes and vested interests among rent beneficiaries. They tend to involve a great deal of discretion; under weak institutional settings, this can lead to arbitrariness on the part of policymakers and politicians, which opens the door for rent seeking.

Many countries in the region and elsewhere engage in vertical policies, but not always for the right reasons, or in a sound way. This chapter draws from the experience of the region, both good and bad. It develops a policy framework to think about priority sectors for countries willing to pursue a productive transformation strategy, and suggests some ideas to make the policy process for sector selection and vertical policies more systematic and safe. Yet because this process of sector selection—sometimes dealing with the emergence of new products and sectors—is a risky and inaccurate exercise grounded less in sharply delineated theories and hard evidence, the analysis in this chapter is more exploratory than the preceding chapters and its conclusions are more tentative.

The Region's Productive Transformation Challenge

Vertical policies are often adopted when countries want to become competitive in a wider, more desirable range of sectors and products. But what constitutes a more desirable range of products? If the market could be relied upon to generate productive transformation in a satisfactory way, the selection of promising sectors for vertical policies would be unwarranted. However, the market has limitations, leading to failures to exploit potential or latent comparative advantages that can be remedied with vertical policies. If latent comparative advantage not accessible by the market is considered, then the question of which sectors should be targeted becomes relevant again.[2]

Through the years, authors have used various concepts to classify products, usually exports, according to some presumably desirable characteristics, such as their value added, their technological content, or their sophistication. Hatzichronoglou (1997), for example, discussed the classification of products (and sectors) according to technological intensity as elaborated by the OECD. Lall, Weiss, and Zhang (2006) developed a measure of sophistication of export goods based on the per capita income of countries that export them. They argue that since more sophisticated products presumably embody greater capabilities and more advanced technologies, it would be desirable for countries to move up the sophistication ladder. Furthermore, they maintain that, to the extent that such upgrading does not happen automatically, their sophistication index could be a useful input to guide development policy. Hausmann, Hwang, and Rodrik (2007) elaborated a similar measure of product sophistication, but went a step further, finding that, other things being equal, countries with more sophisticated export baskets tend to grow faster.[3] Their research suggests that what you export matters for growth, and thus provides some empirical backing to the idea that goods somehow differ in terms of their development value.

More recently, Hidalgo and Hausmann (2009) proposed a new measure of sophistication, which they call "complexity." In a nutshell, products are more complex when they are competitively exported by fewer countries and these countries have dense export baskets, with a great number of products. In turn, a country's complexity, as measured by its Economic Complexity Index (ECI), is the average complexity of the basket of products that it exports competitively. By focusing on the ability of countries to export a wide range of products, including an "exclusive" set of products in which few other countries can compete, the ECI aims to capture the underlying productive capabilities that countries accumulate as they develop. This measure appears to have a stronger empirical backing than the alternatives, for example, as a predictor of growth (Hausmann et al., 2014). Equally important, the way of thinking about economic transformation that emerges from this framework as a process of accumulation of productive capabilities through the redeployment of existing ones is very useful to discuss PDPs, particularly of the vertical variety.[4]

Because they rely on export data, all of these measures of product sophistication display a number of weaknesses. Export product classifications are imperfect and a single trade code may lump together items requiring different skill sets, thus overlooking differences in product quality (an issue analyzed later in more detail). As a result, countries that export similar products may in fact have very different productive capabilities. Furthermore, what is important is not the final product but the actual tasks that are involved in their production (Lederman and Maloney, 2012). Fragmented productive processes across countries further weaken the link between export baskets and actual capabilities, as some countries may be engaged in low-complexity assembly of high-tech goods.[5] Moreover, export baskets include goods only because of lack of data on services, which leaves out an increasingly important segment of international trade.

Finally, none of these measures account for non-traded products, which also involve relevant productive capabilities. However, to the extent that capabilities for non-tradable production are important, underlying ingredients of a country's export competitiveness, they will also be reflected by measures of sophistication that focus on exported goods. For example, if some exportable product requires non-tradable specialized services to be competitive, the fact that the product is exported competitively is in part the reflection of the productive capabilities embodied in the non-tradable services. Thus, while exportable production is sometimes a minor fraction of GDP, new or upgraded exports are the tip of the iceberg of productive transformation because competitiveness in them reflects efficiency gains in the rest of the economy. At the same time, exports also reflect the country's endowment of natural resources, which does not result from productive capabilities and, therefore, may distort the interpretation of these measures.

At the same time that it introduces weaknesses, focusing on competitive exports rather than on the whole range of productive activities also brings key strengths. A country's international competitiveness in a product attests to the value of its productive capabilities. Furthermore, exporting provides an opportunity to scale up production that substantially magnifies the aggregate developmental impact of new productive capabilities, especially for small countries. Consequently, and in spite of the shortcomings, the evolution of export basket sophistication is an effective lens to analyze productive transformation and its challenges.

While any of the previous measures would probably paint a similar picture of the state of affairs in our region, in what follows, Hidalgo and Hausmann's concept of complexity will be used to show the process of productive transformation in the region. As a benchmark for comparison, and to provide a sense of what successful productive transformation looks like, the discussion begins with a portrait of productive transformation in Korea.

Fifty Shades of Grey: Productive Transformation in Korea and Latin America and the Caribbean

To show the process of productive transformation, the export baskets of Korea and Latin America were divided into 34 communities of products, as defined by Hausmann et al. (2014), for the 1984–2010 period (see Figures 9.1a and b). Product communities range from electronics to machinery (including cars), to mining, fruit, garments, and textiles. Each community was assigned a complexity value throughout the period, and a corresponding color.[6] The most complex product community, machinery, is represented by black bars. The rest of the communities are represented by different shades of grey, with darker colors corresponding to more complex communities. The height of each bar, in each year, represents the value share of the product community in the country's total exports. By stacking the bars in a gradation of color from the darker and more complex at the bottom to the lighter and least complex at the top, it is easy to observe the process of productive transformation in action.

Consider Korea, shown in Figure 9.1a. In 1978, the most salient product community was garments, which accounted for 24 percent of total export value. Nowadays, garments comprise just 1.1 percent of total exports, and have been topped by electronics, machinery, and chemicals, among many others. The transformation has been dramatic, aided over the years by strategic policies in support of sectors such as chemicals, electronics, shipbuilding, and cars. By contrast, the figure for Latin America (Figure 9.1b) is much lighter, and despite some moderate progress in the 1980s and 1990s, has not experienced much productive transformation since. This pattern is magnified when considering the export basket of the typical country in the region (Figure 9.1c) rather than that of the region as a whole, which tends to reflect the experience of Brazil and Mexico, which comprise about 60 percent of the region's exports. To some extent, this sluggish transformation toward higher complexity over the last decade or so may be due to the increase in the relative price of simple exports, such as those associated with mining commodities, raising their value share, and displacing less competitive, more complex exports.[7]

What to do with this evidence of slow productive transformation in the region? It would not be correct to simply set faster productive transformation as a policy objective and proceed to execute market interventions to achieve the objective. Distortionary policies that are not designed to mitigate policy failures would be impoverishing and

Figure 9.1 Complexity of Export Baskets in Korea and Latin America and the Caribbean

a. Korea

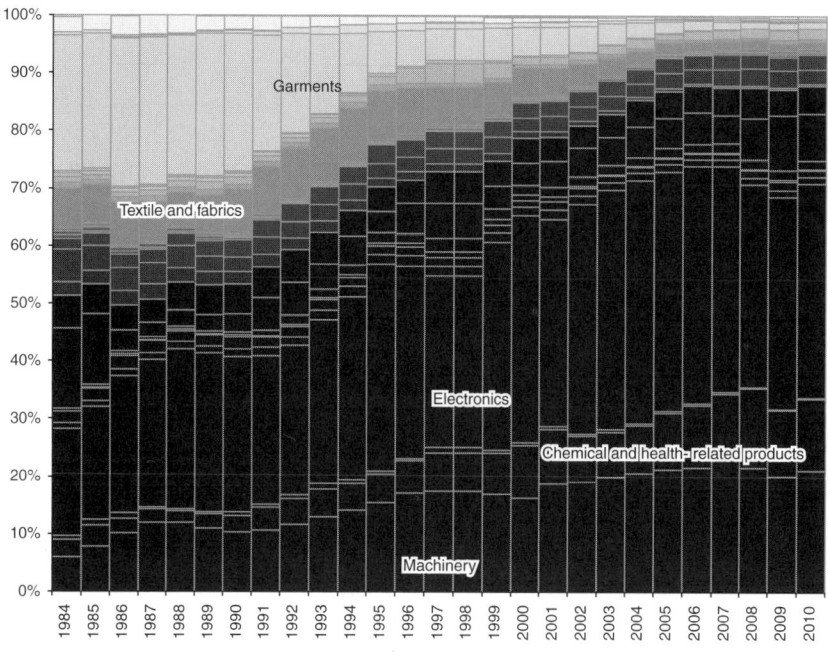

b. Latin America and the Caribbean

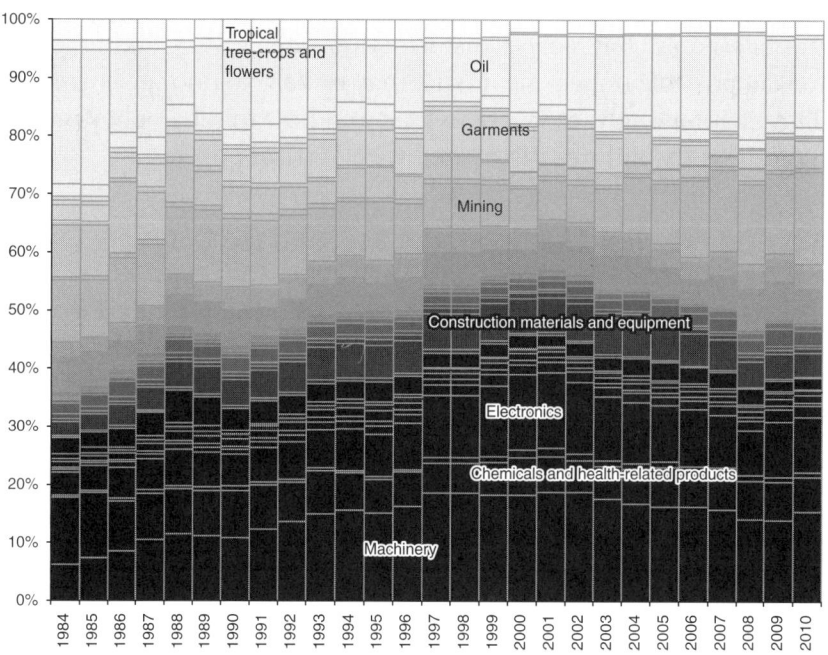

c. Typical Latin American Country

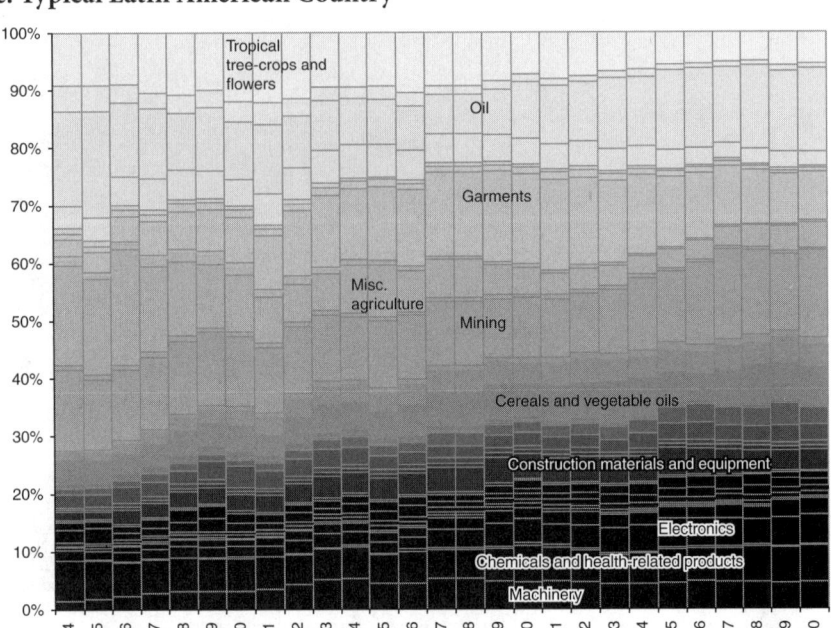

Source: Authors' calculation based on Hausmann et al (2014).

unsustainable. But slow transformation does justify taking a hard look at possible impediments that may be behind poor performance. This chapter analyzes where to look and how to set a policy process to address the failures discovered with vertical policies.

Vertical Policies: The Good, the Bad, and the Ugly

The challenge of fostering productive transformation calls for applying vertical policies to priority sectors with latent comparative advantage that the market fails to seize. However, the policy experience with vertical policies is a mixed bag. First, countries on occasion adopt these policies for the wrong reasons; instead of supporting potentially competitive sectors, they respond to political influence or favoritism to beneficiaries. Second, even when well intentioned, selecting the right sectors is technically difficult and adequately dealing with inputs from multiple stakeholders with differing perspectives, let alone pressures, requires a strong institutional setting. Even though vertical policies are usually an important ingredient of successful productive transformation, unsound vertical policies do more harm than good. This section illustrates these mixed results with some vignettes.

Almost all countries around the world and over time that have achieved substantial economic development have done so by resorting to active PDPs, leading to productive transformation. The successful experience of the East Asian tigers, which substantially transformed their productive sectors with their own versions of industrial policy, is a pointed example of this fact. The experience of Korea transitioning from agriculture to garments and textiles to advanced machinery and electronics shown above is a perfect example. As discussed in Box 8.2 in chapter 8, Ireland is another clear example of a country with strong public institutions that identified priority sectors in a top-down fashion following technocratic criteria, and pursued an aggressive and successful policy of attracting FDI to these sectors.

Even in today's most advanced economies, a free market discourse with respect to the productive sectors has many times in the past been accompanied by de facto interventionist policies to support similar processes of productive transformation. For example, the history of the United States is full of government interventions paving the way for productive transformation, ranging from government support for the diffusion of railways and electric networks to the setting of the system of state universities in the nineteenth century to support agricultural transformation to, more recently, financing the basic and applied research underlying many technological breakthroughs—from the Internet, to the GPS and the smartphone (see Singer, 2014). These active policies took place despite an arduous debate regarding productive development since the very beginning of the nation between Jeffersonians (who thought that free markets were the best way to organize production) and Hamiltonians (who favored active government). Perhaps the success of the United States lies in "talking like Jeffersonians but acting like Hamiltonians."[8]

There are also successful examples in the region. While the development of the aircraft industry in Brazil had its ups and downs and has been the subject of controversy due to the extensive use of government subsidies, undoubtedly, Brazil has become a world leader in regional commercial aircraft as a result of policies with that purpose. The selective attraction of FDI, such as the electronics and medical device sectors in Costa Rica analyzed later in this chapter or the attraction of the auto parts industry to the Mexican state of Durango (see Box 9.1) are good illustrations of vertical policies fostering productive transformation. The role of Fundación Chile in developing, among others, the salmon industry in Chile, is worth highlighting as a very successful model.

Fundación Chile, a private nonprofit corporation created in 1976 through an agreement between the Chilean government and International Telephone and Telegraph, became an instrument for making strategic bets on new and promising industries, by setting up pioneering companies and then selling them off to the private sector. In the late 1970s, it adapted salmon farming technology from Norway to Chilean conditions. It then set up a profitable firm (Salmones Antártica), which it later sold at a large profit to Nippon Suisan, a Japanese food multinational. There was considerable learning-by-looking in the industry, and now Chile exports over $2 billion in cultivated salmon. Fundación Chile played a role in developing other successful export industries following the same develop-and-sell approach, thus ensuring the diffusion of the innovation and the recovery of its commercial return without getting involved in production once the self-discovery was made. Of course, it is in the nature of exploration and strategic bets to also develop activities that do not pan out, and Fundación Chile had its share of them—as it should. The key to its success has resided in the judicious selection of sectors with latent comparative advantages, coupled with its develop-and-sell approach, which ensures that the strategic bet is temporary, whether successful or not. The case of auto parts in Durango is also worth highlighting in this respect, since it offers a good illustration of the sector selection process, which will be discussed in more detail later in the chapter.

Box 9.1 The Case of Auto Parts in Durango

Until recently, the economy of Durango, Mexico, was based on basic primary products such as agriculture, forestry, and mining. In the last decade, however, there has been a significant amount of productive transformation. This transformation did not happen by chance. Rather, it resulted from deliberate efforts, headed by successive state governors, to attract foreign investors in order to diversify the productive structure toward more sophisticated products that could generate good jobs.

The move that got the ball rolling was the successful attraction of Yazaki, one of the global leaders in the production of auto parts and, in particular, of wire harnesses. Why seek wire harnesses? The authorities thought there were good opportunities in the car parts industry, and considered which products would be worth pursuing. After careful consideration, they decided that harnesses offered great potential, provided a large number of jobs, and, given existing capabilities, were within their reach. A wire harness is like a vehicle's spinal cord, distributing electricity and information to the different components. As cars became more complex and the number and sophistication of electronics components have multiplied, harnesses themselves have become more complex, containing a rapidly increasing number of wires. Thus, authorities correctly anticipated that this would be a sector of growing demand.

Having selected a product to target, next came the decision of which firms to approach. Taking into account the relative proximity to Toyota manufacturing plants in the United States, the authorities decided to target Yazaki, Toyota's largest supplier of wire harnesses. In 2002, Ángel Sergio Guerrero Mier, at the time the governor of Durango, visited Yazaki during a promotion tour of Asia and initiated discussions that eventually led to its establishment in the state. It took a generous package to attract Yazaki, including land, buildings, scholarships, and tax exemptions. In cases such as this one, the benefits of attracting a company such as Yazaki extend beyond the direct jobs it can create, or even the productive capabilities that are developed as a result. If the company is successful, it can signal to the world that this location has what it takes to compete in the international marketplace, and that the government is willing and able to provide the type of business environment that allows this to happen. In a way, there is an important information externality, particularly in the case of the first firm that comes to a particular location, which may make generous package offers to entrants taking a worthwhile risk. Equally generous packages for later entrants, in contrast, may not be warranted. As it turns out, Yazaki was just the first car parts manufacturer to set foot in Durango.

> Soon, several others followed, proving that the presumed spillovers associated with the initial investment were in fact real. The sector now employs over 34,000 people, 6,000 of which work in Yazaki plants. And Durango is moving up the complexity scale by engaging in the production of wire harnesses for the aviation industry. The experience of Durango with car parts suggests that a careful selection process that takes into account current capabilities and latent comparative advantage as well as the expected growth of global demand can lead to successful results when the process is done right.

Unfortunately, not all examples are good. Vertical policies are risky and can easily go awry. The dangers of picking winners have been at the core of criticisms of industrial policy—and for good reason. The process of selecting sectors for policy support is usually highly discretionary. Notwithstanding that strong, selective PDPs appear to have been necessary in most cases of successful productive transformation, they are not viable without the right institutional preconditions. If institutions are weak, then discretion can translate into arbitrary behavior by public officials and rent seeking by firms and sectors that use their political clout to obtain favorable treatment. In the extreme, vertical policies may become a vehicle for undue political influence and corruption.

Policies may turn ugly when driven by capture and rent motivations. The protection of the uncompetitive rice sector in Costa Rica, discussed in chapter 2, which distributes rents to large growers without doing anything to increase productivity, suggests that these problems can arise even in countries with relatively strong institutions. These risks are always present and need to be checked in any program of vertical policies. But in cases of weak institutions, the proliferation of vertical policies driven by subjective assessment and capture can lead to pervasive problems that can severely affect the growth and productivity performance of an economy. The problems associated with discretionary tax waivers in Jamaica (very recently eliminated) are a case in point (see Box 9.2).

Box 9.2 Tax Waivers in Jamaica: The Winds Are Changing

Until recently, Jamaica had a very generous system of tax waivers. These waivers were supported by eight different tax incentive laws that provided the basis for a wide variety of tax exemptions for specific sectors, including agriculture, construction, mining, manufacturing, and tourism. To further complicate matters, in addition to the statutory waivers stipulated in these laws, the Constitution of Jamaica grants the Finance Ministry the authority to extend discretionary waivers, without the need to seek legislative approval. While sectorial ministries like Industry, Agriculture, and Tourism did not have the authority to extend waivers, they did have the power to propose them, and negotiate their approval with the Ministry of Finance.

Tax waivers involved a variety of taxes, from corporate income tax to import tariffs, and the benefits varied from case to case. In some cases, waivers were partial; in others, the whole transaction was exempt. In some cases, they were temporary; in others, they provided permanent benefits. How widespread were these incentives? Just as an illustration, in December 2009 alone, the Ministry of Finance extended more than 220 discretionary waivers, for a total of more than US$ 19 million.[9] Altogether, tax waivers peaked at 9 percent of GDP in 2008. In a country in which the debt-to-GDP ratio stands at about 145 percent, this is a big deal.

Not surprisingly, the tax incentive scheme gave way to substantial lobbying and rent seeking, with some sectors receiving particularly sweet deals. One such sector was the car rental industry. In December 2009 alone, 12 car rental companies received a total of $3.2 million in waivers. How did this work? Car imports are subject to very high protection in Jamaica, through a combination of specific and ad valorem tariffs and excises that, in most cases, amount to more than 100 percent. Rental companies were allowed to import vehicles without tariffs. Two years later, they could sell them in the local market, at very significant profits.

The Jamaican case with tax waivers is a good example of what can go wrong when vertical policies are conducted in a discretionary way, without proper attention to reasonable selection criteria. It is also a good example of how vertical policies, especially market interventions, can quickly degenerate when carried out within weak institutional environments. Besides the enormous fiscal costs of out-of-control industrial policy, the economic distortions generated by unjustified PDPs and the high social costs of firms engaged in rent seeking rather than legitimate business activities amount to a heavy burden on Jamaica's productivity and growth, which has lagged far behind that of the typical Latin American and Caribbean country (see Figure B9.1).[10]

Figure B9.1 Productivity Growth in Jamaica and Latin America and the Caribbean

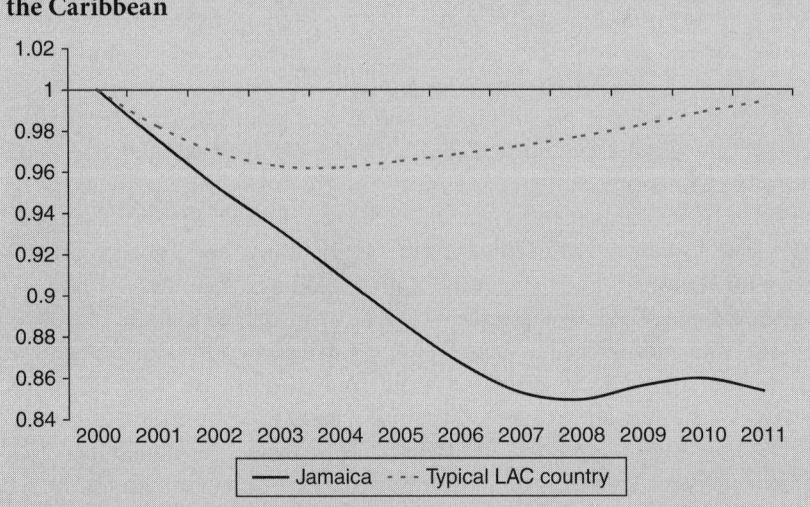

Source: Authors' calculations based on Barro and Lee (2013), and Feenstra, Inklaar, and Timmer (2013).

Fortunately, the winds of tax waivers in Jamaica are changing. In December 2013, in the midst of a standby agreement with the IMF and a tax reform program with the IDB, Jamaica passed important tax reforms. The eight sectorial tax incentives laws were repealed, and replaced by a single, horizontal tax incentive law (the Fiscal Incentives Act) that substantially restricts the type of benefits that can be extended and the type of transactions that are eligible to receive them. Waivers are available only for new investment projects that generate a minimum of formal employment, and apply mostly to the corporate income tax. In particular, waivers for tariffs have been eliminated. Most importantly, the law eliminates the authority of the finance minister to extend tax incentives discretionally. The use of waivers is now more tightly regulated, and tax expenditures have to be reported in the budget, fostering transparency in the tax system.

It is hard to know whether Jamaica is out of the woods with regard to tax incentives. Old habits die hard. The favorable changes observed recently could potentially be reverted under different economic and political circumstances. While the new law restricts the power of the finance minister to discretionally extend waivers, the constitution still empowers the minister to do so. The hope is that reform will be sustained, and Jamaica will continue to strengthen institutions and transition to a set of PDPs that, far from distributing rents, contribute to enhanced productivity and growth. This would be the best antidote to policy reversion.

Clearly, vertical policies that involve picking sectors can be good and bad. Capture and rent seeking are enemies of vertical policies. The strength of the institutions in charge of these policies and, in particular, the ability to conduct policy in an environment that mitigates this risk are key ingredients to enhance the likelihood of success. Chapters 10 and 11 discuss these institutional considerations in detail.

However, political and private capture is not the only risk. Even well-intentioned vertical policies aimed at fostering economic development may go bad simply because of their technical complexity. Guidelines for sector selection, which are discussed later in this chapter, are necessarily imprecise and always leave room for mistakes. Technocrats may embark in the wrong direction and find it difficult to reverse course. The case of the failed 1980s informatics program in Brazil discussed in chapter 1, in contrast to its aeronautics program, may be an example of a sector wrongly selected for technical reasons. While Brazilian informatics initially made some progress with its support, the economy just did not have what it takes to be competitive in such a dynamic industry at the forefront of innovation in advanced countries.

Useful policies for productive transformation need to address market failures that prevent the market from achieving the right outcomes. Willful policies that are not designed to supplement the market by addressing its failures may lead to worse failures of their own. Furthermore, policies pursuing productive transformation should be firmly grounded in achieving international competitiveness: productive transformation against the grain of the country's latent comparative advantage can be very harmful. The next sections will make the theoretical case for vertical policies, and suggest some ideas on how to structure the sector selection process to arrive at sound sector priorities for the application of these policies.

The Case for Vertical Policies

The process of productive transformation advances by redeploying capabilities from products already mastered to new ones of high value—or higher quality—that can be produced and exported competitively. How easy is it to transfer these capabilities? That depends on how similar or "close" the new products are to the existing ones in terms of the competencies involved. One way to operationalize this concept is to measure the proximity between products as the frequency with which they are coproduced by individual countries (Hidalgo and Hausmann, 2009). The assumption is that high frequency of joint production signals similarity in the underlying capabilities. Proximity also signals latent competitiveness because if targets are close by, presumably they will inherit the comparative advantage already revealed in current production. From this viewpoint, countries' prospects for productive transformation in a specific direction depend on how close the new target products are to the products already mastered. For example, the probability that a country will develop a competitive aircraft parts industry increases if it is already competitive in car parts, or other products that require similar capabilities. Evidently, not all directions for productive transformation are equally feasible and costly.

Not all directions for productive transformation are equally valuable either. Expanding a country's product basket in one direction may be more worthwhile than in others, either because it delivers more sophisticated products yielding higher income or because it opens avenues to redeploy productive capabilities into other worthwhile products. As it turns out, some products are more connected than others and are better springboards to expand opportunities for productive transformation. The value of a product as a springboard for productive transformation, or strategic value, is a useful concept when discussing sector selection.[11] Valuable productive transformation does not just depend on moving into new products. Producing the same products with higher quality—a dimension that is missing in the framework of Hausmann et al. (2014)—can also be a very worthwhile way to transform an economy (see Box 9.3). In particular, the value of a product as a springboard for further transformation may also depend on this quality dimension.

Box 9.3   Quality: The Missing Dimension

The discussion of productive transformation until now has focused on the product space. Opportunities for productive transformation depend on the current basket of products that a country produces competitively. Competitive production provides proof of the availability of the required productive capabilities, which may be used to move onto other proximate and valuable products. Yet the discussion so far—as well as the basic complexity framework on which it is built—misses an important dimension: product quality.

Different countries may produce the same product with very different qualities. Producing with higher quality may require very different productive capabilities that may support higher incomes. Moreover, higher quality may open up better opportunities to transition to different products. Producing sophisticated cars may open up opportunities that are not afforded by the production of simple cars. Thus, quality upgrading may also be used as a springboard from which to move to other products.

Within Latin America, there have been countless experiences of transformational quality upgrading. Consider Leonisa, Colombia's main exporter of women's underwear.[12] In the late 1980s, Leonisa's president visited a leading undergarment company in Spain, and discovered that the average price of their products was ten times higher than that of Leonisa. This experience was key in the decision to redirect his business toward higher-value products. The change involved significant technological upgrades: moving from $50,000 looms to $1 million looms capable of producing elastic lace; learning to work with knitted fabrics, rather than woven fabrics; and a complete overhaul of the product design and commercialization processes, allowing Leonisa to quickly tailor production in response to changes in demand. In a few years, the company went from exporting $2 products competing with Chinese producers, to $30 products competing with Italian and French firms. Exports soared.

The story of Leonisa and the array of countries it competed against at different price levels illustrates an important point: as countries develop, they don't just switch to producing new products according to their shifting comparative advantage. Rather, they expand the range of products they produce without necessarily abandoning the previous ones. They tend to produce better-quality varieties of these same products, which they sell at higher prices.

This quality dimension underlies country diversification in the product space, but is not captured by the framework of Hausmann and coauthors utilized in this chapter. Ideally, the framework could be generalized

> by treating different qualities of the same product as altogether different goods. Notwithstanding recent contributions to improve the measurement of quality (see Henn, Papageorgiou, and Spatafora, 2013), data limitations still make this generalization difficult. Nevertheless, the consideration of quality upgrading is central to productive transformation and needs to be part of the policy process.
>
> What factors are important to help countries and firms position themselves to upgrade quality? First, the speed of convergence in quality may not be the same in different products. Henn, Papageorgiou, and Spatafora (2013) find that speed of convergence is faster in manufacturing relative to agriculture or products based on natural resources. Second, Hwang (2007) shows that the speed of convergence in quality within products increases with the distance to the quality frontier. Together, these findings suggest that countries transitioning into rapidly converging products in which there is plenty of "climbing room" (in the sense that there are long quality ladders with plenty of rungs left to climb) can expect to have faster quality upgrading. To the extent that higher quality is associated with higher income, these countries would also experience higher growth.
>
> The Leonisa story has an interesting epilogue. The capabilities accumulated through quality upgrading in underwear were key for the development of a new activity, swimwear, also pioneered by Leonisa. But this firm was not the sole beneficiary of this move. It had important followers, such as Supertex, currently the largest exporter, and Onda de Mar, whose products made it to the cover of *Sports Illustrated's* swimsuit edition. This illustrates how quality upgrading can also lead to important spillovers. This turn of events also suggests that, in the same way that new products can open avenues to further opportunities, quality upgrades can also provide platforms from which to transition into other products.[13]

Does the fact that expansion in some directions may be less costly and more valuable than expansion in another justify policy intervention? Not necessarily!

In principle, the market is in the best position to achieve the delicate cost-benefit balance involved in expanding productive capabilities for productive transformation while preserving international competitiveness. Public policy interventions can be justified only with the purpose of remedying market failures that prevent firms from achieving the right outcome. Active policies that are not intended to supplement the market by addressing its failures may easily lead to worse failures of their own.

The key question is then, when is the market expected to fail to produce the right productive transformation?[14] Private firms care about international competitiveness as reflected in their costs and benefits. They presumably know the costs they would incur to acquire or develop the capabilities needed to produce a new or upgraded competitive product, as well as the price it would fetch in international markets. But do the private costs and benefits that go into market decisions reflect social costs and benefits? In other words, do private firms internalize all the relevant costs and benefits when they make their business calculations and decide to develop new capabilities? If they do, their pursuit of profits would lead to appropriate productive transformation. In this case, the market would be an efficient mechanism for transformation, and policy would only distort it counterproductively. However, if the market fails to pursue productive transformation in this fashion, policy can be useful. In that case, sound policy will be informed by the market shortcomings in order to design appropriate corrective action.

This question of whether and how the market fails is subdivided into two factors: the degree to which it seizes available opportunities for valuable productive transformation and the extent to which it opens up opportunities for development down the road. First, do private firms take the new business opportunities that are available to them to advance to new and better products? Second, do private firms transition to new products that will help them, as well as others, to continue the process of productive transformation down the road? The first question relates to firms' effectiveness in seizing the opportunities afforded by the current production structure. The second question involves their effectiveness in expanding those opportunities.

Missing the Boat: Failure to Seize Opportunities

Under normal circumstances, private firms can be expected to seize worthwhile business opportunities available to them. However, there may be many reasons why the market may fail in this regard.

Why would the market miss business opportunities? When opportunities are collectively profitable to a set of firms, one natural hypothesis is that individual firms fail to coordinate. Lack of market coordination may prevent individual firms from seizing business opportunities that would be available if executed in a concerted fashion, which may merit specific vertical policies. Alternatively, the impediment may be lack of an essential public input (or an outright government failure, for example, public monopolies or undue regulations hindering firm development).

- *Sector coordination failures and missing collective inputs*: Policies attending this class of considerations facilitate coordination among firms in need of certain collective inputs that would benefit all firms, but that no firm has the incentive to provide on its own. For example, atomized producers of perishable food may need a cold chain from plant to port to deliver more sophisticated products to affluent markets. Less obviously, producers may wish to engage in sharing the cost of mutually beneficial research on quality improvement, but find it difficult to avoid free riding and are unable to solve the problem by themselves.
- In these cases, the provision of the missing collective input is justified as long as its cost does not exceed its aggregate benefit. This cost-benefit test implies that the beneficiaries should be willing to pay collectively for the missing input. Therefore, willingness to pay by the private sector is an important test to validate the policy.[15] In some cases, interventions would help the private sector deal with the free-riding problem through the enforcement capacity of the state, at no budgetary cost, as in the case of rice in Entre Ríos discussed in chapter 2. These interventions (which correspond to the vertical public inputs quadrant of the framework in chapter 2) often emerge in the context of cluster development programs. These may be the least controversial vertical policies.
- *Chicken-and-egg coordination failures*: Other more complicated coordination problems involve multiple sectors or activities whose businesses are interdependent, rather than groups of

firms with a similar profile. Some valuable economic activities fail to exist not because productive capabilities are unavailable but simply because the market is unable to coordinate the joint investments across sectors needed for them to emerge. This is a chicken-and-egg situation in which nobody wants to go first. This coordination problem poses a more complex policy challenge not only because of the multiple sectors involved but because it is invisible to policymakers, as the new venture cannot emerge at all. Policies in this case require a vision and a more proactive engagement of the government vis-à-vis the previous ones in which existing producers can explicitly articulate their collective input demands.

- The development of the tourism industry in certain areas requires the simultaneous production of lodging, transportation infrastructure, and other services, as discussed in chapter 2. The prerequisite capabilities may exist, but investment in each sector is not profitable unless all sectors act in a coordinated fashion. Another instance of a chicken-and-egg stalemate may be a sector that does not develop because it lacks some key productive capability—which, in turn, is not forthcoming because it is not in demand. An example of this chicken-and-egg problem may be the lack of specialized labor skills to develop a high-tech industry, such as information technology. Demand for computer engineers, for instance, needs to be coordinated with supply, in terms of both the academic courses offered and students willing to be educated and trained. Solving these coordination failures may take a combination of vertical public inputs and vertical market interventions, such as subsidies or guarantees to those sectors whose coordinated investments are needed to attain a good equilibrium. In these cases, incentives ought to be temporary and discontinued once coordination takes place or it becomes clear it will not take place. However, temporary policies may be difficult to dismantle unless there are strong institutions to make them credibly temporary, an issue discussed in chapters 10 and 11.
- The private market may also miss opportunities because starting up a new sector may require a pioneer to undertake some

investments, at his own expense, that later pave the way for those who follow; if the followers' advantage is large, some collective opportunities requiring the efforts of a pioneer will not be taken and the new ventures will not emerge. This is the case of the so-called infant industry; a pioneer's struggles up a learning curve benefit all firms in the sector as the "industry" matures and becomes competitive. Another example is the self-discovery externality discussed in chapter 2 as applied to certain sectors in which it may be particularly intense. The resulting policy would promote exploration and experimentation in sectors that are especially promising collectively but prone to low appropriability of returns by the pioneer, a sort of selective self-discovery policy.

- *Dynamic spillovers*: These spillovers involve sectors or activities believed to have latent competitiveness that do not emerge spontaneously because no firm has the incentive to jump-start the process.[16] A traditional rationale is learning by doing, which cannot be internalized by the firm because the workforce and know-how could leak to competitor firms that join the sector once it is established. Appropriate policy intervention to help the development of an infant industry on account of the existence of dynamic spillovers would hopefully lead to competitive sectors once they mature.[17] The case of the state of Durango building the auto parts industry from scratch described earlier is an example of a policy betting on a sector with latent comparative advantage and supporting its emergence in the early phases when the pioneer lacks the incentive to do it.
- Like in the case of a chicken-and-egg deadlock, policies concerning infant industries must be temporary until the sector is mature or until it becomes clear that the sector will not become competitive (or it would take too long to justify costly support). However, policies addressing dynamic spillovers are even more forward looking than those addressing coordination problems among existing sectors, and therefore require more vision and may be subject to more risk of failure.

Failure to Expand Opportunities

While in most cases the market can be expected to seize available business opportunities, it cannot be expected to fully pursue the expansion of opportunities. While the benefit from seizing available opportunities tends to match the firm's bottom line, the benefit from expanding opportunities may not be fully appropriated by the firm. Moving to a new product or sector requires the development of new capabilities, but once these exist, they may become building blocks for other firms to venture into other valuable products. Due to span of control or other impediments to firm diversification, the firm that opens new avenues for productive transformation is not expected to take full advantage of all the opportunities it opens up. The presence of this "strategic value" provides a justification for policy intervention.

Thus, the baseline assumption is that externalities associated with the expansion of opportunities justify policy intervention on conceptual grounds. This does not mean that policy intervention is guaranteed; it may or may not be advisable, depending on country circumstances. First, economic analysis is imprecise, and there is a substantial margin of error with respect to the strategic value of the directions for productive transformation that the policymaker favors and the market ignores. Furthermore, this kind of strategic policy intervention is based on tentative theory and evidence, and is therefore especially risky. If the institutions in charge of policy formulation and implementation are weak, the policy remedy may easily be worse than the market disease.[18]

Promoting strategic sectors involves favoring a sector because its development—through the accumulation of productive capabilities—will presumably facilitate the development of other high-value sectors down the road. Policies to target sectors of high strategic value typically include market interventions. They may include incentives such as subsidies for investment in these sectors, special public procurement arrangements, or efforts to attract FDI in specific sectors, products, or processes. In all these cases, the justification for policy intervention is temporary, and ceases once the strategic bet is realized, whether successful or not. The attraction of sterilization services for the medical device industry in Costa Rica, discussed in Box 9.4, is a good example of these strategic vertical policies.

Box 9.4 The Attraction of Sterilization Services in Costa Rica

The medical devices sector was one of a few sectors targeted by Costa Rica, through CINDE, to attract FDI. The sector has been expanding at healthy rates since Baxter first came to Costa Rica in 1987, and is now responsible for nearly $1.5 billion in exports. But not all medical devices are created equal. They range in complexity from simple disposable devices (such as catheters) to surgical and medical instruments (such as biopsy forceps), to therapeutic devices (such as heart valves), which go into the body to stay, to complex medical equipment (such as MRI machines).

As of 2007, Costa Rica had been highly successful in attracting multinationals to the sector. But they were producing mainly low-complexity disposables. Why did they not make, for example, heart valves or other cardiovacular devices? Because in order to sell them, they needed to go through the process of sterilization, not available locally at the time. Producing them in Costa Rica would have required shipping them to the United States to have them sterilized, and then shipping them back for packaging—complicating the logistics and adding greatly to the costs.

Why was there no sterilization? With no heart valves and other similar products in production, there was no demand for sterilization services. It became clear to CINDE that it was a strategic problem that the market would not solve by itself. They had to add the sterilization process, in order for the more complex links of the value chain to develop. Their efforts paid off in early 2009, with the arrival of BeamOne, a contract sterilization processor headquartered in the United States. Next in line was Sterigenics in 2011. Within three years of inauguration of the BeamOne facility, Costa Rica had successfully attracted a number of companies in the cardiovascular sector, including Boston Scientific in 2009, Abbot Vascular in 2010, and St. Jude Medical in 2010. In 2013, Costa Rica exported nearly $300 million in the therapeutics category of medical devices, and an additional $500 million in surgical and medical instruments. The share of disposables fell from 90 percent in the early 2000s to less than half.[19]

Why did CINDE target sterilization? In the language of global value chains, it was trying to move Costa Rica into the more profitable sections of the value chain, in order to capture more value. In the language of this chapter, sterilization opened up important avenues for further development into other complex products. CINDE addressed a failure to expand opportunities by going for strategic value.

Are Vertical Policies Worth the Risk?

The identification of a market failure, finding an answer to the question of why the market is not already investing in productive transformation, is necessary to make a case for a vertical policy, but not sufficient. The degree of institutional strength to control the risk of capture is a key determinant of whether a justified vertical policy is worth undertaking: the lower the strength, the higher the hurdle for the potential benefits of vertical policies. Irrespective of capture risks, even if policymakers conduct policy applying their best judgment, technical assessments are imprecise and, therefore, the yield of vertical policies is uncertain. On these grounds, a prudent approach is to focus only on the cases in which potential benefits are the largest. Limitations to the financial and human resources that can be devoted to these policies would suggest the same. In summary, it is critical to have a sense of the magnitude of the value of the policy opportunities to prioritize and deal only with the most promising ones.

How to assess the potential policy value of a vertical policy? One key metric is the likelihood that such policy leads to new products that are highly competitive. In other words, the policy should lead to uncovering substantial latent comparative advantages. In theory, addressing market failures ensures that any resulting productive transformation is competitive. In practice, given the risks and uncertainties, it is wise to prioritize sectors and vertical policies according to how substantial the latent comparative advantage is expected to be. The key is then to establish a policy process that picks sectors for which there is a case for vertical policies (there is a market failure) and does so attaching a likely value to those interventions in order to yield priority sectors and policies. Such a process produces good vertical policies, limiting their risks, and roots out ill-conceived ones.

A Policy Process to Select and Support Priority Sectors

Sound policies for productive transformation should bring about latent or "dynamic" comparative advantage that the market can be expected to miss. The problem is that identifying latent comparative advantage is often highly subjective, and rationalizing market failures is often highly speculative. Lots of failed bets have been placed in Latin America and around the world in the name of latent comparative advantages that never materialize. The question in this chapter is: How to structure a sound sector selection process for the consideration of vertical policies? Objective analysis of the evidence and independent assessment safeguarded from capture are two key characteristics of a sound process designed to make the case for vertical policies. Before proposing a sector selection process based on the considerations discussed earlier, it is illustrative to discuss a few valuable cases of sector selection drawing from the experience of countries in and outside the region.

Valuable Country Experiences with Sector Selection

Countries use a variety of modalities to carry out these processes. Ireland is a clear example of a country with strong public institutions that identified priority sectors in a top-down fashion following technocratic criteria, and pursued an aggressive and successful policy of FDI attraction in these sectors (see Box 8.2 in chapter 8). The selection process led by the Industrial Development Agency (IDA) considered key features of the Irish economy—availability of skilled labor, small market size, and location—to select low-transport-cost, sophisticated products with high growth potential: information and communication technologies, pharmaceuticals, financial services, and other services.

Within the region, probably the most interesting and systematic effort to proactively select sectors with objective criteria is the "cluster" program in Chile, conducted under the auspices of the National Council of Innovation for Competitiveness (CNIC). In the mid-2000s, the CNIC led a sector selection process based on technical analysis of the capabilities needed to be internationally competitive in both proven sectors with a substantial footprint in the Chilean economy and new sectors on which to bet. This technical analysis from the supply side was matched with forecasts of the world demand growth for each sector, so as to pick competitive sectors that could grow and transform Chile. Interestingly, the CNIC retained the services of the

Boston Consulting Group (BCG) and assigned them an important role in the selection process in order to minimize interference from political as well as private sector interests. Since this strategy was replicated in other countries in the region, it is discussed in more detail in Box 9.5, which also highlights the post-selection process in the specific case of the offshoring sector, the most successful one.

Box 9.5   The Cluster Program and Sector Selection in Chile

The cluster program was the sole vertical component within a largely horizontal set of policies encouraged by the CNIC. This was in line with CNIC's idea of pursuing mostly neutral policies, with some selectivity at the margin. In retrospect, however, the cluster program turned out to be the council's most important initiative.

Engaging in vertical policies and picking sectors are very demanding in terms of the institutional capabilities required. Particularly important are political capabilities to isolate the selection process from undue influence by stakeholders. If not done well, the process can degenerate into a rent-seeking process just like the Jamaica case discussed earlier. The council, presided by Nicolás Eyzaguirre, a prestigious, former finance minister, was perceived as independent and technically solid, and had broad representation from several sectors, which provided good checks and balances.[20]

Once the decision was made to venture into the realm of vertical policies, a key issue was how to choose sectors. The council did not have a selection methodology, so they invited proposals from consulting firms and set up a bidding process, with a budget of $2 million. Four firms presented tenders, and the winner was BCG.

BCG's proposal was to come up with a list of eligible sectors taking into account two key considerations. First, they would identify a number of sectors with high growth potential around the world, focusing initially on a 25-year horizon; second, they would compare the capabilities required to become competitive, to the capabilities that Chile actually possessed.

Regarding the first consideration, BCG offered the advantage of their extensive network of offices around the world, a key strength to engage in a forward-looking market intelligence exercise. As to the second, BCG used a vector of 77 resource or input variables to determine, both qualitatively and quantitatively, how difficult it would be for Chile to become a relevant player in those sectors.[21] After considering both the expected growth in world demand and the effort necessary to produce competently,

BCG, working closely with the CNIC, narrowed the list down to 11 sectors. The selection methodology is summarized in Figure 9.2, where sectors in the upper right-hand corner were the most attractive ones. The selection process also considered the size of the circles in the figure, which represents the expected increase in Chile's sectorial GDP during the subsequent 10 years.

The sectors identified through this process were construction, copper mining and subproducts, aquaculture, financial services, logistics and transport, processed foods for human consumption, telecommunications, offshoring (in particular, IT outsourcing), primary fruit farming, pig farming and aviculture, and tourism (with emphasis on special-interest tourism). While some of the identified sectors confirmed Chile's well-known resources and capabilities (copper mining, or aquaculture), other choices, such as offshoring, were new and surprising. In this last case, CORFO had already begun working with the sector with encouraging results; this experience, combined with the high growth in world demand envisioned for the sector, was key to its selection. Chile had adequate technological infrastructure, including good broadband coverage, and an important geographical advantage: it shared a similar time zone with the United States, the main market, while the main supplier of IT offshoring services, India, was on the opposite side of the world. Within processed foods, functional

Figure B9.2 Sector Selection in the Chilean Cluster Program

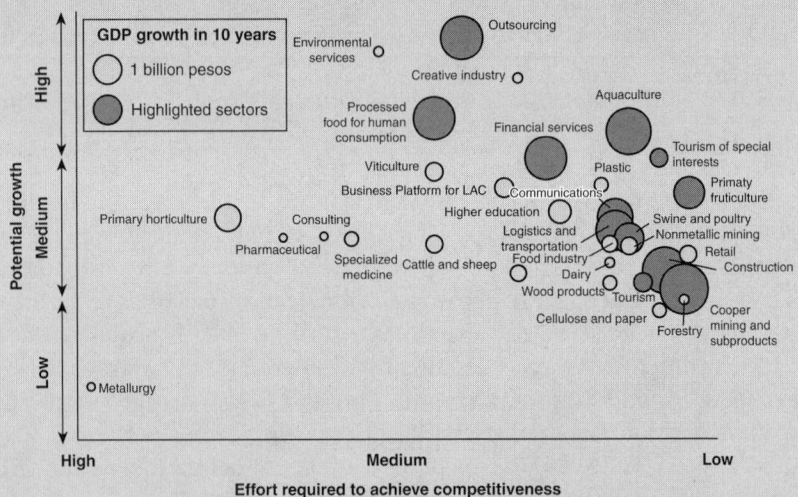

Source: Consejo Nacional de la Innovación para la Competitividad – Chile (2008).

foods were identified as an interesting option. Winemaking, perhaps surprisingly, was left out, because BCG did not expect world demand (and, in particular, Chinese demand) to grow rapidly.

From these 11 sectors, given budget constraints, the CNIC had to choose eight for BCG to do more detailed analysis. In this second round of studies, BCG focused on two things. First, they analyzed the relevant value chains, and identified the key nodes in which the rents were concentrated. For example, in aquaculture, they found that the rents were not necessarily in fish farming but rather in logistics, transportation, and distribution, and discussed how Chile could capture some of those rents. For offshoring, the focus was on skill-intensive, time-sensitive services such as the traffic control system in the city of San Francisco, or activities such as interpreting X-rays where the geographical advantages of Chile would compensate for the higher labor costs.

Second, they identified "derived demands," that is, improvements that would be necessary in order for Chile to become a world-class player in the sector. For example, within offshoring, the most critical of the derived demands identified had to do with the need to increase the human resources available for the sector. Derived demands then led to specific initiatives needed to address them, such as increasing the number of technicians and university graduates in disciplines relevant for offshoring services; aligning the curricula in the relevant programs with the needs of the sector; improving the technicians' and university graduates' proficiency in the use of technical English language; and attracting international professionals (India was specifically targeted) to cover short-term gaps, while the other measures took hold.[22] This last initiative, in turn, required revamping the existing migration policies.

In addition, Chile adopted an aggressive policy to attract foreign companies working in offshoring, in order to jump-start the process. Firms in this sector that set up in Chile included Accenture, Citigroup, and Evaluashare, just to name a few. The offshoring cluster was the most successful. In 2006, exports of offshoring services accounted for around $200 million, and the sector employed 6,700 workers. By 2008, in the span of just two years, exports had reached nearly $850 million, and employment in the sector rose to 20,000. The success of this sector alone would be enough to pay for several failures.

But not everything went smoothly. While sector selection pointed to pig farming, aviculture, and functional foods, the Ministry of Agriculture ended up promoting all food sectors, setting aside identified priorities, arguing that they could not leave out other producers that were asking to be

> included. In some sectors, such as mining, aquaculture, and special-interest tourism, the policy agenda came to be dominated by short-term policies.
>
> The policy of supporting specific sectors was a departure for Chile, which until then had focused mostly on horizontal policies. A key element of the credibility of the program for sector selection was the prestige of the CNIC, which was viewed as a technically sound, neutral body, not subject to political influence. The involvement of a private consulting firm in the process reinforced this perception of neutrality. But while Chile, and the CNIC in particular, proved to have—for the most part—the political capabilities needed to protect the selection process from undue influence, it proved not to have the capabilities needed to sustain the program over time. In spite of its relative success, while some of the public-private bodies created as a result of the programs survived, and some of the initiatives remained under the control of specific sectorial ministries, the cluster program as such was discontinued by the government of President Piñera, which placed the emphasis back on horizontal policies (including the flagship Start-Up Chile program, discussed in detail in chapter 4). At the time of writing, the CNIC is being reinvigorated and it may happen that the cluster program and other vertical policies will be emphasized again in the new Bachelet government, perhaps under new guidelines. Vertical policies for priority sectors is not a settled issue in Chile.

This strategy of asking for technical input from a private consulting company to select sectors was later adopted in Colombia, Mexico, and Panama. In Colombia, the Productive Transformation Program (PTP; formerly the World Class Sectors Program) was more bottom-up in nature, with the participation of the Private Council for Competitiveness, and a process that included calls for proposals from interested sectors—some traditional, and some new. The experience of the PTP, as well as the active participation of the Private Council for Competitiveness, is discussed in chapter 11.

In these cases, the independent analysis from external consultants was an input for policymakers that, in turn, weighed in with additional information and considerations. This second round by policymakers in the selection process poses a trade-off between enriching the independent analysis to make it more appropriate to the policymaking context and weakening the objectivity sought in the first place. Each of these countries reached some intermediate point to retain external advice without outsourcing policy that led to a final selection of sectors. Finally, the last stage of the process was to establish their direct and derived demands in order to refer them to the relevant agencies to design and implement the required vertical policies.

A Systematic Process for Selecting Priority Sectors

These successful models to select sectors of policy interest incorporate some of the relevant elements to make the case for vertical policies. For example, consider the Chilean system described in Box 9.5. It looks at whether the country has the required capabilities to produce a product competitively and, if not, how easy it would be to acquire them; and it looks at whether the product will face growing world demand and its production in Chile can be scaled up to take advantage of it. However, it does not focus on other relevant aspects. First, among the products or sectors for which a country is deemed to have the required capabilities, it makes sense to focus on those that may have some other desirable characteristics beyond a growing world demand. Yet the Chilean selection process does not explicitly look at other features, such as high product sophistication, which may be an important element for sustaining and increasing income.[23] Second, and critical to discipline the overall exercise, the criteria for selecting priority sectors and products are not rooted in the identification of market failures. Looking at plausible market failures preventing the market from investing in the priority sectors is a useful check on the validity of the selection process, as worthwhile sectors unencumbered by market failures are expected to develop on their own. Furthermore, the nature of the market failure is informative regarding which vertical policy would be more suitable when interventions that may be needed in order to seize some of the identified opportunities are discussed in the second stage.

Ideally, a process for sifting through sectors and selecting priority sectors takes into account the previous aspects using analytical criteria as consistent and systematic as possible. In keeping with the analytical approach of this report, the ability of this process to identify a market failure is critical for policy justification concerning candidate sectors. Given the risks of government failure in vertical policies, it is vital to obtain a clear answer to the question of why it is that the market is not already investing in these sectors. Furthermore, the process needs to yield information on the intensity of the latent comparative advantage, so as to allow for setting sector priorities. Priorities are important because, due to the imprecision of these estimations and the risks involved, as well as resource limitations, only the best candidates should be considered for selection.

The following strategic framework builds on Hausmann et al. (2014) to illustrate how these attributes could be brought into the selection process. This framework identifies good candidates worth studying for vertical policies using the complexity/product space-based metrics described above. As mentioned, the frequency with which two products are coproduced in countries' export baskets measures their "proximity." Following Hausmann et al. (2014), a proxy for the overall viability of redeploying the country's productive capabilities to produce a new target product is the "distance" between the target product and the current export basket. Distance is shorter as the number of products in the current basket that are in close proximity to the target grows. This measure of distance also serves as an objective proxy measure of latent comparative advantage, since being close to the existing basket signals the likely availability of the required productive capabilities to competitively produce and export the target product.[24] In traditional economic terms, given that proximate products that presumably utilize similar factors and capabilities are produced competitively, the production of the target product is likely profitable at prevailing wages and other factor prices, perhaps after a learning period. Thus, in their quest for sectors worthy of support, countries need to pay close attention to whether target products and sectors are "near" their current basket, because those are cases in which comparative advantage is more likely and certain to be realized. In that sense, distance can be interpreted as the effort or "cost" of reaching an interesting target.

Detecting failures to seize opportunities: How interesting the target is, or what the "benefit" is of redeploying capabilities to produce a new product, can be proxied by the complexity of the target product. Since more complex products are produced by richer countries, they can be assumed to be capable of sustaining higher wages, and therefore higher profitability at prevailing costs in the economy. Under these assumptions, Figure 9.2 illustrates the cost and benefits associated with the different target product communities in Colombia.

Figure 9.2 Complexity and Distance for Product Communities in Colombia

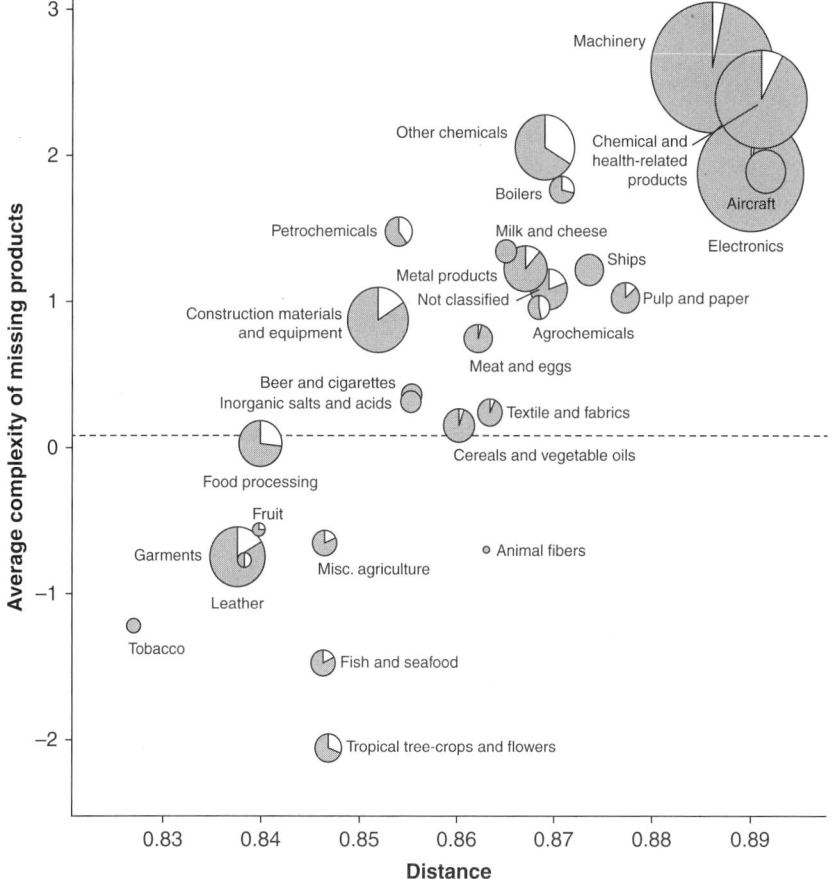

Source: Authors' calculation based on Hausmann et al (2011).

For each product community, the size of the pie represents the size of the community in world trade, and the slice in white corresponds to the share of products in the community currently exported competitively by the country. Targets with low cost and high benefit, depicted in the upper-left quadrant, can be thought of as sweet, low-hanging fruit.

Not surprisingly, the sweeter fruits (such as machinery) tend to be distant, and low-hanging fruits (such as garments) are not so sweet. Seemingly attractive new products that have not prompted market investment, which can be regarded as anomalies, suggest that something may be impeding the market. This does not necessarily imply a market failure, just that a market failure is more likely and may be worthwhile examining further. On the basis of this illustration, products in the petrochemicals community and construction materials and equipment community are candidates for scrutiny to determine what, if anything, is blocking the market. Other chemicals may be of interest, as well. While missing products in this community are farther from the export basket as a whole, they are highly complex, and Colombia is already producing a significant portion of the products in this community.[25]

Once these possibly missed opportunities are identified, the policymaker then explores these cases in conjunction with the relevant private sector actors. If firms are poorly informed and unaware of the costs and benefits associated with presumably profitable target products, this diagnostic tool helps these firms navigate the product space in search of good business opportunities—and no specific policy is needed. However, if firms do not invest because they lack incentives, the policymaker may uncover the fundamental reason why the private sector is not taking advantage of these opportunities. Perhaps the products identified are not as sweet and juicy, or low-hanging, as the preliminary test suggests.[26] By contrast, if this first test is confirmed, this joint review will help identify and design the required policy interventions.

Detecting failures to expand opportunities: While in most cases the market can be expected to seize available business opportunities, it cannot be expected to fully pursue the expansion of opportunities. This is because the benefit from seizing available opportunities (proxied by product complexity) tends to match the firm's bottom line, but the benefit from expanding opportunities (proxied by the strategic value associated with becoming competitive in a new target product) may not be fully appropriated by the firm. Moving to a new product or sector demands developing new capabilities, but once these exist, they may become building blocks for other firms to venture into other valuable products.

Figure 9.3, which depicts a portion of a country's product space, illustrates this discussion. Each circle in the figure is a product, whose complexity is represented by the circle's size. Productive capabilities currently used for existing products can be redeployed (by any firm) for use in nearby products, which are those directly connected by a line. Longer jumps into distant products are more costly, as the capabilities required may differ significantly from existing ones and comparative advantage in them is more uncertain. Consider a firm that currently produces and exports product A. The rest of the products are not being produced competitively. This firm can decide whether to redeploy some of its productive capabilities to produce a nearby product, B, C, or D. Which new product will the firm prefer?

If distance and complexity are closely linked to profitability, as argued above, the firm would likely move into product B, seizing this business opportunity. Products C and D offer less in terms of profitability because they are less complex. Unless a market failure prevents the firm from moving to B, there is no need for policy to push firms in this direction. Product C, however, is attractive from a public policy perspective because, besides its own worth, it has high strategic value, as it opens up avenues for

Figure 9.3 Failure to Seize and Expand Opportunities

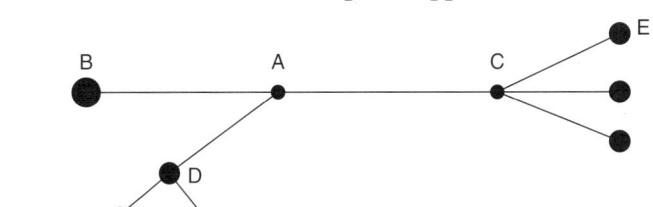

Source: Authors' calculations.

further redeployment of productive capabilities into product E and other high-complexity products. Because these subsequent moves could be exploited by others, the strategic value is not completely internalized by the firm. Policymakers would like firms capable of producing A to move into C. But since C is not very attractive in itself, this may not happen without policy intervention. The case of CINDE aggressively pursuing FDI in sterilization services to unleash the potential of the medical devices cluster discussed in Box 9.4 is a perfect example of a country targeting a process of high strategic value.

The benefit of expanding opportunities that a target product delivers can be represented by the measure of strategic value. Figure 9.4 illustrates the combination of cost and strategic value for Colombia. This tool represents a first pass to explore the areas of high strategic value that may be more easily reached (in the upper-left quadrant).

Figure 9.4   Strategic Value and Distance for Product Communities in Colombia

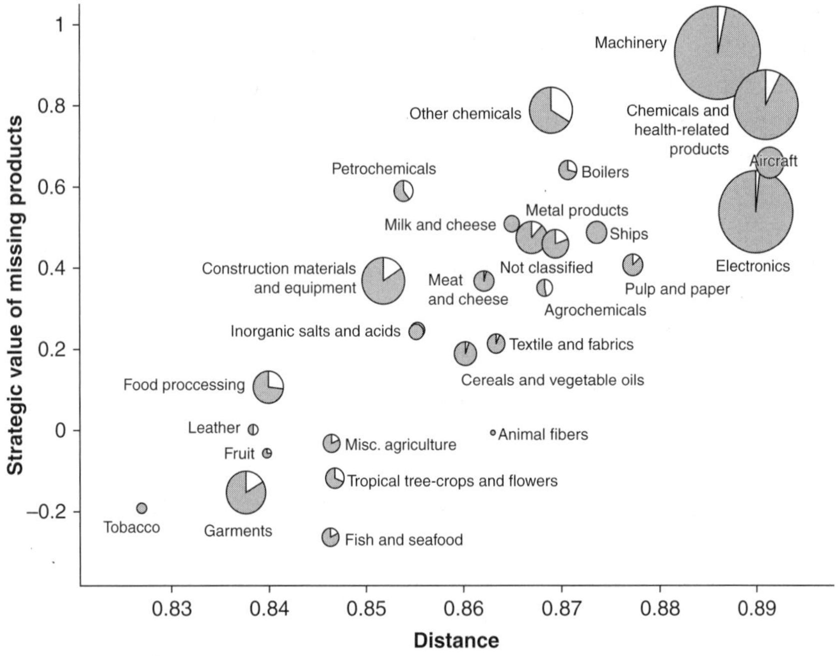

Source: Authors' calculation based on Hausmann et al (2011).

Those may be the subject of specific promotional policies to develop new capabilities, especially if market forces alone are unlikely to produce such a transition because the private benefits are low. Policies favoring certain strategic entry points into complex and well-connected product communities could be justified in this way, provided the effort required is limited. For example, the figure suggests that missing products in petrochemicals might be a strategically valuable sector to consider. Other, possibly more beneficial strategic objectives, such as the communities around the chemicals and health-related products industry, are more costly, farther from current comparative advantages, and thus can be considered riskier strategic bets. Identifying potential strategic directions with this cost-benefit methodology would also help identify the relevant stakeholders for further exploration.

This process for selecting sectors has some important advantages over the ones used in the region. It is anchored in the identification of market failures that would justify policy intervention, and explicitly takes into account the sophistication of products and sectors as an indication of their income-generating potential. However, it also has disadvantages. For example, it does not factor in a forward-looking analysis of market trends to assess the value of new products and sectors, which a consulting firm such as BCG (Box 9.5) or a well-functioning investment promotion agency such as CINDE (Box 9.4) can provide. These approaches are to some extent complementary. Perhaps the key is not to choose one process over the others, but to combine elements of different approaches to take advantage of the best features that each of them has to offer.

A Policy Framework for Productive Transformation: The Policy Mix

How extensively should a country go down the list of priority sectors to pursue vertical policies for productive transformation? How intensely should a country carry out vertical policies, especially concerning new sectors? These questions pertaining to the policy mix need a framework to balance the pros and cons of different PDPs in the specific context of a given country. It may seem that every country would benefit from all cost-effective policies that address a market failure, but this is not so. First and foremost, the risk of government failure due to capture is a key reason why restraint and balance are important. But even if the risk of capture is disregarded, in practice, technical limitations to accurately identify the right policies and uncertainty about their implementation, together with limited resources and time from policymakers, call for guidelines to fix the policy mix.

The nature of this framework to discuss the policy mix is different from the one presented earlier in this book. Chapter 2 presented a conceptual framework for PDPs in which interventions were classified as horizontal or vertical and as market interventions or public inputs, and discussed key considerations for designing and implementing each type of intervention to maximize their value. The question here is different: How should countries decide how much weight to place on policies in the different quadrants to balance potential gains with acceptable risks? When should countries favor a minimalist policy footprint and stick mostly to horizontal policies? Under what conditions should they attempt high-risk/high-reward strategic bets in the vertical/market interventions quadrant? This section tackles some of these questions using the concepts and metrics introduced above (for details on methodology and country illustrations, see Fernández-Arias and Stein, 2014). It derives the kind of policy stance and policy priorities fitting various situations.

When assessing the appropriate policy stance for each country, a starting point is whether a country can expect healthy productive transformation in due course, under normal circumstances. In other words, is it predisposed to make progress naturally, in an evolving process of redeploying existing productive capabilities and factors of production to products that are close to the existing ones? If so, its policy mix could focus on combining horizontal policies with vertical interventions to remove undue burdens and provide essential public inputs to established and emerging sectors. This cautious mix would deliver satisfactory results. By contrast, a country without a natural predisposition for productive transformation does not have the luxury of obtaining satisfactory results with a restrained policy stance and may feel the need to consider more active policies, including thrusting the market into certain new sectors and strategic directions to open doors for transformation. Without this more active policy stance, it could easily get stuck, with no clear way to make progress. This country would face the choice between low-yield policies and potentially high-yield, but risky, policies.

How to tell a country's predisposition for productive transformation? The opportunity value of its export basket, determined by the number and complexity of new target products that are close to it (see Hausmann et al., 2014) is a good first pass. This measure was developed precisely as a way to capture the opportunities for natural productive transformation the current export basket of a country affords. However, a number of additional factors may shift the balance of the policy mix. To begin with, missed opportunities count as no opportunities. Countries with high opportunity value but low effectiveness taking advantage of them, as revealed by their record of actual productive transformation, cannot expect spontaneous productive transformation. It would make sense for these countries to deal with this problem of low effectiveness with active policies to address the root causes. In particular, given a systemic failure to seize the opportunities available, it would be fitting to focus on horizontal policies that encourage the emergence of new products that spin off current productive activities, irrespective of the sector. Furthermore, productive transformation is not the only factor behind catching up with advanced countries. The relative complexity of some products in the export basket may actually erode over time as lower-wage countries gain competitiveness in them (and depress prices through competition). Complexity erosion may completely offset the catching up afforded by productive transformation: countries with highly vulnerable baskets need greater opportunities, and seize them at a reasonable pace, in order to compensate for this dynamic weakness. Countries with high erosion may need to shift the balance of their policy mix toward creating and seizing opportunities more effectively.[27]

Part III

Institutions for Successful Policies

10

The Hard Part: Building Public Sector Capabilities

This book argues that productive development policies (PDPs) are an important component of a successful development strategy. But designing and implementing successful PDPs is not easy. To begin with, the process requires a well-oiled learning mechanism to diagnose market failures amenable to policy intervention, and design sound policy initiatives. Furthermore, it is not enough to get the policy design right; the public sector as a whole and the agencies in charge of specific policies (which we will call productive development agencies or PDAs) must also have the right capabilities to implement them.[1]

The ability to design and implement successful PDPs is influenced by several factors ranging from the organizational structure of the public sector in charge of these policies to the technical, operational and political capabilities (TOP capabilities from here on) of the relevant public agencies.[2] Organizational structures refer to the distribution of responsibilities, decision-making powers, and control over resources among different agencies or units within agencies. The TOP capabilities of PDAs encompass not only the technical ability to deal with PDPs but also the necessary enabling conditions for a successful PDA. These factors are not independent; rather, they interact in fundamental ways. For example, possessing the technical skills to design and implement a certain policy does not mean that the policy will be implemented appropriately. Participants must have the right organizational structure and incentives for these skills to lead to effective policy design and implementation on the ground.

Moreover, if financial resources allocated to specific policies are insufficient, agents will lack the incentives to invest in the technical capabilities needed for sound policy design and implementation. This chapter discusses the organizational structure and TOP capabilities required for successful PDPs. It also discusses how countries can match their PDPs to existing capabilities, as well as expand their capabilities in the long run.

Why Are PDPs Hard?

PDPs are a particularly difficult type of public policy for several reasons.

1. *The need for policy discovery*: For some public policies, the problem, the target beneficiaries, and the solution are all known. For example, a vaccination campaign against hepatitis A involves administering the first dose of the vaccine to children between 12 and 23 months of age, and the second one between 6 and 18 months later. The doses and the delivery mechanism are known and need to meet specific quality criteria defined by standard protocols.

PDPs are different. While in some cases the problems may be known ex ante (for example, there are spillovers in R&D that need to be addressed), in most cases problems need to be discovered as part of the policy process. Even when the problems are known, the best solutions may be hard to identify, as many different instruments can potentially be used to solve a problem; the ideal instrument in a particular country context may not be ideal in another. The target beneficiaries of interventions may not be known, either. For example, the policies to support entrepreneurship discussed in chapter 4 may require identifying young firms with high growth potential—which is not as simple as identifying children between 12 and 23 months of age. To some extent, PDPs need to be set up as search engines, scanning the policy space in order to identify the most important problems, the most appropriate solutions, and the best ways to implement them.[3]

One additional feature of PDPs makes this discovery process more challenging: the effectiveness of PDPs depends not just on public sector actions, but also on voluntary actions of the private sector. For some projects, such as building a road, success or failure depends entirely on actions over which the public sector has direct control. PDPs, in contrast, try to induce changes in the behavior of private agents in response to public sector actions, such as providing a public input or a fiscal incentive. Policies may or may not succeed in inducing the desired changes in private behavior, which provides an additional reason for policy experimentation and adjustment.

2. *Knowledge and technical skills requirements*: Even relatively simple PDPs may require advanced knowledge or technical skills, which are generally in short supply in the public sector, particularly in developing countries. For example, subsidizing R&D may seem to be a straightforward endeavor. However, calculating the level of a subsidy so that it is neither more than what is needed (leading to waste of public resources) nor less than what is needed (leading to failure to induce the desired behavior) may be far from easy. Moreover, designing mechanisms to select the right R&D projects to fund—those likely to give rise to positive externalities—also requires important technical skills. In contrast to the vaccination example, neither the doses nor the delivery mechanism are obvious.

3. *Long delays between policy interventions and results*: In most cases, PDPs yield significant results only many years after they are started. This poses two opposite challenges: on the one hand, policymakers or their constituencies may become impatient and discontinue a worthwhile policy because the expected results have not yet materialized after a number of years. Thus, a policy may be eliminated simply because its "planting to harvest" horizon was longer than what policymakers could or were willing to provide. On the other hand, the expectation of future results can perpetuate a policy that has failed and should be discontinued. In particular, it can help sustain misguided policies that are in place due to capture or simply because those responsible do not like to admit failure.[4]

4. *The need to collaborate with the private sector*: For many PDPs, the public sector will likely have access to only part of the information required to identify what is needed. Much of the information likely resides in the private sector. Thus, collaboration with the private sector and joint exploration of the necessary policies and instruments is an essential ingredient of the policy process. This applies to many

wide-ranging initiatives such as private-public dialogues regarding national competitiveness policies, as well as more focused initiatives such as joint efforts to identify the main obstacles to the development of a sector. At the same time, the private sector may use this information exchange to derive undue benefits from PDPs, which adds an extra layer of difficulty. The challenges of public-private collaboration for productive development policies are many, and will be discussed in detail in chapter 11.

5. *Risk of capture and rent seeking*: PDPs face the risk of capture from the private sector that they are designed to benefit. But the direct beneficiaries are not the only actors that can capture the policy process. Private suppliers hired by public agencies, or even the bureaucracy that works in those agencies, may also capture the policy process to favor their own interests. The intensity of the risk will vary across different types of policies and according to the choice of policy instruments, but it will always be present. Monetary subsidies aimed at a particular sector on an ongoing basis may be an obvious target for rent seeking, but even the provision of horizontal public inputs may be subject to capture by bureaucracies or private sector suppliers of the public sector. Moreover, politicians may use PDPs as vehicles to distribute favors to their constituencies or campaign contributors, in exchange for votes or political support, under the guise of productive policies.

6. *The need to cooperate across multiple public agencies*: In some cases, PDPs can be implemented by a single public agency. These can be thought of as *narrow policies*, either horizontal or vertical. Consider a minister of tourism who engages in a dialogue with the private sector in order to identify the main obstacles to developing a new tourist destination that is considered a high priority. One intervention that may be needed is a public relations and advertising campaign, which a Ministry of Tourism typically handles. This is a good example of a narrow, vertical policy. In other interventions, however, the Ministry of Tourism may need the cooperation of other agencies, whether to pave an access road, build a water treatment plant, and construct an airport, or to train the workforce, for example. While the minister is the one who engages the sector and is in a good position to assess the merits of their demands, he cannot

deliver on what is needed. The minister is not responsible for paving roads and training workers, which are responsibilities of the public works and labor ministers, respectively. These interventions are examples of *wide policies*.

Public development agencies typically do not have authority over the rest of the public sector whose collaboration is required for PDPs to succeed. Inducing the voluntary and hard-to-control collaboration of external public agencies is a difficult challenge. Often, the failure to elicit this type of public-public collaboration derails well-intentioned PDPs, perhaps even more than the failure to induce the voluntary participation of the private sector.

The Organizational Structure of the Public Sector for PDPs

Traditional public sector organizational structures, and in particular sectoral ministries (industry, agriculture, trade, health, education, etc.), tend to be managed by means of a "command and control" approach and are not necessarily well suited for PDPs. What, then, are the alternatives?

There are no unique answers. The most suitable options vary depending on factors such as the scope of PDPs, the instruments used, and the depth of desired cooperation with the private sector. Nevertheless, the organizational structure and design of public sector agencies in charge of PDPs should carefully take into account the six features that make them particularly hard, as described in the previous section. Without pretending to provide ready-made recipes to be applied everywhere, the following are some suggestions on how to do this. The numbering of the suggestions corresponds to the numbering of the difficulties used earlier.

1. *Ensuring flexibility and openness to engage in the policy discovery process*: Traditional public sector organizations, bound by rigid rules and subject to a complex set of controls, authorizations, and an auditing process, may not always have the flexibility and adaptability required to identify the constraints on productivity growth and how best to address them. Traditional public sector organizations are not designed to deal with the experimentation, learning, and adjustment required for PDPs, or to engage in joint discovery

processes with the private sector. There are several options to overcome this obstacle.

First, public-private consultation bodies (whether through presidential-level councils, or regional and/or sectoral bodies) are by definition mixed entities with more flexible rules than purely public organizations (even though they rely on those traditional organizations for policy delivery). Second, some public agencies have more flexible operational rules than others. Taking advantage of this, some countries have engaged public banks, such as BNDES in Brazil or BANCOLDEX in Colombia, to manage their PDPs. Third, some countries have relied on private, generally nonprofit organizations to fulfill some public sector roles, in cooperation with purely public organizations, as in the case of CINDE, a private organization responsible for attracting FDI in Costa Rica, in close, legally enabled cooperation with the Ministry of Foreign Trade. A fourth option is to provide some public organizations with "private-like" operational rules, and to involve the private sector in their governance structure. An example is INTA, the National Agricultural Technology Institute in Argentina, a highly decentralized organization that is deeply engaged with the private sector, and includes private sector representatives in its governance structure. Another example is the Innovation Agency in Uruguay (ANII). It operates according to private law, and is not bound by the rigid purchasing, hiring, and promotion rules of the rest of the public sector.

In many cases, collaboration with the private sector is limited by formal and informal governance rules. In some cases, public institutions are barred from engaging in for-profit activities, thus preventing them from participating in joint research projects with the private sector, as several agricultural institutions in South America have done, sharing the royalties generated by their discoveries. Or it may be simply that within a "command and control" organizational culture, the need to consult, let alone cooperate with the private sector, is an option that is not even considered.

Therefore, the inclusion of legal and administrative mechanisms that facilitate public-private collaboration should be a key element in organizational design. Legal authorization may be needed so that public sector entities can engage in explicit collaboration with the private sector. Administrative mechanisms may be needed to transform the legal authorization into institutional practice. INTA in Argentina (to support agricultural producers) and COMEX in Costa Rica (to attract FDI) are good examples of organizations explicitly designed to collaborate with the private sector.

2. *Availability of highly skilled personnel*: The ability to hire and retain personnel with the skills required by an agency in charge of PDPs will depend, for the most part, on resources, and on hiring and remuneration policies. However, organizational structure may matter as well. In many countries in the region, the rigid pay scales and promotion rules in the public administration, together with the use of civil service positions as a means of political exchange, may make it more difficult to attract and retain top talent within the regular bureaucracy. Some agencies outside of the regular bureaucracy, in contrast, have more flexible operational and administrative rules, which allow them to pay better salaries and provide incentives to attract and retain a highly qualified labor force. Despite the obvious tension this may create within the government, bodies of this kind may be in a better position to deliver results, particularly in countries where the regular bureaucracy is weak, in PDPs that are demanding in terms of the required technical skills required.

Among others, autonomous development banks could be suitable agencies to play this role of "island of excellence." BNDES, for example, offers a very competitive package to recent graduates. These jobs are highly sought after, and staff members often spend their entire careers within the organization. Sectoral experts at BNDES are highly recognized for their knowledge, and often consulted or involved in policy design and implementation. Another example of a development bank involved in a PDP relates to the Productive Transformation Program (PTP) in Colombia. The program identifies sectors with great potential as engines of export growth and productive transformation, and supports these sectors—mainly through vertical public inputs and the resolution of coordination problems—to help them achieve that potential. The PTP was originally under the Ministry of Trade, but was later moved to the Colombian development bank, BANCOLDEX, because it is not subject to the same rigid administrative barriers as the ministries and enjoys more flexibility with regard to salaries and recruitment procedures. As a result of the switch, the quality and stability of the public sector managers of each sector have improved (Eslava, Meléndez, and Perry, 2014).

3. *Providing coherence over time*: PDPs are long-term undertakings. Organizations in charge of them should thus be able to operate with long time horizons. This requires both policy and organizational stability. Organizations launched by executive decree, or that constitute informal working arrangements, usually do not last long, as a change in administration, or even a change in a ministry, is enough for them to be replaced by new organizations or agencies. Similarly, organizations created mainly in response to the availability of grants or concessional loans and that require little financial commitment from local authorities will likely disappear when funding dries up. On the other hand, organizations created by law likely enjoy greater stability, particularly in countries where changing laws is a slow process, or when they are backed by some sort of international commitment.

Like organizations, policies established by law, rather than just at the executive's discretion—and particularly those that are an integral part of an international commitment through membership in international organizations such as the World Trade Organization or trade agreements—will likely be quite stable. In some cases, involving public-private councils in a specific policy, or financing by a multilateral development agency, may help provide policy stability. These actors are not subject to the political cycle, and thus may provide some sort of intertemporal glue. According to Eslava, Meléndez, and Perry (2014), the involvement of the Private Council for Competitiveness in Colombia helped preserve the Productive Transformation Program in the transition from the Uribe to the Santos administration.

Finally, stability of personnel is also required, at least for a core technical team and the essential components of the bureaucracy.[5] Stability can be insured either by civil service regulations or by the specific bylaws of a particular agency. Stability of organizations and personnel is a key factor to elicit the investment in capabilities needed to adequately design and implement PDPs. If public officials know they will not stay within an organization for significant periods of time, they will not have incentives to invest in upgrading their capabilities.

4. *Selecting and empowering credible public sector participants to convene and engage the private sector*: The willingness of the private sector to join and remain involved in PDP processes depends on many factors, but a crucial one is the selection of public sector participants. If those participants are credible and have authority over the resources required by the PDP, participation may be worthwhile for the private sector. In contrast, if the private sector believes that the public sector participants, because of their training, rank, or attitude, are not able or authorized to deliver their end of the bargain, collaboration often breaks down. The private sector will consider that the dialogue is a waste of time, and will not make the necessary investments for public-private dialogue to yield results.

Involving "the highest possible political level," however, is not appropriate or necessary in all cases. As Schneider (2013) notes, it all depends on the nature of the PDP and on where the authority to implement it resides.[6] Having a president participate in a private-public national dialogue may signal to the private sector the high priority that the president assigns to the dialogue, but may also be an indication that both the process and the agreements reached will only last as long as the presidential term.[7] However, when productive development policy is really a top priority for the head of the executive, his or her engagement can be extremely productive, as shown earlier by the experiences of the Republic of Korea and Singapore (Schneider, 2013).

A Solomonic suggestion would be to engage the lowest possible level of public authority with enough standing to convene the relevant parts of the private sector, and the authority to deliver on the commitments resulting from the public-private collaboration process.[8] As will become clear, the standing and authority of the public sector participants will also be crucial to elicit interagency collaboration for "wide" policies, which involve a variety of public agencies providing solutions to private sector challenges.

5. *Protection from capture*: Several features of organizational design can provide protection against private sector capture, although none are perfect (see chapter 11 for a more detailed discussion). Full

public access to the organization's records, budgets, and actions certainly helps, as the organization will be under potentially detailed public scrutiny. Rules and restrictions on the policy instruments the organization is allowed to use can also help: cash outlays under bureaucratic discretion provide ample opportunity for capture and corruption. Programs designed so that only the "right" type of firms self-select into them—for example, with incentives valuable to these firms but not to others—may offer considerable protection from capture. For example, a corporate income tax exemption is valuable for a competitive firm that expects to make profits, but not for a nonprofitable firm that seeks rents. Moreover, the revenue loss in the last case would be zero, since a nonviable company would not pay corporate income taxes anyway. Programs may also rely on private sector agents to do the selection. Such is the case of incubator programs, for example. Provided the incubators themselves are given the right incentives, they will benefit from choosing the right firms and providing them with adequate services (see chapter 4).

Good public sector career paths and adequate remuneration can also help. If technocrats in charge of PDPs have short careers and their best employment opportunities after the public sector are jobs with the same companies that were under their jurisdiction, the temptation to be complacent with those companies is considerable. The temptation will be less if they have job stability, good career paths within the public sector, and incentives related to performance.

Corporate governance of the agencies in charge of PDPs may also mitigate the problem of capture. For example, including in the board of an agency private sector participants that have opposing interests vis-à-vis the beneficiaries—for example, because they compete for the same pool of resources—may partially address the problems associated with the public sector's informational disadvantage. For a more detailed discussion of the role of corporate governance in protection from capture, see Box 10.1.

PDP institutions are also subject to capture by other agents, not just the private sector whose productivity they are supposed to promote. They may be captured by their own bureaucracies, by service providers, or by politicians that use them for clientelistic purposes. For example, Artopoulos and Navarro (forthcoming) argue that to some extent science and technology policies in the region have been captured by the scientific community, which may prefer to research issues in which they are interested, regardless of whether they are useful to the private sector.

> **Box 10.1 The Corporate Governance of Executing Agencies**
>
> Do executing agencies need corporate governance? Or is it enough just to appoint a director who reports to the minister? When an agency manages substantial public resources aimed at addressing market failures and implementing the government's economic policy, a number of problems can arise. Under some circumstances, the agencies may be too focused on the interests of those they report to, and not enough on the real needs of the beneficiaries they are meant to support. On the other hand, concentrating solely on the demands of the beneficiaries may also bring about problems. The agency could be captured by its beneficiaries, and, for example, provide excessive benefits, or avoid terminating a program that is ineffective or no longer justified.
>
> Having good corporate governance can help executing agencies address these problems. It is important for executing agencies to have stable and credible corporate governance with representation not only from the authority under which they operate but also from the direct beneficiaries and society in general. Naming directors who represent the interests of beneficiaries to the board of directors of an agency contributes to reduce informational asymmetries between the agency and the beneficiaries, leading to programs that are more likely to be useful. Including directors who represent the interests of civil society beyond the direct beneficiaries—example, from sectors that may be competing for the same resources—can help prevent the capture to which the agency may be exposed. More generally, it is important to have directors who are not directly related to the government of the day in order to ensure the consistency of the agency's action over time, avoiding changes of strategy that are not justified by technical considerations with every change of government. This is especially important in areas in which policies need more time to mature before generating results—a common characteristic of policies aimed at promoting significant productive transformation.
>
> There are other problems that good corporate governance in executing agencies could help address. For example, an agency that designs the policy that it then implements will usually not be very inclined to evaluate its own performance, or do so with the necessary rigor. It will tend to conclude

> that its results were achieved efficiently and effectively. A corporate government that represents multiple interests, as suggested, can facilitate such evaluation. In addition, the design of the policy may be completely disconnected from what other agencies are doing or planning. This could well create serious problems of coordination when implementing policies that overlap between various public agencies, leading to competition, duplication, and, ultimately, ineffective policies. In this case, having directors who are heads of related agencies can prevent the problem of duplication and help solve the problem of coordination between public agencies so prevalent in our countries.
>
> For example, agencies involved in promoting basic science could have directors who are renowned scientists and academics, together with executive directors from agencies that promote innovation. Their boards could also include specialists in science and higher education along with a representative from the private sector. This diverse board could be chaired by the minister under whom the agency operates, either education or science and technology. Naturally, this board would select the director of the agency.

Protection against supplier and bureaucratic capture can be provided by mechanisms such that: (i) the program or policy is (at least partially) funded by the private sector it is supposed to benefit, and (ii) the private sector participates in program or policy governance. Good examples are agronomic research funded by a self-imposed tax on producers, who in turn oversee how the funds are used, as is the case in some INTA programs, or tourism promotion in Costa Rica, funded by a tax on the industry, which in turn has several seats on the Costa Rican Tourism Institute's marketing board. Political capture may be mitigated by public access to information, for example, with regard to the identity of the program beneficiaries, their geographical location (to prevent benefits that are concentrated in the jurisdiction of the relevant politicians), and the timing of support around elections. Involvement of strong, public-minded private sector organizations in the policymaking process—such as Colombia's Private Council for Competitiveness—may also mitigate political capture.

Finally, systematic program or policy evaluation can provide protection against all forms of capture. In the realm of social policy, Mexico's CONEVAL is responsible for coordinating and regulating the evaluation of national policies in support of social development. This federal agency has the technical capability and the autonomy to generate objective information, perform or contract rigorous evaluations, and in this way inform policymaking in the social areas. While CONEVAL sometimes supports evaluation in other sectors including PDPs, more systematic monitoring and evaluation of these policies would be a welcome development. Interestingly, the productivity law currently being prepared contemplates a requirement to make PDPs subject to monitoring and evaluation, in particular those corresponding to the vertical/market intervention quadrant, in order to mitigate the risk of capture and rent seeking.

No manual exists on how to design an agency to protect it from capture because each case is unique. The examples just presented illustrate the range of issues to be considered, and thus can provide some guidance to policymakers engaged in organizational design.

6. *Cooperation across public agencies*: Public-public cooperation is a challenging issue in PDPs, particularly when policies are wide, because many public agencies must participate and coordinate for policy to be implemented successfully.[9] As discussed earlier with the example of tourism, the minister or public official in charge of the dialogue with a certain sector may be in a good position to assess the sector's public input needs, but may not be in a good position to deliver what is needed. In such cases, in order for the needed public inputs to be delivered, some mechanisms of coordination within the public sector must be in place. But public-public cooperation is not easy. In general, those responsible for the management of public agencies involved in PDPs, from ministries to specialized agencies, do not have the right incentives to cooperate. Rather than solving other agency's priorities, they prefer to focus on their own. As will be shown in chapter 11, the failure to coordinate within the public sector is often one of the most important obstacles to public-private collaboration and the successful implementation of PDPs.

Several organizational structures have been used to address this challenge.

Specialized Cabinets and High-Level Task Forces

One way in which countries have attempted to address the need for coordination across government agencies is by creating specialized cabinets. Mexico is a case in point. Recently, President Peña Nieto created five such cabinets, one for each priority of the National Development Plan. One of them, called "Prosperous Mexico," is the one most closely linked to PDPs. The cabinet, chaired by the president but coordinated by the minister of finance, includes representation from 14 different ministries, as well as the heads of PEMEX, the Federal Electricity Commission, and the Mexican Institute of Social Security, among other agencies. While it does not address all the problems associated with intra-agency coordination discussed above, the specialized cabinet does provide a space for the participating agencies to align their priorities and coordinate policy. The participation of the president, who actually chairs the higher-level meetings attended by the ministers, signals the priority he assigns to these policies.

While interministerial cabinets can sometimes help provide a cross-cutting vision of the needs of the productive sector, they are not always effective in solving coordination issues. The case of Chile and the Regional Productive Development Agencies (ARDP) program discussed in chapter 7 is illustrative in this regard. Initially, the program, whose objective is to promote a number of clusters in each region, received a high priority, as creating the ARDPs was a campaign promise that needed to be fulfilled during the president's first 100 days in office. Given the centralized nature of PDPs in Chile, the program design included an interministerial board at the national level to facilitate high-level policy coordination affecting the selected clusters. As it turned out, however, the national coordination unit barely met. When the ARDPs identify needed public inputs and request help from local representatives of the central level agencies, frequently the response is that they do not have the approval from Santiago to change their annual spending plans.

Clearly, interministerial mechanisms are not the panacea, and can only go as far as the political will behind them takes them.[10]

On occasion, rather than a specialized cabinet in charge of a specific policy area on a more permanent basis, a public sector task force can bring together members of a variety of public entities to collaborate on a temporary basis in a specific task. For these task forces to work, as in the case of specialized cabinets, a primus inter pares is usually required. This may take the form of the chief of staff or the minister of the presidency, or sometimes, a specially appointed minister, with full backing from the president to act on the task assigned, as the voice of the president and with the authority of his or her office. Without such full backing and delegation of authority from the president to the head of the council, these coordinating mechanisms are unlikely to work.

A good example is the case of Intel and Costa Rica. When the government decided to target Intel as a potential investor in Costa Rica, a task force was created that involved all agencies that would have an impact on Intel's decision and success; the president himself chaired it. After Intel set up operations in Costa Rica and the country's ability to host such a high-tech operation was established, the presidential task force was no longer needed. CINDE, the organization in charge of attracting FDI, has been able to pursue other high-tech multinational companies pretty much on its own.

Sometimes cooperation across agencies comes from informal mechanisms and geographical proximity. Recently, Argentina inaugurated the "Polo Científico Tecnológico," a series of buildings that resemble a campus to house the Ministry of Science, Technology, and Productive Innovation (in charge of policy design), the National Innovation Agency for the Promotion of Science and Technology (executing agency), the CONICYT (National Council for Scientific and Technical Research), and a number of interdisciplinary international innovation institutes, including the Buenos Aires Biomedicine Research Institute, in partnership with the Max Planck Society. At the heart of the Polo is the restaurant, which provides a common space for policymakers, researchers, and agency staff to interact informally, and develop the common vision and trust needed to enhance cooperation. Minister Barañao has credited this familiarity with important improvements in the design of policy instruments.

Matrix-Like Organizations

In a matrix-type organization, the vertical organization in charge of the PDP process has a budget to purchase services from horizontal agencies. For example, the Ministry of Tourism might purchase services from the Ministry of Transportation—such as a paved road, a water treatment facility, or an airport—or from the minister of labor. This idea was proposed by Hausmann, Rodrik, and Sabel (2008) for South Africa. It gives the vertical entity extraordinary power to deliver on certain commitments, particularly those related to services provided by other public sector entities. It might also boost the interest and resources invested by the private sector in public-private collaboration, thus increasing the likelihood that such collaboration would be more fruitful. Within the region, Chile presents a case that is fairly consistent with these ideas. In particular, the Ministry of Agriculture has an agreement with CORFO and Fundación Chile through which it "hires" these institutions, transferring financial resources in exchange for their role in implementing PDPs for the sector, which they engage in using their considerable expertise.[11]

Hausmann, Rodrik, and Sabel (2008) propose that rather than assigning a predetermined budget to each vertical agency so they can purchase services from other agencies, a single pool could be set aside with the portion of the budget assigned to this function. The vertical agencies would compete to finance their priority projects under a clear and transparent selection mechanism. While it may require significant changes in the budget procedures of the countries in the region, such a flexible arrangement would match well with the uncertain nature of PDPs.[12]

Public-Private Councils and Other Third Parties

Public-private councils have been a staple of the successful catch-up stories of economic development of the twentieth century, and play a very important role in many developed countries as well. Both the scope and depth of public-private cooperation within these councils can vary enormously, from economy-wide to sector-specific and region-specific, and from a forum in which the government informs the private sector of its policies to one in which in-depth information sharing, policy design, and policy implementation take place.

When broad in scope, these councils can help define the general framework of a country's productive development or competitiveness strategy, ensuring some degree of coherence between the different policy components. If public participation is broad, these councils may provide a space in which those responsible for the different agencies can coordinate and find opportunities for collaboration. Private sector participants may also use these councils as a forum to access different public sector participants and express their needs. When these councils are instituted in a permanent way, they also help provide policy stability beyond the tenure of a particular administration.[13]

Sometimes, coherence across organizations and across time comes from third parties, such as multilateral organizations that provide funding for programs and agencies, and nongovernmental organizations. They can also use their prestige as a force for persuasion and participate in the training of mid-level, nonpolitical bureaucracies. In Costa Rica, for instance, CINDE interacts with many public agencies that have an impact on trade and FDI, and helps provide both coordination and consistency to their actions over time despite not having any formal authority.

TOP Capabilities for PDPs

The second factor that influences the public sector's ability to design and implement successful PDPs is the availability of TOP capabilities. The presence or absence of capabilities is of great relevance for policymakers considering whether to adopt a certain policy. While organizational structures may be amenable to reform, when it comes to capabilities, policymakers often have to work with what they have; they can increase them over time, but only gradually. In this sense, capabilities may be the most important constraint as countries transition to more complex and demanding PDPs.

Technical Capabilities

Technical capabilities comprise all the knowledge and expertise required to perform public sector tasks related to PDPs. This includes the ability to apply highly specialized, advanced knowledge to policy design and implementation, such as scientists working in technological institutes like INTA in Argentina or EMBRAPA in Brazil, or project evaluators in an innovation agency or a public development bank. But technical capabilities go beyond highly specialized skills to the general bureaucratic capabilities to perform all the core functions of the organization, including routine operations in which workers need to follow established procedure with little or no discretion. Technical capabilities are in part determined by factors that affect the selection of personnel and their incentives to invest in their technical capabilities, such as agencies' recruitment and promotion practices, and whether salaries are competitive.

In many countries in Latin America and the Caribbean in which the pool of skilled public administrators is thin, some public agencies such as the Central Bank, regulatory agencies, the revenue service agency, the state development banks, and other such organizations attract an important portion of the highly skilled personnel. This sometimes leaves agencies in charge of PDPs with relatively weak technical staff. In such cases, upgrading the capabilities of the staff through education, training, and career development can be an important step.

When lacking personnel with adequate capabilities, it is sometimes possible to use the capabilities of others. Placing some PDPs under the responsibility of public development banks may be a way to address this. Alternatively, some less developed countries have used the technical staff of relatively more developed countries. For example, Paraguay's Conacyt (the science and technology agency) uses staff from the FONDEF fund in Chile to evaluate their projects. As discussed in chapter 4, Chile, in turn, used Younoodle, a California web-based company that specializes in scoring business plans, to evaluate projects for the Start-Up Chile program.

In some cases, more horizontal regional cooperation can help. The case of PROSUR, a Regional Public Good project financed by the IDB involving nine patent offices in countries in Latin America, is an excellent example. It is not uncommon for foreign firms to want to register the same patents in multiple countries in the region. This implies replicating the due diligence on the patents up to nine times. Given the limited pool of technical experts who can perform this task in many countries, severe work overload is likely. The project generates a common platform such that, when the first office evaluates the patent, the results are made available to all of them. Countries are now working on establishing a single regional trademark system, so firms can protect their trademarks in many countries simultaneously.

Operational Capabilities[14]

Operational capabilities include managerial skills, that is, the ability to run an organization with high professional standards, efficiency, and results. They also allow an organization to set meaningful, measurable goals and evaluate its performance. They also involve the ability to create an environment within which policy experimentation, evaluation, and learning are encouraged, and even required, including setting up appropriate incentives for staff to engage in these activities, and the proper accountability mechanisms. Otherwise, agencies may become set in their way of doing things, even if not effective.

Operational capabilities also involve attributes that enable the organization to collaborate effectively with other relevant public sector organizations, as well as with the private sector. For example, for a PDA in charge of cluster development, operational capabilities would include the ability to effectively organize the engagement with the relevant private counterparts in order to lead a process of identifying public inputs needed for the development of the sector—as well as the obstacles that constrain such development; and the ability to elicit the cooperation of other relevant public agencies that may be critical for the delivery of required public inputs or removal of obstacles.

Some countries have interesting mechanisms to develop these skills, although not necessarily in the realm of PDPs. In the United

States, for example, the terrorist attacks of September 11, 2001, brought into focus the need to break down barriers between the different agencies within the intelligence community (IC). In response to this, the Intelligence Reform and Terrorism Prevention Act of 2004 established the Office of the Director of National Intelligence (DNI), and authorized the director to prescribe personnel policies and programs applicable to the IC, recommending the creation of a joint personnel rotation system, and making "service in more than one element of the IC a condition for promotion to such positions within the community as the Director shall specify." In response to this, the DNI, John Negroponte, created the Civilian IC Joint Duty Program, which established Joint Duty assignments in different agencies of the intelligence community, and issued a directive mandating a Joint Duty requirement for promotions to senior executive levels. The Joint Duty program creates cross-agency expertise, provides senior staff with a wider perspective on intelligence issues, and fosters an environment of information sharing and interagency cooperation.[15]

Political Capabilities

Political capabilities include the ability to both secure political support to accomplish the mission and safeguard against political capture. They involve the ability to access, engage, influence, and secure the support of the relevant authorities: a PDA may require cabinet level support; a governmental program may require support from congress, and so on. In turn, the agency must create a supportive environment among key stakeholders and an effective constituency even as it exercises influence and leadership over key actors and stakeholders above and beyond formal authority lines.

It is also important for agencies to secure a long-term mandate and the institutional setting required to pursue it. For this, they must enjoy adequate and stable funding; merit-based talent recruitment and personnel stability; and protection from undue interference from short-term party politics, clientelistic pressures, and various forms of capture, be it political, bureaucratic, or from direct beneficiaries.[16] Finally, entities must be able to secure the flexibility and autonomy required to engage in policy design and implementation discovery and adjustment.

Clearly, these TOP capabilities are mutually supportive. For example, an entity with little political support will find it difficult to obtain the resources needed to recruit staff with high technical skills, and without them it will be difficult to become a legitimate actor with the private sector. Likewise, without a fluid interaction with private actors, a PDA will have trouble establishing a good support base, which in turn will undermine its capacity to mobilize other entities involved in public policymaking, limit its impact, and further damage its reputation with private actors.

Assessing Public Sector Capabilities

How can the public sector or individual organizations within the public sector assess whether each one of their TOP capabilities is high or low?

Direct measurements of TOP capabilities, as defined, are not readily available either for the public sector as a whole or for individual PDAs. Current research by the IDB constitutes a first attempt at their direct assessment in selected PDAs.[17] Meanwhile, some help is available from the following sources.

Assessment by Policymakers

A well-educated, benevolent policymaker (that is to say, one whose aim is to use PDPs to increase national productivity) will likely form an impressionistic but well-informed evaluation of public sector capabilities. For example, does the agency of interest enjoy considerable independence from vested interests, or is it vulnerable to them? Is it efficient and professionally managed? Do the personnel have the knowledge and training required to deal with the task at hand? Does the organization or agency set for itself meaningful, measurable goals? Does it evaluate its own work, and does it take corrective action when it falls short of its goals? Outside experts—for example, from multilateral organizations—and counterparts in similar agencies in other countries could be used to assess an agency's capabilities. Visits to state-of-the-art counterpart agencies in other countries can be another good way for managers to assess their own capabilities and capability gaps.

Indirect Measurements

There are numerous, albeit imperfect, international indicators of public sector capabilities readily available, such as the World Bank's Worldwide Governance Indicators, the Public Sector section of the Country Policy and Institutional Assessment database, the Bertelsmann Stiftung's Transformation Index (BTI**), and the "Institutions" indicators of the Global Competitiveness Report. In general, these may be too broad, and may be useful only as a first approximation.

Berkman et al. (2013) have compiled indicators of policy features and government capabilities that may prove more directly useful, including indexes for policy stability (the extent to which policies are stable over time), adaptability (the extent to which policies can be adjusted when they fail or when circumstances change), coordination and coherence (the degree to which policies are consistent with related policies, and result from well-coordinated actions among the actors who participate in their design and implementation), quality of implementation and enforcement, and public regardedness (the degree to which policies pursue the public interest).[18] They also include an index of bureaucratic quality, based on a series of institutional diagnostic studies conducted by the IDB in the region. Table 10.1 illustrates the values of these indicators for most Latin American and Caribbean countries.

While all of the indicators mentioned have been calculated for the public sector as a whole and based on answers to opinion surveys (and thus are not hard data), they do provide some guidance. For instance, one would be very cautious before recommending PDPs that require very advanced public-public coordination capabilities in a country like Bolivia or Guatemala, where the global Coordination and Coherence index is very low, without at least recommending additional measures to mitigate potential interagency coordination problems. Ongoing research (see methodology in Chrisney and Kamiya, 2011) is attempting to generate agency- and program-level indicators as well.[19]

Table 10.1 Key Features of Public Policies since the 1980s: Cluster Analysis

Country	Stability	Adaptability	Implementation & enforcement	Coordination	Public regardedness	Bureaucratic quality
Argentina	Medium	Medium	Low	Medium	Low	Medium
The Bahamas	High*				High*	
Belize	High*				Medium*	
Bolivia	Low	Medium	Medium	Low	Low	Low
Brazil	High	High	High	High	Medium	High
Barbados	High*				High	
Chile	High	High	High	High	High	High
Colombia	Medium	High	High	Medium	Low	High
Costa Rica	Medium	High	High	Medium*	High	High
Dominican Rep.	Low	High	High	Medium*	Medium	Medium*
Ecuador	Low	Low	Low	Medium*	Medium	Medium
Guatemala	Low	Low	Low	Low	Medium	Low
Guyana	High*	Low*	Medium*	Low*	Low	Medium
Honduras	Medium	Medium	Medium	Low*	Low	Medium
Haiti	Low*	Low	Low	Low*	Low	Low
Jamaica	Medium	Medium*	High		Medium	High*
Mexico	Medium	Medium	High	Medium	Medium	Medium
Nicaragua	Medium	Low	Medium	Medium*	Low	Medium
Panama	Medium	Medium	Medium	High*	Medium	Low
Peru	Medium	Medium	Medium	Low	Medium	Medium
Paraguay	Low	Medium	Low	Low*	Low	Low
El Salvador	Medium	Medium	High	Low*	Medium	Low
Suriname					Medium	
Trinidad and Tobago	High		Medium*		Medium	
Uruguay	High	High*	High		High	Medium*
Venezuela	Low	Low	Low	Medium	Medium	Low

Notes: The policy index was built including only those countries for which at most one of the components was missing.
*Countries missing half or more of the components of the given index.
Source: Franco Chuaire and Scartascini (forthcoming).

Different Capability Requirements for Different Policy Types

While each individual PDP has unique features, different types of PDPs can be broadly characterized in terms of the key public sector capabilities they require, or by the "relative intensity" with which they demand those capabilities. Some general considerations follow:

- *Wide versus narrow PDPs*: Wide PDPs—that is, those that require the participation of many independent public sector organizations—pose considerable challenges for public sector coordination. Organizational features that facilitate cooperation across public agencies—such as a well-functioning matrix organization, or cross participation in agencies' boards—and operational capabilities regarding public-public coordination—perhaps acquired by rotating senior staff through different PDA agencies so that they understand each other's viewpoints and speak the same language, as in the example of the Joint Duty Program discussed above—will be particularly important. Narrow PDPs—which can be implemented by a single organization or a small group or organizations characterized by clear hierarchical relations—do not present this challenge.
- *Vertical versus horizontal PDPs*: All else being equal, vertical PDPs face a greater risk of private capture than horizontal PDPs. Their benefits accrue to a relatively small group of beneficiaries and can be large, while the costs are often borne by the taxpayers, and are typically small per individual taxpayer. The results are concentrated benefits and widespread costs. Thus, beneficiaries may be able to appropriate funds for private benefit—without corresponding social gains—and without detection or opposition. Accordingly, technical skills to engage in a selection process with due attention to well-justified criteria (see chapter 9) and organizational features and political safeguards that provide protection against capture by sectors with strong lobby capabilities or political connections will be particularly important for vertical policies. Vertical policies are also likely to require in-depth, sector-specific knowledge and technical skills.

- *Avoiding capture of market interventions*: Market interventions may also be easy targets for capture, since they directly impact the firm's financial bottom line. This is true especially when interventions that can be justified on a temporary basis involve recurrent benefits; this creates incentives for the beneficiaries to lobby for continuous support, even after the rationale for intervention is no longer valid.[20] The elimination of market interventions creates losers and, therefore, may be disadvantageous for politicians, particularly during electoral periods. One-off market interventions such as installation subsidies to attract FDI do not pose a similar challenge. However, they may be demanding in terms of probity and technical skills (such as the need to identify the foreign investments worthy of support from a social point of view).
- Careful design can help avoid problems. For those market interventions that attempt to stimulate certain behaviors, capture is less prevalent in cases where, by design, only the firms that exhibit the sought-after behavior receive the benefits. For example, in the case of the subsidy to export pioneers proposed in chapter 2, only the first exporters of a new product receive the subsidy, provided they have followers that benefit from spillovers. Thus, the design of the instrument constrains the scope for policymakers' discretion in selecting beneficiaries and for rent seeking by firms. In such cases, the design of the instrument ensures that only the "right" firms self-select into the program, sparing policymakers the need to "pick winners" in a discretionary (and potentially arbitrary) way. Market interventions that involve discretion in the selection of beneficiaries require organizational features and political skills to protect against capture, insulating the decision process from undue pressures from both politicians and the private sector.
- *Removal of public "bads"*: In the case of public inputs, it is useful to distinguish between policies that remove public bads (such as cumbersome and unnecessary regulations) and policies that provide public inputs. Policies that eliminate excessive regulation are technically relatively easy, but frequently demand the coordinated participation of many independent public agencies.

Coordinating such participation is not just a technical issue; it requires the proper political authority. Examples are the one-stop-shop policies to start a business that have been adopted in several countries in the region.[21] Removal of public bads requires extensive operational capabilities involving public-public coordination and authority over other agencies.

- *Vertical public inputs*: In the case of vertical public inputs, two different stages may be distinguished. First, a decision—based on technical, and not political, criteria—must be made as to which sectors to engage. Second, the main obstacles to the development of a sector must be identified, along with the public inputs needed to unleash the sector's potential. This identification process entails the ability to convene the right actors in the private sector, and engage in a constructive dialogue to define a plan. As with other vertical policies, technical knowledge of the sectors involved is an important requirement. If the needed public inputs require actions by other public sector actors, they involve strong public-public cooperation capabilities, as well as an adequate level of political authority.

From Best Practices to Best Matches: Public Capabilities and Policy Choice

PDPs are hard policies to execute and, to varying degrees, performance depends on capabilities and organizational strengths. How can institutions face the challenge of setting up a PDP portfolio?

In institutional reform projects in the developing world, as Andrews (2013) has argued, the prevailing practice is to identify "best practices" to deal with any given problem, and try to adopt them wherever they are required. At first blush, this seems to make perfect sense: if the "best" way to deal with a problem can be identified, it would be a waste of time to try to reinvent the wheel, and it would be wrong to settle for anything less than the "best" solution.

Recently, however, the notion of adopting "best practices" has been sharply criticized. For the purposes of this chapter, two main arguments seem particularly relevant.

First, if an organization is assigned a task that widely exceeds its capabilities, it may collapse under the strain, just as athletes attempting to lift too much weight before they are ready leave the gym injured, not stronger. Alternatively, an organization that receives funding that is conditional on adopting best practices may try to "go through the motions," pretending to do something it knows it cannot really do, like an athlete who huffs, puffs, and groans loudly in the gym while actually doing very little work. This doesn't produce any gains, either. In both cases, lack of capabilities precludes success.[22]

Second, policies are not applied in a vacuum, but rather in very specific contexts, rich in explicit and tacit "working rules" and behavioral norms that may differ from formal laws (Ostrom, 1990: 51). Local actors know these rules well and follow them while foreign experts may find it more difficult to pick them up. It is the "tacit" part—the unwritten rules of behavior—that makes the adoption of what works well elsewhere so difficult. For example, "best practices" in a setting where behavior is based on mutual trust among policy participants will not work as well in a setting dominated by mistrust. From a slightly different (but not incompatible) perspective, Andrews (2013: 45) describes institutions as icebergs, "suggesting that a large part of any institutional logic is unseen or below the water line because it is informal—implicit, unwritten and seldom visible." The difficulty of transferring "best practices" from one country context to another is that the informal, implicit, unwritten, and seldom visible elements of the institutional setup are practically impossible to replicate. Without them, supposedly "best" practices are unlikely to yield the expected results.

But what, then, is the alternative to "best practices?" The alternative is "best matches" between capabilities, policies, and productive policy goals. Of course, best matches must also take into account the institutional context. The argument in favor of "best matches" is as follows.

First, problems that require PDP solutions can typically be addressed through different policy instruments, not just a single one.[23] Each of these policy instruments require different public capabilities to effectively design and implement them.

Second, the public sectors of different countries, and different public sector agencies within each country, are endowed with different capabilities for policy design and implementation. Some countries may have a deeper pool of people with technical skills. Others may find it easier to align political actors in order to ensure the sustainability of some policies over time, or have better ways to coordinate policies that require multiple agencies. Different agencies may also differ in terms of the capabilities they possess.

Third, and following from the first two points, the choice of policy instruments to be used to achieve broadly defined PDP goals should be guided by the best match between the capability requirements of those policies and instruments and the capabilities available in the relevant parts of the public sector.[24] Countries should assign responsibilities for the design and implementation of policies to agencies that currently have or are close to having the requisite capabilities for those policies. True, policies that are too complex to handle today may be within reach a few years down the road. In the short term, however, it may be wise to refrain from utilizing instruments that require capabilities that countries do not currently possess. More ambitious undertakings can be tackled later as the relevant capabilities develop.

This logic may lead to choosing policies and instruments that are relatively blunt or not the most efficient. Yet choosing less than ideal instruments that roughly match public capabilities may be preferable to choosing state-of-the-art instruments that the public sector is not ready to master and use. There are two complementary reasons for this pragmatic approach. First, if the instruments are less than ideal, but still useful, some progress will be made toward solving the problem that needs to be addressed. Second, by simply starting to do something about the problem, the public sector will deepen its understanding of the problem and increase its capability to deal with it. In the right context, this will lead to upgrades in capabilities and the ability to choose, or create, better policies and instruments.

Policy Learning and Capability Building

While policymakers should decide on the policy mix taking into account available capabilities, they should also be concerned with enhancing those capabilities over time. Just as countries can use existing productive capabilities as springboards to acquire new productive capabilities and change their comparative advantages, the public sector can also use their existing capabilities as a point of departure to expand them, thus allowing them to tackle more complex PDPs.

There is certainly a role for capability upgrading through traditional methods: personnel policies that attract the right talent; competitive salaries to retain that talent; promotion policies that reward performance and technical and managerial skills; rotation policies to encourage cooperation across agencies; good training programs focused on required capabilities; and so on. Improving organizational structures along the lines discussed in this chapter may contribute to upgrade capabilities as well. Countries should devote sufficient resources to capability upgrading. As important as these methods might be, however, the process of acquiring capabilities involves much learning by doing. In fact, as argued by Pritchett, Woolcock, and Andrews (2010), it is in the process of identifying problems and learning how best to address them through iteration and adaptation that capabilities for policy design and implementation really develop. In other words, the same discovery processes that spark policy learning and improvement may also expand capabilities for policy design and implementation.

In line with these ideas, this chapter proposes that policy learning and capability upgrading require three distinct but complementary conditions: an enabling environment; a sound method for improvement; and the correct set of incentives.

Enabling Environment

An enabling environment comprises a set of "minimum conditions," without which improving capabilities is simply out of the question, and a set of "desirable conditions" under which capability upgrading may be easier. The lists provided below are meant as a first step in exploring this question; they do not pretend to be exhaustive or final.

The *minimum conditions* are stability and flexibility: Stability (of policy, organization, and personnel) is needed because without it, learning—and therefore improving—is simply not possible; knowledge is not accumulated, but rather lost when policies change very quickly; organizations have short lives, and personnel rotates at high rates. Flexibility is needed because learning leads to discovering new things to do and new ways of doing them; an organization that discourages its staff from trying new things cannot translate learning into improved capabilities and performance. Table 10.1 shows which countries in the region have better indicators in terms of policy stability as well as flexibility (adaptability), and may thus offer more fertile ground for upgrading capabilities. A culture of monitoring and evaluation is also a requirement, since it provides a way for policymakers to derive lessons from the policy experiences. An enabling environment for capability upgrading does not just happen by chance, but rather as a result of conscious decisions to provide such an environment, and requires substantial political support.

Desirable conditions include adequate resources; participation in knowledge and practice networks; access to training; qualified, highly skilled personnel who are encouraged to develop their own capabilities; and so on. An environment of trust, respect for the professional abilities of the personnel, and a reasonable degree of autonomy from political pressure for decision makers at different organizational levels may also help, as well as systematic interaction with policy beneficiaries and other stakeholders.

A Method for Improvement

An enabling environment is not enough. Organizations need methods that create new knowledge and translate it into both policy improvement and capability. "Best practices" and traditional training have attempted to achieve these goals, but the results have been less than satisfactory. These disappointing results should not be grounds for discarding the study of successful practices or dismissing the usefulness of training and advanced education. However, a method for improvement should complement these efforts by incorporating other important features. Recent work by authors such as

Sabel, Zeitlin, Pritchett, Woolcock, and Andrews (see references) has produced important insights on this issue.

Sabel and Zeitlin (2012) emphasize that the exact nature of the problems faced by the "street-level bureaucrat" or frontline worker of the public sector is often not known; when this is the case, the best way of solving those problems, given the particular features of each case, cannot be known ex ante at the central levels of any organization. Therefore, sufficient discretion must be granted to the street-level bureaucrat, but this discretion—which is to say, the ability to try new things or new ways of doing old things—needs to be integrated into a system that creates new knowledge and improved organizational performance. The bureaucrat can deviate from organizational norms, but the deviation needs to be justified, and the results evaluated. Within this paradigm, street-level bureaucrats must provide detailed information on what exactly was done, how it was done, and why, as well as what results were obtained. In fact, accountability within this paradigm relates more to the proper provision of this information in order to allow joint learning, rather than to the actual effectiveness of the delivery.

Typically this method of learning and capability upgrading involves not just one street-level bureaucrat delivering a service, but many, thus speeding up the joint learning process. As a result of what is learned, norms and instructions are adjusted, discarded, or created, and the cycle starts again. Within this method, which these authors call "experimentalist governance," there is no clear separation between policy design and implementation. It is in the process of implementing that learning takes place, capabilities are upgraded, and policy design adapts. The program of Start-Up Chile discussed in chapter 4 has some elements of experimentalist governance: the program was rolled out with a minimalist design, and was adjusted on the go as learning took place.

Andrews, Pritchett, and Woolcock (2012) have independently developed a method that shares many elements with Sabel and Zeitlin's. They call their method PDIA: problem-driven iterative adaptation. The initial focus, they argue, should not be on some ready-made, imported "solution" (such as best practices), developed and applied in a different context, but rather on understanding the exact nature of the local problem. Then, different possible approaches to solving the problem should be outlined and tried out (perhaps simultaneously, if the policy is being applied at the same time in different regions, or to different groups of beneficiaries), and the results evaluated. Based on this, improved solutions can be tried or, if the problem has been solved, the next problem can be tackled. Iteration thus leads to adaptation, and the process begins anew. Moreover, it is in the process of solving specific problems that capabilities are accumulated. The experimentalist governance and PDIA approaches apply to policymaking in general, but are especially relevant to PDPs, in which often the exact nature of the problems and the best way to address them are not known ex ante.

While these two groups of authors have developed their approaches independently, the similarities are obvious. The process outlined in what follows, inspired by their ideas, will be characterized as an EFA Cycle that begins with Experimentation, as in Sabel and Zeitlin (2012), ends with Adaptation, as in Pritchett, Woolcock, and Andrews (2010), and has a Feedback loop in the middle.

Experimentation
In the words of American philosopher John Dewey, policies should be "experimental in the sense that they will be entertained subject to constant and well-equipped observation of the consequences they entail when acted upon, and subject to ready and flexible revision in the light of observed consequences" (Sabel and Simon, 2011: 78). Experimentalism does not necessarily call for formal, statistically meaningful experiments, but rather for a space in which different approaches to solving a given problem are allowed, and their results systematically evaluated. US President Franklin Delano Roosevelt made the point even more forcefully in the depths of the Great Depression in 1932: "The country needs and, unless I mistake its temper, the country demands bold, persistent experimentation. It is common sense to take a method and try it: if it fails, admit it frankly and try another. But above all, try something" (Roosevelt, 1932).

While room for "trying out new things" might seem like a commonsense requirement in order to learn whether there are better ways to achieve current goals, or even to revise those goals, creating such room goes against the grain of the dominant paradigm in public administration in Latin America. Within this paradigm, desirable features for public service delivery involve clear, and ideally simple, rules and procedures, designed by technocratic experts facing well-defined problems that can be tackled with well-defined, known technologies, minimizing bureaucratic discretion at the point of delivery. Moreover, as noted by Aghion et al. (2010), in societies with low levels of trust there is a tendency to impose even more strict and detailed regulations on public sector actions, as a means to stop corruption. While such strict, detailed regulations may help mitigate wrongdoing by public officials, they are exactly the contrary of what room for experimentation requires. But this is exactly what has happened in many Latin American countries, where regulations and controls are increasingly abundant, and where the work of agencies in charge of them, such as Comptrolling Offices (*Contralorías*) frequently has a paralyzing effect on the rest of the public administration. This is, of course, not an argument against accountability and proper control of public funds. But controls and accountability could be more focused on policy outcomes rather than on red tape and procedure. In other words, less emphasis on ex ante, and more emphasis on ex post control.

Feedback Loops
The second component of the approach is the "feedback loop." This is perhaps the most difficult component of all from a technical point of view.

The general idea is simple enough: in order to improve, an organization needs to obtain data that identifies things that work and things that don't work through "constant and well equipped observation of the consequences" of policies and projects (to use Dewey's expression). But just identifying what has worked and what has not is not enough to improve performance: this information must flow back into the decision-making process in order to discard that which didn't work, adopt that which has worked, and continue to tinker with it to make it better. Hence, the complementarity between feedback loops and experimentation.

In order to be useful for decision making, feedback needs to be received in a timely fashion. A comprehensive, rigorous evaluation of a program that is delivered years after program completion, while invaluable for learning about its impact and whether it merits continued support and replication, is of little use for policymakers involved in the program's design. Thus, agencies need to combine more formal and time-consuming evaluations with provisional, impressionistic evaluations of what seems to be working and what is not, and equally impressionistic attempts at identifying reasons for this differential performance.[25] While the more formal evaluations are underway, they will have to do more of what seems to be working, less of what seems not to be working, and observe the results. They may resort in some cases to systematically trying out several different options, or "crawl the design space" (Pritchett, Samji, and Hammer, 2012): that is to say, to go back to experimentation, and to evaluate, at least informally, the results of different approaches to solving one particular problem.

Adaptation

The ultimate goal of experimentation and feedback is organizational adaptation. The idea is not just to try out new things, and to observe and evaluate their effect. The idea is to use experimentation and feedback loops to systematically generate new knowledge, and to use this new knowledge to change organizations, policies, and practices: that is, to use this new knowledge to increase organizational capabilities.

This is possible, however, only if organizations have some flexibility. Without it, experimentation would not be possible, but even if it did take place, in the margins and under the radar, it would not lead to large-scale—and therefore visible—changes in organizational structure, policies, operating procedures, organizational culture, and accepted norms of behavior. The case of the produce funds in Mexico, discussed in Box 10.2, is a good example of the EFA cycle at work.

Box 10.2 The EFA Cycle at Work: The Experience with Produce Foundations in Mexico

Promoting the use of scientific capacities to help small and medium agriculture producers is a sensible thing to do. In principle, it also appears to be a simple and straightforward policy: put some resources on the table and make an open call to the research community to present applied R&D proposals to deal with the challenges and opportunities that producers face in their localities. Sounds easy. But the experience of the Produce Foundations in Mexico highlights the unexpected complexities involved in moving from theory to reality.

The Produce Foundations were established in every Mexican state. Their purpose was to provide financial support to applied research projects that would address relevant local technological challenges in the agricultural area. The resources were assigned through open and contestable calls. Luring researchers to apply for the funds wasn't difficult. On the contrary, many proposals were presented. However, the managers of the funds began to notice that the projects weren't really addressing the needs of the local producers, but were instead responding to the interest of the researchers. Although the terms of reference and the evaluation criteria were adjusted in successive calls, the research community still managed to stick to its previous agenda, finding creative ways to "camouflage" proposals so they would be eligible. After many trials, managers decided to radically change the operational model of the fund. Instead of waiting for the researchers' proposals, they went to the communities and met with local producers and organizations to identify the main problems they faced; then they organized calls for R&D projects that would address precisely those problems. Resources were directed to pre-investment studies in order to assess the technological feasibility and the productive relevance of the challenges put forward by the producers. Obviously this also meant a profound change in the competence profile of fund personnel.

Source: Ekboir et al. (2009).

Incentives for Improvement

An enabling environment and a method for improvement are necessary but not sufficient conditions for capability upgrading. Somebody has to do the upgrading—so that somebody better have a good reason to proceed with the always difficult and risky task of deviating from accepted practice and creating new norms and policies. The puzzle is still missing one piece: incentives and motivation.

On this issue the extant literature is divided into two conflicting strands. On the one hand, a pessimistic strand is associated with the public choice theory and part of the political economy literature, which views bureaucrats and politicians as pursuing narrowly defined self-interested goals, rather than the social welfare. On the other hand, Sabel and Zeitlin's ideas on experimentalist governance as well as Andrews, Pritchett, and Woolcock's ideas on "positive deviation" and "Problem Driven Iterative Adaptation" take a more optimistic view that, given the right institutional framework—which includes important elements of accountability—public servants will implement policy in the service of the general interest. In reality, both "public-minded" behavior and "self-interested behavior" occur, so perhaps the more interesting question is what prompts policy participants to behave one way or the other.

What prompts a bureaucrat to do his or her job well, to seek outstanding performance and great results? Several factors may come into play, including the following:

- Belonging to a prestigious organization—possibly one with high admission barriers, having a well-defined and attractive career path within the public sector, and perhaps after leaving it, in the private sector.[26]
- Being part of a (possibly global) "community of practice," with well-defined standards of acceptable practice and quality.
- Prestige and community respect. This may be strengthened through formal recognition of extraordinary performance. The US federal government, for example, has instituted the Samuel J. Heyman Service to America Medals, known as the Sammies, which have earned a reputation as the "Oscars" of public service.[27]
- Having long enough time horizons for investments by bureaucrats to develop their own capabilities or those of the organization to have time to pay off.

- Salaries that are indicative of a high social valuation of the profession or activity, perhaps with a contingent component dependent on performance.
- Strong mechanisms of accountability.

Is Any of This Realistic?

The preceding subsections present an argument about the minimum institutional conditions required for upgrading the capability of the public sector. Whatever the theoretical merits of the approach, is it realistic to try to implement it (or something similar to it) in Latin America and the Caribbean? Doesn't "room for experimentation" open the door for arbitrary behavior on the part of public agencies? And isn't the idea of establishing feedback loops with empowered stakeholders embedded in the decision-making process just plain utopia?

No, it is not. Throughout the region there are many examples of PDAs that are engaged in experimentalism, learning from their policy results, with feedback loops that use this newly acquired knowledge to guide continuous processes of policy adjustment and capability upgrading. Fundación Chile and CORFO in Chile, CINDE in Costa Rica, the ANII in Uruguay, the Innovation Agency in Argentina, and the agricultural technology institutes in Argentina, Brazil, and Uruguay are just a few organizations that have, to a greater or lesser extent, carved out some room for experimentation, worked closely with the private sector, attracted and developed top-level talent, and created a strong organizational "ethos" of high performance and professional excellence. Some have dedicated units charged with implementing policy studies and carrying out impact evaluations, indicating a strong focus on learning and results, rather than on procedure and ex ante controls.

The case of INTA in Argentina illustrates some of these points. This institution has decentralized units deployed in the territory that function with a considerable amount of autonomy. It provides their staff significant discretion at the point of delivery, and lots of space for joint experimentation with the private sector. It also provides their staff with the right monetary incentives for discovery, which has produced very successful results. The development of new rice varieties discussed in chapter 2 is a case in point. Not only did the experts at the local INTA unit come up with a variety well adapted to the needs of the local growers in the Entre Ríos province; in the process of solving this problem, they acquired world-class technical capabilities for rice technology that led to even more important developments down the road. In other words, their efforts to solve a specific local problem led to the solution of that problem, and the accumulation of further technical capabilities.

Even though these high capability organizations are not the norm, they prove that even in unfavorable contexts, their creation is indeed possible. High-capability PDAs should be seen as potential "templates" to be used as guides in a more general effort to upgrade PDP-relevant public capabilities. Successful PDAs in Latin America should be treated not as irreproducible exceptions but rather as institutions deserving of careful study in order to identify the elements in their experience that can be used to guide a broader effort to create high-performing PDP institutions in the region. The ongoing IDB research project on "Building Capabilities for PDAs" aims precisely at this.

11

Two to Tango: Public-Private Collaboration

In the traditional view of productive development policies (PDPs), the roles of government and the private sector are completely separated. Market forces are powerful, and largely lead to desirable outcomes. When a market failure does arise that requires government intervention, a public sector entity identifies the problem and designs a solution. Government sets the rules and conditions, pursuing some collective goals, and firms act within those rules and conditions, attempting to maximize profits. If the rules are well designed, the individual and profit-seeking behavior of the firms leads to good results. In that context, with very well-informed governments, there is limited room for public-private interaction in productive development policy. Each side can do its part independently of the other.

This chapter deviates from that view. At the very least, the public sector cannot hope to have all the required knowledge to assess the needs for intervention and design appropriate policy, for the fundamental reason that some of that information is held by private firms (Rodrik, 2008). In such cases, government needs to extract the information, yet the profitability of those firms is affected by the shape and size of the resulting policy. At the heart of this informational asymmetry lies a classic principal-agent problem: the challenge for government as the principal is to conduct this interaction in a manner that induces firms to provide their complete information truthfully, rather than manipulating it in order to bias the policy in their favor.

More generally, in many cases, the design, implementation, feedback, and redesign of policy cannot be done by the public sector without interaction and perhaps collaboration with private agents. The problem of lack of trust due to differing motivations of public and private agents is only one of the impediments to their interaction. This process is further complicated by other issues such as communication, coordination, and the manner in which private agents interact with one another, not only with government.

Actually, unlike the static theoretical exercises in which government is first faced with a one-shot problem and then posits a one-shot solution upon which firms react, some of the most interesting and successful policy efforts are often dynamic processes by which new questions and challenges emerge and are solved, and the relevant information is learned gradually by all participants. Yes, there is a danger of capture, which needs to be dealt with.[1] But the main interest goes beyond just avoiding capture to understanding how private and public agents can truly cooperate in a constructive manner, especially as some of the PDPs with more potential *require* private engagement. The process of acquiring knowledge and using it jointly is an integral part of the policy question, and the nature of effective public-private interaction is one of the main topics of this chapter.

As Hausmann, Rodrik, and Sabel (2008: 5) emphasize, a government should evaluate its productive development policy framework by asking if it has "set up the institutions that engage the bureaucrats in an ongoing conversation of pertinent themes with the private sector,... has the capacity to respond selectively, yet also quickly and using a variety of updated policies, to the economic opportunities that these conversations are helping identify." This approach turns on its head the traditional focus of productive development policy analysis, shifting it from static policy design in isolation to a discussion about the institutions of productive development policy and, in particular, about their ability to interact with the private sector. This chapter reexamines some of the issues discussed in the report through this lens, deepening the analysis of public institutional capabilities in chapter 10.

The Private Sector as a Partner

The manner by which government can engage the private sector to obtain the knowledge it needs, adequately implement policy, and react to new developments varies with the depth of the engagement. There is no best way of doing things: what is useful depends on capabilities and circumstances. In some instances, the public-private interaction is limited to government consulting with the private sector about its intended policies and attempting to extract from the private sector information relevant to policy design through informal dialogue.[2] In other situations, the private sector is integrally involved in the design and/or implementation of policies. Sometimes, the involvement extends to the monitoring, evaluation, and redesign of those policies. Finally, as some cases later in this chapter illustrate, government may yield the initiative on certain PDPs, or even partial or total control and authority to make the relevant decisions, to the private sector. How the public sector interacts with the private sector is one of the keys to obtaining useful information and applying the policy effectively.

In a pure consultation process, by definition, the public sector "listens" to the private sector, but then makes decisions by itself. However, there is a continuum to the depth of the consultation process, as Devlin (2013) notes, that starts with "mere talk," progresses to "consultation" in which issues are discussed but the government then makes decisions on its own, and culminates in "dialogue," which aims to develop a consensus among participants so that the private sector will assume ownership and lend credibility and political support to the policy. Or, as Schneider (2010) puts it, the process ranges from "cheap talk" to "expensive exchanges" to "collaborative learning." The scope of the consultation process can also vary widely. Very broad discussions about the whole policy spectrum include cases of public-private alliances around long-term, national development strategies, studied in Devlin (2013) and Devlin and Moguillansky (2009a, b). However, consultation like that performed in preparation of trade negotiations frequently involves much narrower and more technical issues; when effective, it empowers government not only with legitimacy but also with superior information and wider options. Numerous examples of these narrower interactions, in which vertically specialized institutions engage in different degrees of consultation with their constituencies, are described by Schneider (2010).

Joint policy design takes the collaboration a step further, presumably under certain preestablished rules to prevent the pursuit of consensus from becoming a case of capture by the private parties of public roles. The more extensive process that Devlin (2013) calls "dialogue" can be thought of as straddling the divide between pure consultation and joint policy design. The differentiating element is that the private sector would not just be lodging complaints or raising issues reactively, but also be actively involved in assessing the main problems and designing possible solutions. This would require not just in-depth knowledge of the practical problems that they face, but also skills that would enable private actors to evaluate proposals made by the public sector and make technically sound proposals of their own. It would also require that private actors understand and value public policy objectives, just as the policymaker understands private goals. Other types of cooperation may include academia and third parties working together, for example, to design research programs aimed at increasing the productivity of a particular economic activity or to evaluate existing programs.

Successful international experience studied in Devlin (2013) offers useful examples along this range. For example, in South Korea up until the mid-1980s, a public-private council included only the business sector and the public sector. The government used the council to inform the business sector of the policies it would pursue and, in fact, impose on them. At the other extreme, in Ireland, a council that included business leaders, academia, nongovernmental organizations (NGOs), and labor unions engaged in an open dialogue to define a national development and competitiveness strategy. The Latin American cases studied in Schneider (2013) do not reach this level of interaction but do show substantial experience with public-private councils with economy-wide, competitiveness mandates, such as the Foro de Desarrollo Productivo in Chile in the 1990s, the Council for Economic and Social Development created in Brazil in 2002, and the National Competitiveness Council created in Colombia in 2006.

The scope and depth of public-private cooperation within public-private councils can vary enormously, from economy-wide to sector-specific and region-specific, and from a forum in which the government informs the private sector of its policies to one in which in-depth information sharing, policy design, and policy implementation take place. Whatever the modality of interaction with the private sector that appears useful and feasible in a given situation, the effective engagement of the private sector is fundamental for a robust portfolio of PDPs.

What the Private Sector Brings to the Table

The public sector has substantial uncertainty about both the *what* and the *how* of appropriate PDPs. In contrast to the private sector, it does not have readily available signals to guide its performance in fulfilling its objectives or a process of competition to automatically weed out ineffective decisions; the private sector receives information from prices, feedback from profitability, and benefits from the natural selection of the most efficient initiatives and firms through competition. Identifying and carrying out socially beneficial PDPs requires elaborate information that the government usually does not have, including detailed productive knowledge about the production, trade, and usage of goods and services. Such knowledge may reside in the private sector, mainly in firms and industry associations that own and use the technology in the market. They know by direct experience the problems they face or the cost such problems impose, and can better evaluate the repercussions that alternative conditions would have. While the public sector still needs to validate and integrate the pieces of information it may gather in a fragmented fashion from private sector sources, there is clearly much to be gained by engaging the private sector in public policy issues. The process of identifying policies and then implementing them through all its phases (design, execution, monitoring/evaluation) can substantially benefit from public-private collaboration, if only to guide the process at each stage.

Likewise, the private sector also has incomplete information. Information from both sectors is complementary: the private sector benefits from the comprehensive public perspective on issues that are relevant for business but are outside the direct experience of individual firms or the sector. In some instances, the basis for collaboration may not even be information sharing, but "learning sharing." In these cases, the motivation for public-private interaction may be the need to engage in co-exploration of new directions unknown to both the public and the private sectors, to their mutual benefit.

The private sector may also be interested in trying to influence the productive development policy selected by the public sector. For example, most activities require the provision of sector-specific collective inputs (such as certification, storage, or communications), and the private sector has an interest in demonstrating the need for such inputs to the public sector. In so doing, private demands may contribute to the cooperation of the relevant public sector units, usually in their own functional silos in the public administration. The private partner may be a coalescing force for the public sector.

Private sector engagement also helps to protect productive development policy from undue influences of the political cycle. This engagement may bring a long-term perspective to policy by providing a safeguard for the policies to survive changes in key public officials and, especially, election-induced reshuffling. Public-private collaboration can help create a consensus above the political fray (Stiglitz, 1998), and can be a substitute for the stability that a grand political agreement on state policies in this area would provide. It is not uncommon for governments to seek to engage the private sector simply to help preserve their policies over time. In the right proportions, engagement of the private sector may provide the balance between stability over the political cycle and a healthy flexibility to make room for the policy perspectives of new governments.

The Perils of Private Sector Engagement

For all its important benefits, private sector engagement in productive development policy also involves serious perils that need to be contained. The challenge is that those parties with the information that the government needs also have a profit motive that may distort the information they may be willing to share. While good productive development policy is, for the most part, presumably also in the interest of the private sector subject to it, other inefficient but self-serving policies may be even better for their private bottom line. In that case, private sector engagement may not help and may hinder policy quality. In some cases, this contradiction is particularly salient. For example, the information advantage of the private sector may lead to biased information or half-truths that may impede the discovery and implementation of the best policies. In the extreme, private sector engagement may end up being a mechanism for seeking privileges, or rent seeking, rather than information sharing of any kind. In other words, the policymaker may be subject to capture, due to the informational asymmetry that governs the relationship.

Other potential problems range from the private parties assuming complete control of the policy instruments by political maneuver to the private sector never engaging, demonstrating enthusiasm, or developing sufficient trust in government agents to even participate. Lack of trust may stem from the firm's own lack of information (it may doubt the intentions of the government, or fear that a competitor may end up being the main beneficiary at its expense), or its own pessimism about the effectiveness with which government does anything, especially if it requires coordination.

The risk of capture and rent seeking by the private party at the expense of the policymaker, and the risk of limited engagement due to trust issues, depends on the type of policy in question. Vertical policies, by design, can create benefits for some firms at the expense of others, and are therefore more prone to rent seeking. They also make capture likelier in the long run since a concentrated impact on a few agents gives them strong incentives to try to influence decision makers, because for them the stakes are very high. In this regard, vertical policies tend to be riskier than horizontal policies. Policies of market intervention are also risky because, by directly impacting firms' financial bottom lines, they create a strong constituency against discontinuing promotional instruments even if they do not work. For this reason, these policies are riskier than the provision of public inputs, which usually fulfill a permanent production need, and whose costs can be shared with beneficiaries. It follows that vertical market interventions are doubly risky. This is especially so in the case of strategic bets, which, in contrast to policies aimed at incrementally improving already established sectors, entail substantial uncertainty concerning their potential competitiveness. Conversely, horizontal public inputs, the least controversial policies, are also the least risky.

There are other margins along which this tension may rise or fall. Consider a case where government is trying to assess the size of the transfer to a particular sector to compensate for a negative externality that prevents the sector from growing to its optimal size. In this case, the objective of the firm would be to provide incorrect information that inflates the size of the externality and thus of the subsidy received. Alternatively, consider a government trying to figure out the technical specifications of a necessary public input, or a precise question that requires some research. In these examples, the best interest of the firm would be for the government to get as accurate information as possible, and there is no tension.

These perils are real because opportunities for capture abound. For example, consider the temporary credit subsidy for low-income housing in Panama studied by Fernández (2011). When the subsidy was due to expire, a powerful lobby for the construction industry made sure it was renewed. They also made sure that only families purchasing new housing—rather than existing housing—would be eligible for the credit subsidy. Thus, while the original intention of the subsidy was to help the lives of the poorest, it also turned into an instrument that ensures the profitability of the construction industry. Not surprisingly, there is skepticism about the advisability of implementing productive development policy in Latin America—even if the effectiveness of such policy in other regions is accepted. Skepticism hinges, in equal parts, on legitimate doubts about government's ability to "pick winners" and on the likelihood that such policies will be used to transfer rents to private groups with privileged access to power, rather than to increase productivity (Rodrik,

2008). Public-private collaboration needs to successfully deal with both concerns.

The perils of private sector engagement concerning capture are in the nature of the system everywhere; it is not a problem specific to Latin America. Recent empirical research on lobbying activities to Congress in the United States shows that the exchange of contributions for rents, as opposed to the exchange of information for the benefit of Congressional committees or "information lobbying," is central to what lobbyists do (Bertrand, Bombardini, and Trebbi, 2011). Lobbyists not only take advantage of superior information, but once the lobby contacts the policymaker, then it can offer a reward in exchange for a policy that is more favorable to the sector. Private sector engagement may actually create the opportunity for rent seeking and capture.

Most countries have made progress in modernizing the state and deepening democratic transparency and accountability. Improvements have also been made in policy design and evaluation. However, an antidote for capture has not been found. Capture remains an important peril for more ambitious PDPs, which invite more opportunities for abuse. It would be naïve to assume that the risk of capture has disappeared—and open the floodgates to private engagement without appropriate institutions to keep tabs on it. In particular, some of the more ambitious vertical policies discussed in chapter 9 are more susceptible to capture—and require sufficient capabilities and institutional design to run them well.

Matching Public and Private Counterparts

It takes two to tango. Public-private collaboration requires strong counterparts with compatible characters. The success of PDPs is in good measure dependent on the quality of the counterparts.

The Private Sector Counterpart

Successful public-private collaboration requires appropriate private sector capabilities. If the private sector has weak capabilities, fails to trust the government counterparts, lacks enthusiasm about the possibility of success, or is represented by the wrong parties, it will be difficult for effective policy to emerge. The key question in this section is: How can the capabilities and expertise of the private sector best be fostered for this purpose?

In practice, motivation is a key problem: how can individual firms be encouraged to develop expertise and become involved in costly engagement with the public sector that will benefit all firms in the sector? Individual firms would like to free ride on the others to support information exchange. Industry organizations have multiple ways to solve this coordination problem among member firms and to assess the quality and intentions of government, and for this reason are often suitable counterparts.[3] The government may want to help such organizations "upgrade" so that they become better counterparts for collaboration.[4]

However, the reliability of business associations for public-private collaboration is unclear. On the one hand, Doner and Schneider (2000) provide numerous examples of business associations that have contributed significantly to economic development both by pushing for better market-supporting institutions, such as property rights, and by participating in the provision of market-complementing services, such as setting standards and coordinating joint efforts to upgrade quality. For example, the association of Colombian flower exporters, Asocolflores, has been very effective in dealing with coordination failures and promoting collective inputs that allowed the sector to take off as a competitive exporter (see Box 11.1). On the other hand, this optimistic picture contrasts with the view that business associations are rent-seeking interest groups, usually associated with Mancur Olson and others, which is often confirmed by experience. There are plenty of examples of industry associations that focus on lobbying for short-term matters, whose association executives are less aware of the long-term matters than individual firms themselves. Lack of expertise may also limit the usefulness of business associations. For example, industry associations play a constructive role in some trade agreements, but the truly detailed information useful for elaborating negotiation positions must come from individual firms themselves.

Box 11.1 The Smell of Success in Colombia's Flower Sector

The "discovery" of the Colombian flower sector can be traced to the evolution of the US flower industry. Growing flowers is intensive in land and labor, requires long sunny days and moderate temperatures, or, alternatively, costly airtight greenhouses and high heating costs. Yet until the 1940s, production in the United States was concentrated in the northeast: New York, Pennsylvania, and Massachusetts. Why? Because flowers are delicate and perishable, there was no air transportation, and that is where the market was. As air transportation developed, production moved to warmer locations, but conditions were still not ideal. US growers were looking for alternative locations.

In 1966, a student at Colorado State University, David Cheever, wrote a thesis identifying the Sabana of Bogotá as the ideal place to grow flowers for the US market: fertile soils, long sunny days, cheap land and labor, and proximity to the airport made Bogotá an irresistible location. Three years later, Cheever put his money where his mouth was, and, together with other partners, founded Floramérica, the flower export pioneer.

The pioneer was soon followed by many others, and flowers in Colombia became a huge success. By 1980, Colombia was the most important exporter to the United States. By the late 2000s, exports exceeded $1 billion. But on the way to success, several key obstacles had to be overcome, from phytosanitary problems to air transportation, to reception and storage at the Miami airport, to ensuring access to the US market. Solving these problems required coordinated action. Asocolflores, created in 1973, played a predominant role in addressing them.

Take air transportation, for example: Colombia was served by few airlines, most of them with relatively old planes. Flowers were transported in the luggage hold, since there were no dedicated cargo planes. Narrow cabins and doors required manual loading and unloading, adding to transportation costs. Asocolflores hired a charter, and asked each exporter to commit to sending a certain number of flower boxes to Miami at the same time. Once this proved profitable, other US-based cargo carriers jumped in.

Flowers at the Miami airport were frequently damaged due to the lack of special equipment to unload them, or cold facilities to keep the flowers in storage awaiting inspection by the US Department of Agriculture. Through Asocolflores, exporters established a joint company (Transcold) responsible for loading and unloading and keeping flowers in refrigerated rooms. Colombian growers had to face protectionist pressures from US growers, who filed claims with the US Department of Commerce asking for countervailing duties. Asocolflores responded by creating the Florida

> Importers Association, an independent US entity, to protect the interests of flower growers outside the United States. In addition, it hired lawyers and technical advisors to lobby US authorities, and has since had a permanent presence in Washington, DC.
>
> Undoubtedly, industry associations can and do engage in rent-seeking activities to benefit their firms, sometimes at the expense of the state. But, as the case of Asocolflores clearly shows, they can also be a powerful instrument of collective action in pursuit of needed collective public inputs.
>
> *Source*: Arbeláez, Meléndez, and León (2012)

What leads some associations to serve constructive roles while others engage largely in rent-seeking activities? Why in some countries (Brazil) do industry associations serve as the government counterparts in deliberations on productive development policy, while in others (Chile), "representative" firms or individuals are preferred? The answers to these questions are important in order to understand the role of business associations in public-private collaboration.

The strength of business associations is certainly important for their effectiveness to reach their own objectives—but not necessarily for their socially beneficial contribution to PDPs. Strength is defined in terms of their degree of representation and capacity to execute different actions by inducing its members to commit resources and abide by association rules and decisions. Strength derives mostly from the ability to provide crucial benefits only to members, thereby making membership valuable and making exit costly. It is precisely this ability that allows associations to resolve the free-rider problem and coordinate collective actions—a critical feature of an effective counterpart in productive development policy. However, strong business associations can direct their efforts to productive development activities or to lobbying for rents. The negative example of Costa Rican rice, described in chapter 2, is the result of a strong industry association, so the characterization of strong associations as the best counterpart is not always applicable. In summary, institutional capability is neutral: associations can use it for good or ill depending on circumstances (Doner and Schneider, 2000).

The behavior of industry associations may actually be shaped by public sector capabilities. Associations may fail to be geared toward constructive productive development policy when they expect little from the public sector's ability to deliver. Perhaps associations are organized for rent seeking because they have found too few opportunities for constructive interaction and too many for capturing rents. The bottom line is that the public sector may hold the key to orient strong business associations to collaborate by being more responsive to legitimate demands and by not offering channels of communication for undue demands. The paucity of collaborative business associations in Latin America and the Caribbean may be a reflection of low public sector capabilities.[5]

Picking the Right Private Sector Partner

The private sector is not monolithic; firms across and within sectors may have not only different capabilities but also different interests and, consequently, different policy preferences. As Pritchett and Werker (2012) note, some segments of the private sector may not be interested in sound productive development policy. Schneider (2013) makes the case that public-private collaboration and policy outcomes depend on the structure, capabilities, and preferences of the main business interlocutors. A series of country studies by the IDB on the political economy of PDPs, and the accounts of experienced consultants for competitiveness-enhancing programs, show how different groups split in favor of or against particular policies, and display different abilities, attitudes, and roles. The importance of selecting the appropriate counterparts at the outset is one of the key determinants of the policy's eventual success or failure.[6]

Private sector heterogeneity should be carefully considered when designing the process by which the public sector interacts with the private sector. In particular, constituencies must be built to make sure that policies will be supported over time. Supportive constituencies may collaborate in policy identification and design, but would also be useful even in those cases in which the public sector had already identified, from the start, what needs to be done. Private sector ownership of good productive development policy is critical for success, and sometimes the leadership of some private sector actors provides legitimacy, as they can convey the credibility of policy to other firms better than government officials. Nevertheless, constituency building may be particularly hard for policies that aim to transform the productive structure of an economy, which are likely to be opposed by those who may lose importance or assets from the transformation. Deeply transformational development strategies may require the public sector to enjoy considerable independence from the private sector (as in the cases of the Republic of Korea and Taiwan), or a widespread social consensus regarding the strategy (as in the case of Ireland) (Khan and Blankenburg, 2009 and Paus, 2005, respectively).

The question of how to interact with the private sector is key for modern productive development policy. One option is for the government to adopt an "open architecture" (Hausmann and Rodrik, 2006) that gives great latitude to the specifics of the organization and relies on the self-selection of private sector participants, which are supported in their technical capabilities and encouraged to take the initiative.

On occasion, private-private coordination may be a problem that the public sector can help solve. As mentioned, firms in an industry often vary widely in terms of their interests and levels of access to policymakers, which makes it difficult to create a cohesive private counterpart that reflects all views. The public sector may play a role in helping the sector articulate a unified view. A good illustration is the case of the tourism cluster in Colonia (Uruguay), where public officials in charge of the program spent much of their initial energy overcoming differences and grudges among the private sector actors. Some actors, such as the *Buquebus* transportation company, the Hotel Chamber, and the Gastronomy Chamber, were well-established and organized actors; some had good access to the local and national authorities. Other cluster participants, such as the association of handicraft makers and the rural tourism providers, did not have their voices heard. The public sector was instrumental in making sure that the interests of these weaker actors were taken into account. Their success has been one of the most important and durable successes of the program (Pittaluga et al., 2014).

In some cases, and notwithstanding its best efforts to pursue an open process, the government may have to pick the sectors or actors that have the capacity to interact with the public sector. In other words, the priority of which sectors/policies to engage first may be influenced not only by the value and urgency of the actions involved, but also by the feasibility that the interaction will lead to the desired policies in the first place. Sectors with a less confrontational history, stronger leaders, a more concrete knowledge of their problems and opportunities, better coordination and communication skills, or stronger relations with academia and other institutions may take priority.

Another way to facilitate interaction with a poorly organized private sector counterpart could be to partner with economically dominant firms or conglomerates. However, this is a risky strategy because these firms may be in the best position to capture the public sector because of their economic and political influence. Korea's experience of structuring productive development policy through very close collaboration with economic conglomerates (*chaebols*) was successful because it was led by a strong public sector able and willing to negotiate performance conditions and enforce them. This is not an argument necessarily for interaction with *large* counterparts, but rather with *effective* counterparts.

The modality of interaction with the private sector depends on the type of policy it is meant to support. Horizontal policies call for private counterparts cutting across sectors, be they broad collectives (such as chambers of exporters), well-selected representative individuals from various industries, or private sector organizations that are well positioned to promote certain strengths or attributes (such as innovation councils). By contrast, vertical policies call for sector-specific or subsector-specific private counterparts that match the selectivity of such policies. These councils or ad hoc consultation groups are often regional rather than national, which helps confirm and amplify the specific information that is shared.

Vertical policies concerned with solving coordination problems, often around the provision of public inputs, typically rely on narrow public-private councils delimited by the type of coordination problem that the policy is designed to address. These public-private councils can deal with the firms to which the vertical policy is applicable, through parallel links (as in similar firms in need of a collective input), backward/forward links (as in the case of a cluster or productive chain), or the need for investment coordination to resolve a "chicken-and-egg" problem. Which public-private councils are worth forming? The process must contemplate listening to private demands and setting up specific councils to deal with problems that may require policy solutions. At the same time, the public sector may unilaterally identify certain councils that appear to offer good opportunities for productive development policy. For example, the criteria suggested in chapter 9 to identify productive transformation anomalies meriting further study (good business opportunities that the market misses) may be a good basis for setting up certain councils to explore opportunities collaboratively.

Vertical market intervention policies, however, may call for broad private counterparts when they involve strategic bets, typically designed to foster sectors that are not yet established. These kinds of transformational policies may call for private counterparts such as the successful public-private alliances outside the region analyzed in Devlin and Moguillansky (2009a). This high-level collaboration may validate criteria used for selecting priority sectors to be promoted and generate consensus around a development strategy. A good basis for identifying interesting cases for further study are the criteria suggested in chapter 9 for identifying potentially good candidates for high-value strategic productive transformation that the private sector can be expected to miss.

However, the ability to engage the relevant private sector counterpart in productive interaction cannot be taken for granted. To support a productive exchange of information and collaboration in policymaking, the public sector initiative must be seen as credible, meaning that there is a credible commitment to pursue the resulting policies. Otherwise, the private sector has no good reason to engage and participate in it. More generally, productive dialogue requires mutual trust, or at least a trust-building process. The case can be made that lack of trust (or outright mistrust) between the public and private sectors has limited public-private collaboration in many countries in the region (as in Chile) and compromised the depth and success of public-private alliances in Latin America (Devlin and Moguillansky, 2009b).

Making the Public Sector a Better Partner

Given the importance of the private sector to productive development policy, the public sector needs to adapt in order to engage constructively with the private sector. The nature of public sector participation is driven by the productive structure of the relevant private sector counterpart, so that the public sector must have the organizational capacity to coordinate among various relevant agencies (as discussed in chapter 10). In this case, coordination means the ability to provide a consistent public sector counterpart that can latch onto the private sector (so that it is able to "speak the same language") and adapt (so that it supports integral solutions to productive problems as they actually occur, not as they are reflected in the organizational chart of public sector agencies). This requires public sector managers who share the culture of their private sector counterpart and have access to the network of public sector agencies for support and delivery. As discussed in chapter 10, there are alternative choices for the authority structure of the public sector counterpart to ensure that specific PDPs are delivered. In all cases, the very participation of the private sector may act as a catalyst to induce public sector engagement, empowering the industry-oriented institution in charge of *designing* the PDP to influence the stronger, more broadly oriented institution that holds the ways and means necessary to implement the PDP.

All productive development agencies need to be imbued with some measure of private sector culture. For example, as discussed in chapter 6, smart development banks may also exploit their relations with producers to uncover bottlenecks and view the potential development impact of various policies from a wide perspective. Development banks with a vocation for learning may be able to aggregate private sector needs and advise on productive development policy on par with other top public sector agencies.[7]

The case of emerging sectors is perhaps the most demanding in terms of the public sector fine-tuning its ability to engage, because these sectors suffer from weak representation and low visibility. At the same time, providing public inputs to help them establish themselves and develop may offer a very high policy payoff. This case may merit creating a specialized intelligence unit charged with the task of searching for information and identifying promising emerging sectors, with whom it can then interact and mainstream the dialogue.

Public-Private Interaction in Practice

This section draws heavily on case studies conducted by the IDB on the subject of public-private collaboration for productive development. The experiences analyzed are from Argentina, Chile, Colombia, Costa Rica, and Uruguay.[8] The cases display an interesting diversity: different countries; some successes and some failures; some featuring task forces to address a very specific problem in limited time, and others involving permanent development programs; and some umbrella efforts ranging across the whole economy with involvement at the highest level, other programs addressing horizontal policies, and other industry-specific projects. The following is a short summary of some of the main observations about how public-private collaboration is conducted in practice.

An Extensive Menu of Options and Results

Public-private interaction takes multiple forms. In some instances, it assumes a consultative role, where government simply informs the private sector about its policy choices and decisions through dialogue and in a participatory process. Instead of just soliciting information, the government sometimes engages private agents in the discussion about what to do, through the joint design of the policy instruments and joint implementation. In some interesting and perhaps the most successful instances, the public-private cooperation and implementation of policy is a dynamic process with joint learning, and amounts to a long-term effort with evolving policies and objectives.

In extreme cases, on one hand, the roles of the public and private sectors may be reversed, with the latter having a majority or a leading role over the institutions in charge. Public-private agencies are sometimes used successfully to combine private expertise with public control or oversight. For example, the Costa Rican Institute of Tourism is an autonomous public institution, but industry leaders are always represented in its board of directors (Cornick, Jiménez, and Román, 2014).[9] On the other hand, some private entities are entrusted with public policy tasks, perhaps with public sector representatives on their boards of directors, as is the case of Fundación Chile (Agosin, Larraín, and Grau, 2010) or CINDE, the Costa Rican agency tasked with attracting FDI.[10] In between is a whole range of mixed agencies and task forces that are often created as tools of public sector authorities in charge of productive development policy.

The degree of engagement of the private sector in the policy-making process is influenced not only by the nature of the policy, the sector, and the problem, but also by the political traditions and expectations of the population in place. In some countries, such as Costa Rica, business is expected to be near the policy design process on matters that affect it directly. In others, such as Chile, government (especially high-level officers) keeps a distance. As a result, policies in Chile tend to be top-down, while policies in Costa Rica tend to follow a more participatory, bottom-up approach.

Interestingly, the by-products of public-private interaction may turn out to be more valuable than their explicit objectives. For example, the value of the process may stretch beyond the resulting policy and impact on intangibles like trust, market expectations, or the disposition for future policy engagement. Dialogue in itself is valuable, and in some instances the policy in question may simply provide a platform to initiate deeper interaction between the parties. In practice, the existence of a flexible means of engagement among the parties facilitates responses that can expand upon or modify the original purpose. For example, it was the trust and goodwill generated by public and private agents jointly administering the temporary incentive program to develop tourism in Costa Rica (discussed in chapter 9) that made it possible to launch the world-class country initiative "Costa Rica: No Artificial Ingredients" down the road.

Dangers of Lack of Coordination in Both Sectors

The organizational structure of most governments is largely—but not exclusively—to blame for coordination problems impeding public-private interaction. Small, industry-specific ministries and institutions oversee the interaction with private agents in the industry, and are tasked with their progress, but the policy instruments to do so are not at their command. The example discussed in chapter 10, of the Chilean decentralization program creating regional development agencies that went awry for lack of effective coordination mechanisms across national agencies, is a typical case. Another related problem is the possible coexistence of two public counterparts: one formal, technical dialogue and the other informal interactions that may be dominated by political concerns at odds with the technical interaction (see the Colombia study by Eslava, Meléndez, and Perry, 2014).

Private-private coordination may also be a problem for interaction with the public sector. As mentioned, the tourism cluster in Colonia (Uruguay) was mired with internal friction that the public sector helped to repair. The presence of heterogeneous, sometimes conflicting interests is common in cases in which public-private collaboration involves different actors within a product's value chain. In Santa Fe, Argentina, for example, the dairy cluster brings together milk producers and processing plants. While they both want to develop the sector, they have been engaged in a deep-rooted conflict over the producer's price of milk. Distrust in such cases can be difficult to overcome.

Collaboration Free from Capture Is Commonplace

In the case studies prepared for this report, capture was indeed an issue but not a prevalent one. In most of the cases, the private sector was so keenly interested in the implementation and success of sound policy that the information exchange that took place was direct and frank. Such was the case, for example, of Empleartec, a collaborative program between Argentina's Software and IT Services Chamber of Commerce and the Labor Ministry focused on overcoming the most salient constraint faced by the rapidly growing industry: the lack of adequately trained human resources (Bisang et al., 2014). More generally, in efforts whose sole purpose is to achieve a very specific, short-term objective—like the Empleartec case, the rice case in Entre Ríos discussed in chapter 2, or the case of Asocolflores in Colombia in Box 11.1—private and public parties exchange information easily, commit resources, trust one another, and play fewer games. There is ample scope for effective PDPs in small endeavors, especially the provision of specific collective inputs, implemented with limited regard for private gamesmanship. For this set of policies, collaboration appears to flow naturally, without the need for restrictive institutional designs to align incentives.

In other cases, collaboration is more open-ended, taking the form of co-exploration. For example, in the case of the sugarcane sector in Tucumán, Argentina, farmers must replace their plantings with new varieties every five or six years to control disease. Farmers, sugarcane processors, and others came together with the state government and research center, the Agricultural Experimental Station Obispo Colombres (EEAOC), to develop new hybrid varieties well adapted to the local conditions, multiply them in order to obtain seedlings under strict scientific protocols, and distribute them to farmers. While the EEAOC is a public institution, it operates under a private board, using private sector administrative procedures. Funding for the research center comes to a large extent from a tax on sugarcane sales. As in the case of Empleartec, the collaboration was fruitful, leading to a drastic reduction in diseases and a 3 percent per year increase in yields.

Some of the key aspects of public-private collaboration that determine success or failure relate to practical problems of organization, communication, and trust. As long as they trust the public sector's intentions and abilities, private agents are willing to incur significant costs and dedicate significant human resources to collaborative efforts, even when their direct reward is not obvious and there are incentives to free ride. In fact, payoffs can be high because sometimes cooperation leads to virtuous cycles by which private and public actors bring out the best in each other to their mutual benefit. Because so often in the past, especially in times of more heavy-handed interventionism, mistrust has emerged between the parties, many barriers are removed only with constructive attitudes on all fronts.

The Risk of Capture Is Alive

The studies revealed limited capture but did not turn up policy features designed to control it that could account for this finding; the observation of scarce capture in this set of case studies may simply indicate that it includes mostly safe policies, perhaps because riskier ones are seldom attempted. A closer look reveals a latent risk of capture.

The studies show that whether things work out well in this regard depends largely on the underlying design, as well as the circumstances that shape the incentives of the private sector to engage in productive collaboration or revert to demands for protection. The Street Design Circuits program in the fashion design sector in Argentina is illustrative in this regard. The program, which created a series of urban tours centered on fashion design stores, with the goal of positioning Argentina as a fashion design hub, brought together the textile chapter of the National Institute for Industrial Technology (INTI) and Pro-Tejer, an NGO created in 2003 to promote the interests of the country's textile and apparel industry.[11] Pro-Tejer initiated the program and provided a substantial portion of the funding for what turned out to be a constructive and successful collaboration. But by 2011, the government of Argentina had increased its protectionist stance through a stringent system of discretionary import licenses. Under these circumstances, Pro-Tejer lost interest, which led to the termination of the program.[12] This case illustrates the latent risk that exists if policy design and circumstances are not appropriate.

Designing and implementing appropriate PDPs in declining sectors is also at higher risk of capture.

In particular, when a country has a competitive edge (actual or latent) in a particular activity, and the need for policy emerges from the desire to bring about, enhance, or take advantage of that edge, the gains from doing so are potentially large enough for the participants to engage with fully aligned objectives. However, when an industry is declining, uncompetitive, or phasing out, although feasible policies that increase productivity and reduce/minimize the problems would be valuable, it is far more tempting for the private sector to aspire to transfers or distortions that help it at the expense of others, rather than pursuing solutions that truly strengthen its prospects. The cases in Costa Rica studied by Cornick, Jiménez, and Román (2014) illustrate this disparity clearly: a competitive sector like coffee prompts constructive collaboration, while declining sectors, such as fisheries and rice, breed rent seeking.

Making the Marriage Work

Relationships are never easy; public-private collaboration in PDPs is no exception. A system abused by capture and riddled with rent seeking—as was often the case in the past—is clearly faulty; avoiding these risks by severing the private sector from the process of productive development policy would also be a failure. Both "public-minded" and "rent-seeking" behaviors can be rational responses by private counterparts; the key for government is to create an environment that favors the former and discourages the latter. In this regard, the first task is to determine whether existing institutions for public-private interaction offer a good foundation to build on.

Ideally, the incentives for collaboration on the part of the private sector would be self-enforcing—meaning that the environment for interaction is shaped in such a way that it is in the self-interest of the private sector to engage, collaborate in the design, and then support sound productive development policy. This section will discuss a number of ideas to help align public and private incentives in this way. Alternatively, monitoring and carrots/sticks—depending on observed behavior—may be needed to stimulate private sector collaboration. This section also offers ideas in this regard.

Abstain from Riskier Policies

As discussed, in well-conceived PDPs, firms benefit from the provision of a public input only to the extent that they use it in production, and in so doing increase productivity. Firms would reap benefits only from succeeding in the marketplace. A market intervention policy, in contrast, may yield profits for the firms without productivity gains or any effort at all on their part. By barring or discouraging the demand for risky policies, risk is controlled and the incentives for collaborating on sound policies increase.

The Productive Transformation Program in Colombia, which organizes public-private collaboration in a number of selected sectors, is an example of preventing capture by excluding risky policies from consideration for public-private collaboration. The program requires that the conversations relate to public inputs, coordination problems, and other initiatives that contribute to the sector's productivity. By design, subsidies and protectionist measures are not part of the conversation.[13] Countries with weak institutional capabilities may need to restrict vertical public-private councils to a discussion of productive bottlenecks and coordination problems that can be addressed with the provision of public inputs and refuse to consider policies of market intervention that would open up the discussion to requesting subsidies.

Share the Burden

Some policies may impose a bigger cost on the government than the benefit perceived by private agents. That makes them inefficient, yet firms may still demand them. If a cost-benefit analysis is conducted to guide decision making, firms would have the incentive to exaggerate the benefit. Given their informational advantage, they stand a good chance of convincing the public bureaucracy. While this may not be the prevalent case, it is important to address this risk.

The incentive-compatible solution to this problem is to ask the private counterpart to engage and contribute to the costs or sacrifices necessary for the policy, thus confirming its worth. While cost sharing also saves fiscal resources, which are costly to raise, the argument here is not so much about fiscal costs but rather about how to align incentives to ensure that only sound policies are carried out. Ideally, the share of the cost that the private counterpart would contribute should correspond to the benefit it would enjoy; if benefits are concentrated and the private sector counterpart covers all beneficiaries, the input should be fully paid by the private sector. In practice, an arrangement to share a substantial portion of the costs would go a long way toward introducing discipline in the demand for public inputs, based on willingness to pay. This cost-sharing principle can also be applied to signal the intensity with which firms may demand a variety of alternative public inputs and in this way prioritize their provision.[14]

The key problem with burden sharing is coordination. Individual firms benefiting from a collective input ("a club good") would rather not contribute and let the rest pay for the cost. The private sector can participate in cost sharing only if it is able to coordinate among its firms to agree on this collective action, because otherwise no individual firm would be willing to pay. If individual firms can be excluded from the benefits of a collective input (such as certification of product quality), cost sharing can be implemented through user fees or a "member-only" restriction. If that is not the case (for example, a research center), then an external incentive is needed to compel individual firms to contribute. The authority of the public sector may be the solution to this coordination problem. Box 11.2 discusses an institutional innovation proposed by Paul Romer (1993) that would address these issues in a precise way.

Box 11.2 Self-Organizing Investment Boards

Problems of collective action can sometimes be a severe obstacle for the development of an industry. Even if industry participants were able to identify a set of collective goods that would benefit the sector as a whole, in the absence of some coordinating device each individual firm would have incentives to free ride on the efforts of others, resulting in underprovision, or outright non-provision, of the collective good. In 1993, noted American economist Paul Romer proposed an institutional innovation designed to facilitate collective action at the industry level. He called this innovation "self-organizing investment boards."

To use the generic example provided by Romer, consider a sector producing widgets. Widget makers come together and identify one or more collective inputs that would be in the interest of the industry as a whole.

> Perhaps different participants disagree on what the most important inputs would be. Some argue that what is needed is to help fund research regarding widget design at the local universities. Others think that it would be more valuable to stimulate the development of suppliers of specialized widget-making equipment, or to train the labor force in appropriate widget-making techniques.
>
> Romer's proposal would have the sector petition the state to impose a tax on their sales in order to fund the vertical collective inputs selected. After certifying that the collective inputs in play address genuine collective needs, the state would hold an election among industry participants to vote on whether the tax should be imposed. With sufficient support, a tax would be imposed and the self-organizing investment boards would be set up, one for each collective input identified and validated by the sector.
>
> Each firm would decide how to allocate its tax money among the various boards depending on how much it values each of the collective inputs identified. Members elected to manage each board would autonomously decide how to spend resources for the specified purpose. Boards linked to collective inputs that are no longer deemed necessary would not receive any funding, which effectively implies that there would be a sunset clause.
>
> Romer's proposal creates a very flexible and potent instrument of collective action through which the sectors decide what they need, provide the necessary financing, and thus contribute to solve their own problems. The state's role, beyond perhaps contributing to provide (but not finance) some of the collective inputs identified, is to help solve the free-riding problem, through its capacity to enforce the tax.
>
> Sectors actually petitioning to be taxed? Does this sound far-fetched in Latin America? The example of rice in Entre Ríos, Argentina, discussed below and in chapter 2, suggests that it is not.

An example of such an alignment of incentives is that of a collaboration in Argentina between PROARROZ (a corporation of rice growers in Concepción in the province of Entre Ríos) and INTA, discussed in chapter 2. To secure funding for INTA's efforts to develop a new rice variety in a way that would solve free riding, PROARROZ asked the government of the province to levy a tax on rice producers. The receipts were to be used to finance research efforts (otherwise, presumably, any grower could benefit from the new seed without making a contribution). Since rice growers will be paying for a significant part of the research, this should reduce their incentives to ask for an investment that is larger than what is socially desirable. It is interesting to note that while the government could unilaterally enact a tax scheme of this sort, in this case PROARROZ asked to be taxed; this clearly added legitimacy and facilitated the enactment of the tax. A private counterpart would ask to be taxed only if it believes that otherwise the public input would not be provided. It is important to note that cost sharing requires not only private sector coordination to pay but also commitment by the public sector not to fund the public input in the absence of the tax.

Conditionality or Performance-Based Policies

The social value of a productive development policy may be enhanced if private beneficiaries of the policies are induced to maximize the social benefits. This may be achieved by aligning incentives of the private parties to policy goals. For example, productive development policy to boost firm innovation and spark positive spillovers through dissemination would be more effective if incentives were added to make dissemination more attractive. For instance, subsidies to foster innovation may favor research done by a consortium, as discussed in chapter 3. A market-friendly mechanism could be to calibrate the size of the subsidy to the number of firms that adopted the research and entered the market; that is, the greater the number of followers, the larger the subsidy. The proposed policy to favor self-discovery discussed in chapter 2 is an example in this regard. Yet another mechanism could be to condition the benefit to sharing the innovation research or adoption with would-be followers.

Information and Policy Demands

The private sector party has better knowledge than its public sector counterpart, but does not share the same objective; it is a biased expert, in economics jargon (Grossman and Helpman, 2001). Thus, it is critical to devise methods that encourage the flow of better knowledge, while controlling for biased distortions. One possibility is to utilize peer-to-peer monitoring, including additional experts with opposing biases, so that they check on each other. Additional experts may be from competing sectors, academia, or perhaps the same sector in other countries (or even individual firms or individuals within the sector that may have particular reasons to collaborate with the public sector). In particular, cross-sectoral programs introduce checks and balances by bringing in sectors with different interests, making collusion between the private sector and the authorities more difficult.[15]

Another approach could be to invite the private sector counterpart to present proposals to express policy demands and make it accountable for their content in light of ex post performance evaluation. This approach would work best if proposals need to comply with certain standards. For example, if the policy demand is justified based on expected positive spillovers, the proposal should state so and provide indicators of performance after the policy is put in place. Such an approach would facilitate ex ante evaluation of the proposed policy, conditioned on the information provided, and would also facilitate testing the accuracy of such information based on ex post performance. Unbiased experts would conduct the testing and reach a conclusion about the accuracy of the information based on the relevant circumstances. If the test is favorable, the private counterpart could be rewarded with continued collaboration; if the test is not favorable, future interactions would be more guarded, and less accommodating. This "trust but verify" approach would in turn provide better incentives for less biased proposals, since highballing benefits would be costly.

Good Performance before Renewing Policy

Even without any biases or impediments to collaboration, it is technically difficult to select the right policies. Thus policymakers willing to try PDPs ought to be prepared to fail sometimes. However, it should be feasible to spot failed policies after the fact. This is an area where private agents may play a role. It is important to define evaluation methods that are suitable to assess the degree to which the original policy justification was verified in actual performance and how the policy could be improved. All too often, there are no clear goals or evaluation criteria for productive development policy, let alone actual evaluations. A sound system would allow a reasonable number of policy experiments to go wrong and also have a systematic way to weed them out (Rodrik, 2007a).

Policies involving market intervention tend to generate "addiction," that is, an interest in prolonging the promotional policy ad infinitum, regardless of performance. To stop those policies that are not justified, evaluation is key. One solution is to apply sunset clauses so policies expire unless reapproved.[16] For this system to work, both the process of evaluation and acting upon evaluation need to be systematic. It is important to include all policies under this system so that policies benefiting private interests do not find refuge in loopholes to avoid scrutiny. In practice, the policies more hidden from scrutiny are often those that provide implicit subsidies in the form of tax exemptions, a favorite of rent seekers. Sunset clauses should apply to both explicit and implicit benefits. These evaluation checks are critical to contain the risk of capture because the benefit of rent seeking diminishes in a system in which only sound policies survive over time.

Evaluation must be strict and binding. Independent participants are often needed to ensure there is no conflict of interest to cover mistakes, or, worse, capture. Negative evaluations should have consequences: within the learning paradigm, it is critical that evaluation be a learning experience leading to redesign. Beyond the technical aspects of evaluation, stronger collaboration requires the kind of political capabilities discussed in chapter 10 to ensure that evaluation is not pro forma, but an instrument to effectively separate the wheat from the chaff.

Checks and Balances

Appropriate internal controls in the public organizational structure may be useful to check capture. The distribution of authority across agencies, such as separation between design and implementation or regional delegation subject to central oversight, may provide desirable checks and balances. At the same time, there is a trade-off between controls and effectiveness. These mechanisms should not take forms that excessively weaken the public sector, impede action, or make the already challenging public-public coordination problems unmanageable.

Providing appropriate incentives to public officials is also important. Compensation (both monetary and career pride) must be sufficient to protect against some forms of capture. While it is reasonable for the public sector to hire experts with specialized, sector-specific knowledge originally developed in the private sector, if the career path of technocrats and managers who have moved to the public sector entails a quick return to the private sector, the integrity of their work may be compromised. To avoid this, once the transition to the public sector has been made, an attractive career path should lie ahead, and a cooling-off period, with adequate compensation, should be mandatory before key public servants responsible for a certain PDP can return to work for the segment of firms with an interest in it. The bottom line is not necessarily that "revolving doors" should not exist, but when they do, the rules and standards should be clear.

Transparency and Accountability

All of the steps described would greatly benefit from transparency. Just as sunlight is a good disinfectant, exposing policy proposals, the way policies are chosen and costs shared, and performance evaluations to interested parties and the wider public would shine light on issues worth probing and allow scrutiny from adversarial viewpoints. Ideally, transparency standards for productive development policy would be established, and an independent agency would regulate and monitor them.

However, informal consultations may in some cases be necessary, either as a preliminary step to more formal collaboration or as a complement to formal processes. In fact, complete openness is not always the best environment for exploratory dialogue. But caution is necessary: The tension between probity in the use of public resources and responsiveness/discretion on the part of bureaucrats is especially high in these instances. Since responses to specific problems of productive sectors cannot be codified in advance, officers need room to maneuver and react, albeit at the cost of some risk. This kind of flexible interaction will be accepted as legitimate and incorporated in mainstream policymaking only if it is known and transparent. This requires well-known rules and procedures for participation in the dialogue and for receiving policy benefits, as well as transparency in their application. Transparency should not be confused with an undue formality that impedes fluid dialogue, or with inclusiveness with no clear purpose.

Accountability is a necessary complement to transparency. The results of the interaction process should be evaluated credibly, and the evaluation should be disseminated to key stakeholders and the public at large. Every collaborative scheme ought to make sure that there is a mechanism for the private sector to hold the public sector accountable for following up on the decisions that are reached and for receiving feedback during the implementation of policies in response to perceived needs.

Notes

1 Rethinking Productive Development

1. The "typical" country is the average country; the income of the typical country is the average income across countries.
2. The East Asian tigers are Hong Kong, Malaysia, Singapore, South Korea, and Thailand.
3. This assumes that government failures are not to blame or cannot be corrected.
4. This section is based on Agosin (2013).
5. The most drastic example of these was Decision 24 of the Andean Pact—established in 1966 by Bolivia, Chile, Colombia, Ecuador, Peru, and Venezuela—which limited profit remittances and capital repatriations, and required foreign companies to invest as minority shareholders alongside domestic partners.
6. Rodrik (1992) hammers home this argument on theoretical grounds with the use of a formal model. Other papers arguing for temporary and moderate protections include Bruton (1989) and Greenwald and Stiglitz (2006).
7. Consider a final good whose international price is $100, with a tariff rate of 30 percent. The domestic producer will be able to sell it at $130. If the product uses imported inputs for $50 and these are not subject to tariffs, the producer will be able to obtain a net revenue of $80 for a domestic value added of $50, consistent with an effective level of protection of value added in the sector of 60 percent.
8. These experiences are described in detail in Amsden (1989) for the Republic of Korea, and in Wade (1990) for Taiwan.
9. The EMBRAER story is described in Bonelli and Pinheiro (2008) and in Goldstein (2002). A description of the informatics policy can be found in UNCTC (1988: 190–91).
10. See Petkantchin and Coimbra (2004).
11. For example, while local content provisions regulated by the WTO agreements on public purchases are voluntary and often not subscribed by countries in the region, typically they are strongly limited by North-South free-trade agreements.
12. Nontariff measures have been prohibited since the beginning of the GATT in 1948. However, as in the case of other disciplines, this prohibition does not apply to agriculture, which has been largely excluded from WTO disciplines.

13. Unless more than 9 percent of that total is sourced in developing countries.
14. In Latin America and the Caribbean, these countries included Bolivia, Guatemala, Nicaragua, and the Dominican Republic.
15. Some importing countries continue to practice protectionism, particularly in agriculture, perhaps because this sector continues to be beyond discipline of the WTO. But even in manufacturing, protection abounds. Nonetheless, tariff levels are significantly lower than they were before 1980.
16. Among others, Matthew Andrews, Ricardo Hausmann, Lant Pritchett, and Charles Sabel have advanced this approach, and have generously shared their views, to the benefit of this report.

2 A Conceptual Framework for Productive Development Policies

1. The distinction between vertical and horizontal policies is useful conceptually, but is not always easy to make in practice. A policy may be targeted at a broad sector such as agriculture, or at a narrow product such as rice, and it may be difficult to decide where to draw the line. Furthermore, some policies classified as horizontal may affect some sectors more than others. For example, policies that foster investment in research and development (R&D) will have stronger effects on sectors that are intensive in R&D.
2. A special case of vertical policies relates to interventions that favor individual firms. The stakes are even higher in this type of intervention, and the scope for rent-seeking behavior is even stronger. Moreover, policies that focus on individual firms discourage competition. Aghion et al. (2012) present evidence showing that interventions tend to have more beneficial effects (greater social returns) in the presence of competition. The link between competition and innovation policies is explored in more detail in chapter 3.
3. Job training and other policies related to human capital are discussed in chapter 5.
4. The analysis might be different if this is the first machine of its type in this market and its adoption might reveal its true value, so that if profitable it will lead to imitation. In this case, the justification would not be linked to the investment in the machinery per se, but rather to a risky innovation.
5. See Rodríguez-Clare (1996), and Monge-González, Rivera, and Rosales-Tijerino (2010).
6. If the training received is specific to an industry, it may be desirable to facilitate the coordination among competing firms in order to have the industry itself—rather than the government—pay for most of the training through a specific tax, thus internalizing the spillover.
7. Obviously, these spillovers are not easily measured.
8. In the case of benefits that are extended over time, some taxes may be better than others. Benefits associated with the corporate income tax have the advantage that they only attract firms that expect to be competitive and

generate profits. Firms that do not generate profits will not receive benefits, and thus would not impose fiscal costs.

9. See Agosin, Larraín, and Grau (2010) for a detailed account of this policy intervention.
10. One potential problem that remains is that of wasteful duplication of experimentation efforts. This could be addressed through policies that foster collaboration among firms, such as the innovation consortia discussed in chapter 3. If discovery is done in collaborative fashion, the subsidy would be shared by the collaborating firms.
11. Stein (2012) also discusses implementation issues such as how to identify the pioneer, what data is required, how to prevent firms from gaming the system, how to define the size of the subsidy, etc.
12. See WTO Agreement on Subsidies and Countervailing Measures, Article 27.10.
13. The use of intermediary agents in the delivery of PDPs is not restricted to this quadrant. They could in principle play a role in the delivery of collective inputs for a specific sector (in the vertical public input quadrant), as well as in the case of sector-specific market interventions.
14. Rather than proper alignment of incentives, in some cases the policy is captured by the intermediaries in such a way that they, and not the firms, become the real beneficiaries of government programs.
15. Chapter 6 explores the case of commercial banks intermediating financing from second-tier development banks.
16. The fact that the state may be needed to help solve the coordination problems among firms that preclude them from providing the collective good themselves does not mean that the state itself should be the provider. The state could potentially coordinate the contributions of the beneficiaries, and rely on a private sector intermediary agent to provide the missing input.
17. Rodrik (2004) has emphasized this point.
18. Most of the airlines operating in Argentina had exited the market in the wake of the 2001 crisis.
19. For a more formal elaboration and references, see the survey in Harrison and Rodríguez-Clare (2010).
20. The bailout to the leading automobile firms in the United States in the crisis of 2008 is a good example. That move arguably saved this traditional US industry (at essentially no fiscal cost).

3 Investing in Ideas: Policies to Foster Innovation

1. This is an average figure. Not all countries report these figures for every year. So for some countries, data begin in 1999. In others, data end in 2008.
2. Once produced, new knowledge can be used simultaneously by many different firms because the new "blueprints" are not normally associated with

physical constraints. This characteristic is an extreme form of decreasing marginal costs as the scale of use increases: although the costs of the first use of new knowledge may be large, in that it includes the costs of its generation, further use can be done at negligible or small incremental costs (Aghion, David, and Foray, 2009).
3. The nonexcludable nature of knowledge refers to the difficulty and cost of trying to retain exclusive possession of it while, at the same time, putting it to use.
4. Technological knowledge is also more likely to be protected by intellectual property rights (IPRs). IPRs provide innovating firms the right to temporarily exclude others from using a new idea commercially so the originators can appropriate the rents of their investments in innovation. In exchange for this, the owner must disclose the invention so anyone can improve upon it. However, IPRs can also generate unintended consequences, as they cause a static market distortion in the form of monopoly power and slower technology diffusion for producers that must pay a higher cost to transfer protected technology. In other words, IPRs also create market distortions that might or might not be compensated by the increased incentives to innovate (De Ferranti et al., 2003).
5. It has also been suggested that traditional R&D statistics do not capture the innovation effort carried out by natural resource-intensive industries well. For example, investments in mining prospecting are not considered part of R&D, so mining is an activity that is more knowledge-intensive than the official statistics suggest. Given that the bulk of Latin American countries are very intensive in these activities, this measurement problem may overestimate the gap between the typical Latin America country and say, South Korea. However, when the comparison is done with developed countries well endowed with natural resources, such Australia and Canada, the investment gaps remain and are still significant. Accordingly, the natural resource curse is not the explanation for the gap.
6. In both periods there is a residual not explained by those variables included in the analysis. Several omitted factors are included in this residual. For example, Katz (2001) puts forward the hypothesis that macroeconomic volatility typical of the Latin American and Caribbean development process might have affected entrepreneurs' "animal spirits," making them reluctant to spend on highly risky and sunk investments such as R&D. An alternative hypothesis could be the differences in the size distribution of firms. Unfortunately, the authors lack detailed comparable information of R&D by size of the firm, and thus could not include this factor in the analysis.
7. An early example of this is the US decision to upgrade agricultural productivity through the land-grant universities during the second half of the nineteenth century (with the passing of the Morrill Act of 1862 by Congress). Another example is the establishment of Israel's Institute of Technology (Technion) during the early 1920s.

8. Such as energy technologies, microelectronics, aerospace, health, and, in some cases, the defense sector.
9. Such as the National Institute of Industrial Technology (INTI) and the National Institute for Agricultural Technology (INTA) of Argentina, the Agricultural Research Corporation (EMBRAPA) of Brazil, the Technological Institute (INTEC) of Chile, and the Institute for Industrial Technology and Technical Norms (ITINEC) of Peru.
10. The fact that knowledge is a public good does not necessarily mean that it needs to be provided by the public sector, at least in its entirety.
11. Conditional loans are a risk-sharing financial instrument by which loans could be partially or even totally written off on the basis of three criteria: the success of the investment, the technological risk, and spillovers of an innovation project. In Israel, for example, the repayment of conditional loans is done through royalties of between 2 percent and 5 percent of the sales of the innovated product until the original grant is fully repaid.
12. A nice feature of subsidies is that they can also provide signaling on the quality of an externally assessed innovation project. Tax incentives are normally ex post, so they are less suitable to alleviate financial constraints and have no signaling power.
13. Several evaluations in developed countries suggested that indeed this could be the case (Irwin and Klenow, 1996; Branstetter and Sakakibara, 1998; Czarnitzki and Fier, 2003).
14. In the OECD (2005b) framework, the concept of "fully developed outside" is close in spirit to the idea of "innovation new to the firm."
15. See Ezell and Atkinson (2011) for a review on this topic. The earliest examples of TEPs are found in agriculture in both continental Europe and the United States (Steinmueller, 2010).
16. In a similar line, several developed countries have put in place fiscal incentives (mostly in the form of a tax deduction) on those profits generated from IPRs royalties or sales (see, for example, the UK Patent Box act).
17. See, for example, Lach, Parizat, and Wasserteil (2008) and Mohnen and Lokshin (2010).
18. For evidence on the effectiveness of business innovation programs in developed countries, see the summaries by David, Hall, and Toole (2000) and Westmore (2013).
19. Chudnovsky et al. (2006) found that crowding-in effects were particularly strong in the case of new innovators.
20. In particular, propensity score matching (PSM) techniques.
21. Chapter 8 discusses the potential benefit of combining and sequencing innovation and export promotion programs.
22. This evaluation links beneficiary data with Argentina's social protection dataset. This allows the beneficiaries and controls to be tracked over a long period of time at low cost. The trade-off is that productivity as such cannot

be measured. In this chapter, productivity is approximated by the average wages paid by the firm.
23. For more on PROFO, see chapter 7.
24. This is particularly true when measures of technology adoption such as the one reported in Table 3.5 are considered. Less conclusive are the findings on yields. In many cases, yields seem not to be affected in the short run (which, in some cases is the only time frame considered in the evaluations), but increased over longer periods. The available evidence seems to confirm that for agricultural TEPs also, positive effects on productivity require a certain period of gestation; in the short run, producers may experience some adjustment costs to the new technology and practice, which may lead to null or even negative short-run effects on productivity.
25. Given that spillovers surround scientific and generic technological research, there is clearly a role for public research and technology centers. However, without the right institutional arrangements, these organizations may end up being captured by scientific elites and carry out their activities in complete isolation from societal needs (Artopoulos and Navarro, forthcoming). There is some consensus that successful public research and technology centers should have a funding mechanism that allows them to build capabilities over the long term but at the same time also connect their research agenda to the needs and demand of the private sector. This can be achieved by combining long-term core funding regulated by performance agreements negotiated every four to five years with competitive finance though matching grants funds and authorizations to provide contract research to the private sector. Researches should also be promoted based on performance and enjoy at least some of the benefits of the intellectual property that they are generating. Finally, and most importantly, the private sector should be represented on the boards that control these institutions (Maloney and Perry, 2005).

4   The Start-Up and Scale-Up of High-Productivity Firms

1. These factors, of course, are mitigated if the new firms can "borrow" these capabilities from related existing firms.
2. Shane (2009) makes this argument very eloquently.
3. Shane (2009: 147) provides the example of two firms. One is a personal cleaning business started by an entrepreneur without much educational background pursuing the customers of another personal cleaning business, capitalized with $10,000 of the founder's savings. The other is an Internet company started by a former employee of a global software company with an MBA, a master's degree in computer science, and plenty of industry experience, capitalized with $250,000 and backed by a group of business angels.

While the comparison is deliberately extreme, it is effective in driving home the point that some projects and firms are more likely to have high growth potential than others.
4. See, for example, the conclusions of Bonilla and Cancino (2011) regarding the SERCOTEC Seed Capital Program in Chile, a program that combined financing with training. While the program had an impact on employment, the beneficiaries tended to be very small and lacked significant growth prospects. Moreover, the program did not lead to further financing for the beneficiaries. The authors conclude that the program looked more like social policy, and less like productive development policy.
5. It is not obvious that having more entrepreneurs is necessarily better. What matters is their quality. In fact, the *Global Entrepreneurship Monitor* shows a negative correlation between their indicator of the *stock* of entrepreneurs—which includes the self-employed—and the country's income per capita. The recent World Bank report on Latin American entrepreneurs (Lederman et al., 2014) presents data from Gindling and Newhouse (2012) in which the overall share of "entrepreneurs" (employers plus the self-employed) is also negatively correlated with GDP per capita. However, once they exclude the self-employed and focus just on employers, the correlation with GDP per capita becomes positive.
6. The figure excludes countries such as Uruguay and several Caribbean countries, classified by the International Monetary Fund (IMF) as financial offshore centers, where residents of other countries can create firms as investment vehicles.
7. Exits of manufacturing firms in Latin America are comparable to those in the OECD countries, according to Bartelsman, Haltiwanger, and Scarpetta (2009); approximately one out of every five firms exits before its second birthday, and two out of five exit before their fourth. The data correspond to the 1990s, and include only four Latin American countries.
8. If the rate of high-growth firms over formal firms is similar and the rate of formal firms per working-age population is lower in Latin America, it follows that the rate of high-growth firms per working-age population must be lower, as well.
9. A project may have an expected social rate of return of 15 percent in a context in which the cost of capital is 10 percent. But if because of taxes or spillovers, the firm expects a private rate of return of only 7.5 percent (if appropriability $\alpha=0.5$) it will not undertake the project.
10. Lazear argues that even hiring a specialist requires some minimum knowledge of that specialty.
11. Start-Up Chile is a recent intervention to help deal with the lack of high-potential entrepreneurs. It is discussed in detail below.
12. For example, Hsieh and Klenow (2012) find that Mexican plants exhibit slower growth in employment than their US counterparts, although the

difference in average growth seems apparent only around a decade after they have been launched. Regarding new products for export, Wagner and Zahler (2013) show that export pioneers tend to be outgrown by some of their early followers with regard to export volumes. These limits of pioneers to scale up may amplify the so-called self-discovery problems.

13. See Gompers and Lerner (1998) on the effect of capital gains taxes on venture capital. In 2009, Chile also initiated a tax credit for firms acquired by private equity, reducing taxation above a certain return, in order to encourage entry of more risky projects, and in this way to increase deal flow for the early stages of venture capital.

14. One way to change entrepreneurial culture is by celebrating the most worthwhile projects that have failed. For example, during Stanford University's Entrepreneurship Week, organized by the Stanford Technology Ventures program, a prize is awarded for the biggest failure, with the idea that failing and earning from failure can be very valuable. As Bob Sutton puts it in his blog about the failure award, "failure sucks but instructs" (http://bobsutton.typepad.com/my_weblog/2008/03/the-winner-of-1.html).

15. Policy reformers should understand that bankruptcy regulations are there for a reason. The goal of reform is to eliminate excessive and inefficient regulations, but not all regulation. There should not be a race to reduce bankruptcy delays to zero days. Efficient renegotiation and restructuring also take some time.

16. Pledging a house as collateral in a mortgage contract improves the probability that the borrower will pay the bank, thereby increasing pledgeability, and consequently the probability that the bank will be willing to finance the house. Adelino, Schoar, and Severino (2013) show how increases in housing prices increase the entry of small entrepreneurs (defined as the self-employed). Venture capital is also a mechanism to increase pledgeability. Monitoring entrepreneurs, using convertible shares, or having additional control rights over key firm decisions are ways to increase the credibility that a venture capital firm can later appropriate some of the benefits created by the assets that need to be financed.

17. Gompers and Lerner (1998) show how in the United States, the reduction in capital gain taxes also generated a massive increase in venture capital funding.

18. An often-cited figure is that venture capitalists make more than 70 percent of the returns on only 8 percent of the dollars they have invested, although they could not know ex ante which investments would be so successful.

19. The INOVAR program in Brazil, discussed in some detail below, also created various signals of credibility with respect to pension funds.

20. It is hard to raise funds for seed and venture capital in Latin America; and since fees to fund managers tend to be proportional to the fund size, highly skilled managers often try to move to later-stage private equity. This is less of

an issue in countries in which the size of the market for ideas is large enough and thus allows more fund-raising for seed and venture funds.
21. As mentioned before, these distinctions between the real and financial sides of policies are not always clear in practice.
22. *NuevaMente* is a pilot program to improve the prospects of re-entrepreneurship and also to favor the efficient termination of unsuccessful businesses. It was developed with the support of local partners and the IDB's MIF.
23. In fact, evidence suggests that richer subnational regions around the world are characterized by a higher endowment of well-educated managers (Gennaioli et al., 2013).
24. There are 12 categories of criteria that enter into the decision to extend the subsidy to incubators. These criteria have different weights according to the stage of development of the incubator, as well as the nature of its sector(s) and technology/technologies.
25. The use of equity to incentivize incubators is clearly not something new, either in the country or in the world, but the reform introduced clear regulation. In fact, before this reform many incubators and accelerators asked for substantial equity, beyond what could have been considered a fair valuation of the incubator's contribution, leaving incubated firms at a disadvantage and limiting the interest of later investors.
26. For example, it was featured in *The Economist*.
27. For more information on Start-Up Chile, see Melo (2012) and the Harvard Business School case by Applegate et al. (2012).
28. Having the common brand "Start-up-[country-name]" does not necessarily mean that the institutions and the rules of operation are the same across countries. In general, it appears that other countries have been less committed than Chile to attracting foreign entrepreneurs, focusing relatively more on incubating domestic entrepreneurs.
29. See, for example, Sabel and Zeitlin (2012).
30. Universities are another interesting source of spin-offs. Policies in universities may encourage or discourage university-firm interactions in general. For example, in the United States in the 1980s, the Bayh-Dole Act facilitated the sharing of IPRs of the university and faculty, easing constraints for entrepreneurship and spin-offs from universities.
31. They were able to identify an employee spin-off either when the director/manager moved from a parent in the same industry or when one-quarter of the employees shifted from a common parent company to a new firm.
32. The importance of spin-offs seems to be generalized, and not restricted to these countries. Mostafa and Klepper (2011) document the success of spin-offs for the textile sector in Bangladesh, while Klepper and Sleeper (2005) do so for the laser industry in the United States.
33. In some sectors, the impact of venture capital is much larger. For example, the *Venture Impact* report states that in 2010, venture-backed companies

employed 74 percent of workers and generated 80 percent of revenues in the biotechnology industry (NVCA and IHS Global Insight, 2011).
34. The importance of deal flow to make a venture capital fund viable cannot be overstated. Given the high-risk, high-return nature of the typical projects backed by venture capital and the correspondingly high failure rate, it is necessary to pool a sufficiently large group of viable projects so that the success of the few outweigh the losses of the many. This is even more important in smaller markets, where even the successful projects may not lead to huge returns.
35. Venture capital is naturally lumpy. In countries with few players and low funding, a few investments could strongly impact the relative ranking among Latin American countries. A similar figure using data from Thomson One (available in Stein and Wagner, 2013) shows a different ranking among Latin American countries; however, the big gap with respect to developed economies, China, and India remains the same.
36. Limited partners invest in the fund, but have no managerial responsibilities and no legal liability for the business beyond the amount invested.
37. For more details about the program, see Leamon and Lerner (2012). The main lessons from the program are discussed in detail in Lerner, Leamon, and García-Robles (2013).
38. In a sample of 46 countries in the 1980s, Rajan and Zingales (1998) show that two-thirds of growth in industries comes from growth within the firm.
39. Hsieh and Klenow (2009) pioneered an entire research agenda quantifying misallocation in an economy by measuring the extent to which marginal revenue created by the last unit of input differs across firms; they have named this the *dispersion* of TFP measured as revenue.
40. Buera, Kaboski, and Shin (2011) argue that financial constraints could be a powerful explanation for low growth, accounting for almost 40 percent of losses in TFP, especially in sectors that operate at a large scale. In contrast, Midrigan and Xu (2009) find that in a sample of South Korean firms, (calibrated) financial constraints explain less than 7 percent of TFP losses due to misallocation.
41. Banerjee and Moll (2010) argue that these differences in marginal productivity could be self-correcting, as productive firms without access to finance would reinvest a higher fraction of their profits to make their business grow over time, so the financial constraint would become less and less binding. These authors are more worried about firms that do not even start up because they do not have the tools to escape the vicious cycle in which they lack capital.
42. Bloom et al. (2012) show that average management practices are systematically worse in their sample of firms in four Latin American countries (Argentina, Brazil, Chile, and Mexico), compared to firms in developed countries. They also show that management practices are systematically

worse in family-owned firms in which the chief executive officer (CEO) is the founder or a family member, compared to firms owned by dispersed shareholders, private equity, or even family-owned firms with CEOs who are not family members. Bloom et al. (2013), in turn, using randomized experiments in India, show that better management practices lead to increased productivity.
43. These authors show that firms in Latin America, Asia, and Southern Europe are worse at decentralizing managerial decisions than their counterparts in the United States and Northern Europe.
44. Caliendo, Monte, and Rossi-Hansberg (2012) use the Garicano (2000) model to show how a cost curve with a W-shape, as in Figure 4.7, emerges when there is a discontinuous decision on how to organize a firm in layers. A new layer has a fixed cost, but makes the work of the other layers more efficient.
45. Moreover, within the more challenging contracting environment in countries in Latin America—where, for example, hiring additional management to scale up projects may be more difficult—the gap between the local optimal production q_1 and $\hat{q}$, the critical quantity to justify a leapfrog in scale, could be wider and more difficult to bridge.
46. For more information, visit http://www.techba.org/.
47. While it has never been easier to create a high-tech start-up with a website in order to promote and sell a product, the broad definition of marketing includes the definition of the product, which is very sensitive to a good understanding of demand. The majority of the dollars that demand products in the world are not Latin American and do not necessarily speak Spanish. There may be failures in how potential entrepreneurs understand the needs of foreign customers.

5 Beyond the Classroom: Preparing People to Produce

1. Glewwe et al. (2011) note that development agencies have also increased their aid to developing countries in education projects, practically doubling the amount allocated to this sector.
2. In terms of expenditure per pupil, Latin American countries also spend far less than the highly developed member-countries of the OECD. For example, while average expenditure per pupil in primary education in OECD countries is $6,670, in Chile it is $2,981, in Mexico $2,158, in Argentina $2,398, and in Brazil $1,696 (at the same level). Spending on secondary education averages $9,312 across OECD countries, well above the level of spending in Latin American countries at this level (Argentina, $3,932; Brazil, $2,235; Chile, $2,892; and Mexico, $2,536) (OECD, 2012b).
3. Only 46 percent of young people of secondary school age graduate on time, and only 52 percent do so before age 26 (Bassi, Busso, and Muñoz, 2013).

4. Only 30 percent of adults (aged 35–64) and 40 percent of young adults (25–34) in the region achieved secondary education (either complete or incomplete).
5. See Huneeus, de Mendoza, and Rucci (2013) for an analysis of funding and allocation of public resources for training for work in Latin America.
6. Urzúa and Puentes (2010) analyze a large number of studies on the impact of training programs on job performance worldwide. The results suggest considerable heterogeneity in the impacts, which precludes any conclusion about whether training programs have effectively improved the productivity of the beneficiaries.
7. In practice, graduates from the technical secondary scheme continue higher education at lower rates than graduates of general secondary education (either because they receive weaker academic preparation or because technical education in itself attracts students who intend to enter the workforce after completing their secondary studies).
8. In Brazil, students can opt for the integrated scheme (similar to the model in Argentina and Chile) or the independent technical courses of formal academic education, which do not require pre-certification or provide eligibility for postsecondary studies. In Mexico, technical secondary education includes technological baccalaureate and technical vocational studies of varied scope and length.
9. In the four MERCOSUR countries alone, software exports increased almost tenfold between 2000 and 2008, reaching nearly $1.8 billion in this last year. See ECLAC (2008).
10. Peng (2011); Aho et al. (2011); BIBB (2012); Cuddy (2012); and Mourshed, Farrell, and Barton (2013).
11. Levels 1–4, national certificates. Levels 5–6, national diplomas. Level 7, university degree, diplomas, and degree certificates. Level 8, graduate diplomas and certificates, honors degree. Level 9, masters. Level 10, doctorate.
12. Bassi et al. (2012), based on interviews at Volkswagen's Pacheco plant with the coordinator of formal education in June 2010.

6 Giving Credit to Productivity

1. Data are from Beck et al. (2012). For a survey of the evidence on the relationship between financial development and economic growth, see Levine (2005). This chapter focuses on credit because in developing and emerging market countries, few firms have access to the equity market. The data in Figure 6.1 refer to total credit to the private sector, including lending to households. However, most theoretical models suggest that financial development should affect growth by providing access to credit to firms (Levine, 2005; Beck et al., 2012). Unfortunately, cross-country data on credit to the corporate sector have limited coverage and are insufficient to present more precise evidence. Nevertheless, there is a tight correlation between credit to the private sector and the share of firms that have bank loans.

2. The data are from Beck et al. (2012) and are averages for the 2007–10 period.
3. For a discussion of causality in the relationship between TFP growth and financial depth, see Pagés (2010).
4. The chapter focuses on credit and bank financing because capital markets are relatively underdeveloped in Latin America and the Caribbean (for a discussion of the Latin American bond market, see Borensztein et al., 2008).
5. According to the World Bank Enterprise Survey (World Bank, 2013), the average Latin American firm needs to post collateral equal to nearly 200 percent of the borrowed funds (the developing country average is 177 percent).
6. It is in the nature of credit (as opposed to equity or, rarely used, equity-like contingent debt contracts) that when projects go well, firms keep all the returns in excess of contractual debt service, but when projects fail, firms can only lose the collateral. This asymmetry increases with leverage and leads firms to act as if they were risk lovers (the opposite of being risk averse). Higher interest rates are no cure because they attract riskier projects.
7. Social returns may also be lower than private returns, as in the case of environmentally damaging investments.
8. Other possible reasons for intervention include giving access to banking services to residents of isolated areas or smoothing the credit cycle. However, these interventions are justified by social or macroeconomic objectives and have a much more tenuous link with productivity. In fact, such interventions may have a positive effect on productivity as they preserve social capital or allow investment during recessions, but may also reduce productivity if they slow down the process of resource reallocation.
9. Since this chapter focuses on credit, it does not discuss the role of policies aimed at improving the working of the capital market. The list of such policies would include, among other things, the regulation of primary and secondary markets (listing and disclosure requirements) and the creation of benchmark yield curves.
10. Colombia's well-designed bankruptcy law (implemented in 2006) and movable collateral law (implemented in 2013) are examples of the value of educating lawmakers about the benefit of strong creditors' rights.
11. They can also indirectly affect firms with full access to financing, which would see their cost of capital marginally decline because of somewhat lower default risk. This additional borrowing would finance lower-return projects, a partial offset to the beneficial expansion of credit-constrained firms. They may also be a way to alleviate regulatory capital charges that discourage banks from extending loans, even to safe borrowers. The optimal response to this distortion would be to change bank regulation, but if it is difficult to change, guarantees can be an effective method to reduce capital charges and relax credit constraints.
12. For a discussion of the fiscal costs of public guarantees schemes and their pricing, see Anginer, de la Torre, and Ize (2011).

13. The costs associated with public credit guarantees are equal to the difference between the price of the guarantee and the expected loss. The costs associated with the subsidized funding costs are equal to the difference between the funding interest rate and the social costs of funds.
14. This is consistent with Anginer, de la Torre, and Ize (2011), who conclude that, by itself, the presence of social spillovers does not justify the extension of a public guarantee because spillovers are better dealt with through subsidies. However, they also suggest that the presence of coordination problems may tilt the balance in favor of public guarantee schemes.
15. Beck, Demirgüç-Kunt, and Maksimovic (2005) show that size is the main obstacle to access to finance in developing countries. IDB (2004) finds that strong creditors' rights are relatively more important for small firms. Kuntchev et al. (2012) develop a measure of actual credit constraints and show that SMEs are more likely to be credit-constrained than large firms.
16. A recent survey of 90 national development banks in 60 developing and transition economies (de Luna-Martínez and Vicente, 2012) found that 12 percent of surveyed institutions have a specific mandate concerning SMEs and that 92 percent of the surveyed institutions actively target SMEs.
17. Well-functioning credit bureaus can provide lenders with quick and affordable information about potential borrowers and thus reduce the fixed lending and monitoring costs that are the main source of credit constraints for small borrowers. However, many countries in Latin America and the Caribbean have had credit bureaus for more than a century, and credit bureau coverage tends to be higher in Latin America than in other developing regions. As a consequence, lack of credit bureaus does not appear to be the most important constraint to financial development in the region.
18. For further evidence on the productivity gap of Latin American SMEs, see Ibarrarán, Maffioli, and Stucchi (2009). Van Biesebroeck (2005) provides evidence for Africa, and Ayyagari, Demirgüç-Kunt, and Maksimovic (2011) provide worldwide evidence, showing that productivity growth is positively correlated with firm size.
19. Nevertheless, while identifying high-productivity firms from scratch may be overly costly for a bank, independent evaluations conducted for other purposes—for example, qualification for support in productive development programs (such as obtaining an innovation grant)—may be a useful signal to enable screening.
20. In fact, bank credit may not be the best way to discover new high-productivity firms. For a discussion of start-up financing, see chapter 4.
21. This may be especially true if growth leads to the formalization of previously informal firms.
22. Even if it were, the thorny issue of screening remains. Focusing on sectors structurally more dependent on external financing may help in such selection (in the spirit of Rajan and Zingales, 1998).

23. This risk may be mitigated through "reverse factoring," in which the lender purchases accounts receivable only from high-quality buyers, so that the credit risk is that of a high-quality customer.
24. Chrisney and Monge-González (2013) show that these complementary nonfinancial services are important and closely associated with accesses to credit.
25. In May 2000, Mexico passed a Law of Conservation of Electronic Documents, which gives data messages the same legal validity as written documents. In April 2003, the legislative approve an Electronic Signature Law, which allows secure transactions substituting electronic signatures for written signatures. In January 2004, the Fiscal Code was modified to include necessary amendments for electronic factoring, including digital certification.
26. They also benefit because interest charges are tax deductible—a fiscal expenditure.
27. In most countries, these guarantee schemes are further sweetened, with regulations permitting lower required reserves on guaranteed loans, a source of financial risk.
28. FOGAPE increased its participation within total bank loans from 2.8 percent to 10 percent from 2007 to 2011.
29. Larraín and Quiroz (2006) show that average firms benefitting from a FOGAPE guarantee are 14 percent more likely to get a loan compared to similar nonparticipating firms and that the scheme contributed to an increase in the volume of credit by 40 percent, while sales in the firms increased by 6 percent.
30. This assumes that the development bank does not have an efficiency advantage in financial intermediation over the private system. Collection privileges, such as those concerning the right to seize collateral or appropriate tax receipts, may be an exception. However, these strengths may be more than offset by collection weakness because of political pressures to favor borrowers.
31. The operation of development banks that target specific projects or sectors needs to be justified by the presence of spillovers that render socially profitable projects unattractive from the point of view of individual investors. Such spillovers relate either to individual projects with high social returns or to variants of the "Big Push" model first discussed by Rosenstein-Rodan (1961) and formalized by Murphy, Shleifer, and Vishny (1989).
32. This is also the case outside Latin America and the Caribbean (OECD, 2013c). The resurgence of state-owned banks was partly a response to the financial crisis, as there is evidence that lending by state-owned banks is less procyclical than private bank lending (Micco and Panizza, 2006).
33. Colby (2013) describes in detail the different sectors targeted by BNDES since its creation in 1952. For instance, the productive development policy program implemented by President Lula in 2008 focused on sectors that were

thought to have large positive spillovers: software, semiconductors, capital goods, pharmaceutical, biotechnology, and nanotechnology.
34. Employees are not hired in mid-career, which further protects staff from political dominance.
35. Nevertheless, Carvalho (2014) finds that BNDES lending tends to favor firms in regions where incumbents allied with the federal government face political competition. He also finds that manufacturing firms that benefit from this increase in BNDES loans expand employment, but that such politically motivated loans have no effect on investment or firm valuation.
36. A renewed interest for a development mandate may lead to cyclical behavior that de la Torre, Gozzi, and Schmukler (2007) have labeled the Sisyphus Syndrome.
37. Colby (2013), for instance, claims that BNDES may be too conservative because the development impact of a loan is hard to evaluate but defaults are easy to measure and employees can be punished for loans that default. Employees end up being too risk averse and maximize its financial health, rather than maximizing the bank's development impact.
38. Nevertheless, a captured development bank may face difficult-to-evaluate credit risks driven by undue pressures to condone debts.
39. The point is that such practice diminishes the bank's development impact, even if cross-subsidization by sound borrowers ensures overall financial safety.
40. They find a positive impact on employment and export growth but no effect on productivity. Credit had an impact only on the intensive margin of exports (firms that were already exporters increased their exports) but not on the probability of becoming an exporter.
41. de Luna-Martínez and Vicente (2012) found that in their world sample, 12 percent of the institutions covered in their survey operate as second-tier institutions, 36 percent as first-tier, and the remaining 52 percent blend first- and second-tier operations. Among the banks that are members of the Association of Latin American Development Banks, 47 percent are first-tier, 34 percent are second-tier, and the remaining 19 percent are dual institutions.
42. Similarly, banking regulation aimed at productive development policy objectives by favoring lending to certain activities or sectors (as in the current Bolivian Law of Financial Services enacted in 2013) leads to penalizing those that are not favored through bank cross-subsidization, and ultimately hurts financial development. Using financial regulation as productive development policy has no direct fiscal cost. There is thus a theoretical argument for it. In practice, however, it is very distortive and overly risky in terms of unintended consequences.
43. At the end of the 1990s and beginning of the new millennium, various countries (such as Colombia, El Salvador, Mexico, Nicaragua, Paraguay, and

Peru) implemented legal reforms that created new second-tier institutions or transformed first-tier banks into second-tier institutions. About 50 percent of the development banks that operate in Latin America and the Caribbean now offer second-tier services.

44. Problems related to the excessive risk aversion of private banks can be mitigated by combing second-tier lending with a credit guarantee scheme.
45. This concern over the subsidy was often mentioned during the interviews carried out for this DIA and summarized in Fernández-Arias, Hausmann, and Panizza (2013).
46. For example, in Bolivia, El Salvador, and Nicaragua, the second-tier institutions were transformed via legislative changes in order to include first-tier activities. Also, the National Financing Corporation (NAFIN) in Mexico, and the Investment and Foreign Trade Bank in Argentina, have opened or reinforced their first-tier windows in order to finance renewable energy projects.
47. El Salvador's Development Bank (Banco de Desarrollo or BANDESAL) is in the early stages of implementing a similar strategy.
48. This is in line with Hart, Shleifer, and Vishny's (1997) finding that subcontracting dominates direct provision of public goods when the characteristic of the public good can be fully specified.
49. Second-tier banks are at an informational disadvantage (see Box 6.1). Second-tier banks would need to make adjustments to their operations in order to be able to focus on this role, as in the case of Germany's KfW, a second-tier bank, which claims to be able to do so.
50. Banks can learn about constraints to economic growth by screening loans applications, even in the case that the loan is not approved. An analysis of the reasons for refusing to fund a particular project can yield valuable information about the conditions under which the project would have been profitable, and the main obstacles to the creation of new firms and activities.

7 More Than the Sum of Its Parts: Cluster-Based Policies

1. Of course, carrying out a transaction also involves costs, as shown by Olivier Williamson (1998).
2. The categories may overlap, but reflect an effort to focus on the main differentiating factors among a very large variety of policy measures.
3. This logic also applies to the supply of intermediate inputs in a specific cluster.
4. Along these lines, Paul Romer proposes the creation of self-organizing industry investment boards as a way for the private sector to identify and finance their own solutions (Romer, 1993). For more details, see Box 11.2 in chapter 11.

5. This is similar to the protection offered by a regime of Free Zones but not necessarily associated with exports.
6. MERCOSUR is a customs union that allows import taxes between country members, with the exception of exports from the Free Zones of Tierra del Fuego in Argentina and Manaus in Brazil.
7. The European Commission traces the cluster approach to industrial policies as far back as the early 1980s (EC, 2008).
8. Early PCPs were also present in Taiwan and China (Guerrieri, Iammarino, and Pietrobelli, 2003; Guerrieri and Pietrobelli, 2006).
9. A few years later the program added two more clusters, taking the number of supported clusters to 11.
10. An early example of an intervention was the provincial tax on sugarcane production in Tucuman, Argentina. It was established in the early 1900s to fund the applied research done by the local agricultural research station. It thus solved a coordination failure aimed at providing a public input.
11. Since the early 2000s, the IDB has supported more than 20 projects at the national and subnational levels, mostly in the Southern Cone, encompassing nearly 200 clusters.
12. A Chilean program that created regional development agencies in each of that country's 15 regions is a good example. In each of the regions, the newly created agencies were expected to support at least three clusters. Since Chile's policies are still very centralized in the national government, the program design included an interministerial board at the national level to facilitate high-level policy coordination affecting the selected clusters. At the local level, the program created instances in which local representatives of national PDP agencies could coordinate their instruments to meet the identified demands of each clusters. As it turned out, the national-level coordination unit barely met, while at the local level there were many instances in which previously uncoordinated interventions improved their joint actions around each cluster's strategic plans.
13. In Portuguese, Serviço Brasileiro de Apoio às Micro e Pequenas Empresas of São Paulo.
14. This was a national-level technical association that had not been active in that region before.
15. As Andersson et al. (2004) point out, there are only a few thorough evaluations of specific cluster initiatives and they have focused on only a few countries. Few solid attempts have been made to assess whether first-best results have been obtained, whether they go beyond efficiency in the use of given resources to encompass other economic results, or take into account interactions and synergies in the performance of different actors. Further, most evaluations of cluster policies still focus on single tools, which fit poorly with the systemic notion of cluster policy.
16. Although the randomization among eligibles or applicants is always theoretically possible, in many cases the number of potential beneficiaries is so

small that the randomization would be of limited use in practice. As discussed at length elsewhere (Giuliani et al., 2013; Pietrobelli, Maffioli, and Stucchi, forthcoming), this methodological drawback has some costs. First, nonexperimental evaluations are based on stronger assumptions than RCTs, and therefore usually have more limited validity. Second, many nonexperimental methods require a great amount of data, in both cross-sectional and longitudinal terms, making the implementation of these second-best options also rather challenging—particularly when secondary and administrative data are not available.
17. Crespi, Maffioli, and Meléndez (2011) show that it can take three to five years to observe the effect of PDPs on firm's productivity.
18. For a complete discussion on this issue, see Giuliani et al. (2013) and Pietrobelli, Maffioli, and Stucchi (forthcoming).
19. When SNA is not viable, studies have approximated the existence of linkages through proximity measures, mainly geographic proximity. For instance, Falck, Heblich, and Kipar (2010) and Nishimura and Okamuro (2011) use the location in the same district to define the existence of potential linkages among firms. Similarly, Falck, Heblich, and Kipar (2010) evaluate a German cluster program, aimed at fostering innovation and regional competitiveness through cooperation. They find that the program increased the likelihood of becoming an innovator in the targeted industry. Nishimura and Okamuro (2011) evaluate the Industrial Cluster Project in Japan. They found not only that the program expanded the industry-university-government network but also that the linkages with the university were the main driver for the positive effect on firms' R&D.
20. Labor mobility has been used extensively to measure spillover effects in trade and FDI literature. For a review on this topic, see Castillo et al. (2014b).
21. Thanks to an employer-employee dataset, the study tracks qualified workers who moved from beneficiary firms to nonbeneficiary firms, and defines these latter firms as potential indirect beneficiaries of the knowledge generated by the program.

8 A World of Possibilities: Internationalization for Productive Development

1. For a critical survey of the literature on the links between openness and economic growth, see Harrison and Rodríguez-Clare (2010).
2. On the negative side, if firms that are currently exporting fail to meet contractually agreed upon delivery standards, then not only their reputation may suffer, but they may also create a negative externality for their peers. Egan and Mody (1992) report the case of a US bicycle importer whose bad experience with a supplier from a country not known for supplying quality bicycles spread to other buyers and independent bicycle dealers. Such negative

externalities might also provide a rationale for public action. For instance, the government of Taiwan launched a program to compensate return shipments of defective bicycles when Taiwanese firms started to export as a way of preventing reputational damage (Egan and Mody, 1992).
3. Domestic suppliers may learn how to become more efficient, upgrade their technological capabilities and their products, meet international quality standards, and achieve on-time delivery (Humphrey and Schmitz, 2000; Paus and Gallagher, 2008).
4. Mion and Opromolla (2013) find that an increase in a firm's share of managers with export experience acquired in a previous company is associated with a higher probability of starting to export. Koenig, Mayneris, and Poncet (2010) uncover a positive relationship between the number of firms exporting a certain product to a certain destination from a certain geographical area and the probability that a firm located in the same area will begin to sell the product in the market in question. In a related paper, Álvarez, Faruq, and López (2010) show that the probability that firms in Chile introduce given products to new countries or different products to the same countries increases with the number of peers exporting those products and to those destinations, respectively.
5. The results suggest that if the number of firms in a given municipality selling a given good to a given market increases by 100, the probability that a firm from the same municipality exports the same good to the same market increases by 0.75 percent.
6. The presence of followers is certainly not a necessary condition for spillovers to exist.
7. The picture does not change significantly when the sample is restricted to those new products that survive from the first to the second year, or a minimum threshold in terms of export value is imposed in identifying new export products. It is worth noting that the share of the respective foreign sales that pioneers account for tend to decrease rapidly and, in some cases, followers for all practical purposes took over the export business in a relatively short period of time.
8. Evidence of positive horizontal spillovers is accordingly much weaker than evidence of vertical spillovers.
9. Benefits derived from FDI may also depend on the degree of financial development, intensity of competition and level of openness, infrastructure, and local R&D and learning efforts (Alfaro et al., 2004; Wang and Blomström, 1992; Borensztein, De Gregorio, and Lee, 1998; Blalock and Gertler, 2002), whereas those from GVC are also contingent on firms' strategies and capabilities (Gereffi, Humphrey, and Sturgeon, 2005; Pietrobelli and Rabellotti, 2011). The entry of Wal-Mart into Mexico provides interesting insights in this regard. This chain provides manufacturers of consumer goods with a larger market but puts pressure on these suppliers to improve their products'

appeal. As a result of this entry, high-quality, upstream suppliers of merchandise and food expanded their sales and became more productive, whereas low-quality suppliers suffered in both areas (Iacovone et al., 2011).
10. Broadly defined, *trade costs* include all costs incurred in delivering a good to the final user: transport costs, tariffs and nontariff measures, information costs, costs arising from the use of different currencies, legal and regulatory costs, and local distribution costs (Anderson and van Wincoop, 2004).
11. Nevertheless, these new policies still have components of their predecessors, such as fiscal incentives (rebates, drawbacks, exemptions from value-added, indirect, or profit taxes), financial incentives (those granted by public banks, such as Brazil's BNDES, Colombia's BANCOLDEX, and Mexico's BANCOMEX), incentives for trade in services (drawbacks, deferred payment of tariffs in capital goods, credit for acquisition of domestic services by foreign buyers, and credit for the development and dissemination of new services), and export-processing zones.
12. This section draws on Jordana, Volpe Martincus, and Gallo (2010) and Volpe Martincus (2010) and the results of the survey presented therein.
13. These activities may have a regional dimension. For example, some EPOs such as PROCHILE help firms take advantage of the business opportunities created by the trade agreements signed by their countries.
14. Additional services include facilitation of production linkages with MNCs (PROCOMER) (discussed below) and support for initiatives to increase the value added and quality of products (PROEXPORT).
15. *Marcas Sectoriales* is an initiative aimed at increasing the penetration of foreign markets. It supports the design, implementation, and international positioning of sectoral trademarks representing particular sectors in Chile through a public-private collaboration.
16. While exports of goods account for most of the promotion efforts of EPOs, exports of services are no longer neglected. The resources allocated to assist firms that export services vary significantly by country in the region. Some EPOs have only a few staff members working on a part-time basis on exports of services, while others, such as PROCHILE and PROEXPORT, have specialized service units within their organizational arrangements.
17. Investment aftercare is considered to play an important role in fostering FDI (UNCTAD, 2007).
18. The way IPOs handle inquiries from investors is rated based on the "*competence and responsiveness of the organization's staff, including timeliness, quality and credibility of informational content*," whereas the quality of their websites is rated based on "*whether they contain relevant, clear and credible information presented in an attractive and user-friendly way*" (Harding and Javorcik, 2013).
19. The advantages of combined organizations can include better coherence and coordination in trade and investment issues, common ground for

policy advocacy in the area of national competitiveness, better service delivery through a single point of contact in government, cross-fertilization in general and synergies in overseas promotion in particular, and sharing of support services and office space. Possible disadvantages include the risks of fragmented responsibilities and loss of focus given different objectives and core activities, different time frames—with a longer time perspective in investment promotion in general—different clients and contact points in companies, different skills requirements for staff, and problems in managing staff with different mindsets (UNCTAD, 2009).
20. According to data from Jordana, Volpe Martincus, and Gallo (2010) and the World Development Indicators, the average share of an EIPO's budget in central public sector expenditures is 0.06 percent in Latin America and the Caribbean, and 0.09 percent in other regions.
21. Cooperation with foreign partners could be a possible strategy to overcome the limitations imposed by size. Regional initiatives such as Caribbean Export are an example in this regard. The same holds for the collaboration agreement signed by URUGUAY XXI with counterparts in other countries (Jordana, Volpe Martincus, and Gallo, 2010).
22. Needless to say, not everything comes down to size and budget. Some relatively small organizations, such as Costa Rica's Ministry of Foreign Trade (COMEX), play an important role in their countries.
23. In PROEXPORT, base salaries are comparable to those of the Ministry of Trade, Industry, and Tourism, but there are economic incentives in the form of a variable bonus (up to about 25 percent of base salary) based on the degree of achievement of individual goals. In addition, the organization has established other incentives for employees with outstanding performance. Besides providing incentives for good performance, the scheme has allowed PROEXPORT to remain competitive in a context in which private firms attract well-trained employees, offering them higher wages (Obando and Gómez Escalante, 2008).
24. For instance, with only a few exceptions, EPOs do not participate in the selection of the commercial attachés or in their evaluation.
25. An alternative worth exploring would be to outsource some export assistance services in specific market niches to specialized companies.
26. Data on the costs of foreign offices are not readily available. Information kindly provided by PROEXPORT for 2006 indicates that the overall budget of the entire network of offices in that year was $6 million (on average, $500,000 per office). Combining these data with the estimated effect of having an office in the destination on total bilateral exports—according to a regression similar to that carried out in Volpe Martincus, Carballo, and Gallo (2011)—suggests that each additional dollar spent in these offices is associated with a median increase of $182 in exports to the respective countries. These figures are only indicative; given the challenges that

typically confront such estimations, these results should be viewed with caution.
27. One of the most sophisticated strategies in this regard is FINPRO's signal gathering. The organization's representatives around the world follow business news in relevant media and register those events in a common system, across different areas of activities. This information is then centrally and systematically analyzed to uncover emerging and consolidating business opportunities for Finnish companies.
28. A t-test of difference in means suggests that these means are significantly different from each other. These tests are available from the authors upon request.
29. These estimates have been obtained by estimating a linear probability model whose dependent variable is a binary indicator that takes the value of 1 if the product-destination began to be exported and zero otherwise. The model includes the product's and destination's fixed effects. This model has been estimated on a cross-section of data drawn from the 2007–09 period. A table with these estimation results is available from the authors upon request.
30. The picture does not significantly change when followers that receive trade support are excluded. Yet, it should be taken into account that PROCHILE is the EPO in the region with the largest network of offices abroad. This is likely to affect its ability to retrieve relevant business information. Hence, its experience with targeting should not be considered representative of other EPOs in the region, particularly those without a direct presence abroad.
31. Specific activities within sectors could also be targeted. For instance, in Panama, assembly plants can be established in the free zone but not in the "knowledge city," which admits only training and design centers supported by MNCs.
32. In most cases, these are the so-called high-tech or knowledge-intensive sectors such as electronics and electrical equipment, information and communication technologies (ICTs), and industrial machinery and equipment. Charlton et al. (2004) show that electronics and electrical equipment, tourism and tourist amenities, industrial machinery and equipment, ICT, food and kindred products, and crop agriculture were targeted by more than 40 percent of the organizations in a sample of mostly developed countries. These sectors are widely believed to generate more positive spillovers in general, and allow for more substantive technology transfer in particular, thereby helping increase the average productivity of the host economies (Charlton et al., 2004; OECD, 2012a).
33. The average investment-promotion organization spent $90,000 per targeted sector. Combining the benefit and the cost sides, it can be concluded that a dollar spent on *investment promotion* leads to $189 of FDI inflows. Alfaro and Charlton (2007) also found a strong, positive relationship between

sector targeting and sector FDI inflows, but in a sample of mostly developed countries.
34. In order to make an overall assessment of export-promotion programs, the analysis must consider the cost side of the equation. Based on data on EPOs' budgets and the results of the impact evaluation of export-promotion programs in Argentina, Chile, Colombia, Costa Rica, Peru, and Uruguay reported in Volpe Martincus (2010), each additional dollar allocated to *trade promotion* resulted in increased foreign sales of $25. Given the limitations of the analysis, these figures should be viewed with caution.
35. Authors could obtain consistent information on trade promotion assistance by service category only for this period. This short sample period does not allow a proper assessment of how services interact with one another over time, and the relative effectiveness of their alternative sequencing.
36. An EPO's counseling and information services can provide firms with information about a country and product lines of interest before going abroad. This knowledge helps managers learn what to expect from and how to properly behave with buyers from the target markets, and define the right range of products to present as well as the appropriate promotion material to use, and may facilitate acquisition of experiential knowledge once in the country. Missions and fairs can help generate and increase awareness of on-site potential customers about products and obtain contacts and leads. Setting up face-to-face meetings with potential buyers may help transform these contacts and leads into concrete exports (Branch, 1990; Hibbert, 1990; Spence, 2003).
37. These export indicators might also account for productivity differences among firms, although in an imperfect manner.
38. For technical details on estimation procedures, see Volpe Martincus and Carballo (2010).
39. In addition, specific combinations of two services are associated with better export performance than their individual components for comparable firms.
40. Unfortunately, the authors were not able to obtain data on the costs of the programs.
41. For instance, employees trained by MNCs have moved to domestic firms (or started their own businesses), thereby helping them increase their productivity (Monge-González, Leiva Bonilla, and Rodríguez-Álvarez, 2012a). These companies are also helping to upgrade technical education in the country, particularly in science and engineering (Larraín, López-Calva, and Rodríguez-Clare, 2001; Paus and Gallagher, 2008; OECD, 2012a). Moreover, a significant proportion of Costa Rican providers of goods and services to MNCs engaged in some training with them, and have modified their organizational practices (and changed their product varieties) because of their relationships with these companies. This was particularly the case with Intel (Larraín, López-Calva, and Rodríguez-Clare, 2001).
42. CRP was initially a component of the Supplier Development Project for High-Technology Multinational Companies, which was launched in 1999

with support from the IDB and initially administered by FUNCENAT (High Technology National Center Foundation). In 2004, CRP was transferred to PROCOMER.
43. It also attempts to create business opportunities through small projects between local SME suppliers and MNCs to help the SMEs become global suppliers.
44. The number of SMEs participating in the project grew from 23 to 455 from 2003 to 2009 (MIF, 2010).
45. In particular, while a few domestic firms have succeeded in becoming successful suppliers of other products, packaging and printing materials and different services account for the largest shares of inputs that foreign firms based in Costa Rica source locally.
46. Recently, the Costa Rican government decided to provide more support to firms participating in CRP through better coordination with other programs. Thus, beneficiaries of the program will be assisted in obtaining resources from PROPYME. Provided that this program actually helps firms expand their innovation activities, this could improve their chances of succeeding in establishing and expanding their commercial relationships with MNCs (OECD, 2012a; Monge-González and Rodríguez-Álvarez, 2013).
47. The members are the Ministry of Foreign Trade (COMEX); the Ministry of Economy, Industry, and Commerce; the Ministry of Science and Technology; the Coalition of Development Initiatives (CINDE); the Chamber of Industries of Costa Rica; the Chamber of Exporters of Costa Rica; the Association of Free Trade Zone Companies; the National Council for Scientific and Technological Research (CONICYT); and PROCOMER.
48. *Bumiputera* is the term used to describe the Malay race and other indigenous people of Southeast Asia. In 1970, the Malaysian government started implementing policies in different areas to favor this ethnic group.
49. Feedback effects from exporting are also possible. In particular, contacts with foreign customers through exporting activities may allow firms to enhance their knowledge bases, thus raising their technological capabilities to innovate—and, specifically, to perform R&D (see, for example, Aw, Roberts, and Winston, 2007; Girma, Görg, and Hanley, 2008).
50. If participation in these other programs is time-invariant over the sample period, its impact can be automatically controlled by the estimation procedures that identify the effects of interest, based on the time variation. If firms' participation in other assistance programs is instead a time-varying variable that is overrepresented in the group of supported firms and these other forms of assistance positively influence the outcome in question, then conventional procedures would overestimate the true causal effects of the program on this outcome.
51. Further lags do not seem to matter. Macroeconomic factors are controlled by year fixed effects. Alternatively, firm fixed effects are used, with similar results.

52. There may be different organizational formulas to achieve coordination. For instance, in Finland, a representative from TEKES, the Finnish innovation promotion agency, is a member of the board of FINPRO, the Finnish trade and investment promotion organization.
53. A limitation of the current analysis is that, by focusing on exporting firms, the impacts of the programs on the entry to international markets cannot be established. A more complete assessment of these programs would require studying whether and how participation would help firms become exporters. In order to explore the incidence on this firm-extensive margin, access to the entire business register (at least for firms in tradable sectors) would be needed. More generally, patterns of complementarities may differ across sets of programs within countries, as well as across countries.

9 Selecting Priority Sectors for Productive Transformation: An Elephant in the Room?

1. This approach to economics is usually associated with Austrian-American economist Joseph Schumpeter (1934). The relative importance of the static and dynamic channels for increased productivity varies by country.
2. At the same time, targeting sectors irrespective of why the market fails to undertake them are adventures that may easily turn sour.
3. While Lall, Weiss, and Zhang (2006) use shares in world exports as the weights for their calculation of sophistication, Hausmann, Hwang, and Rodrik (2007) use revealed comparative advantage.
4. Furthermore, it provides a robust characterization of the process because it does not depend on any preconceived notion of what kind of productive capability adds more value.
5. See Lall, Weiss, and Zhang (2006) for a discussion of this issue. Lederman and Maloney (2012) refer to this as a problem of "tasks vs. goods," and provide the example of China as an exporter of the iPod, based on work by Linden, Kraemer, and Dedrick (2009).
6. Complexity for the product community is given by the simple average of the 2010 product complexity index of its constituent products.
7. This would amount to a "Dutch Disease" slowing down complexity.
8. *The Economist* (2013) and Mazzucato (2013).
9. See http://www.mof.gov.jm/taxpolicy/publicdocs/Waivers?page=3. December 2009 is the first month for which detailed data are reported on the website. An important portion corresponds to charitable waivers.
10. While the typical country in Latin America and the Caribbean has had an annual growth rate of 2.09 percent over the period 2000–10, the corresponding growth rate for Jamaica was 0.26 percent.
11. Hausmann et al. (2014) introduce the concept of *opportunity value* of a country as the prospects for productive transformation afforded by the country's

existing export basket and measure it by looking at the extent to which there are unexploited fruits that are low-hanging (that is, in close proximity) and also sweet and juicy (complex). For a formal definition of opportunity value, see Hausmann et al. (2014). This concept will be discussed in more detail below, in the section on the policy mix. The *strategic value* of a target product, that is, the extent to which it is a springboard for productive transformation by opening up further opportunities, can then be operationalized as the increase in opportunity value associated with "conquering," or achieving competitiveness, in that target product.

12. For a detailed account of the Leonisa case, see Arbeláez, Meléndez, and León (2007).
13. This is consistent with the findings in Kugler, Stein, and Wagner (2007), who show that the likelihood that a new export sector will emerge increases with the quality in the surrounding product space.
14. This is also the key question in Greenwald and Stiglitz (2013), in which industrial policy is motivated by distortions in the production and dissemination of knowledge. In this chapter, knowledge is materialized in productive capabilities and disseminated through production.
15. If there are beneficiary firms outside the sector in question, this test would involve willingness to cofinance to a sufficient degree.
16. This is similar to self-discovery, but applies to known or at least presumed (dynamic) advantages that are developed, rather than discovered.
17. Infant industries in developing countries also need to overcome the hurdle of competing with mature peers in pioneering countries (Harrison and Rodríguez-Clare, 2010).
18. Chapters 10 and 11 analyze the institutional capabilities required to effectively implement these types of policies.
19. For more on Costa Rica's upgrading in the medical devices global value chain, see Bamber and Gereffi (2013).
20. It had representation from five ministries: finance, education, mining, agriculture, and public works. It also had different representatives from the scientific, innovation, and education communities, and included the heads of CORFO and CONICYT.
21. While these variables included attributes related to existing human capital, availability of natural resources, access to technology, adequacy of infrastructure and logistics, etc., the exact definition of the variables and weighting system used to calculate the size of the effort necessary to become competitive were not disclosed.
22. The original sector study by BCG called for 5,100 international professionals between 2007 and 2010.
23. Although the selection process does consider where high value is generated within each value chain, this is done only in the second stage, once the sectors have been identified. It may happen that higher value links exceed the country's capabilities.

24. In fact, Hausmann et al. (2014) show empirically that this measure of distance has predictive power: the probability that a new competitive product will emerge is tightly linked to its distance to the existing basket.
25. In order to think about these policy issues in specific countries, the analysis should be done at the level of individual products, rather than at the level of product communities. Communities of products are used here as the unit of analysis solely for purposes of exposition.
26. It could be, for example, that for these specific products complexity is not a good proxy for profitability.
27. For measures of effectiveness in seizing opportunities and complexity erosion, see Fernández-Arias and Stein (2014).

10 The Hard Part: Building Public-Sector Capabilities

1. By PDAs we mean all the agencies involved in the design, implementation, evaluation, and oversight of PDPs, including the relevant ministries. While there may be important differences among them (for example, some may specialize in design and others in implementation), we will only make these distinctions to the extent that they are necessary for the analysis.
2. At a more general level, other critical factors include political institutions, the features of the policymaking process, and the interests, capabilities, and distribution of power between the key actors in the process (Spiller, Stein, and Tommasi, 2008). These are outside the scope of this report.
3. In this regard, the design and implementation of PDPs may not be as much a science as it is an art.
4. The long delays also complicate the evaluation of the programs, since many things may change during these maturation periods, making it more difficult to attribute particular outcomes to specific PDPs.
5. In cases in which public officials interact with private actors, high rotation of public officials can be a powerful disincentive for the private sector to engage for at least two reasons: first, rotation may impose high transaction costs on the private actors, who have to explain the situation to the newcomers again and again; second, agreements reached with the public actor today may not be respected tomorrow by their replacements.
6. Naturally, participation in national strategic councils requires a different type of public participation than the implementation of a specific policy instrument.
7. Moreover, if frequent and periodic meetings at the highest level are held on an issue that is not a high priority, the president or other high-ranking officials will begin sending delegates rather than attend the meetings themselves. Soon the private sector will follow suit, and what was meant to be a high-level political exercise will evolve into a low-level bureaucratic one.

8. Inducing changes in the behavior of the private sector requires more than just choosing the right public sector participants. Issues of policy and instrument design are essential, but this discussion focuses on organizational design.
9. The distinction between wide policies that involve many agencies and narrow ones that involve only one or a few should not be confused with the distinction between vertical policies that impact only a specific sector of economic activity and horizontal policies that impact all sectors of economic activity.
10. Uruguay is another country with specialized cabinets. The "Productive Cabinet," which is composed of ministries that deal with the productive sector, includes the minister of economics and finance, industry, energy and mining, labor and social security, livestock, agriculture and fishing, and tourism and sports, as well as the office of planning and budget. This cabinet oversees the sectorial councils, a group of 14 public-private councils charged with identifying obstacles and solutions to the development of these sectors. The productive cabinet, however, does not have a clear leader, does not meet very frequently, and has not been very effective as a mechanism for coordination.
11. While not in the specific area of PDPs, the example of the Defense Logistics Agency (DLA) is also a good illustration of this idea. The agency is responsible for providing supplies and services to America's military forces worldwide, including food, fuel, medical supplies, and weapons. Interestingly, the DLA does not have its own budget to provide these services. The budget is controlled by the different branches of the armed forces, which can hire the services of the DLA, or choose to hire other logistics providers, if the DLA proposal is not to their liking (see Bilmes and Gould, 2009: 64–79).
12. Alternatively, priority actions identified during the year could be accommodated in the budget of the following year (see Hausmann et al., 2011).
13. For more discussion on public-private councils, see chapter 11, as well as Devlin (2013) and Schneider (2013).
14. Care should be taken not to confuse "organizational structure" and "organizational skills"; the former refers to how organizations are structured; the latter refers to what an organization knows how to do.
15. In 2008, the IC Civilian Joint Duty Program won the Innovations in American Government Award by the Ash Institute of Harvard University's Kennedy School of Government as a "key to improved national security" and an "innovative solution for improving cross-agency understanding."
16. These capabilities would be made possible by fostering transparency and governance structures that bring to bear the interests of all relevant stakeholders.
17. See the terms of reference for the project on Building Institutional Capabilities for Productive Development Policies. See http://www.iadb.org/en/research-and-data/project-details,3187.html?id=3266.

18. This paper updates the policy indexes that were developed originally in Stein et al. (2005).
19. These authors define desirable attributes for institutions and policy instruments and attempt to grade them according to their perspectives for creating effective and efficient interventions. The institutional attributes include coverage, coordination, efficiency, client focus, accountability, and learning. Each criterion is distinguished by a specific indicator (ranging from 0 to 2, depending on the degree of compliance or presence of the attribute), which can then be used to evaluate institutions. The focus is on benchmarking their performance and method of operation, rather than on explaining the conditions that allow them to act effectively and build the required capabilities.
20. In contrast, public inputs tend to be one-off interventions (such as passage of a law to safeguard intellectual property needed to develop the biotechnology sector, or the development of a new rice variety) or an ongoing response to permanent needs (such as the provision of phytosanitary services or the creation of an electrical engineering major in the public university). Thus, the temporal mismatch between policy justification and instrument does not typically arise.
21. See chapter 4 for an analysis of the impact of these policies.
22. The first case is described as "premature load bearing" and the second as "isomorphic mimicry" in Pritchett, Woolcock, and Andrews (2010).
23. Rodrik (2007b) has stressed the point more generally in his book *One Economics, Many Recipes*.
24. Similar considerations apply when assigning specific policy instruments to specific public agencies, which also have different capabilities.
25. In some cases, feedback from users or beneficiaries might be crucial, as well.
26. See discussion of "revolving doors" in chapter 11.
27. Interestingly, in many cases, Sammies have been awarded on the basis of achievements obtained through interagency collaboration.

11   Two to Tango: Public-Private Collaboration

1. *Capture* refers to the result by which, whether government knows it or not, the collective objectives that it pursues are supplanted by individual rent seeking of the private participants. The classical manner in which this happens is by taking advantage of informational asymmetry, but other means can lead to the same result including, but not limited to, corruption.
2. It may even be the case that the objective of the dialogue is not so much to extract information from the private sector, as to legitimize or obtain support for policies as they have been designed. Similarly, the private party's interest

in engaging in dialogue may not be as much about influencing the playing field as about anticipating the direction in which things are moving.
3. At the same time, enlarging the private sector counterpart beyond the point required for effective information exchange provides no real gain. For example, unless the issues under discussion are of general interest, dealing with a chamber of commerce instead of individual associations only dilutes expertise.
4. In addition to free riding, the private sector may not trust the public sector or, at least, the public sector's ability to do its part and deliver effectively.
5. This is consistent with the successful experience of East Asian countries in granting benefits to associations in return for enhanced economic performance by their member firms and sectors, a grand bargain based on the ability of imposing discipline on business associations if they do not hold their end of the bargain.
6. See, for instance, Eslava and Meléndez (2009) for Colombia; Urbiztondo et al. (2009) for Argentina; Alston, Libecap, and Mueller (2010) for Brazil; and Aninat et al. (2010) for Chile.
7. In Brazil, for example, sector specialists at the state development bank, BNDES, are among the most knowledgeable in the nation, and participate actively in the design of vertical public policies.
8. The cases dealt with the fashion, software, biodiesel, and sugar industries, along with an entrepreneurship program, in Argentina (Bisang et al., 2014); the tourism, global services, and aquaculture clusters, along with the innovation programs in health-care implements and fruits, in Chile (Benavente et al., forthcoming); the "umbrella" competitiveness program and the productive transformation programs in the cosmetics, cleaners, business processing, and palm oil industries in Colombia (Eslava, Meléndez, and Perry, 2014); experiences in rice, tourism, fisheries, and coffee, and in attracting FDI, in Costa Rica (Cornick, Jiménez, and Román, 2014); and the beef, blueberries, biotech, tourism, and shipbuilding industry programs in Uruguay (Pittaluga et al., 2014).
9. The authors also point out the cautionary tale of CONARROZ, which was set up in the same way as the tourism agency, but resulted in a particularly bad case of capture. The board of CONARROZ is dominated by large rice producers and processors, with only two of eleven seats in the board corresponding to public actors. See also Box 2.2 in chapter 2.
10. CINDE operates with private funds, but with objectives and duties that are very similar to those of government offices like the Irish Development Agency or ProChile.
11. The name Pro-Tejer is suggestive: *tejer* means to weave or to knit. However, *proteger* with a "g" means to protect.
12. See Bisang et al. (2014) for a detailed account of this and other collaborative programs between INTI and Pro-Tejer.

13. Unfortunately, this does not preclude rent seeking from taking place through other, sometimes more informal channels.
14. One difficulty with cost sharing is that sometimes the most deserving policy beneficiaries are not in a position to contribute sufficient financial resources, hence the signal of the worthiness of the engagement needs to be verified by their active involvement and other sacrifices.
15. Bringing in more public agencies may also make collusion more difficult. Multiple agencies with decisive power may in many cases explain the low levels of capture observed. However, the beneficial effects of this scheme may be overwhelmed by the coordination challenges they introduce.
16. This assumes a recurring need for policy. If not, policies should consist of one-off incentives rather than recurring benefits. For example, policies to attract FDI could involve up-front grants, rather than tax exemptions that may generate expectations of and lead to pressures for continuity.

References

Adelino, M., A. Schoar, and F. Severino. 2013. House Prices, Collateral and Self-Employment. NBER Working Paper No. 18868. National Bureau of Economic Research, Cambridge, MA.
Aghion, P., Y. Algan, P. Cahuc, and A. Shleifer. 2010. Regulation and Distrust. *Quarterly Journal of Economics* 125(3): 1015–49.
Aghion, P., N. Bloom, and J. V. Reenen. 2013. Incomplete Contracts and the Internal Organization of Firms. NBER Working Paper No. 18842. National Bureau of Economic Research, Cambridge, MA.
Aghion, P., P. A. David, and D. Foray. 2009. Science, Technology and Innovation for Economic Growth: Linking Policy Research and Practice in "STIG Systems." *Research Policy* 38(4) May: 681–93.
Aghion, P., M. Dewatripont, L. Du, A. Harrison, and P. Legros. 2012. Industrial Policy and Competition. NBER Working Paper No. 18048. National Bureau of Economic Research, Cambridge, MA.
Agosin, M. R. 2013. Productive Development Policies in Latin America: Past and Present. Working Paper No. 382. Facultad de Economía y Negocios, Universidad de Chile, Santiago.
Agosin, M. R., C. Larraín, and N. Grau. 2010. Industrial Policy in Chile. IDB Working Paper No. 170. Inter-American Development Bank, Washington, DC.
Aho, M., R. André, I. Echeverry, and V. Roca-Rey. 2011. Taking Youth to Market: Expanding Formal Labor Market Access through Public-Private Collaboration. White Paper. Americas Society/Council of the Americas (AS/COA), New York. Available at http://www.as-coa.org/sites/default/files/ASCOA_MarketAccessYouthReport.pdf. Accessed January 2014.
Aitken, B., G. H. Hanson, and A. E. Harrison. 1997. Spillovers, Foreign Investment, and Export Behavior. *Journal of International Economics* 43(1–2) August: 103–32.
Aitken, B., and A. E. Harrison. 1999. Do Domestic Firms Benefit from Direct Foreign Investment? Evidence from Venezuela. *American Economic Review* 89(3) June: 605–18.
Albuquerque, R., and H. A. Hopenhayn. 2004. Optimal Lending Contracts and Firm Dynamics. *Review of Economic Studies* 71(2): 285–315.
Alfaro, L., A. Chanda, S. Kalemli-Ozcan, and S. Sayek. 2004. FDI and Economic Growth: The Role of Local Financial Markets. *Journal of International Economics* 64(1) October: 89–112.
Alfaro, L., and A. Charlton. 2007. Growth and the Quality of Foreign Direct Investment: Is All FDI Equal? CEP Discussion Paper No. 830. Centre for Economic Performance, London School of Economics and Political Science, London.
Alfaro, L., and M. X. Chen. 2012. Surviving the Global Financial Crisis: Foreign Ownership and Establishment Performance. *American Economic Journal: Economic Policy* 4(3) August: 30–55.

Alfaro, L., and A. Rodríguez-Clare. 2004. Multinationals and Linkages: An Empirical Investigation. *Economía* 4(2) Spring: 113–69.

Alston, L. J., G. D. Libecap, and B. Mueller. 2010. Interest Groups, Information Manipulation in the Media, and Public Policy: The Case of the Landless Peasants Movement in Brazil. NBER Working Paper No. 15865. National Bureau of Economic Research, Cambridge, MA.

Álvarez, R., J. J. Benavente, and J. J. Price. 2013. Policy Changes in the Incubators Program in Chile. Inter-American Development Bank, Washington, DC. Unpublished.

Álvarez, R., G. Crespi, and C. Cuevas. 2012. Public Programs, Innovation, and Firm Performance in Chile. IDB Technical Note No. 375. Inter-American Development Bank, Washington, DC.

Álvarez, R., G. Crespi, G. Imbens, and C. Volpe Martincus. 2013. Timing versus Duration of Treatment and Sequential Unconfoundedness. Inter-American Development Bank, Washington, DC. Unpublished.

Álvarez, R., H. Faruq, and R. A. López. 2010. Is Previous Exporting Experience Relevant for New Exports? Working Paper No. 599. Central Bank of Chile, Santiago.

Álvarez, R., and R. A. López. 2005. Exporting and Performance: Evidence from Chilean Plants. *Canadian Journal of Economics* 38(4) November: 1384–1400.

Amsden, A. H. 1989. *Asia's Next Giant: South Korea and Late Industrialization*. New York: Oxford University Press.

Anderson, J. E., and E. van Wincoop. 2004. Trade Costs. *Journal of Economic Literature* 42(3) September: 691–751.

Andersson, T., S. Schwaag Serger, J. Sörvik, and E. Wise Hansson. 2004. *The Cluster Policies Whitebook*. Malmö, Sweden: International Organisation for Knowledge Economy and Enterprise Development.

Andrews, M. 2013. *The Limits of Institutional Reform in Development: Changing Rules for Realistic Solutions*. New York: Cambridge University Press.

Andrews, M., L. Pritchett, and M. Woolcock. 2012. Escaping Capability Traps through Problem-Driven Iterative Adaptation (PDIA). Working Paper No. 299. Center for Global Development, Washington, DC.

Anginer, D., A. de la Torre, and A. Ize. 2011. Risk Absorption by the State: When Is It Good Public Policy? Policy Research Working Paper No. 5893. World Bank, Washington, DC.

Aninat, C., J. M. Benavente, I. Briones, N. Eyzaguirre, P. Navia, and J. Olivari. 2010. The Political Economy of Productivity: The Case of Chile. IDB Working Paper No. 105. Inter-American Development Bank, Washington, DC.

Applegate, L. M., W. R. Kerr, J. Lerner, D. D. Pomeranz, G. A. Herrero, and C. Scott. 2012. Start-Up Chile: April 2012. HBS Case No. 812–158. Harvard Business School, Boston, MA.

Aranguren, M. J., and I. Navarro. 2003. La política de clusters en la Comunidad Autónoma del País Vasco: una primera valoración. *Ekonomiaz* 53(2): 90–113.

Arbeláez, M. A., M. Meléndez, and N. León. 2007. The Emergence of New Successful Export Activities in Colombia. FEDESARROLLO, Bogotá. Unpublished.

———. 2012. The Emergence of Fresh Cut-Flower Exports in Colombia. In C. Sabel, E. Fernández-Arias, R. Hausmann, A. Rodríguez-Clare, and E. Stein, eds., *Export Pioneers in Latin America*. Washington, DC: Inter-American Development Bank; and Cambridge, MA: David Rockefeller Center for Latin American Studies, Harvard University.

Arráiz, I., F. Henríquez, and R. Stucchi. 2013. Supplier Development Programs and Firm Performance: Evidence from Chile. *Small Business Economics* 41(1) June: 277–93.

Arrow, K. J. 1962. The Economic Implications of Learning by Doing. *Review of Economic Studies* 29(3): 155–73.

Arrow, K. J., and R. C. Lind. 1970. Uncertainty and the Evaluation of Public Investment Decisions. *American Economic Review* 60(3) June: 364–78.

Artopoulos, A., D. Friel, and J. C. Hallak. 2010. Challenges of Exporting Differentiated Products to Developed Countries: The Case of SME-Dominated Sectors in a Semi-Industrialized Country. IDB Working Paper No. 166. Inter-American Development Bank, Washington, DC.

Artopoulos, A., and J. C. Navarro. Forthcoming. La política de la política pública en ciencia, tecnología e innovación en América Latina: modelo conceptual y casos estilizados. IDB working paper. Inter-American Development Bank, Washington, DC.

Aw, B. Y., M. J. Roberts, and T. Winston. 2007. Export Market Participation, Investments in R&D and Worker Training, and the Evolution of Firm Productivity. *World Economy* 30(1) January: 83–104.

Axèle, G., and B. Delane. 2008. Policies Promoting MNE Linkages in Host Economies: A Comparison between Brazil and Malaysia. Paper presented at the OECD Global Forum on International Investment VII, March 27–28, Paris.

Ayyagari, M., A. Demirgüç-Kunt, and V. Maksimovic. 2011. Small vs. Young Firms across the World: Contribution to Employment, Job Creation, and Growth. Policy Research Working Paper No. 5631. World Bank, Washington, DC.

Balassa, B. 1989. Outward Orientation. In H. Chenery and T. N. Srinivasan, eds., *Handbook of Development Economics.* Volume 2. Amsterdam: North-Holland.

Balsvik, R. 2011. Is Labor Mobility a Channel for Spillovers from Multinationals? Evidence from Norwegian Manufacturing. *Review of Economics and Statistics* 93(1) February: 285–97.

Bamber, P., and G. Gereffi. 2013. Costa Rica in the Medical Devices Global Value Chain: Opportunities for Upgrading. In G. Gereffi, P. Bamber, S. Frederick, and K. Fernández-Stark, eds., *Costa Rica in Global Value Chains: An Upgrading Analysis.* Durham, NC: Duke University Center on Globalization, Governance and Competitiveness.

Banerjee, A. V., and B. Moll. 2010. Why Does Misallocation Persist? *American Economic Journal: Macroeconomics* 2(1) January: 189–206.

Barrios Cobos, S., H. Görg, and E. Strobl. 2003. Explaining Firms' Export Behaviour: R&D, Spillovers and the Destination Market. *Oxford Bulletin of Economics and Statistics* 65(4): 475–96.

Barro, R. J., and J. W. Lee. 2013. A New Data Set of Educational Attainment in the World, 1950–2010. *Journal of Development Economics* 104(C) September: 184–98.

Barry, F., and J. Bradley. 1997. FDI and Trade: The Irish Host-Country Experience. *Economic Journal* 107(445) November: 1798–1811.

Bartelsman, E., J. Haltiwanger, and S. Scarpetta. 2009. Measuring and Analyzing Cross-Country Differences in Firm Dynamics. In T. Dunne, J. B. Jensen, and M. J. Roberts, eds., *Producer Dynamics: New Evidence from Micro Data.* Chicago: University of Chicago Press.

Barth, J. R., G. Caprio, Jr., and R. Levine. 2013. Bank Regulation and Supervision in 180 Countries from 1999 to 2011. *Journal of Financial Economic Policy* 5(2) April: 111–219.

Bassi, M., M. Busso, and J. S. Muñoz. 2013. Is the Glass Half Empty or Half Full? School Enrollment, Graduation, and Dropout Rates in Latin America. IDB Working Paper No. 462. Inter-American Development Bank, Washington, DC.

Bassi, M., M. Busso, S. Urzúa, and J. Vargas. 2012. *Disconnected: Skills, Education, and Employment in Latin America.* Washington, DC: Inter-American Development Bank.

Battat, J., I. Frank, and X. Shen. 1996. Suppliers to Multinationals: Linkage Programs to Strengthen Local Companies in Developing Countries. Foreign Investment Advisory Service Occasional Paper No. 6. International Finance Corporation and World Bank, Washington, DC.

Becattini, G. 1989. Sectors and/or Districts: Some Remarks on the Conceptual Foundations of Industrial Economics. In E. Goodman and J. Bamford, eds., *Small Firms and Industrial Districts in Italy.* London: Routledge.

Beck, T., B. Büyükkarabacak, F. K. Rioja, and N. T. Valev. 2012. Who Gets the Credit? And Does It Matter? Household vs. Firm Lending across Countries. B.E. *Journal of Macroeconomics* 12(1) March: 1–46.

Beck, T., A. Demirgüç-Kunt, and V. Maksimovic. 2005. Financial and Legal Constraints to Growth: Does Firm Size Matter? *Journal of Finance* 60(1) February: 137–77.

Beck, T., R. Levine, and N. Loayza. 2000. Finance and the Sources of Growth. *Journal of Financial Economics* 58(1–2): 261–300.

Beltrán, C., and A. Gutiérrez. 2007. La vinculación de suplidores domésticos con multinacionales en Costa Rica. Departamento de Economía, Universidad de Costa Rica, San José. Unpublished.

Benavente, J. M., C. Bravo, D. Goya, and A. Zahler. Forthcoming. Public-Private Cooperation in Productive Development Policies: Case Studies from Chile. IDB working paper. Inter-American Development Bank, Washington, DC.

Benavente, J. M., and G. Crespi. 2003. The Impact of an Associative Strategy (the PROFO Program) on Small and Medium Enterprises in Chile. SPRU Working Paper No. 88. Science and Technology Policy Research, University of Sussex, Falmer, Brighton, UK.

Benavente, J. M., G. Crespi, and A. Maffioli. 2007. Public Support to Firm-Level Innovation: An Evaluation of the FONTEC Program. OVE Working Paper No. 05/07. Office of Evaluation and Oversight, Inter-American Development Bank, Washington, DC.

Berkman, H., D. Focanti, M. Franco, C. Scartascini, E. Stein, and M. Tommasi. 2013. Political Institutions, State Capabilities, and Public Policy: An International Dataset. Database. Inter-American Development Bank, Washington, DC. Available at http://www.iadb.org/en/research-and-data/publication-details,3169.html?pub_id=dba-012. Accessed April 2014.

Bernard, A. B., and J. B. Jensen. 2004. Why Some Firms Export. *Review of Economics and Statistics* 86(2) May: 561–69.

Bernstein, S. 2012. Does Going Public Affect Innovation? Research Paper No. 2126. Graduate School of Business, Stanford University, Stanford, CA.

Bértola, L., and J. A. Ocampo. 2012. *The Economic Development of Latin America since Independence.* Oxford, UK: Oxford University Press.

Bertrand, M., M. Bombardini, and F. Trebbi. 2011. Is It Whom You Know or What You Know? An Empirical Assessment of the Lobbying Process. NBER Working Paper No. 16765. National Bureau of Economic Research, Cambridge, MA.

BIBB (Federal Institute for Vocational Education and Training). 2012. Desarrollo de competencias profesionales junto con socios alemanes para mejorar la empleabilidad: 8 historias de éxito en Latinoamérica. BIBB, Bonn, Germany. Available at http://www.imove-germany.de/cps/rde/xbcr/imove_projekt_de/p_iMOVE_Success-Stories-Latinoamerica_spanish_2012.pdf. Accessed January 2014.

Bilmes, L. J., and W. S. Gould. 2009. *The People Factor: Strengthening America by Investing in Public Service*. Washington, DC: Brookings Institution Press.

Binelli, C., and A. Maffioli. 2007. A Micro-econometric Analysis of Public Support to Private R&D in Argentina. *International Review of Applied Economics* 21(3): 339–59.

Bisang, R., A. González, J. C. Hallak, A. López, D. Ramos, and R. Rozemberg. 2014. Public-Private Collaboration on Productive Development Policies in Argentina. IDB Working Paper No. 478. Inter-American Development Bank, Washington, DC.

Blalock, G., and P. Gertler. 2002. Technology Diffusion from Foreign Direct Investment through Supply Chain. Haas School of Business, University of California, Berkeley, CA. Unpublished.

Blomström, M., and A. Kokko. 2003. The Economics of Foreign Direct Investment Incentives. In H. Herrmann and R. Lipsey, eds., *Foreign Direct Investment in the Real and Financial Sector of Industrial Countries*. Berlin, Heidelberg, and New York: Springer-Verlag.

Bloom, M. 1992. *Technological Change in the Korean Electronics Industry*. Paris: Organisation for Economic Co-operation and Development (OECD).

Bloom, N., B. Eifert, A. Mahajan, D. McKenzie, and J. Roberts. 2013. Does Management Matter? Evidence from India. *Quarterly Journal of Economics* 128(1) February: 1–51.

Bloom, N., C. Genakos, R. Sadun, and J. Van Reenen. 2012. Management Practices across Firms and Countries. NBER Working Paper No. 17850. National Bureau of Economic Research, Cambridge, MA.

Blyde, J. S., C. Daude, and E. Fernández-Arias. 2010. Output Collapses and Productivity Destruction. *Review of World Economics* 146(2) June: 359–87.

Bonelli, R., and A. C. Pinheiro. 2008. New Export Activities in Brazil: Comparative Advantage, Policy or Self-Discovery? Research Network Working Paper No. R-551. Inter-American Development Bank, Washington, DC.

Boneu, F., V. Castillo, D. Giuliodori, A. Maffioli, A. Rodríguez, S. Rojo, and R. Stucchi. Forthcoming. El impacto del apoyo al cluster de TICs de la Ciudad de Córdoba. IDB technical note. Inter-American Development Bank, Washington, DC.

Bonilla, C. A., and C. A. Cancino. 2011. El impacto del Programa de Capital Semilla del Sercotec en Chile. IDB Working Paper No. 279. Inter-American Development Bank, Washington, DC.

Borensztein, E., K. Cowan, B. Eichengreen, and U. Panizza, eds. 2008. *Bond Markets in Latin America: On the Verge of a Big Bang?* Cambridge, MA: MIT Press.

Borensztein, E., J. De Gregorio, and J.-W. Lee. 1998. How Does Foreign Direct Investment Affect Economic Growth? *Journal of International Economics* 45(1) June: 115–35.

Brainard, W. C., and R. N. Cooper. 1968. Uncertainty and Diversification in International Trade. *Studies in Agricultural Economics, Trade, and Development* [Food Research Institute] 8(3): 257–85.

Branch, A. E. 1990. *Elements of Export Marketing and Management*. London: Chapman and Hall.

Branstetter, L. G., F. Lima, L. J. Taylor, and A. Venâncio. 2010. Do Entry Regulations Deter Entrepreneurship and Job Creation? Evidence from Recent Reforms in Portugal. NBER Working Paper No. 16473. National Bureau of Economic Research, Cambridge, MA.

Branstetter, L., and M. Sakakibara. 1998. Japanese Research Consortia: A Microeconometric Analysis of Industrial Policy. *Journal of Industrial Economics* 46(2) June: 207–33.

Bruhn, M. 2011. License to Sell: The Effect of Business Registration Reform on Entrepreneurial Activity in Mexico. *Review of Economics and Statistics* 93(1) February: 382–86.

Bruhn, M., and D. McKenzie. 2013. Using Administrative Data to Evaluate Municipal Reforms: An Evaluation of the Impact of Minas Fácil Expresso. Policy Research Working Paper No. 6368. World Bank, Washington, DC.

Bruton, H. 1989. Import Substitution. In H. Chenery and T. N. Srinivasan, eds., *Handbook of Development Economics*. Volume 2. Amsterdam: North-Holland.

Bucarey, A., and S. Urzúa. 2013. El retorno económico de la educación media técnico profesional en Chile. *Estudios Públicos* 129(Summer): 1–48.

Buera, F. J., J. P. Kaboski, and Y. Shin. 2011. Finance and Development: A Tale of Two Sectors. *American Economic Review* 101(5) August: 1964–2002.

CAF (Corporación Andina de Fomento), ed. 2013. *Emprendimientos en América Latina: desde la subsistencia hacia la transformación productiva*. Bogotá: CAF.

Calderón-Madrid, A. 2011. A Micro-Econometric Analysis of the Impact of Mexico's R&D Tax Credit Program on Private R&D Expenditure. Paper presented at the international conference, Mind the Gap: From Evidence to Policy Impact, June 15–17, Cuernavaca, Mexico.

Caliendo, L., F. Monte, and E. Rossi-Hansberg. 2012. The Anatomy of French Production Hierarchies. NBER Working Paper No. 18259. National Bureau of Economic Research, Cambridge, MA.

Carvalho, D. R. 2014. The Real Effects of Government-Owned Banks: Evidence from an Emerging Market. *Journal of Finance* 69(2) April: 577–609.

Castillo, V., A. Maffioli, S. Rojo, and R. Stucchi. 2014a. The Effect of Innovation Policy on SMEs' Employment and Wages in Argentina. *Small Business Economics* 42(2) February: 387–406.

———. 2014b. Knowledge Spillovers of Innovation Policy through Labor Mobility: An Impact Evaluation of the FONTAR Program in Argentina. IDB Working Paper No. 488. Inter-American Development Bank, Washington, DC.

Cattaneo, O., G. Gereffi, S. Miroudot, and D. Taglioni. 2013. Joining, Upgrading and Being Competitive in Global Value Chains: A Strategic Framework. Policy Research Working Paper No. 6406. World Bank, Washington, DC.

CENIT (Centro de Investigaciones para la Transformación) and CPA Ferrere. 2010. Evaluación de impacto de un programa de financiamiento público a actividades de innovación en Uruguay—Programa de Desarrollo Tecnológico. Unpublished.

Charlton, A., N. Davis, M. Faye, J. Haddock, and C. Lamb. 2004. Industry Targeting for Investment Promotion: A Survey of 126 IPAs. Oxford Investment Research, London. Unpublished.

Chrisney, M. D., and M. Kamiya. 2011. Institutions and Productive Development Programs in Latin America and the Caribbean: Methodological Approach and

Preliminary Results. IDB Technical Note No. 305. Inter-American Development Bank, Washington, DC.

Chrisney, M. D., and R. Monge-González. 2013. Los servicios de desarrollo productivo y el papel de los bancos públicos de desarrollo. In F. de Olloqui, ed., *Bancos públicos de desarrollo: ¿hacia un nuevo paradigma?* Washington, DC: Inter-American Development Bank.

Chrisney, M. D., and J. Prats Oriol. 2012. Where Are the Formal SMEs in Latin America and the Caribbean? The Role of Structural and Institutional Factors. In A. Corbacho, coord., *The Fiscal Institutions of Tomorrow*. Institutions for People series. Washington, DC: Inter-American Development Bank.

Chudnovsky, D., A. López, M. Rossi, and D. Ubfal. 2006. Evaluating a Program of Public Funding of Private Innovation Activities: An Econometric Study of FONTAR in Argentina. OVE Working Paper No. 16/06. Office of Evaluation and Oversight, Inter-American Development Bank, Washington, DC.

CNIC (Consejo Nacional de Innovación para la Competitividad). 2008. *Hacia una estrategia nacional de innovación para la competitividad*. Volume 2. Santiago: CNIC.

Coelho, D. S. C., and J. A. de Negri. 2011. Impacto do financiamento do BNDES sobre a produtividade das empresas: uma aplicação do efeito quantílico de tratamento. ANPEC Working Paper No. 119. Associação Nacional dos Centros de Pós-Graduação em Economia, Niterói, RJ, Brazil.

Colby, S. 2013. Searching for Institutional Solutions to Industrial Policy Challenges: A Case Study of the Brazilian Development Bank. Ph.D. dissertation, School of Advanced International Studies (SAIS), Johns Hopkins University, Washington, DC.

Conference Board, The. 2013. Total Economy Database™. January. Available at http://www.conference-board.org/data/economydatabase/. Accessed April 2014.

Corbacho, A., V. Fretes Cibils, and E. Lora, eds. 2013. *More than Revenue: Taxation as a Development Tool*. Development in the Americas series. Washington, DC: Inter-American Development Bank, and New York: Palgrave Macmillan.

Cornick, J. 2012. PPC for Successful PDPs (PP4PD): What Is Required from the Public Sector? Paper presented at the workshop, Public-Private Collaboration for Productive Development Policies, March 5–6, Washington, DC.

Cornick, J., J. Jiménez, and M. Román. 2014. Public-Private Collaboration on Productive Development Policies in Costa Rica. IDB Working Paper No. 480. Inter-American Development Bank, Washington, DC.

Crespi, G., A. Maffioli, and M. Meléndez. 2011. Public Support to Innovation: The Colombian COLCIENCIAS' Experience. IDB Technical Note No. 264. Inter-American Development Bank, Washington, DC.

Crespi, G., G. Solís, and E. Tacsir. 2011. Evaluación del impacto de corto plazo de SENACYT en la innovación de las empresas panameñas. IDB Technical Note No. 263. Inter-American Development Bank, Washington, DC.

Crespi, G., and E. Tacsir. 2012. Effects of Innovation on Employment in Latin America. IDB Technical Note No. 496. Inter-American Development Bank, Washington, DC.

Cuddy, N. 2012. The Construction Sector in the UK. Case Study. Unpublished.

Cuddy, N., T. Leney, and C. Ward. 2010. Case Studies on Lifelong Learning and Labor Competencies in the OECD: Austria, England, Czech Republic, Finland, and Spain. Unpublished.

Czarnitzki, D., and A. Fier. 2003. Publicly Funded R&D Collaborations and Patent Outcome in Germany. ZEW Discussion Paper No. 03-24. Zentrum für Europäische Wirtschaftsforschung GmbH [Centre for European Economic Research], Mannheim, Germany.

Dal Bó, E., and F. Finan. 2014. State Capabilities for Productive Development Policies: A Simple Theoretical Framework. Unpublished.

Damijan, J. P., M. Knell, B. Majcen, and M. Rojec. 2003. The Role of FDI, R&D Accumulation and Trade in Transferring Technology to Transition Countries: Evidence from Firm Panel Data for Eight Transition Countries. *Economic Systems* 27(2) June: 189–204.Daude, C., and E. Fernández-Arias. 2010. Aggregate Productivity: The Key to Unlocking Latin America's Development Potential. In C. Pagés, ed., *The Age of Productivity: Transforming Economies from the Bottom Up*. Development in the Americas series. New York: Palgrave Macmillan, and Washington, DC: Inter-American Development Bank.

David, P. A., B. H. Hall, and A. A. Toole. 2000. Is Public R&D a Complement or Substitute for Private R&D? A Review of the Econometric Evidence. *Research Policy* 29(4) April: 497–529.

De Ferranti, D., G. E. Perry, I. Gill, J. L. Guasch, W. F. Maloney, C. Sánchez-Páramo, and N. Schady. 2003. *Closing the Gap in Education and Technology*. Washington, DC: World Bank.

de Groote, R. 2005. Costa Rica: Proyecto de desarrollo de proveedores para empresas multinacionales de alta tecnología (ATN/ME-6751-CR). Final Evaluation. Inter-American Development Bank, Washington, DC.

de la Torre, A., J. C. Gozzi, and S. L. Schmukler. 2007. Innovative Experiences in Access to Finance: Market Friendly Roles for the Visible Hand? Policy Research Working Paper No. 4326. World Bank, Washington, DC.

de Luna-Martínez, J., and C. L. Vicente. 2012. Global Survey of Development Banks. Policy Research Working Paper No. 5969. World Bank, Washington, DC.

de Negri, J. A., M. Borges Lemos, and F. de Negri. 2006a. Impact of P&D Incentive Program on the Performance and Technological Efforts of Brazilian Industrial Firms. OVE Working Paper No. 14/06. Office of Evaluation and Oversight, Inter-American Development Bank, Washington, DC.

———. 2006b. The Impact of University Enterprise Incentive Program on the Performance and Technological Efforts of Brazilian Industrial Firms. OVE Working Paper No. 13/06. Office of Evaluation and Oversight, Inter-American Development Bank, Washington, DC.

de Olloqui, F., ed. 2013. *Bancos públicos de desarrollo: ¿hacia un nuevo paradigma?* Washington, DC: Inter-American Development Bank.

del Castillo, J., and J. Paton. 2010. Política de promoción y reconversión industrial. *Ekonomiaz* 25[Anniversary] (3): 96–123.

Devlin, R. 2013. National Public-Private Economic Councils: Their Governance Matters. Inter-American Development Bank, Washington, DC. Unpublished.

Devlin, R., and G. Moguillansky. 2009a. Alianzas público-privadas como estrategias nacionales de desarrollo a largo plazo. *Revista CEPAL* 97 (April): 97–116.

———. 2009b. Alianzas público-privadas para una nueva visión estratégica del desarrollo. Project Document No. 283. United Nations Economic Commission for Latin America and the Caribbean (ECLAC), Santiago.

———. 2012. What's New in the New Industrial Policy in Latin America? Policy Research Working Paper No. 6191. World Bank, Washington, DC.

Didier, N., and C. Pérez González. 2012. Perfil del capacitando en Chile: variables que inciden en el acceso. *Revista Latino-americana de Estudos do Trabalho* 17(27): 165–90.

Dini, M. 2009. Capital social y programas asociativos: reflexión sobre instrumentos y estrategias de fomento de CORFO. In O. Muñoz Gomá, ed., *Desarrollo productivo en Chile: la experiencia de Corfo entre 1990 y 2009*. Santiago: Corporación de Fomento de la Producción (CORFO), FLACSO-Chile, and Editorial Catalonia.

Djankov, S., R. La Porta, F. López-de-Silanes, and A. Shleifer. 2002. The Regulation of Entry. *Quarterly Journal of Economics* 117(1): 1–37.

Dobles Madrigal, R. 2012a. Encadenamientos para la exportación. Promotora del Comercio Exterior de Costa Rica (PROCOMER), San José. Unpublished.

———. 2012b. *Informe anual: comisión de encadenamientos para la exportación*. San José: PROCOMER.

Doner, R. F., and B. R. Schneider. 2000. Business Associations and Economic Development: Why Some Associations Contribute More Than Others. *Business and Politics* 2(3) December: 261–88.

Duque, J. F., and M. Muñoz. 2011. Evaluating SME Support Programs in Colombia. In G. López-Acevedo and H. W. Tan, eds., *Impact Evaluation of Small and Medium Enterprise Programs in Latin America and the Caribbean*. Washington, DC: World Bank.

Dussel Peters, E. 2010. Mexico's Economic Relationship with China: A Case Study of the PC Industry in Jalisco, Mexico. *Cuadernos de trabajo* [Centro de Estudios China-México] 1: 1–24.

Dussel Peters, E., L. M. Galindo Paliza, and E. Loría Díaz. 2003. *Condiciones y efectos de la inversión extranjera directa y del proceso de integración regional en México durante los noventa: una perspectiva macro, meso y micro*. Mexico City: Plaza y Valdés and Universidad Nacional Autónoma de México (UNAM), and Buenos Aires: INTAL/IDB.

EC (European Commission). 2008. The Concept of Clusters and Cluster Policies and Their Role for Competitiveness and Innovation: Main Statistical Results and Lessons Learned. Europe INNOVA/PRO INNO Europe Working Paper No. 9. Office for Official Publications of the European Communities, Luxembourg.

ECLAC (United Nations Economic Commission for Latin America and the Caribbean). 2008. La transformación productiva 20 años después: viejos problemas, nuevas oportunidades. ECLAC, Santiago. Available at http://www.eclac.org/publicaciones/xml/7/33277/2008-117-SES.32-Latransformacion-WEB_OK.pdf. Accessed February 2014.

———. 2013. CEPALSTAT—Databases and Statistical Publications. ECLAC, Santiago. Available at http://estadisticas.cepal.org/cepalstat/WEB_CEPALSTAT/Portada.asp?idioma=i. Accessed March 2014.

Economist, The. 2013. Schumpeter: The Entrepreneurial State. August 31, p. 59.

Egan, M. L., and A. Mody. 1992. Buyer-Seller Links in Export Development. *World Development* 20(3) March: 321–34.

Ekboir, J. M., G. Dutrénit, G. Martínez V., A. Torres Vargas, and A. O. Vera-Cruz. 2009. Successful Organizational Learning in the Management of Agricultural Research and Innovation: The Mexican Produce Foundations. 2009. Research Report No. 162. International Food Policy Research Institute (IFPRI), Washington, DC.

Ellison, G., E. L. Glaeser, and W. R. Kerr. 2010. What Causes Industry Agglomeration? Evidence from Coagglomeration Patterns. *American Economic Review* 100(3) June: 1195–1213.

Eslava, M., and J. Haltiwanger. 2012. Young Businesses, Entrepreneurship, and the Dynamics of Employment and Output in Colombia's Manufacturing Industry. CAF Working Paper No. 2012/08. Corporación Andina de Fomento, Caracas.

Eslava, M., A. Maffioli, and M. Meléndez. 2012a. Second-Tier Government Banks and Access to Credit: Micro-Evidence from Colombia. IDB Working Paper No. 308. Inter-American Development Bank, Washington, DC.

———. 2012b. Second-Tier Government Banks and Firm Performance: Micro-Evidence from Colombia. IDB Working Paper No. 294. Inter-American Development Bank, Washington, DC.

Eslava, M., and M. Meléndez. 2009. Politics, Policies and the Dynamics of Aggregate Productivity in Colombia. IDB Working Paper No. 101. Inter-American Development Bank, Washington, DC.

Eslava, M., M. Meléndez, and G. Perry. 2014. Public-Private Collaboration on Productive Development Policies in Colombia. IDB Working Paper No. 479. Inter-American Development Bank, Washington, DC.

European Cluster Observatory. 2012. Global Cluster Initiative Survey 2012. Survey Summary Report. European Commission, Brussels.

Ezell, S. J., and R. D. Atkinson. 2011. International Benchmarking of Countries' Policies and Programs Supporting SME Manufacturers. Report. Information Technology and Innovation Foundation (ITIF), Washington, DC. September.

Falck, O., S. Heblich, and S. Kipar. 2010. Industrial Innovation: Direct Evidence from a Cluster-Oriented Policy. *Regional Science and Urban Economics* 40(6) November: 574–82.

Fama, E. F. 1985. What's Different about Banks? *Journal of Monetary Economics* 15(1) January: 29–39.

FAO (Food and Agriculture Organization of the United Nations). 2013. FAOSTAT. Database. FAO, Rome. Available at http://faostat.fao.org/. Accessed March 2014.

Feenstra, R. C., R. Inklaar, and M. Timmer. 2013. The Next Generation of the Penn World Table. NBER Working Paper No. 19255. National Bureau of Economic Research, Cambridge, MA.

Feldman, M. P., and D. B. Audretsch. 1999. Innovation in Cities: Science-Based Diversity, Specialization and Localized Competition. *European Economic Review* 43(2) February: 409–29.

Fernández, M. A. 2011. Políticas de desarrollo productivo en Panamá: auto-descubrimiento y fallas de coordinación. IDB Working Paper No. 172. Inter-American Development Bank, Washington, DC.

Fernández-Arias, E. 2014. Productivity and Factor Accumulation in Latin America and the Caribbean: A Database (2014 Update). Research Department, Inter-American Development Bank, Washington, DC. Available at http://www.iadb.org/research/pub_desc.cfm?pub_id=DBA-015. Accessed June 2014.

Fernández-Arias, E., R. Hausmann, and U. Panizza. 2013. Smart Development Banks and Productive Development Policies. Inter-American Development Bank, Washington, DC. Unpublished.

Fernández-Arias, E., R. Hausmann, and E. Stein. 2001. Courting FDI: Is Competition Bad? Inter-American Development Bank, Washington, DC. Unpublished.

Fernández-Arias, E., and U. Panizza. 2013. A Framework for Financial Interventions. Inter-American Development Bank, Washington, DC. Unpublished.

Fernández-Arias, E., and E. Stein. 2014. Pursuing Productive Transformation: A Strategic Policy Framework. Inter-American Development Bank, Washington, DC. Unpublished.

Figal Garone, L., A. Maffioli, C. M. Rodríguez, G. Vázquez, and J. A. De Negri. 2012. Assessing the Impact of Cluster Policies: The Case of the *Arranjos Productivos Locais* in Brazil. SPD Working Paper No. 1203. Inter-American Development Bank, Washington, DC.

Findlay, R. 1978. Some Aspects of Technology Transfer and Direct Foreign Investment. *American Economic Review* 68(2) May: 275–79.

FMC (Foundation for MSME Clusters). 2007. Policy and Status Paper on Cluster Development in India. FMC, New Delhi. November. Available at http://msmefoundation.org/folder/Publication/48.pdf. Accessed February 2014.

———. 2008. Cluster Development and Poverty Alleviation. Study. FMC, New Delhi. May. Available at http://msmefoundation.org/folder/Publication/54.pdf. Accessed February 2014.

Franco Chuaire, M., and C. Scartascini. Forthcoming. The Politics of Policies: Revisiting the Quality of Public Policies and Government Capabilities in Latin America and the Caribbean. IDB policy paper. Inter-American Development Bank, Washington, DC.

Frankel, J. A., and D. Romer. 1999. Does Trade Cause Growth? *American Economic Review* 89(3) June: 379–99.

Fundación Chile. 2012. Fuerza laboral de la Gran Minería Chilena 2012–2020: diagnóstico y recomendaciones. Report. Innovum, Centro de Innovación en Capital Humano, Fundación Chile, Santiago.

Garicano, L. 2000. Hierarchies and the Organization of Knowledge in Production. *Journal of Political Economy* 108(5) October: 874–904.

Gennaioli, N., R. La Porta, F. López-de-Silanes, and A. Shleifer. 2013. Human Capital and Regional Development. *Quarterly Journal of Economics* 128(1): 105–64.

Gereffi, G. 1999. International Trade and Industrial Upgrading in the Apparel Commodity Chain. *Journal of International Economics* 48(1) June: 37–70.

Gereffi, G., J. Humphrey, and T. Sturgeon. 2005. The Governance of Global Value Chains. *Review of International Political Economy* 12(1) February: 78–104.

Gereffi, G., and T. Sturgeon. 2013. Global Value Chains and Industrial Policy: The Role of Emerging Economies. In D. K. Elms and P. Low, eds., *Global Value Chains in a Changing World*. Hong Kong: Fung Global Institute (FGI), Singapore: Nanyang Technological University (NTU), and Geneva, Switzerland: World Trade Organization (WTO).

Gil-Pareja, S., R. Llorca-Vivero, J. A. Martínez-Serrano, and F. Requena-Silvente. 2011. Regional Export Promotion Offices and Trade Margins. Universidad de Valencia, Valencia, Spain. Unpublished.

Gindling, T. H., and D. Newhouse. 2012. Self-Employment in the Developing World. Policy Research Working Paper No. 6201. World Bank, Washington, DC.

Girma, S., H. Görg, and A. Hanley. 2008. R&D and Exporting: A Comparison of British and Irish Firms. *Review of World Economics* 144(4) December: 750–73.

Giuliani, E., A. Maffioli, M. Pacheco, C. Pietrobelli, and R. Stucchi. 2013. Evaluating the Impact of Cluster Development Programs. IDB Technical Note No. 551. Inter-American Development Bank, Washington, DC.

Giuliani, E., A. Matta, and C. Pietrobelli. Forthcoming. Impact Evaluation with Social Network Analysis Methods: Program for Supply Chain Development in the Province of Córdoba, Argentina. In C. Pietrobelli, A. Maffioli, and R. Stucchi, eds., *The Evaluation of Cluster Development Programs*. Washington, DC: Inter-American Development Bank.

Giuliani, E., C. Pietrobelli, and R. Rabellotti. 2005. Upgrading in Global Value Chains: Lessons from Latin American Clusters. *World Development* 33(4) April: 549–73.

Giuliodori, D., and R. Giuliodori. 2012. Incentivos tributarios para la I+D+i en Argentina: una evaluación de las políticas recientes. IDB Discussion Paper No. 240. Inter-American Development Bank, Washington, DC.

Glaeser, E. L., ed. 2010. *Agglomeration Economics*. Chicago: University of Chicago Press.

Glass, A. J., and K. Saggi. 1998. International Technology Transfer and the Technology Gap. *Journal of Development Economics* 55(2) April: 369–98.

———. 2002. Multinational Firms and Technology Transfer. *Scandinavian Journal of Economics* 104(4) December: 495–513.

Glewwe, P. W., E. A. Hanushek, S. D. Humpage, and R. Ravina. 2011. School Resources and Educational Outcomes in Developing Countries: A Review of the Literature from 1990 to 2010. NBER Working Paper No. 17554. National Bureau of Economic Research, Cambridge, MA.

Goldstein, A. 2002. The Political Economy of High-Tech Industries in Developing Countries: Aerospace in Brazil, Indonesia and South Africa. *Cambridge Journal of Economics* 26(4): 521–38.

Gompers, P., and J. Lerner. 1998. What Drives Venture Capital Fundraising? *Brookings Papers on Economic Activity: Microeconomics* 1998(July): 149–92.

Gompers, P., J. Lerner, and D. Scharfstein. 2005. Entrepreneurial Spawning: Public Corporations and the Genesis of New Ventures, 1986 to 1999. *Journal of Finance* 60(2) April: 577–614.

González, I., and L. Pittaluga. 2007. Uruguay. In A. López, coord., *Complementación productiva en la industria del software en los países del Mercosur: impulsando la integración regional para participar en el mercado global*. Montevideo: Red Mercosur de Investigaciones Económicas.

Granovetter, M. 1985. Economic Action and Social Structure: The Problem of Embeddedness. *American Journal of Sociology* 91(3) November: 481–510.

Greenaway, D., N. Sousa, and K. Wakelin. 2004. Do Domestic Firms Learn to Export from Multinationals? *European Journal of Political Economy* 20(4) November: 1027–43.

Greenwald, B., and J. E. Stiglitz. 2006. Helping Infant Economies Grow: Foundations of Trade Policies for Developing Countries. *American Economic Review* 96(2) May: 141–46.

———. 2013. Industrial Policies, the Creation of a Learning Society, and Economic Development. In J. E. Stiglitz and J. Y. Lin, eds., *The Industrial Policy Revolution I: The Role of Government beyond Ideology*. New York: Palgrave Macmillan.

Griffith, R., S. Redding, and J. Van Reenen. 2004. Mapping the Two Faces of R&D: Productivity Growth in a Panel of OECD Industries. *Review of Economics and Statistics* 86(4) November: 883–95.

Griliches, Z. 1979. Issues in Assessing the Contribution of Research and Development to Productivity Growth. *Bell Journal of Economics* 10(1) Spring: 92–116.

Grossman, G. M., and E. Helpman. 2001. *Special Interest Politics.* Cambridge, MA: MIT Press.

Grossman, G. M., and E. Rossi-Hansberg. 2010. External Economies and International Trade Redux. *Quarterly Journal of Economics* 125(2) May: 829–58.

Guerrieri, P., S. Iammarino, and C. Pietrobelli, eds. 2003. *The Global Challenge to Industrial Districts: Small and Medium-Sized Enterprises in Italy and Taiwan.* Cheltenham, UK: Edward Elgar.

Guerrieri, P., and C. Pietrobelli. 2006. Old and New Forms of Clustering and Production Networks in Changing Technological Regimes: Contrasting Evidence from Taiwan and Italy. *Science, Technology and Society* 11(1) March: 9–38.

Gutiérrez, E., H. P. Rudolph, T. Homa, and E. Blanco Beneit. 2011. Development Banks: Role and Mechanisms to Increase Their Efficiency. Policy Research Working Paper No. 5729. World Bank, Washington, DC.

Hall, B. H., and J. Lerner. 2010. The Financing of R&D and Innovation. In B. H. Hall and N. Rosenberg, eds., *Handbook of the Economics of Innovation.* Volume 1. Amsterdam: North-Holland.

Hall, B. H., J. Mairesse, and P. Mohnen. 2010. Measuring the Returns to R&D. *Handbook of the Economics of Innovation.* Volume 2. Amsterdam: North-Holland.

Hall, R. E., and S. E. Woodward. 2010. The Burden of the Nondiversifiable Risk of Entrepreneurship. *American Economic Review* 100(3) June: 1163–94.

Hallberg, K. 2000. A Market-Oriented Strategy for Small and Medium Scale Enterprises. IFC Discussion Paper No. 40. International Finance Corporation, Washington, DC.

Haltiwanger, J. 2012. Job Creation and Firm Dynamics in the United States. *Innovation Policy and the Economy* 12(1) January: 17–38.

Haltiwanger, J., R. S. Jarmin, and J. Miranda. 2013. Who Creates Jobs? Small versus Large versus Young. *Review of Economics and Statistics* 95(2) May: 347–61.

Hanushek, E. A., and L. Woessmann. 2008. The Role of Cognitive Skills in Economic Development. *Journal of Economic Literature* 46(3) September: 607–68.

———. 2010. *The High Cost of Low Educational Performance: The Long-Run Economic Impact of Improving PISA Outcomes.* Paris: OECD Publishing.

———. 2011. How Much Do Educational Outcomes Matter in OECD Countries? *Economic Policy* 26(67) July: 427–91.

———. 2012a. Do Better Schools Lead to More Growth? Cognitive Skills, Economic Outcomes, and Causation. *Journal of Economic Growth* 17(4) December: 267–321.

———. 2012b. Schooling, Educational Achievement, and the Latin American Growth Puzzle. *Journal of Development Economics* 99(2) November: 497–512.

Harding, T., and B. S. Javorcik. 2011. Roll Out the Red Carpet and They Will Come: Investment Promotion and FDI Inflows. *Economic Journal* 121(557) December: 1445–76.

———. 2012. Foreign Direct Investment and Export Upgrading. *Review of Economics and Statistics* 94(4) November: 964–80.

———. 2013. Investment Promotion and FDI Inflows: Quality Matters. *CESifo Economic Studies* 59(2) June: 337–59.

Harrison, A., and A. Rodríguez-Clare. 2010. Trade, Foreign Investment, and Industrial Policy for Developing Countries. In D. Rodrik and M. Rosenzweig, eds., *Handbook of Development Economics.* Volume 5. Amsterdam: North-Holland.

Hart, O., A. Shleifer, and R. W. Vishny. 1997. The Proper Scope of Government: Theory and an Application to Prisons. *Quarterly Journal of Economics* 112(4) November: 1127–61.

Hatzichronoglou, T. 1997. Revision of the High-Technology Sector and Product Classification. STI Working Paper No. 1997/02. Directorate for Science, Technology and Industry, Organisation for Economic Co-operation and Development, Paris.

Hausmann, R., C. A. Hidalgo, S. Bustos, M. Coscia, A. Simoes, and M. A. Yildirim. 2014. *The Atlas of Economic Complexity: Mapping Paths to Prosperity.* Cambridge, MA, and London: MIT Press.

Hausmann, R., C. A. Hidalgo, J. Jiménez, R. Lawrence, E. Levy Yeyati, C. Sabel, and D. Schydlowsky. 2011. Construyendo un mejor futuro para la República Dominicana: herramientas para el desarrollo. Technical report. Center for International Development, Harvard University, Cambridge, MA.

Hausmann, R., J. Hwang, and D. Rodrik. 2007. What You Export Matters. *Journal of Economic Growth* 12(1) March: 1–25.

Hausmann, R., A. Rodríguez-Clare, and D. Rodrik. 2005. Towards a Strategy for Economic Growth in Uruguay. Economic and Social Study Series Paper No. RE1-05-003. Inter-American Development Bank, Washington, DC.

Hausmann, R., and D. Rodrik. 2003. Economic Development as Self-Discovery. *Journal of Development Economics* 72(2) December: 603–33.

———. 2006. Doomed to Choose: Industrial Policy as Predicament. Paper presented at the Blue Sky Conference, September 9–10, Cambridge, MA.

Hausmann, R., D. Rodrik, and C. F. Sabel. 2008. Reconfiguring Industrial Policy: A Framework with an Application to South Africa. CID Working Paper No. 168. Center for International Development, Harvard University, Cambridge, MA.

Hausmann, R., and R. Wagner. 2014. Public Procurement: Industrial Policy by Stepping Stones. Unpublished.

Henn, C., C. Papageorgiou, and N. Spatafora. 2013. Export Quality in Developing Countries. IMF Working Paper No. 13/108. International Monetary Fund, Washington, DC.

Hibbert, E. P. 1990. *The Management of International Trade Promotion.* London: Routledge.

Hidalgo, C. A., and R. Hausmann. 2009. The Building Blocks of Economic Complexity. *Proceedings of the National Academy of Sciences of the U. S. A.* 106(26) June: 10570–75.

Hoff, K. 2001. Beyond Rosenstein-Rodan: The Modern Theory of Coordination Problems in Development. In B. Pleskovic and N. Stern, eds., *Annual World Bank Conference on Development Economics 2000.* Washington, DC: World Bank.

Hoffman, N. 2011. *Schooling in the Workplace: How Six of the World's Best Vocational Education Systems Prepare Young People for Jobs and Life.* Cambridge, MA: Harvard Education Press.

Hsieh, C.-T., and P. J. Klenow. 2009. Misallocation and Manufacturing TFP in China and India. *Quarterly Journal of Economics* 124(4): 1403–48.

———. 2012. The Life Cycle of Plants in India and Mexico. NBER Working Paper No. 18133. National Bureau of Economic Research, Cambridge, MA.

Hummels, D., and P. J. Klenow. 2005. The Variety and Quality of a Nation's Exports. *American Economic Review* 95(3) June: 704–23.

Humphrey, J., and H. Schmitz. 2000. Governance and Upgrading: Linking Industrial Cluster and Global Value Chain Research. IDS Working Paper No. 120. Institute of Development Studies, University of Sussex, Brighton, East Sussex, UK.

Huneeus, C., C. de Mendoza, and G. Rucci. 2013. Una visión crítica sobre el financiamiento y la asignación de recursos públicos para la capacitación de trabajadores en América Latina y el Caribe. IDB Discussion Paper No. 265. Inter-American Development Bank, Washington, DC.

Hurst, E., and B. W. Pugsley. 2011. What Do Small Businesses Do? *Brookings Papers on Economic Activity* 43(2) Fall: 73–118.

Hwang, J. J. 2007. Patterns of Specialization and Economic Growth. Ph.D. dissertation, Economics Department, Harvard University, Cambridge, MA.

Iacovone, L., and B. S. Javorcik. 2012. Getting Ready: Preparation for Exporting. CEPR Discussion Paper No. 8926. Centre for Economic Policy Research, London.

Iacovone, L., B. S. Javorcik, W. Keller, and J. R. Tybout. 2011. Supplier Responses to Wal-Mart's Invasion of Mexico. NBER Working Paper No. 17204. National Bureau of Economic Research, Cambridge, MA.

Ibarrarán, P., A. Maffioli, and R. Stucchi. 2009. SME Policy and Firms' Productivity in Latin America. Discussion Paper No. 4486. Institute for the Study of Labor (IZA), Bonn, Germany.

IDB (Inter-American Development Bank). 2002. *Beyond Borders: The New Regionalism in Latin America*. Economic and Social Progress in Latin America: 2002 Report. Washington, DC: IDB.

———. 2004. *Unlocking Credit: The Quest for Deep and Stable Bank Lending*. Economic and Social Progress in Latin America: 2005 Report. Washington, DC: IDB.

———. 2010a. Demand for Skills Survey (DSS) — Argentina, Brazil, and Chile. Education Division, Inter-American Development Bank, Washington, DC. Unpublished.

———. 2010b. Science, Technology, and Innovation in Latin America and the Caribbean: A Statistical Compendium of Indicators. Inter-American Development Bank, Washington, DC. Available at http://idbdocs.iadb.org/wsdocs/getdocument.aspx?docnum=35384423. Accessed January 2014.

———. 2011. Bancarización de clusters: la experiencia de la Provincia de San Juan, Argentina. IDB Discussion Paper No. 178. Inter-American Development Bank, Washington, DC.

———. 2012. Productivity and Human Resources Survey. Inter-American Development Bank, Washington, DC. Unpublished.

———. 2013. Case Study of the São Paulo Cluster Program. Inter-American Development Bank, Washington, DC. Unpublished.

IFC (International Finance Corporation). 2007. Linkage Programs to Develop Small and Medium Enterprises. IFC Monitor Note No. 46002. IFC, World Bank, Washington, DC.

Ingtec and USP Research Group. 2013. Productive Development Policies and Innovation Spillovers through Labor Force Mobility: The Case of the Brazilian Innovation Support System. IDB Working Paper No. 459. Inter-American Development Bank, Washington, DC.

Irwin, D. A., and P. J. Klenow. 1996. High-Tech R&D Subsidies: Estimating the Effects of Sematech. *Journal of International Economics* 40(3–4) May: 323–44.

Jaffe, A. B., M. Trajtenberg, and R. Henderson. 1993. Geographic Localization of Knowledge Spillovers as Evidenced by Patent Citations. *Quarterly Journal of Economics* 108(3) August: 577–98.

Jäntti, M., J. Saari, and J. Vartiainen. 2005. Growth and Equity in Finland. World Bank, Washington, DC. Unpublished.

Jaramillo, M., and J. J. Díaz. 2011. Evaluating SME Support Programs in Peru. In G. López-Acevedo and H. W. Tan, eds., *Impact Evaluation of Small and Medium Enterprise Programs in Latin America and the Caribbean*. Washington, DC: World Bank.

Javorcik, B. S. 2004. Does Foreign Direct Investment Increase the Productivity of Domestic Firms? In Search of Spillovers through Backward Linkages. *American Economic Review* 94(3) June: 605–27.

Javorcik, B. S., and M. Spatareanu. 2009. Tough Love: Do Czech Suppliers Learn from Their Relationships with Multinationals? *Scandinavian Journal of Economics* 111(4) December: 811–33.

Jordana, J., C. Volpe Martincus, and A. Gallo. 2010. Export Promotion Organizations in Latin America and the Caribbean: An Institutional Portrait. IDB Working Paper No. 198. Inter-American Development Bank, Washington, DC.

Kannebley, Jr., S., and G. Porto. 2012. Incentivos fiscais à pesquisa, desenvolvimento e inovação no Brasil: uma avaliação das políticas recentes. IDB Discussion Paper No. 236. Inter-American Development Bank, Washington, DC.

Kantis, H., J. Federico, M. Gonzalo, S. I. García, C. Menéndez, S. Rojo, V. Castillo, L. Tumini, L. Llorente, D. Amorín, and D. Guariniello. 2013. Dinámica, crecimiento y productividad empresarial en el período 1996–2011 (Argentina). Inter-American Development Bank, Washington, DC. Unpublished.

Kaplan, D. S., E. Piedra, and E. Seira. 2011. Entry Regulation and Business Start-ups: Evidence from Mexico. *Journal of Public Economics* 95(11–12) December: 1501–15.

Kappaz, C. 2013. Lifelong Learning in Mexico. Inter-American Development Bank, Washington, DC. Unpublished.

Karikomi, S. 1998. The Development Strategy for SMEs in Malaysia. APEC Study Center Working Paper No. 4. Institute of Developing Economies, Japan External Trade Organization, Chiba Prefecture, Japan.

Katz, J. 2001. Structural Reforms and Technological Behaviour: The Sources and Nature of Technological Change in Latin America in the 1990s. *Research Policy* 30(1) January: 1–19.

Keesing, D. B. 1967. Outward-Looking Policies and Economic Development. *Economic Journal* 77(306) June: 303–20.

Keesing, D. B., and A. Singer. 1991. Development Assistance Gone Wrong: Failures in Services to Promote and Support Manufactured Exports. In P. Hogan, D. B. Keesing, and A. Singer, eds., *The Role of Support Services in Expanding Manufactured Exports in Developing Countries*. Washington, DC: World Bank.

Khan, M. H., and S. Blankenburg. 2009. The Political Economy of Industrial Policy in Asia and Latin America. In M. Cimoli, G. Dosi, and J. E. Stiglitz, eds., *Industrial Policy and Development: The Political Economy of Capabilities Accumulation*. New York: Oxford University Press.

Klepper, S., and S. Sleeper. 2005. Entry by Spinoffs. *Management Science* 51(8) August: 1291–1306.

Klepper, S., and P. Thompson. 2010. Disagreements and Intra-Industry Spinoffs. *International Journal of Industrial Organization* 28(5) September: 526–38.
Koenig, P., F. Mayneris, and S. Poncet. 2010. Local Export Spillovers in France. *European Economic Review* 54(4) May: 622–41.
Krueger, A. O. 1974. The Political Economy of the Rent-Seeking Society. *American Economic Review* 64(3) June: 291–303.
Kugler, M., E. Stein, and R. Wagner. 2007. Product Space, Product Quality and the Emergence of New Export Sectors. PowerPoint presentation. Center for International Development, Harvard University, Cambridge, MA. April 2.
Kuntchev, V., R. Ramalho, J. Rodríguez-Meza, and J. S. Yang. 2012. What Have We Learned from the Enterprise Surveys Regarding Access to Finance by SMEs? World Bank Research and Working Paper. World Bank, Washington, DC.
La Porta, R., F. López-de-Silanes, and A. Shleifer. 2002. Government Ownership of Banks. *Journal of Finance* 57(1) February: 265–301.
Lach, S., S. Parizat, and D. Wasserteil. 2008. The Impact of Government Support to Industrial R&D on the Israeli Economy. Final report. E. G. P. Applied Economics Ltd., Tel-Aviv, Israel.
Lall, S. 2001. *Competitiveness, Technology and Skills.* Cheltenham, UK: Edward Elgar.
Lall, S., J. Weiss, and J. Zhang. 2006. The "Sophistication" of Exports: A New Trade Measure. *World Development* 34(2) February: 222–37.
Landier, A. 2005. Entrepreneurship and the Stigma of Failure. Toulouse School of Economics, Toulouse, France. Unpublished.
Larraín, C., and J. Quiroz. 2006. Estudio para el Fondo de Garantía de Pequeños Empresarios (Study of the Guarantee Fund for Small Business Owners). BancoEstado, Santiago. Unpublished.
Larraín, F., L. F. López-Calva, and A. Rodríguez-Clare. 2001. Intel: A Case Study of Foreign Direct Investment in Central America. In F. Larraín, B. Álvarez, G. Esquivel, C. García López, M. Jenkins, L. F. López-Calva, A. Rodríguez-Clare, J. D. Sachs, and J. Tavares, eds., *Economic Development in Central America: Volume 1: Growth and Internationalization.* Cambridge, MA: Harvard University Press.
Lazear, E. P. 2005. Entrepreneurship. *Journal of Labor Economics* 23(4) October: 649–80.
Leamon, A., and J. Lerner. 2012. Creating a Venture Ecosystem in Brazil: FINEP's INOVAR Project. Working Paper No. 12-099. Harvard Business School, Boston, MA.
Lederman, D., and W. F. Maloney. 2003. R&D and Development. Policy Research Working Paper No. 3024. World Bank, Washington, DC.
———. 2012. *Does What You Export Matter? In Search of Empirical Guidance for Industrial Policies.* Washington, DC: World Bank.
Lederman, D., J. Messina, S. Pienknagura, and J. Rigolini. 2014. *Latin American Entrepreneurs: Many Firms but Little Innovation.* Washington, DC: World Bank.
Lederman, D., M. Olarreaga, and L. Payton. 2010. Export Promotion Agencies: Do They Work? *Journal of Development Economics* 91(2) March: 257–65.
Lederman, D., and L. Saenz. 2005. Innovation and Development around the World, 1960–2000. Policy Research Working Paper No. 3774. World Bank, Washington, DC.
Lee, K. 2013. How Can Korea Be a Role Model for Catch-Up Development? A "Capability-Based View." In A. K. Fosu, ed., *Achieving Development Success: Strategies and Lessons from the Developing World.* Oxford, UK: Oxford University Press.

Leland, H. E., and D. H. Pyle. 1977. Informational Asymmetries, Financial Structure, and Financial Intermediation. *Journal of Finance* 32(2) May: 371–87.

Lerner, J. 1999. The Government as Venture Capitalist: The Long-Run Impact of the SBIR Program. *Journal of Business* 72(3) July: 285–318.

Lerner, J., A. Leamon, and S. García-Robles. 2013. Best Practices in Creating a Venture Capital Ecosystem. Multilateral Investment Fund (MIF), Washington, DC. Available at http://lavca.org/wp-content/uploads/2013/12/Best-Practices-in-Creating-a-VC-Ecosystem.pdf. Accessed January 2014.

Lerner, J., and A. Schoar. 2005. Does Legal Enforcement Affect Financial Transactions? The Contractual Channel in Private Equity. *Quarterly Journal of Economics* 120(1): 223–46.

Levine, R. 2005. Finance and Growth: Theory and Evidence. In P. Aghion and S. N. Durlauf, eds., *Handbook of Economic Growth*. Volume 1A. Amsterdam: North-Holland.

Levy Yeyati, E., A. Micco, and U. Panizza. 2007. A Reappraisal of State-Owned Banks. *Economía* 7(2) Spring: 209–47.

Lin, J. Y. 2011. New Structural Economics: A Framework for Rethinking Development. *World Bank Research Observer* 26(2): 193–221.

Linden, G., K. L. Kraemer, and J. Dedrick. 2009. Who Captures Value in a Global Innovation Network? The Case of Apple's iPod. *Communications of the ACM* 52(3) March: 140–44.

Lipsey, R. E., and F. Sjöholm. 2005. The Impact of Inward FDI on Host Countries: Why Such Different Answers? In T. H. Moran, E. M. Graham, and M. Blomström, eds., *Does Foreign Direct Investment Promote Development?* Washington, DC: Peterson Institute for International Economics and Center for Global Development.

Little, I. M. D., T. Scitovsky, and M. Scott. 1970. *Industry and Trade in Some Developing Countries: A Comparative Study.* Oxford, UK: Oxford University Press for the OECD Development Center.

Loewendahl, H. 2001. A Framework for FDI Promotion. *Transnational Corporations* 10(1) April: 1–42.

López, A., A. M. Reynoso, and M. Rossi. 2010. Impact Evaluation of a Program of Public Funding of Private Innovation Activities: An Econometric Study of FONTAR in Argentina. OVE Working Paper No. 03/10. Office of Evaluation and Oversight, Inter-American Development Bank, Washington, DC.

López, F., and A. Maffioli. 2008. Technology Adoption, Productivity and Specialization of Uruguayan Breeders: Evidence from an Impact Evaluation. OVE Working Paper No. 07/08. Office of Evaluation and Oversight, Inter-American Development Bank, Washington, DC.

López-Acevedo, G., and H. W. Tan, eds. 2011. *Impact Evaluation of Small and Medium Enterprise Programs in Latin America and the Caribbean.* Washington, DC: World Bank.

López-Acevedo, G., and M. Tinajero-Bravo. 2011. Evaluating Enterprise Support Programs Using Panel Firm Data. Paper presented at the Sixth IZA/World Bank Conference: Employment and Development, May 30–31, Mexico City.

López-Córdova, J. E. 2002. NAFTA and Mexico's Manufacturing Productivity: An Empirical Investigation Using Micro-Level Data. Inter-American Development Bank, Washington, DC. Unpublished.

Maffioli, A. 2005. The Formation of Network and Public Intervention: Theory and Evidence from the Chilean Experience. ISLA Working Paper No. 23. Centre for Research on Latin American Studies and Transition Economies (ISLA), Università Bocconi, Milan, Italy.

Maffioli, A., F. Pusterla, and D. Ubfal. 2011. Public Support to Firm's Innovation: The FOMOTEC Experience in Panama. Inter-American Development Bank, Washington, DC. Unpublished.

Maffioli, A., D. Ubfal, G. Vázquez-Baré, and P. Cerdán-Infantes. 2011. Extension Services, Product Quality and Yields: The Case of Grapes in Argentina. *Agricultural Economics* 42(6) November: 727–34.

———. 2013. Improving Technology Adoption in Agriculture through Extension Services: Evidence from Uruguay. *Journal of Development Effectiveness* 5(1) March: 64–81.

Maggi, C., and M. Dini. 2012. Examen de prácticas y evidencias de políticas de desarrollo productivo con foco en articulación productiva. Inter-American Development Bank, Washington, DC. Unpublished.

Maloney, W. F., and G. Perry. 2005. Towards an Efficient Innovation Policy in Latin America. *Cepal Review* 87 (December): 25–43.

Maloney, W. F., and A. Rodríguez-Clare. 2007. Innovation Shortfalls. *Review of Development Economics* 11(4) November: 665–84.

Marshall, A. 1920. *Principles of Economics*. Eighth edition. London: Macmillan and Co.

Mayneris, F., and S. Poncet. 2013. Chinese Firms' Entry to Export Markets: The Role of Foreign Export Spillovers. Policy Research Working Paper No. 6398. World Bank, Washington, DC.

Mazzucato, M. 2013. *The Entrepreneurial State: Debunking Public vs. Private Sector Myths*. London and New York: Anthem Press.

Meléndez, M., and G. Perry. 2010. Industrial Policies in Colombia. IDB Working Paper No. 126. Inter-American Development Bank, Washington, DC.

Melo, A., and A. Rodríguez-Clare. 2006. Productive Development Policies and Supporting Institutions in Latin America and the Caribbean. IDB Working Paper No. C-106. Inter-American Development Bank, Washington, DC.

Melo, H. 2012. Prosperity through Connectedness (Innovations Case Narrative: Start-Up Chile). *Innovations: Technology, Governance, Globalization* 7(2) Spring: 19–23.

Mercer-Blackman, V. 2008. The Impact of Research and Development Tax Incentives on Colombia's Manufacturing Sector: What Difference Do They Make? IMF Working Paper No. 08/178. International Monetary Fund, Washington, DC.

Micco, A., and U. Panizza. 2006. Bank Ownership and Lending Behavior. *Economics Letters* 93(2) November: 248–54.

Micco, A., U. Panizza, and M. Yañez. 2007. Bank Ownership and Performance: Does Politics Matter? *Journal of Banking and Finance* 31(1) January: 219–41.

Midrigan, V., and D. Y. Xu. 2009. Accounting for Plant-Level Misallocation. Paper presented at the 2009 Annual Meeting of the Society for Economic Dynamics (SED), July 2–4, Istanbul.

———. 2014. Finance and Misallocation: Evidence from Plant-Level Data. *American Economic Review* 104(2) February: 422–58.

MIF (Multilateral Investment Fund). 2010. Evaluación de impacto del Proyecto para desarrollar suplidores para empresas multinacionales de alta tecnología en Costa Rica:

informe final. MIF, Inter-American Development Bank, Washington, DC. Available at http://www.fomin.org/Portals/0/Impact%20Evaluation/Evaluación_de_Impacto_Costa_Rica_FullReport.pdf. Accessed April 2014.

Ministry of Education of Chile. 2010. Estadísticas de la educación 2010. Report. Studies Center, Ministry of Education of Chile, Santiago.

Mion, G., and L. D. Opromolla. 2013. Managers' Mobility, Trade Performance, and Wages. Working Paper No. 1596. European Central Bank, Frankfurt, Germany.

Mohnen, P., and B. Lokshin. 2010. What Does It Take for an R&D Tax Incentive Policy to Be Effective? In V. Ghosal, ed., *Reforming Rules and Regulations: Laws, Institutions, and Implementation*. Cambridge, MA: MIT Press.

Monge-González, R., J. C. Leiva Bonilla, and J. A. Rodríguez-Álvarez. 2012a. Inversión extranjera directa, movilidad laboral y derrames de conocimiento en Costa Rica. *Tecnología en Marcha* 25(5): 103–15.

———. 2012b. Movilidad laboral y derrames de conocimiento desde las compañías multinacionales en Costa Rica: nuevos emprendimientos y externalidades positivas sobre las empresas locales. Inter-American Development Bank, Washington, DC; Comisión Asesora en Alta Tecnología (CAATEC), San José, Costa Rica; and Instituto Tecnológico de Costa Rica, Cartago, Costa Rica. Unpublished.

Monge-González, R., L. Rivera, and J. Rosales-Tijerino. 2010. Productive Development Policies in Costa Rica: Market Failures, Government Failures, and Policy Outcomes. IDB Working Paper No. 157. Inter-American Development Bank, Washington, DC.

Monge-González, R., and J. A. Rodríguez-Álvarez. 2013. Impact Evaluation of Innovation and Linkage Development Programs in Costa Rica: The Cases of PROPYME and CR Provee. IDB Working Paper No. 461. Inter-American Development Bank, Washington, DC.

Moreira, M. M., C. Volpe Martincus, and J. S. Blyde. 2008. *Unclogging the Arteries: The Impact of Transport Costs on Latin American and Caribbean Trade*. Washington, DC: Inter-American Development Bank, and Cambridge, MA: David Rockefeller Center for Latin American Studies, Harvard University.

Moretti, E. 2012. *The New Geography of Jobs*. New York: Houghton Mifflin Harcourt.

Morrison, A., C. Pietrobelli, and R. Rabellotti. 2008. Global Value Chains and Technological Capabilities: A Framework to Study Learning and Innovation in Developing Countries. *Oxford Development Studies* 36(1): 39–58.

Mostafa, R., and S. Klepper. 2011. Industrial Development through Tacit Knowledge Seeding: Evidence from the Bangladesh Garment Industry. Unpublished. Available at http://citeseerx.ist.psu.edu/viewdoc/download?doi=10.1.1.193.9519&rep=rep1&type=pdf. Accessed January 2014.

Mourshed, M., D. Farrell, and D. Barton. 2013. Education to Employment: Designing a System that Works. Report. McKinsey Center for Government, McKinsey and Company, Washington, DC.

Mowery, D. C. 2010. Military R&D and Innovation. In B. H. Hall and N. Rosenberg, eds., *Handbook of the Economics of Innovation*. Volume 2. Amsterdam: North-Holland.

Muendler, M.-A., J. E. Rauch, and O. Tocoian. 2012. Employee Spinoffs and Other Entrants: Stylized Facts from Brazil. *International Journal of Industrial Organization* 30(5) September: 447–58.

Murphy, K. M., A. Shleifer, and R. W. Vishny. 1989. Industrialization and the Big Push. *Journal of Political Economy* 97(5) October: 1003–26.

National Science Board. 2006. *Science and Engineering Indicators 2006*. Volumes 1 and 2. Arlington, VA: National Science Foundation.

Nelson, R. R. 1959. The Simple Economics of Basic Scientific Research. *Journal of Political Economy* 67(3) June: 297–306.

Nishimura, J., and H. Okamuro. 2011. R&D Productivity and the Organization of Cluster Policy: An Empirical Evaluation of the Industrial Cluster Project in Japan. *Journal of Technology Transfer* 36(2) April: 117–44.

Nooteboom, B. 1992. Towards a Dynamic Theory of Transactions. *Journal of Evolutionary Economics* 2(4): 281–99.

Ñopo, H., and M. Bassi. 2013. Technical High School and Vocational Training in Latin America. Paper presented at the 2013 LACEA-LAMES Conference, November 1, Mexico City.

NVCA (National Venture Capital Association) and IHS Global Insight. 2011. Venture Impact: The Economic Importance of Venture Capital-Backed Companies to the U.S. Economy. Study. NVCA, Arlington, VA, and IHS Global Insight, Englewood, CO. Available at http://www.nvca.org/index.php?option=com_content&view=article&id=255&Itemid=103. Accessed March 2014.

Obando, M., and A. Gómez Escalante. 2008. Experiencia de la remuneración variable en PROEXPORT. Paper presented at the Tenth Annual Meeting of the Ibero-American Network of Trade Promotion Organizations, June 24–26, San José, Costa Rica.

OECD (Organisation for Economic Co-operation and Development). 2005a. *Innovation Policy and Performance: A Cross-Country Comparison*. Paris: OECD Publishing.

———. 2005b. *Oslo Manual: Guidelines for Collecting and Interpreting Innovation Data: The Measurement of Scientific and Technological Activities*. Third edition. Paris: OECD Publishing, and Luxembourg City: Eurostat.

———. 2007. *Competitive Regional Clusters: National Policy Approaches*. Paris: OECD Publishing.

———. 2009. *OECD Reviews of Innovation Policy: Korea*. Paris: OECD Publishing.

———. 2010. R&D Tax Incentives: Rationale, Design, Evaluation. OECD, Paris.

———. 2011. *OECD Reviews of Innovation Policy: Peru*. Paris: OECD Publishing.

———. 2012a. Attracting Knowledge-Intensive FDI to Costa Rica: Challenges and Policy Options. Making Development Happen Series No. 1. OECD Publishing, Paris.

———. 2012b. *Education at a Glance 2012: OECD Indicators*. Paris: OECD Publishing.

———. 2013a. Knowledge-Based Capital, Innovation and Resource Allocation. In, *Supporting Investment in Knowledge Capital, Growth and Innovation*. Paris: OECD Publishing.

———. 2013b. *OECD Economic Surveys: Brazil*. Paris: OECD.

———. 2013c. The Role of Public Financial Institutions in Fostering SMEs' Access to Finance. OECD, Paris. Unpublished.

OECD/ECLAC (Organisation for Economic Co-operation and Development and United Nations Economic Commission for Latin America and the Caribbean). 2012. *Latin American Economic Outlook 2013: SME Policies for Structural Change*. Paris: OECD Publishing.

Ostrom, E. 1990. *Governing the Commons: The Evolution of Institutions for Collective Action*. Cambridge, UK: Cambridge University Press.

Pack, H., and K. Saggi. 2006. Is There a Case for Industrial Policy? A Critical Survey. *World Bank Research Observer* 21(2) Fall: 267–97.

Padilla-Pérez, R. 2005. Estudio sectorial de la industria electrónica en México. Instituto Tecnológico Autónomo de México (ITAM), Mexico City. Unpublished.

———. 2008. A Regional Approach to Study Technology Transfer through Foreign Direct Investment: The Electronics Industry in Two Mexican Regions. *Research Policy* 37(5) June: 849–60.

Pagés, C., ed. 2010. *The Age of Productivity: Transforming Economies from the Bottom Up.* Development in the Americas series. New York: Palgrave Macmillan, and Washington, DC: Inter-American Development Bank.

Parra Torrado, M. 2011. Exenciones fiscales para la I+D+i: experiencias en América Latina y retos pendientes. IDB Discussion Paper No. 247. Inter-American Development Bank, Washington, DC.

Paus, E. 2005. *Foreign Investment, Development, and Globalization: Can Costa Rica Become Ireland?* New York, NY, and Houndmills, Basingstoke, UK: Palgrave Macmillan.

Paus, E. A., and K. P. Gallagher. 2008. Missing Links: Foreign Investment and Industrial Development in Costa Rica and Mexico. *Studies in Comparative International Development* 43(1) March: 53–80.

Pavitt, K. 1984. Sectoral Patterns of Technical Change: Towards a Taxonomy and a Theory. *Research Policy* 13(6) December: 343–73.

Peng, J. 2011. Apuntes sobre el caso coreano. Unpublished.

Petkantchin, V., and M. C. Coimbra. 2004. Keep Subsidies out of Aircraft Competition. *Financial Post*, June 28, p. 17.

Pietrobelli, C., A. Maffioli, and R. Stucchi, eds. Forthcoming. *The Evaluation of Cluster Development Programs*. Washington, DC: Inter-American Development Bank.

Pietrobelli, C., and R. Rabellotti, eds. 2006. *Upgrading to Compete: Global Value Chains, Clusters, and SMEs in Latin America*. Washington, DC: Inter-American Development Bank, and Cambridge, MA: David Rockefeller Center for Latin American Studies, Harvard University.

———. 2011. Global Value Chains Meet Innovation Systems: Are There Learning Opportunities for Developing Countries? *World Development* 39(7) July: 1261–69.

———. 2012. Innovation Systems and Global Value Chains. In C. Pietrobelli and R. Rasiah, eds., *Evidence-Based Development Economics: Essays in Honor of Sanjaya Lall*. Kuala Lumpur: University of Malaya Press.

Pietrobelli, C., and C. Staritz. 2013. Challenges for Global Value Chain Interventions in Latin America. IDB Technical Note No. 548. Inter-American Development Bank, Washington, DC.

Pittaluga, L., A. Rius, A. Bianchi, C. Bianchi, and M. González. 2014. Public-Private Collaboration on Productive Development in Uruguay. IDB Working Paper No. 501. Inter-American Development Bank, Washington, DC.

Poole, J. P. 2013. Knowledge Transfers from Multinational to Domestic Firms: Evidence from Worker Mobility. *Review of Economics and Statistics* 95(2) May: 393–406.

Potter, J. 2002. Embedding Foreign Direct Investment. OECD, Paris. Available at http://www1.oecd.org/gov/regional-policy/2489910.pdf. Accessed February 2014.

Pritchett, L., S. Samji, and J. Hammer. 2012. It's All about MeE: Using Structured Experiential Learning ('e') to Crawl the Design Space. CID Working Paper No. 249. Center for International Development, Harvard University, Cambridge, MA.

Pritchett, L., and E. Werker. 2012. Developing the Guts of a GUT (Grand Unified Theory): Elite Commitment and Inclusive Growth. ESID Working Paper No. 16/12. Effective States and Inclusive Development Research Centre, University of Manchester, Manchester, UK.

Pritchett, L., M. Woolcock, and M. Andrews. 2010. Capability Traps? The Mechanisms of Persistent Implementation Failure. Working Paper No. 234. Center for Global Development, Washington, DC.

Proksch, M. 2004. Selected Issues on Promotion and Attraction of Foreign Direct Investment in Least Developed Countries and Economies in Transition. *Investment Promotion and Enterprise Development Bulletin for Asia and the Pacific* [United Nations] 2: 1–18.

Rajan, R. 2012. The Corporation in Finance. NBER Working Paper No. 17760. National Bureau of Economic Research, Cambridge, MA.

Rajan, R., and L. Zingales. 1998. Financial Dependence and Growth. *American Economic Review* 88(3) June: 559–86.

Rauch, J. E. 1996. Trade and Search: Social Capital, Sogo Shosha, and Spillovers. NBER Working Paper No. 5618. National Bureau of Economic Research, Cambridge, MA.

Reikard, G. 2011. Total Factor Productivity and R&D in the Production Function. *International Journal of Innovation and Technology Management* 8(4) December: 601–13.

RICYT (Red de Indicadores de Ciencia y Tecnología). 2013. Base de datos de indicadores. RICYT, Buenos Aires. Available at http://www.ricyt.edu.ar. Accessed March 2014.

Rius, A. 2013. Coordinación institucional y la colaboración de los sectores público y privado: estudio de caso Uruguay sobre la cooperación de actores múltiples. Inter-American Development Bank, Washington, DC. Unpublished.

Rivas, G., R. de Groote, C. Maggi, R. Saldias, and R. Sanhueza. 2012. Integrando servicios financieros y no financieros en el desarrollo empresarial. In H. M. M. Lastres, C. Pietrobelli, R. Caporali, M. C. C. Soares, and M. G. P. Matos, eds., *A nova geração de políticas de desenvolvimento produtivo: sustentabilidade social e ambiental*. Brasília: Confederação Nacional da Indústria, Rio de Janeiro: Banco Nacional de Desenvolvimento Econômico e Social, and Washington, DC: Inter-American Development Bank.

Rodríguez-Clare, A. 1996. Multinationals, Linkages, and Economic Development. *American Economic Review* 86(4) September: 852–73.

———. 2007. Clusters and Comparative Advantage: Implications for Industrial Policy. *Journal of Development Economics* 82(1) January: 43–57.

Rodríguez-Pose, A., and D. Hardy. 2012. Industrial Parks, Technology Parks or Just Amusement Parks? Assessing Their Impacts in Lagging Areas. Inter-American Development Bank, Washington, DC. Unpublished.

Rodrik, D. 1992. Closing the Productivity Gap: Does Trade Liberalization Really Help? In G. K. Helleiner, ed., *Trade Policy, Industrialization, and Development: New Perspectives*. New York: Oxford University Press.

———. 2004. Industrial Policy for the Twenty-First Century. KSG Faculty Research Working Paper No. 04–047. Kennedy School of Government, Harvard University, Cambridge, MA.

———. 2007a. Industrial Development: Some Stylized Facts and Policy Directions. In United Nations, ed., *Industrial Development for the 21st Century: Sustainable Development Perspectives*. New York: United Nations.

———. 2007b. *One Economics, Many Recipes: Globalization, Institutions, and Economic Growth*. Princeton, NJ: Princeton University Press.

———. 2008. The Real Exchange Rate and Economic Growth. *Brookings Papers on Economic Activity* 39(2) Fall: 365–412.

Romer, P. M. 1993. Implementing a National Technology Strategy with Self-Organizing Industry Investment Boards. *Brookings Papers on Economic Activity: Microeconomics* 2: 345–90.

Roosevelt, F. D. 1932. Commencement address. Oglethorpe University, Atlanta, GA. May 22.

Rosenstein-Rodan, P. N. 1943. Problems of Industrialisation of Eastern and South-Eastern Europe. *Economic Journal* 53(210/211) June–September: 202–11.

———. 1961. Notes on the Theory of the Big Push. In H. S. Ellis (with H. C. Wallich), ed., *Economic Development for Latin America*. New York: St. Martin's Press.

Rucci, G. 2010. Chile: capacitación en el sistema de formación continua basado en competencias laborales. Avances, desafíos y recomendaciones de política. IDB Technical Note No. 155. Inter-American Development Bank, Washington, DC.

Rudolph, H. P. 2009. State Financial Institutions: Mandates, Governance, and Beyond. Policy Research Working Paper No. 5141. World Bank, Washington, DC.

Sabel, C. F., and W. H. Simon. 2011. Minimalism and Experimentalism in the Administrative State. *Georgetown Law Journal* 100(1): 53–93.

Sabel, C. F., and J. Zeitlin. 2012. Experimentalist Governance. In D. Levi-Faur, ed., *The Oxford Handbook of Governance*. New York: Oxford University Press.

Sagasti, F. 2011. *Ciencia, tecnología, innovación: políticas para América Latina*. Lima: Fondo de Cultura Económica.

Sánchez, G., I. Butler, and R. Rozemberg. 2011. Productive Development Policies in Argentina. IDB Working Paper No. 193. Inter-American Development Bank, Washington, DC.

Sánchez, G., I. Butler, R. Rozemberg, and H. Ruffo. 2012. The Emergence of Blueberry Exports in Argentina. In C. Sabel, E. Fernández-Arias, R. Hausmann, A. Rodríguez-Clare, and E. Stein, eds., *Export Pioneers in Latin America*. Washington, DC: Inter-American Development Bank, and Cambridge, MA: David Rockefeller Center for Latin American Studies, Harvard University.

Schmitz, H. 1995. Collective Efficiency: Growth Path for Small-Scale Industry. *Journal of Development Studies* 31(4): 529–66.

Schmitz, H., and K. Nadvi. 1999. Clustering and Industrialization: Introduction. *World Development* 27(9): 1503–14.

Schneider, B. R. 2010. Business-Government Interaction in Policy Councils in Latin America: Cheap Talk, Expensive Exchanges, or Collaborative Learning? IDB Working Paper No. 167. Inter-American Development Bank, Washington, DC.

———. 2013. Institutions for Effective Business-Government Collaboration: Micro Mechanisms and Macro Politics in Latin America. IDB Working Paper No. 418. Inter-American Development Bank, Washington, DC.

Schumpeter, J. A. 1934. *The Theory of Economic Development: An Inquiry into Profits, Capital, Credit, Interest, and the Business Cycle*. Cambridge, MA: Harvard University Press.

SEGPRES (Ministerio Secretaría General de la Presidencia). 2013. Informe de empleo en empresas según la edad, 2006–2009. Departamento de Estudios, SEGPRES, Government of Chile.

Shane, S. 2009. Why Encouraging More People to Become Entrepreneurs Is Bad Public Policy. *Small Business Economics* 33(2) August: 141–49.

Shapira, P., J. Youtie, D. Cox, C. Downing, A. Gok, and J. Rogers. 2013. Institutions for Technology Diffusion: Technology Extension Services—Operation, Cases and Insights. Inter-American Development Bank, Washington, DC. Unpublished.

Singer, P. L. 2014. Federally Supported Innovations: 22 Examples of Major Technology Advances That Stem from Federal Research Support. Report. Information Technology and Innovation Foundation, Washington, DC. Available at http://www2.itif.org/2014-federally-supported-innovations.pdf. Accessed March 2014.

Smith, K. 2006. Measuring Innovation. In J. Fagerberg, D. C. Mowery, and R. R. Nelson, eds., *The Oxford Handbook of Innovation*. New York: Oxford University Press.

Solow, R. M. 1957. Technical Change and the Aggregate Production Function. *Review of Economics and Statistics* 39(3) August: 312–20.

Spence, M. M. 2003. Evaluating Export Promotion Programmes: U.K. Overseas Trade Missions and Export Performance. *Small Business Economics* 20(1) February: 83–103.

Spiller, P. T., E. Stein, and M. Tommasi. 2008. Political Institutions, Policymaking, and Policy: An Introduction. In E. Stein and M. Tommasi (with P. T. Spiller and C. Scartascini), eds., *Policymaking in Latin America: How Politics Shapes Policies*. Washington, DC: Inter-American Development Bank, and Cambridge, MA: David Rockefeller Center for Latin American Studies, Harvard University.

Stein, E. 2012. ¿Cómo estimular nuevos exportadores? Una propuesta de política. Buenos Aires. Unpublished.

Stein, E., M. Tommasi, K. Echebarría, E. Lora, and M. Payne, coords. 2005. *The Politics of Policies*. Economic and Social Progress in Latin America: 2006 Report. Washington, DC: Inter-American Development Bank, and Cambridge, MA: David Rockefeller Center for Latin American Studies, Harvard University.

Stein, E., and R. Wagner. 2013. Venture Capital in Latin America: A Comparative Perspective. Paper prepared for the Seventh Micro Evidence on Innovation in Developing Economies Conference, November 7–8, Santiago.

Steinmueller, W. E. 2010. Economics of Technology Policy. In B. H. Hall and N. Rosenberg, eds., *Handbook of the Economics of Innovation*. Volume 2. Amsterdam: North-Holland.

Stiglitz, J. E. 1998. Towards a New Paradigm for Development: Strategies, Policies, and Processes. Ninth Raúl Prebisch lecture delivered at UNCTAD, Geneva, Switzerland, October 19.

Stiglitz, J. E., and A. Weiss. 1981. Credit Rationing in Markets with Imperfect Information. *American Economic Review* 71(3) June: 393–410.

Suyderhoud, J. P. 1999. The Malaysian Economic Development Challenge: Can Productivity Growth Coexist with Income Redistribution? Paper presented at the Seventh Tun Abdul Razak International Conference (Part Two), December 2–4, Penang, Malaysia.

Székely, M. 2012. Analysis of IDB Operations for Technical and Vocational Education and Training at the Secondary Level: Mexico. Inter-American Development Bank, Washington, DC. Unpublished.

Tan, H. W. 2011. Evaluating SME Support Programs in Chile. In G. López-Acevedo and H. W. Tan, eds., *Impact Evaluation of Small and Medium Enterprise Programs in Latin America and the Caribbean.* Washington, DC: World Bank.

Tether, T. 2008. Statement Submitted to the Subcommittee on Terrorism, Unconventional Threats and Capabilities. House Armed Services Committee, US House of Representatives, Washington, DC.

Thompson, P., and J. Chen. 2011. Disagreements, Employee Spinoffs and the Choice of Technology. *Review of Economic Dynamics* 14(3) July: 455–74.

Trindade, V. 2005. The Big Push, Industrialization and International Trade: The Role of Exports. *Journal of Development Economics* 78(1) October: 22–48.

UNCTAD (United Nations Conference on Trade and Development). 1996. Incentives and Foreign Direct Investment. Current Studies, Series A. United Nations, New York and Geneva.

———. 2000. Tax Incentives and Foreign Direct Investment: A Global Survey. ASIT Advisory Studies No. 16. United Nations, New York and Geneva.

———. 2007. Aftercare: A Core Function in Investment Promotion. Investment Advisory Series—Series A, No. 1. United Nations, New York and Geneva.

———. 2009. Promoting Investment and Trade: Practices and Issues. Investment Advisory Series—Series A, No. 4. United Nations, New York and Geneva.

———. 2010. Integrating Developing Countries' SMEs into Global Value Chains. United Nations, New York and Geneva. Available at http://unctad.org/en/Docs/diaeed20095_en.pdf. Accessed March 2014.

———. 2011. Best Practices in Investment for Development: How to Create and Benefit from FDI-SME Linkages—Lessons from Malaysia and Singapore. Investment Advisory Series—Series B, No. 4. United Nations, New York and Geneva.

UNCTC (United Nations Centre on Transnational Corporations). 1988. *Transnational Corporations in World Development: Trends and Prospects.* New York: United Nations.

UNESCO Institute for Statistics. 2013. UIS.Stat. Database. UNESCO Institute for Statistics, Montreal, Quebec, Canada. Available at http://data.uis.unesco.org/. Accessed April 2014.

UNIDO (United Nations Industrial Development Organization). 2010. Independent Thematic Evaluation: UNIDO Cluster and Networking Development Initiatives. Evaluation report. UNIDO, Vienna. Available at http://www.unido.org/fileadmin/user_media/About_UNIDO/Evaluation/Project_reports/e-book_cluster-report.PDF. Accessed March 2014.

Urbiztondo, S., M. Cristini, C. Moskovits, and S. Saiegh. 2009. The Political Economy of Productivity in Argentina: Interpretation and Illustration. IDB Working Paper No. 102. Inter-American Development Bank, Washington, DC.

Urzúa, S., and E. Puentes. 2010. La evidencia del impacto de los programas de capacitación en el desempeño en el mercado laboral. IDB Technical Note No. 268. Inter-American Development Bank, Washington, DC.

Van Biesebroeck, J. 2005. Firm Size Matters: Growth and Productivity Growth in African Manufacturing. *Economic Development and Cultural Change* 53(3) April: 545–83.

Volpe Martincus, C. 2010. *Odyssey in International Markets: An Assessment of the Effectiveness of Export Promotion in Latin America and the Caribbean.* Washington, DC: Inter-American Development Bank.

Volpe Martincus, C., and J. Blyde. 2013. Shaky Roads and Trembling Exports: Assessing the Trade Effects of Domestic Infrastructure Using a Natural Experiment. *Journal of International Economics* 90(1) May: 148–61.

Volpe Martincus, C., and J. Carballo. 2010. Export Promotion: Heterogeneous Programs and Heterogeneous Effects. IDB Working Paper No. 206. Inter-American Development Bank, Washington, DC.

Volpe Martincus, C., J. Carballo, and A. Gallo. 2011. The Impact of Export Promotion Institutions on Trade: Is It the Intensive or the Extensive Margin? *Applied Economics Letters* 18(2): 127–32.

Volpe Martincus, C., J. Carballo, and A. Graziano. 2013. Customs as Doorkeepers: What Are Their Effects on International Trade? Inter-American Development Bank, Washington, DC, and University of Maryland, College Park. Unpublished.

Volpe Martincus, C., A. Estevadeordal, A. Gallo, and J. Luna. 2010. Information Barriers, Export Promotion Institutions, and the Extensive Margin of Trade. *Review of World Economics* 146(1) April: 91–111.

Volpe Martincus, C., and A. Gallo. 2009. Institutions and Export Specialization: Just Direct Effects? *Kyklos* 62(1) February: 129–49.

Wade, R. 1990. *Governing the Market: Economic Theory and the Role of Government in East Asian Industrialization.* Princeton, NJ: Princeton University Press.

Wagner, R. 2014. Is Finance a Most Binding Constraint or Complaint? Unpublished.

Wagner, R., and A. Zahler. 2013. New Exports from Emerging Markets: Do Followers Benefit from Pioneers? Unpublished. Available at http://sites.tufts.edu/rodrigowagner/files/2012/04/Pioneers.pdf. Accessed March 2014.

Wang, J.-Y., and M. Blomström. 1992. Foreign Investment and Technology Transfer: A Simple Model. *European Economic Review* 36(1) January: 137–55.

Wasserman, N. 2012. *The Founder's Dilemmas: Anticipating and Avoiding the Pitfalls That Can Sink a Start-up.* Princeton, NJ: Princeton University Press.

Westmore, B. 2013. R&D, Patenting and Growth: The Role of Public Policy. Economics Department Working Paper No. 1047. OECD Publishing, Paris.

Westphal, L. E. 1990. Industrial Policy in an Export-Propelled Economy: Lessons from South Korea's Experience. *Journal of Economic Perspectives* 4(3) Summer: 41–59.

Williamson, J. 2003. Overview: An Agenda for Restarting Growth and Reform. In P.-P. Kuczynski and J. Williamson, eds., *After the Washington Consensus: Restarting Growth and Reform in Latin America.* Washington, DC: Peterson Institute for International Economics.

Williamson, O. E. 1998. Transaction Cost Economics and Organization Theory. In G. Dosi, D. J. Teece, and J. Chytry, eds., *Technology, Organization, and Competitiveness: Perspectives on Industrial and Corporate Change.* New York: Oxford University Press.

World Bank. 2008. Chile: Toward a Cohesive and Well Governed National Innovation System. Report. World Bank, Washington, DC.

———. 2010a. Enterprise Surveys: What Businesses Experience. Database. World Bank, Washington, DC. Available at http://www.enterprisesurveys.org/About%20Us/. Accessed March 2014.

———. 2010b. World Development Indicators. Database. World Bank, Washington, DC. Available at http://data.worldbank.org/data-catalog/world-development-indicators/wdi-2010. Accessed March 2014.

———. 2012. Doing Business—Entrepreneurship. Database. Available at http://www.doingbusiness.org/data/exploretopics/entrepreneurship. Accessed April 2014.

———. 2013. Enterprise Surveys: What Businesses Experience. Database. World Bank, Washington, DC. Available at http://www.enterprisesurveys.org. Accessed March 2014.

Wyckoff, A. W. 2013. The OECD Innovation Strategy: Science, Technology and Innovation Indicators and Innovation Policy. In F. Gault, ed., *Handbook of Innovation Indicators and Measurement*. Cheltenham, UK: Edward Elgar.

Yusuf, S., K. Nabeshima, and S. Yamashita, eds. 2008. *Growing Industrial Clusters in Asia: Serendipity and Science*. Washington, DC: World Bank.

Zeng, D. Z., ed. 2010. *Building Engines for Growth and Competitiveness in China: Experience with Special Economic Zones and Industrial Clusters*. Washington, DC: World Bank.

Index

adaptation, 88, 217, 349, 351–2, 354
Adelino, M., 398n16
Agencia San Juan de Desarrollo de Inversiones, 189
agglomeration, 115–16, 204–7, 231, 239, 248
Aghion, 68, 96, 139, 353, 392n2, 394n2
Agosin, Manuel, 377, 451
Aitken, B., 37, 243
Albuquerque, R., 184
Alfaro, L., 233, 236, 243, 257, 259, 413n33
Álvarez, R., 86, 94, 127, 243, 274–6
Amsden, A. H., 15, 20, 391n8
Anderson, J. E., 244, 411n10
Andersson, T., 408n14
Andrews, Matthews, 346–7, 349, 351–2, 356, 392n16
Anginer, D., 190, 404n14
APEX-Brazil, 251
Aranguren, M. J., 211
Arbeláez, M. A., 370
Argentina
  blueberry production, 39–40
  CDPs and, 216–18, 228
  credit and, 176, 189–90
  EIPOs and, 250–1, 253
  exports, 100
  FONTAR, 84–5
  GDP and, 152
  high-productivity firms and, 109–10, 133
  human capital and, 154–5, 159
  innovation investment, 63–4, 87, 92
  innovation policies, 101–2, 357
  INOVAR and, 136
  INTA and, 326–7, 338
  internationalization and, 57, 234–6
  MERCOSUR and, 208
  "Polo Científico Tecnológico," 335
  private sector, 176
  productivity, 176–7
  public inputs and market interventions, 182
  public support for TEPs, 90, 94
  public-private interaction in, 376, 378–80, 384
  rice production, 44, 48–9
  self-discovery, 39–41
  spillovers and, 98–100
  Support Program for Organizational Change (PRE), 94
  testing output, 95
  tourism, 52
  venture capital and, 133, 136
  vertical public inputs and, 44, 48–9
  Volkswagen and, 164, 168, 172–3
Arráiz, I., 230
Arrow, K. J., 67, 190
Artopoulos, A., 243, 330, 396n25
Autonomous Community of the Basque Country (CAPV), 210–13

BANCOLDEX, 195, 326–7
bankruptcy, 117, 120–1, 181
Bassi, Marina, 154–5, 159
Benavente, 127
Blyde, Juan, 55, 246, 278
BNDES (Banco Nacional de Desenvolvimento Econômico e Social), 12, 56, 190, 195–6, 201–2, 326
Boston Consulting Group (BCG), 45, 305–7, 315

Brazil
  aircraft industry, 288
  APEX-Brazil, 251
  APL, 229
  Argentina and, 48
  BNDES, 12, 56, 190, 195–6, 201–2, 326
  Bolsa Escola, 149
  Caribbean and, 52–3
  CDPs and, 216, 218–19, 221
  cluster policies, 218–19
  Council for Economic and Social Development, 362
  credit and, 56, 176
  development banks and, 196
  EIPOs and, 251, 253
  EMBRAER, 16–18
  EMBRAPA, 338
  FDI and, 248
  high-productivity firms, 125, 129, 131
  human capital and, 149, 152, 154–5, 159
  industrial policy, 15, 370
  informatics program, 16–18, 293
  innovation and, 63–4, 85–7, 101
  INOVAR and, 134–6
  level of development in, 234–6
  manufacturing sector, 22
  MERCOSUR and, 208
  Minas Fácil Expresso program, 125
  policy capabilities, 101–2
  private sector and, 176
  productive transformation and, 284
  productivity and, 176–7
  reforms, 152
  regulatory issues, 118, 124
  SENAI, 216
  spillovers and, 98–100
  tourism and, 52
  venture capital and, 134–6

Cadenas Productivas, 186–7
Caffarena, Francisco, 39–40
CARICOM countries, 52
Casaburi, Gabriel, 451
Catalonia, 211
Charlton, A., 233, 257, 259, 413n33
Chen, M. X., 236

Chile
  agricultural value chains in, 224–5
  CDPs and, 213–14, 216, 224–6
  Chile Califica, 167
  cluster program, 45, 304–9
  CONICYT, 96
  CORFO, 12, 96, 126–8, 214, 216, 226, 336, 357
  credit and, 176–7, 188
  EIPOs and, 252–3
  FOGAPE, 188
  FONDEF, 338
  FONTEC, 94
  Foro de Desarrollo Productivo, 362
  Fundación Chile, 288, 336, 357, 377
  GDP per capita, 152–3
  high-productivity firms and, 108, 110, 118–19
  human capital and, 152–5, 158–60
  incubator policy, 43
  innovation and, 63–4, 86–7, 90, 92, 96–7, 101–2, 260, 274
  INOVAR and, 136
  level of development and, 234–6
  matrix-like organizations and, 336
  MGSs and, 182
  mining sector, 140, 164, 168–71
  new products introduced, 240–1
  NuevaMente program, 120
  PDPs and, 334
  private sector and, 362, 370, 374, 376–8
  productivity, 95, 177
  PROFO, 94, 213–14
  reforms, 152
  regulatory issues, 118
  reintegro simplificado, 21, 41
  Start-Up Chile, 126, 128–30, 351
  supplier development program, 226, 230
  venture capital and, 133
CIDETER, 217–18
CINDE, 249, 258–9, 302, 314–15, 326, 335, 337, 357, 377
cluster development programs (CDPs)
  in action, 216–26
  in advanced countries, 209–11
  Autonomous Community of the Basque Country and, 211–13

CIDETER, 217–18
effectiveness and evaluation of, 227–32
Latin America and, 213–16
cluster-based policies
  Brazil and, 218–22
  CDPs, 204, 209–32
  Chile and, 224–6
  overview, 203–4
  Uruguay and, 222–4
  value chain programs, 204
  why public policies make sense for interlinked firms, 204–9
  Zonamerica, 208–9
Colombia
  BANCOLDEX, 195, 326
  credit and, 176
  EIPOs and, 251, 253
  exports and, 245, 260, 263–4, 274, 295
  floral industry, 206, 238, 368–70
  GDP per capita, 152
  high-productivity firms and, 108, 110
  human capital and, 158, 164
  innovation and, 63–4, 86–7, 92, 190
  INOVAR and, 136
  level of development and, 234–6
  National Competitiveness Council, 362
  new products and, 240–1
  Private Council for Competitiveness, 328, 332
  product communities and, 311–12, 314
  productivity and, 177, 185
  PROEXPORT, 249
  PTP, 45–6, 308, 327, 382
  public-private interaction in, 376, 378–9
  regulatory restrictions and, 118
  strategic value and, 314
  TEPs and, 90
  venture capital and, 133
CORFO (Corporación de Fomento de la Producción), 12, 96–7, 126–9, 182, 213–14, 216, 224, 226, 306, 336, 357
Cornick, Jorge, 49, 377, 381
Costa Rica
  CINDE, 326, 337, 357, 377
  COMEX, 327
  credit and, 176
  EIPOs and, 251, 253

exports and, 267–8
FDI and, 248–9, 258–60, 265, 326–7, 337
innovation and, 63–4
Intel and, 44, 140, 335
level of development and, 234–6
market interventions, 47–50
medical device sector, 288, 301–2
MNCs and, 260, 268–70
new products and, 240, 242
productivity and, 177
public-private interaction in, 376, 381
rice sector, 48–9, 290, 370
sterilization and, 302
strategy-setting capabilities, 101
TEPs and, 90
tourism, 50–1, 332, 377
vertical public input and, 44
credit, productivity and
  combining credit with nonfinancial services, 189–90
  credit to private sector, 176
  financial depth and productivity growth, 177
  financial policies as PDPs, 180–5
  government ownership of banks, 192–3
  interest rates on loans with maturity greater than 1 year, 176
  market failures and rationale for intervention, 178–80
  market interventions, 181–3
  offering credit guarantees, 187–8
  overview, 175–8
  public development banks, 190–200
  public inputs, 181–3
  relaxing constraints on collateral through factoring, 185–7
  small firms and, 183–5
  technical loans, 189–90
Crespi, Gustavo, 86, 94
Cuevas, C., 86, 94

de la Torre, A., 190, 404n14
de Olloqui, Fernando, 188, 191, 193, 195–7
debt crisis of 1980s, 18
Dewey, John, 352–3
Dominican Republic, 110, 158, 176–7, 234–5, 343

Dovat, Orlando, 208
Dual Plan, 173

economic intelligence, 199–201
EEAOC (Agricultural Experimental Station ObispoColombres), 379
EFA cycle, 352, 354–5
EMBRAER (Empresa Brasileira de Aeronáutica), 15–18
EMBRAPA, 338
European Cluster Observatory, 210
European Union (EU), 211–13
Export and Investment Promotion Organizations (EIPOs), 246, 250–3, 259, 260–2, 278
export promotion organizations (EPOs), 246–7, 249, 252, 254–5, 259–60, 262, 265, 274

Faruq, H., 410n4
Federation of Industries of the State of São Paulo (FIESP), 218–21
feedback loops, 352–4, 357
Fernández-Arias, Eduardo, 3, 55, 178, 199–200, 248, 316
fiscal incentives
  see subsidies; tax incentives
FONDEF, 94–5, 274–6, 338
FONTAR, 84–5, 92, 99
foreign direct investment (FDI)
  attracting, 37–8, 247, 258, 287–8, 301–2, 304, 335, 345, 377
  Brazil and, 248
  Costa Rica and, 248–9, 258–60, 265, 302, 314, 326–7, 337
  evidence for, 243–4
  exports and, 250, 277
  GVC and, 9, 31
  high-productivity firms and, 121
  incentives for, 248–9
  internationalization and, 233, 235, 243–4, 248–9
  level of development and, 235
  linkage programs and, 265–73
  Mexico and, 272
  PDPs and, 23
  restrictions on, 11
  spillovers and, 37–8, 243, 265, 272, 290
  start-ups and, 121, 126
  targeting and, 257–9
  tax breaks and, 37–8
  technology-based, 76
  Uruguay and, 129, 235
Friel, D., 243

General Agreement on Tariffs and Trade (GATT), 11
global value chains (GVCs), 233–4, 237–8, 243–5, 250, 265, 269–70, 277
Griliches, Z., 62
gross domestic product (GDP)
  per capita decomposition, 5
  relative GDP per capita, 4
Guatemala, 64, 90, 109–10, 115, 176, 234–6, 251, 253, 342

Hallak, J. C., 243
Harrison, A. E., 37, 243
Hausmann, Ricardo, 39, 44–5, 116, 140, 199–200, 207, 233, 237–8, 248, 281–4, 294–5, 310–11, 314, 317, 336, 360, 372, 392n16, 416n3
Henriquez, F., 230
Hidalgo, C. A., 282–3, 294
high-productivity firms, start-up and scale-up
  constraints to expected private returns, 114
  constraints to financing of new ventures, 117–19
  CORFO and, 126–8
  how to encourage firms, 142–3
  impact of one-stop shops, 124–5
  improving productivity of start-ups, 126–32
  INOVAR and, 134–6
  Latin America and, 124–5
  mapping policy space, 119–22
  overview, 107–11
  policy examples, 122–4
  Portugal and, 124–5
  rationale for policy intervention, 111–14
  scaling up high-productivity firms, 136–42
  Start-Up Chile and, 128–32
  venture capital in Latin America, 132–6

hiring, 40, 75, 100, 102, 128–9, 132, 137, 157, 172, 193, 208, 243, 324, 326–7, 336, 369–70, 388
Honduras, 155, 158, 176–7, 234–6, 251, 253
Hopenhayn, H. A., 184
horizontal policies
  CDPs and, 216
  cluster program and, 305, 308
  development banks and, 190
  innovation and, 74, 78–80, 101
  market interventions, 22, 36–43, 245
  matrix-like organizations, 336
  MGSs, 182
  overview, 6
  PDPs and, 344
  policy-coordination, 101–2
  private sector and, 365–6, 373, 376
  productive transformation and, 279–80, 316–17, 324
  public inputs, 33–6, 44, 119, 178
  regional cooperation and, 338
  targeting and, 255
  value chains and, 204
  see also horizontal policies; public policy
human capital
  Argentina and, 154–5, 159
  Brazil and, 149, 152, 154–5, 159
  Chile and, 152–5, 158–60
  Colombia and, 158, 164
  Latin America and, 149–68
  Mexico and, 149, 152, 159, 167–8
  overview, 145–9
  sectoral initiatives in Latin America and Caribbean, 168
  Uruguay and, 155–8, 164, 168
Hwang, J. J., 233, 238, 281, 416n3

imports, 10–14, 48, 208, 214, 233, 245–6, 251, 291, 380
import-substitution industrialization (ISI) model, 11–13, 15, 18–19
incubation, 42–3, 109, 120–2, 126–8, 131–2, 136, 142–3, 198, 272, 330
Industrial Development Agency (IDA), 258, 270, 304
Industrial Policy Framework, 212

information and computer technology (ICT), 18, 78, 120, 156, 211, 228, 230, 266
innovation policy
  building through catch-up, 76–7
  Chile and, 96–7
  competition and impacts of grants, 96–7
  demand side approach, 79
  fiscal incentives, 81–6
  fostering innovation, 74–5
  impacts on firm performance, 93–6
  impacts on innovation investment, 91–3
  innovation toolbox, 80–1
  keys to success, 100–3
  knowledge spillovers, 98–100
  Latin America and, 77–80
  learning from impact evaluations, 90–1
  monitoring and evaluation capabilities, 102–3
  overview, 72–4
  policy-coordination capabilities, 101–2
  policy-implementation capabilities, 102
  South Korea and, 76–7
  strategy-setting capabilities, 101
  supply side approach, 78–9
  systemic approach, 79–80
  technology extension programs, 88–90
  United States and, 74–5
INOVAR, 134–6
  see also Brazil
insolvency, 122, 181
Intel, 44, 140, 258, 335
intellectual property rights (IPR), 20–2, 44, 62, 72–3, 78–9, 96, 206
intelligence community, 340
International Monetary Fund (IMF), 292
internationalization
  balancing social costs and benefits of intervention, 244
  Costa Rica and, 258–9
  dosage, 260–4
  evaluation of effectiveness, 259–60
  export and investment promotion services, 246–7
  exports and, 235, 239–43
  FDI and, 235, 243–4, 248–9
  GVC and, 243–4
  Ireland and, 258

internationalization—*Continued*
  lessons learned, 277–8
  linkage programs and FDI, 265–73
  merit pay, 252–3
  number of subsidiaries and level of development, 236
  overview, 233–6
  PDP interaction to shape, 273–6
  policies, past and present, 244–6
  presence abroad, 253–5
  private sector and, 250
  public intervention and, 237–9
  size and, 251–2
  specialization-coordination trade-off, 249–50
  targeting and, 255–9
Ireland, 87, 101, 249, 251, 253, 258–9, 270, 287, 304, 362, 372
Ize, A., 190, 404n14

Joint Duty Program, 340, 344

KfW, 200–2
knowledge production, 62, 67, 80, 205
knowledge use, 80

Leonisa, 295–6
lobbyists, 367
López, R. A., 243

Maffioli, Alessandro, 91–2, 95, 195, 228
Maloney, W. F., 178–82, 184, 189, 193, 196, 199, 205–6
market failure
  credit and, 189, 193, 196, 199
  CRP and, 269
  defensive PDPs and, 55
  dosage and, 261
  FDI and, 130, 138, 265
  fiscal incentives and, 81, 89–90
  government failure and, 28–30
  high-productivity firms and, 114, 142
  horizontal market interventions and, 36–7, 39–40
  human capital, 161
  identifying, 33, 36–7, 43, 174, 303–4, 309–16

innovation and, 93, 100, 103
internationalization and, 272
ISI and, 11
knowledge and, 67, 69
policy intervention and, 8, 22, 25, 111–12, 178–82, 205–6, 237, 244–6, 296
private sector and, 45
productive transformation and, 293, 296
public sector and, 321, 331, 359
SMEs and, 184
value chains and, 206, 214
market interventions
  Argentina and, 48–9
  Costa Rica and, 48
  horizontal, 36–43
  vertical, 47–54
Meléndez, M., 370
MERCOSUR, 208
merit pay, 252–3
Mexico
  auto parts industry and, 288–90
  CONEVAL, 333
  CONOCER, 167–8
  credit and, 176–7, 186
  EFA cycle and, 354–5
  EIPOs and, 250
  exports and development, 234–6
  FDI and, 272
  high-productivity firms, 109–10, 118, 124–5, 138–9, 141
  human capital and, 149, 152, 159, 167–8
  innovation and, 63–4, 87, 92, 101, 109–10
  INOVAR and, 136
  manufacturing and, 22, 90
  Nacional Financiera, 12, 186
  NAFIN, 198
  NAFTA and, 142
  PEMEX, 334
  productive transformation and, 284
  PROMEXICO, 250–3
  public support for TEPs, 90
  regulations in, 118, 124
  sector selection and, 308
  TechBA program, 141
  venture capital and, 133

Microsoft, 123, 164
Mion, G., 239, 410n4
Monge-González, 266
multilateral reciprocal guaranteeschemes (MGSs), 181–2
multinational companies (MNCs), 236–8, 243–4, 247–50, 260, 265–73

Nacional Financiera (NAFIN), Mexico, 12, 186–7, 195, 198
narrow policies, 324
National Institute for Industrial Technology (INTI), Argentina, 380
Navarro, J. C., 330, 396n25
Navarro, L., 211
Negroponte, John, 340
Nelson, R. R., 67
New Zealand, 162, 164–7, 173, 249
Nicaragua, 176–7, 234–5, 343
nonfinancial services (NFS), 189
North American Free Trade Area (NAFTA), 142

Opromolla, 239, 410n4
Organisation of Economic Co-operation and Development (OECD), 65–6, 69–74, 86, 109–10, 149, 151, 153, 181–3, 196, 210, 213, 281

Panama, 63–4, 92, 95, 155, 158, 176–7, 234–5, 251, 253, 308, 343, 366
Panizza, Ugo, 199–200
payroll taxes, 158, 163, 171
PDP interventions
  horizontal market interventions, 36–43
  horizontal public inputs, 35–6
  types, 33–5
  vertical market interventions, 47–54
  vertical public inputs, 43–7
PDP types
  avoiding capture of market interventions, 345
  careful design of, 345
  removal of public "bads," 345–6
  vertical public inputs, 346
  vertical vs. horizontal, 344
  wide vs. narrow, 344

PDPs, explained
  avoiding capture of market interventions, 345
  constructive, 54–5
  defensive, 54–6
  vertical vs. horizontal, 344
  wide vs. narrow, 344
"picking winners," 19, 23, 41, 43, 290
Pietrobelli, Carlo, 204–6, 214, 228, 246, 269, 273
pledeability, 117–18, 178, 181, 184
policy learning and capability building
  enabling environment and, 349–50
  experimentation, 352–3
  feedback loops, 353–4
  method for improvement, 350–2
  overview, 348–9
Portugal, 124–5, 218, 222
Price, J. J., 127
Pritchett, Lant, 392n16
PROCHILE, 240, 242, 247, 251–3, 256–7, 274–6
PROCOMER, 240, 242, 251–2, 265, 267
productive transformation
  Chile and, 305–8
  Costa Rica and, 302
  experiences with sector selection, 304–9
  failure to expand opportunities, 301
  failure to seize opportunities, 297–300
  Jamaica and, 291–2
  in Korea, Latin America, and Caribbean, 283–6
  Mexico and, 289–90
  overview, 279–81
  policy framework for, 315–17
  policy process to select and support priority sectors, 303–4
  quality and, 295–6
  regional challenges, 281–6
  systematic process for selecting priority sectors, 309–15
  vertical policies, 286–94, 303
Productive Transformation Program (PTP), Colombia, 45, 308, 327
PROMEXICO, 250–3
protectionism, 11, 17, 19, 22, 369, 380, 382
Pro-Tejer, 380

proximity, 229–30, 294, 310, 335
public development banks
　bank managers and, 200
　BNDES, 201–2
　economic intelligence, 199–202
　first-tier, 196–9
　government ownership of, 192–3
　KfW, 202
　new role for, 199–200
　overview, 190–6
　second-tier, 196–9
public policy
　innovation, 72–103 (*see also* innovation policy)
　pervasiveness of coordination failures, 68–9
　problem of asymmetric information and uncertainty, 67–8
　rationale for, 66
　reassessing innovation investment gap, 69–70
　spillovers and "public good" nature of knowledge, 67
　theory-based justifications, 66–9
　weighing social returns, 70–2
　see also horizontal policies; vertical policies
public sector capabilities, building for successful PDPs
　different capability requirements for different policy types, 344–6
　difficulties with, 322–5
　EFA cycle, 355
　knowledge and technical skills requirements, 323
　matrix-like organizations, 336
　need for policy discovery, 322–3
　need to collaborate with private sector, 323–4
　need to cooperate across multiple public agencies, 324–5
　organizational structure of public sector, 325–34
　overview, 321–2
　policy learning and capability building, 348–58
　public capabilities and policy choice, 346–8

　public-private councils and other third parties, 336–7
　risk of capture and rent seeking, 324
　specialized cabinets and high-level task forces, 334–6
　TOP capabilities for PDPs, 337–42 (*see also* TOP capabilities)
public-private collaboration
　avoiding risk and, 381–2
　capture and, 378–81
　checks and balances, 387–8
　in Colombia, 369–70
　dangers of lack of coordination, 378
　making public sector better partner, 375–6
　making the marriage work, 381–9
　matching public and private counterparts, 367–76
　menu of options and results, 376–7
　information and policy demands, 385–6
　overview, 359–60
　performance-based policies, 385–7
　perils of private sector engagement, 364–7
　picking right private sector partner, 371–5
　in practice, 376–81
　private sector as partner, 361–3
　private sector counterpart, 367–71
　private sector strengths, 363–4
　self-organizing investment boards, 383–4
　sharing burden, 382–5
　transparency and accountability, 388–9

randomized control trials (RCTs), 227
Rasteletti, Alejandro, 452
Rodríguez-Álvarez, 131, 266, 268–9, 414n41
Rodriguez-Clare, A., 207, 243
Roosevelt, Franklin D., 352
Rodrik, D., 39, 44–5, 116, 207, 233, 237–8, 281, 336, 360, 372
Rucci, Graciana, 158, 167

Sabel, Charles, 129, 336, 351–2, 360, 356, 392n16
Schoar, A., 118, 398n16

Schumpeter, Joseph, 177
Scotland, 211
self-organizing investment boards, 383–4
SENAI, 216, 221
Severino, F., 398n16
small and medium enterprises (SMEs), 25, 36, 42, 77, 80–2, 88–9, 94, 100, 122, 183–6, 202, 213–14, 217–20, 226, 265–6, 271
social network analysis (SNA), 227–8
Spain, 63–4, 87, 133, 142, 211–13, 251, 253, 295
Special Zone, 207
spillovers
  asymmetric information and, 67–8
  Brazil and, 16
  Caribbean and, 53
  CDPs and, 204, 209, 214, 227, 229–30
  cluster-based policies, 203–4
  coordination failures and, 68
  credit and, 178, 196, 200
  dynamic, 300
  EPOs and, 256, 262
  FDI and, 37–8, 243, 265, 272, 290
  fiscal incentives and, 81–6
  impact evaluations nad, 91
  innovation and, 28, 67, 73–5, 105
  intervention and, 37–9, 105, 112, 180, 183, 237–9, 244, 277, 345
  low appropriability and, 115–16
  market failures and, 36–7, 206
  Marshallian, 54
  MNCs and, 265, 268
  PDPs and, 322
  performance-based policies and, 385–6
  "public good" nature of knowledge and, 67
  reforms and, 79
  search for, 98–100
  self-discovery and, 40
  subsidies and, 38–41
  tax breaks and, 37
  venture capital and, 134, 290
  Zonamerica and, 209
state-owned enterprises (SOEs), 11, 19
Stein, Ernesto, 41, 133, 248, 316
Steinmueller, W. E., 66
Stucchi, R., 228, 230

subsidies
  credit and, 182–3, 185, 188, 190–1, 194–5, 197
  EMBRAER and, 17
  EPOs and, 247
  exports and, 14–15, 39–40, 246
  FDI and, 247–8, 345
  horizontal policies and, 280
  human capital and, 323
  innovation and, 9, 23, 80–4, 86, 91
  interventions and, 34–3, 46–52, 78, 277
  ISI and, 19
  level of development and, 236
  private sector and, 46–7, 136, 180
  productivity and, 127, 382
  public policy and, 207
  rent seeking and, 324
  trade agreements and, 19–21
  venture capital and, 136
  vertical policies and, 288, 299

targeting, 80–1, 89, 93, 100, 121, 147, 183, 193, 220, 245, 255–9, 266, 314
tariffs, 11, 13–14, 21, 34–5, 41, 48, 245–6, 277, 291–2
tax incentives
  CDPs and, 208–9
  credit and, 182
  FDI and, 37–9, 248, 258, 271, 273
  high-productivity firms and, 112, 116–17, 131
  human capital and, 158, 163, 171
  income tax exemptions, 21
  innovation and, 73, 76, 78–84, 86
  interventions and, 23, 36, 43, 49, 387
  PDPs and, 9, 24
  public inputs and, 34–5, 66
  spillovers and, 37
  tourism, 34, 50, 291
  vertical policies and, 280, 289–92
technology extension programs (TEPs), 80, 88–90, 93–6, 100
technology loans, 189–90
temporary shocks, 55
TOP capabilities
  assessing public sector capabilities, 341–2
  assessment by policymakers, 341–2

TOP capabilities—*Continued*
  cluster analysis of public policies, 343
  indirect measurements, 342
  operational, 339–40
  overview, 337
  PDPs and, 321–2, 337–43
  political, 340–1
  technical, 338–9
tourism
  Argentina and, 52
  Caribbean and, 52–3, 291
  Chile and, 306, 308
  Costa Rica and, 50–1, 332, 377
  EPOs and, 249
  matrix-type organizations and, 336
  PDPs and, 324
  private investment and, 299
  public agencies and, 324, 333
  tax breaks for, 34, 291
  Uruguay and, 216, 222–4, 372, 378
  vertical market intervention and, 34, 43, 46, 50–1
transparency, 54, 82–3, 103, 162, 166, 181, 183, 189, 194–5, 273, 292, 336, 367, 388–9
Trejos, Alberto, 453

Uruguay
  cluster program, 222–4, 372
  construction sector, 171, 164, 168
  credit and, 176–7
  EIPOs and, 250–3
  exports and level of development, 234
  FDI and, 129, 235
  GDP per capita, 152
  globalization and, 115
  human capital and, 155–8, 164, 168
  Innovation Agency in Uruguay (ANII), 326, 357
  innovation investment, 63–4, 87, 92
  innovation policy, 101–2
  private sector and, 250, 378
  productivity, 176–7
  public policies, 343
  public support for TEPs, 90
  self-discovery and, 42
  service sector, 216

testing output, 95
tourism, 372, 378
WTO and, 20–1
Zonamerica and, 207–8
Urzúa, Sergio, 160

value chain, 9, 31, 57, 189, 203–4, 206, 210, 214, 216, 218, 224–6, 230, 233, 272, 302, 307, 378
van Wincoop, E., 244, 411n10
Venezuela, 64, 176–7, 234–6, 343
vertical policies
  case for, 293–304
  CDPs and, 214, 216
  cluster program and, 305, 308–10
  development banks and, 190, 327
  failure to expand opportunities, 301
  failure to seize opportunities, 297–300
  FDI and, 234
  focalized, 56
  innovation and, 78, 80
  internationalization and, 245
  market interventions, 21–2, 47–54, 74, 190, 365–7
  matrix-like organizations, 336
  narrow policies, 324
  overview, 6, 33–5
  private sector and, 362, 365–7, 373–4, 382
  productive transformation and, 280–2, 286–8, 290–1, 293, 315–16
  public inputs, 43–7, 346
  risks, 303
  spillovers and, 243
  targeting and, 255
  tax incentives and, 280, 289–92
  value chains and, 204, 206, 216
  see also horizontal policies; public policy
volatility, 56, 175
Volkswagen, 164, 172–3
Volpe Martincus, Christian, 243, 245–6, 250, 252–4, 261, 263–4, 278

Wagner, Rodrigo, 133, 138, 140, 243
Washington Consensus, 18–19, 61, 73, 79
Williamson, John, 18–19

workforce training
　construction in Uruguay, 171
　continuous training system for productive development, 165–7
　education and skills, 149–56
　enrollment in secondary technical/vocational education, 160
　impact of education on productivity, 150
　mining sector in Chile, 169–71
　national certification systems, 167–8
　overview, 145–9
　sectoral initiatives, 168–73
　survey of skill demand, 155
　technical education and training for work, 157–65
　Volkswagen in Argentina, 172–3
World Bank, 35, 101, 109–10, 116, 122, 125, 138, 154, 342
World Trade Organization (WTO), 17, 19–22, 41–2, 328
World War II, 11, 61

Younoodle, 130, 338

Zeitlin, J., 351–2, 356
Zonamerica, 207–9

Printed in the United States of America